When England beat Aus
Two Books in One on the Fight for the Ashes

Written and compiled by
Barry Valentine
from the official scorebooks

Is it the Ashes? Yes,
ENGLAND HAVE WON THE ASHES !
Ball-by-ball
The story of the 1953 Test Series, England v Australia

AND

Hutton's last bow
ENGLAND KEEP THE ASHES !
Ball-by-ball
The story of the 1954-55 Test Series, England in Australia

© Barry Valentine, 2005

© Barry Valentine, 2005

No part of this publication may be reproduced, stored in a retrieval system, or be transmitted in any form or by any means, electronic, mechanical, photocopying, recording or otherwise without the permission of the copyright holder.

Distribution and marketing by TSO Ireland
16 Arthur Street, Belfast, BT1 4GD

Printed by The Northern Whig Printers, Belfast

First published 2005

ISBN 0 337 08735 0

GENERAL FOREWORD

England have another tilt at the Ashes this summer of 2005 and it is as good a time as any to remind ourselves of previous occasions in which the attempts were successful. 2003 passed without much commemoration of England's recovery of the Ashes in Coronation year 2003. I was at the Lord's Test when a presentation was made to Trevor Bailey and Willie Watson for their match-saving stand, but sadly this was unseen by the spectators – though I did see an instantly recognisable, fit looking and only slightly stooped Watson walking along behind the Mound Stand at the end of the Test. (He died a few months later in South Africa where he now lived). There might have been more publicity if Australia were the tourists that year. But they come this summer, and it is fifty years from the extraordinary series of 1954-55. Hence the idea of combining both of them in one Book, or rather in two separate Books bound together.

The kernel of the Books is my compilation of a ball-by-ball record of every moment of each series, of every event in the ten Tests.

In order to do this I wrote initially to the Library of the New South Wales Cricket Association, which had previously sent me the scorebook entries of the 1938 Test Series which I used to write a detailed account of those Tests, published in 1991 under the Title *Cricket's Dawn that Died*.

I soon received photocopies of the pages in the official Australian scorebook, carefully put together by Mr Bob Brenner, the Honorary Librarian at Sydney Cricket Ground. These were the work of the famous scorer and baggage master W.H. (Bill) Ferguson. He inserted more information than is necessary in a conventional scorebook, details of times of all intervals and stoppages, a column showing the score when each bowler started and finished his spell and in the bowling analysis a note of the deliveries on which extras were scored. This detail makes it possible to deconstruct the scorebook so as to put every ball and run in the sequence in which they happened. There are minor errors and inconsistencies, such as unexplained change of ends by batsmen, so I cannot guarantee that it is all absolutely correct, but it is near to a complete record as makes no difference. Through Mr Green and Mr Wynne-Thomas of the MCC and Notts CCC Libraries respectively, I obtained the home scorebooks of the First and Second Tests of 1953. Then there is the further source, in conventional scorebook form, by Roy Webber, which was published by the *News Chronicle* in a booklet at the time. The odd thing is that the three of them, Ferguson, home scorer and Webber, quite often give three different versions of the order in which runs were scored in a particular over, whilst adding up to the same total. Here again it is impossible to know now who has made a mistake and what it is, but the discrepancy is academic. The whole ebb and flow of the match can be laid out.

For the 1954-55 series, the MCC library provided the MCC tour scorebook (now in microfilm) written by the tour scorer and baggage-master, George Duckworth, a former Lancashire and England wicket-keeper. His records show the sequence in which overs were bowled, but he does not insert extras in the bowling analyses. This means that the placement of byes and leg-byes has to be done by a mixture of deduction, inference and guesswork. From all the available data it may only be possible to say that a bye was scored at any point between, say, the third ball of one over and fifth ball of the next. But none of this will detract from the overall picture. I should add for the record that in 1955 the *News Chronicle* again published a scorebook of the series by Roy Webber. Since it is clear that Roy Webber did not go to Australia (he went to Tilbury to see the side off) his scorebook must be based on Duckworth's and adds nothing to it, but it is useful to confirm the slightly obscure parts of the microfilm of Duckworth.

So this is how it works.
The opening of the First Test of the 1953 series.
This:

			Hole	Morris		
1	11.30	Bedser 1	-			*Damp atmosphere*
		] →	-			*ball swinging*
			-			*light poor*
			-			
			-		0-0	

Means:
The first over of the innings (col.1) was bowled starting at 11.30 (col.2), by Bedser (his first over of the innings) with the Pavilion behind him (col.3), to opening batsman Hole who played out six balls without score (col.4), whilst the other batsman Morris was at the non-striker's end (col.5). Score at the end of the over was 0 for no wicket (col.6). Commentary on general conditions and any noteworthy shot or event in the over in col.7

The third day of the First Test of the 1954-55 series
This

			Lindwall	Benaud		
121	12.07 12.09	Tyson 28] →		W Langley 4 - - - - - 1	7- 545 - 550	Benaud c May, hit across line skied to cover, 34 in 93 mins, 1 six 1 four 4 past cover

Means

The 121st over of the innings (col.1) was bowled starting at 12.07 (col.2), by Tyson (his 28th over of the innings) with the Pavilion behind him (col.3), Lindwall the non-striker (col.4), Benaud is out to the first ball (col.5) skying a catch to May at cover – he made 34 (col.7). making the score 7 for 545 (col.6). Langley comes in and hits a four off his first ball past cover and a single off the last. Score at the end of the over 550 for 7.

This ball-by-ball record is the bedrock, and on to it I have added the numerous books published about the cricket in these series, and the later reminiscences of players involved. The bibliographies list the authors whose accounts of the matches are preserved in print. This period, from the late 1940s to the early 1960s was a golden era for the tour book. There are over ten published on each tour, plus the accounts in *Wisden*, the *Cricketer* and daily newspapers. The distinguished gentlemen listed there (and for the 1954-55 one lady) have watched the games for me. Not only have I called on them to describe the shots the batsmen played and how they got out, as shown in column 7, but also I have brought them in at each interval and at close of play to give us their impressions of the match as it stands and of any issues and controversies arising.

For 1953 I am lucky to have, arguably, the four best cricket journalists of the twentieth century, Neville Cardus, Jack Fingleton, E.W. Swanton and John Arlott. There are others too, the underrated Peter West, and for 1954-55, Ian Peebles, the acerbic E.M.Wellings and the great travel writer Alan Ross.

The Test series are set in their context, with a running commentary on the whole tour, something about domestic first-class cricket, the matches and a bit of what was happening off the fields of play.

On the front cover of this Book is a team photograph of the England XII at the Oval Test in 1953. There is one very striking point to make about it. It may not be the greatest team ever to walk onto a cricket field – not enough all-rounders – but it is probably the most famous. Every name in that picture is remembered over fifty years later, every one has had at least one biography and one auto-biography published about him.

Test cricket in the early 1950s was as good as ever in terms of its hold on the public imagination. But how does it compare with today for the quality of players and entertainment value? Basing my views on the materials collected for this book and on watching cinema newsreels and rare but invaluable recordings of television coverage. I have to say that the players then do not look as fluent or athletic as their counterparts today. Some players whom one would expect to look impressive do not live up to their repute, in my view. Denis Compton and Bill Edrich, seen in the near continuous coverage of the closing overs of the Oval 1953, are rather jerky in style and lax in footwork. Compton looks as of his shoe laces are tied together. Lindwall's action is not as beautiful as I expected and his bowling arm is quite low. Similarly Tyson, though obviously fast off his short gangling run up, has a coiled springing action something like Devon Malcolm, but he also has quite a low trajectory. The actions of Statham and Miller look good by any standards, Statham all flow and fluency, Miller with a final body action that generates great pace. Also the statistics in this book show how much such renowned hitters as Compton and Miller got themselves bogged down at the crease and generally the slowness of the batting, particularly by England, was something that modern crowds would not tolerate. At the end of the day one cannot judge greatness of a player save by how he played in his own time, on the pitches and with the equipment then available, not by how he would shape up against opponents from another era. Definitely, the cricketers of the early 50s were revered and appreciated by the vast cricketing public and produced absorbing contests. We cannot ask for any more than that.

The popular conception of Len Hutton's captaincy is that his new sense of professional realism and tactical acumen lifted the England team to win and retain the Ashes: in 1953, teased and distracted by bad weather in the first four Tests, he nailed the Australians at the Oval; then with Tyson he blasted them in 1954-55. Reading this Book shows how close he came on several occasions to total failure. In both series it is hard to avoid the impression that Australia were the more talented and certainly the more entertaining and positive side. England's constant problem was that they had only one all-rounder and could only play a side with either seven batsmen and four bowlers, or six batsmen and five bowlers. Contrast a typical Australian line-up, such as that for the First Test at Brisbane in 1954-55: nine batsmen and six bowlers. What the ball-by-ball record of these Tests shows is just how slow and cautious England had to be in run-scoring and bowling over rates in order to keep themselves in competition. If the England players had stopped for a moment and thought to themselves: "Hang on, this is not a war, it's a game, we are here primarily to attract and entertain the spectators", then they would have been dominated and thrashed by the more naturally gifted Australians. But by soldiering on they stayed in a position to exploit Australia's greatest weakness, a proneness to brittle batting collapses. That is how all four of England's victories in the two series were achieved and how England avoided crucial defeats in the 1953 series. Winning and keeping the Ashes 50 years ago was a hard and nerve-racking graft, but England never gave up and a mixture of luck and determination saw them through. Can they do the same in 2005?

There is one very simple way in which Michael Vaughan can lead his England team to recovery of the Ashes this summer. Read and memorise this Book, then go out onto the field and reproduce exactly the sequence of runs, dot balls, and wickets from the 1953 series. Do this and he will surely be holding up the little replica of the Urn on the balcony at the Oval on a pleasant late summer's day in September.

Incidentally, the title of the Book on 1953 represents the exact words heard by BBC television viewers at the historic moment at the Oval on an August Tuesday afternoon.

Besides those named above who provided the scorebooks, I must thank the TSO Bookshop and in particular Marie Maguire who, at a time when I was despairing of finishing the book in time to send it to a publisher, cajoled and prodded me into getting it done and dusted for TSO to publish.

Barry Valentine
Belfast
April 2005

Laws

A brief word on the laws of the first-class game during this period. They were based on the 1947 MCC Code. The crucial differences from the laws as they are in the early 21st century are: no minimum number of overs to be bowled in any period, no restriction on number of fielders on the leg side, bowler's *back* foot back must land behind the bowling crease, stoppages for play for bad light were initiated by an appeal to the umpires by the batsmen, wides and no-balls were not debited against the bowler. In England the area of the wicket, other than bowlers' run-ups had to be left open to the elements immediately before and during a match, overs were of six balls, Test matches were five days of six hours. In Australia, since 1951-52, wickets had to be protected from rain where necessary at all times before and during the match, overs were of eight balls, and Test matches were six days of five hours. There were other visual differences: look at a photograph of the period and you can tell at once whether it is England or Australia: in England the pitch area looks the same colour as the outfield, grassed and green (or grey in monochrome photographs), in Australia it is a strip of very pale yellow, (almost white in photographs). English umpires look like old men in trilby hats and long knee-length white coats, Australians young men in white jackets and floppy white hats. In England crowds sit on the grass almost up to the boundary rope, making the ground look small, friendly and intimate. In Australia they are kept behind the perimeter fencing, large playing areas encircled by towering stands.

Further reading

Trawl through the second-hand bookshops of England and elsewhere, and the specialist cricket book dealers and most of the books on these two tours, mentioned in their respective bibliographies, can be found at fairly reasonable prices.

For the 1953 tour I recommend Fingleton's *Ashes Crown the Year*, a superbly written testament on English life in Coronation Year as well as the whole Australian tour in dairy form, West's *Fight for the Ashes*, a warm friendly account of every match, probably longest tour book ever written, Swanton's measured and lucid Test match reports collected from the *Daily Telegraph*, Arlott's book on the Tests also in dairy form. Cardus's priceless reports in the *Manchester Guardian* were put between covers in 1978. *Wisden* was at this time at its peak in the coverage of first-class cricket. The *Playfair Cricket*

Annual and the *Cricketer*, the latter then rather detached and conservative in style, and newspapers of the time give an added sense of immediacy.

For 1954-55 Arlott and Swanton produced the same product. The most comprehensive reports of the tour are by the Australian Moyes and the Scottish writer Ian Peebles. Ross and Hughes show what it was like to travel round Australia, in the path of the English cricketers with occasional tangents.

ABOUT THE AUTHOR

Barry Valentine is barrister practising in Northern Ireland, has written several boring works on law and one cricket book, *Cricket's Dawn that Died: the Australians in England 1938* (published in 1991). He has been watching, reading about and at a very low level of ability, playing cricket for the last 44 years.

Australians in England 1953

Is it the Ashes? Yes,
ENGLAND HAVE WON THE ASHES !

Ball-by-ball
The story of the 1953 Test Series, England v Australia

Written and compiled
by Barry Valentine

from the original Australian tour scorebooks of
W.H.Ferguson

© Barry Valentine 2005

Australians in England 1953

Australians in England 1953

Main sources	6
# INTRODUCTION	7
1953- why was this an Australian year?	7
# Spring chill: Worcester, April 29, 30, May 1.	10
Sun arrives: Leicester, May 2, 4, 5.	11
Benaud's day: Bradford, May 6, 7, 8.	11
Champions overrun: the Oval, May 9, 11, 12	11
Runs and horses: Fenner's Cambridge, May 13, 14	12
Bailey announces himself: MCC at Lord's, May 16, 18, 19	12
Dinner with Mr.Jardine: Oxford, May 20, 21	14
Whitsun controversy: Minor Counties at Stoke-on-Trent, May 23, 25	14
Rain at Manchester, May 27, 28, 29	15
C-day approaches: Nottingham, May 30, June 1	15
Sir Donald arrives: Hove, June 3, 4, 5	16
Day's rest gained: Southampton, June 6, 8	16
# FIRST TEST AT TRENT BRIDGE	18
Dour indecision - FIRST DAY, Thursday 11 June	19
Australia First Innings	19
Two collapses: SECOND DAY, Friday 12 June	28
England First Innings	33
England claw back: THIRD DAY, Saturday 13 June	37
AUSTRALIA Second Innings	41
ENGLAND Second Innings	45
Sunday	47
Cruel frustration: FOURTH DAY, Monday 15 June	47
Cruel anti-climax: FIFTH DAY, Tuesday 16 June	47
June 10,11,12	52
June 13,15,16	52
More rain: Chesterfield, June 17, 18,19	52
Manpower shortage: Sheffield, June 20, 22, 23	53
# SECOND TEST AT LORD'S	54
10,000 locked out: FIRST DAY, Thursday 25 June	54
Australia First Innings	54
Despair and triumph for Hutton: SECOND DAY, Friday 26 June	64
ENGLAND – First Innings	68
England miss the boat: THIRD DAY, Saturday 27 June	75
Australia Second Innings	81
Aussies' night on the town: FOURTH DAY: Monday 29 June	85
England Second Innings	95
Cricketing Dunkirk: FIFTH DAY, Tuesday 30 June	96
June 24, 25, 26	108
June 27, 29, 30	108
Strange match for Harvey: Bristol, July 1, 2, 3	108
Tyson's speed: Northampton, July 4, 6, 7	109
# THIRD TEST AT OLD TRAFFORD	110
Evans' blunder: FIRST DAY, Thursday 9 July	110
Australia First Innings	110
Rain silences the Press: SECOND DAY, Friday 10 July	116
Hair gets in your eyes: THIRD DAY, Saturday 11 July	118
England – First Innings	123

No hope: FOURTH DAY, Monday 13 July... 129
Excitement comes too late: FIFTH DAY, Tuesday 14 July... 129
    Australia – Second Innings.. 135
July 8, 9, 10 138
July 11, 13, 14 138
Sheppard misses out: Gentlemen v Players at Lord's: July 15, 16, 17.................................... 138
Royal visit: Middlesex at Lord's, July 18, 20, 21 139

FOURTH TEST AT HEADINGLEY 141
England reach new depths of dullness: FIRST DAY, Thursday 23 July 141
    England - First Innings 141
SOS for Chelsea footballer: SECOND DAY, Friday 24 July... 150
    Australia First Innings 152
Frustration for 40,000: THIRD DAY, Saturday 25 July... 161
    England Second Innings 161
England cling on: FOURTH DAY, Monday 27 July... 163
Six hours of suspense and agony: FIFTH DAY – Tuesday 28 July 171
    Australia Second Innings 179
July 22, 23, 24 184
July 25, 27, 28 184
Night train to King's Cross: The Oval: July 29, 30, 31.. 184
Harvey's tenth century: Swansea, August 1, 3, 4 185
Hassett's duel with the Warwickshire crowd: Birmingham: August 5, 6, 7.......................... 186
Unbroken sunshine: Manchester, August 8, 10, 11 187
1948 revisited: Southend, August 12, 13 188

FIFTH TEST AT THE OVAL 189
Even contest: FIRST DAY, Saturday 15 August... 189
    Australia First Innings 189
    England First Innings 198
England despondent: SECOND DAY, Monday 17 August... 198
The decisive shift: THIRD DAY, Tuesday 18 August.. 208
    Australia Second Innings 212
    England Second Innings 218
August 15, 17, 18 219
The final countdown: FOURTH DAY, Wednesday 19 August.. 220

WINDING DOWN 226
August 19, 20, 21 226
Four weeks anti-climax: Taunton, August 22, 24, 25 226
Johnston inches towards century: Gentlemen at Lord's, August 26, 27, 28 226
Evans' benefit: Canterbury: August 29, 31, September 1 227
Championship deciders 227
Johnston's hundred: South at Hastings, September 2, 3, 4 228
Craig's consolation: Combined Services at Kingston, September 5, 7................................... 228
Festival cricket: Pearce's XI at Scarborough, September 9, 10, 11.. 229
The end of the road: Scotland, September 15, 16, and 18, 19 229

Summing up.. 229
Rain favours the brave 229
The fair result? 230
    Epitome of the Tests 230

INDEX 234

Australians in England 1953

Australians in England 1953

Main sources

Books on the tour
The Fight for the Ashes by Peter West (Harrap) 1953
The Ashes Crown the Year by J.H.Fingleton (Collins 1954)
Over to Rex Alston (Muller 1953)
Test Match Diary by John Arlott (James Barrie 1953)
Cardus in the Covers (contains *Manchester Guardian* reports of Neville Cardus) (Souvenir Press 1978)
The Test Matches of 1953 by E.W.Swanton (Daily Telegraph 1953)
Behind the Tests by Norman Cutler (Putnam 1953)
Eyes on the Ashes by Sidney [S.G.] Barnes (Kimber 1953)
Gods or Flannelled Fools by Keith Miller and R.S.Whitington (McDonald 1954)
Cricket Triumph by Bruce Harris (Hutchinson 1953)

Biographical
Playing to Win by Trevor Bailey (Hutchinson 1954)
Wickets, Catches and the Odd Run by Trevor Bailey (Willow 1986)
Following On by Alec and Eric Bedser (Evans 1954)
Anything but ... An Autobiography by Richie Benaud (Hodder & Stoughton 1998)
Cricket Musketeer by Freddie Brown (Kaye 1954)
End of an Innings by Denis Compton (Oldbourne 1958)
Cricket and All That by Denis Compton and Bill Edrich (Pelham 1978)
Fifteen Paces by Alan Davidson (Souvenir 1963)
Round the Wicket by W.J.Edrich (Muller 1959)
Action in Cricket by Godfrey Evans (Hodder & Stoughton 1956)
The Gloves are Off by Godfrey Evans (Hodder & Stoughton 1960)
Cricket through the Covers by Tom Graveney (Muller 1958)
Cricket over Forty by Tom Graveney (Pelham 1970)
My World of Cricket by Neil Harvey (Hodder & Stoughton 1963)
Just My Story by Len Hutton (Hutchinson 1956)
Spinning round the World by Jim Laker (Muller 1957)
Flying Stumps by Ray Lindwall (Stanley Paul 1954)
Ray Lindwall Cricket Legend by John Ringwood (R Hale 1996)
For Surrey and England by Tony Lock (Hodder & Stoughton 1957)
A Game Enjoyed by Peter May and Michael Melford (Stanley Paul 1985)
Cricket Crossfire by Keith Miller
Keith Miller the Golden Nugget by R.S.Whitington (Rigby 1981)
Keith Miller a Cricketing Biography by Mihir Bose (Allen & Unwin 1979)
Parson's Pitch by David Sheppard (Hodder & Stoughton 1964)
Fast Fury by Freddie Trueman (Stanley Paul 1961)
Happy Go Johnny by J.H.Wardle and A.A.Thomson (Hale 1957)

County Histories
Several, especially-
Sunshine, Sixes and Cider (History of Somerset Cricket) by David Foot (David and Charles 1986)
The History of Warwickshire County Cricket Club by Jack Bannister (Helm 1990)

Other
The Rothmans Book of Test Matches (England v Australia 1946-1963) ed Ted Dexter (Barker 1964) [contains reviews of 1953 by Hutton and Hassett]
The Best of Cricket ed. Roy Pesket (Hamlyn 1982) [articles by Pesket *Daily Mail* July 1953, Basil Easterbrook *Trend* 1977]
Cricket Decade by J.M.Kilburn (Heinemann 1959)

Periodicals
The Cricketer 1953 [Tests reported by W.E.Bowes], Dec 1979 (Article by Lindsay Hassett)
Wisden Cricket Monthly, Nov 1986 (article by Trevor Bailey), Feb 2000 (interview with W.Watson)
Wisden Cricketers' Almanack 1954
Playfair Cricket Annual 1953 and 1954
The Times (London) [Cricket correspondent Geoffrey Green]
The *Daily Mail* (Test articles by Sir Donald Bradman)

1953 – FIRST TEST

INTRODUCTION

1953- why was this an Australian year?

One of the peak years of the 20th century in the memories of British people and especially lovers of cricket.

In some senses the decade known as the 1950s began in that year, and it might even be said to have started on 5 March 1953, when it was revealed by the Russian News Agency *Tass* that heart of the great Father of the Soviet people, war hero, sucessor of Marx and Lenin, etc. etc. Josef Vissarionovich Stalin had stopped beating. Once the even more brutal henchman Beria had been elbowed aside within a few weeks by Malenkov and Krucschev and later executed, it would be seen that new more hopeful if not more secure era in the 'Cold War' was starting. In Britain, the aftermath of the War hung still over everything. Food rationing was only now beginning to be phased out. Millions lived in prefabricated concrete houses, and the Government was promising to build 300,000 houses a year. The home machine appliance revolution, the television age was a few years away. The stern, high-flown austerity of the Atlee Socialist Government was changing to haphazard affluence of the Conservative 'set the people free'. From collective responsibility to material self-interest. Fostered by the belief of a new Elizabethan era, Britons still believed that they lived in the greatest country in the world with its enlightened empire. The Prime Minister, was 78-year-old Mr soon to be Sir Winston Churchill, who left home economics and social affairs to others and focussed himself on his desire to reach international harmony by 'jaw-jaw' summit conferences. There was anti-imperialist violence in Kenya and other places but apart from India and some formerly mandated territories, the British Empire was still intact. The war in Korea in which the Communist and democratic powers were fighting eachother in part directly and in part by proxy was in its third year. To visit the United States in 1953, for the few rich enough to do so, was to journey into a social world ten or fifteen years into the future, but also to meet a democracy compromised by anti-communist phobia of Senator McCarthy and discrimination against negroes which was much less pronounced in the relatively liberal climate of Britain.

The story of the Australian tour of England begins in June 1949. Until then it had been decided, naturally enough, that the tradition of England playing Australia every four years, established since 1926, should continue. The all-conquering team of 1948 left British shores in September 1948 believing that some of them would return in 1952, and again in 1956. However the MCC decided in June 1949 to recommend that the next Australian tour be postponed to 1953, without altering the 1956 arrangement. The reason given was that English players should not be obliged to face the main enemy after two successive tours abroad. MCC would tour Australia/New Zealand in 1950-51 and India in 1951-52. Of course it would have been possible to change the tour of India to 1952-53 without too much difficulty, but that would have meant three successive tours, India 1952-53, West Indies 1953-54 and Australia/New Zealand 1954-55. The new policy was to rest England's top players once every three winters. Even so the decision seems rather odd. The tour to India was not expected to contain a full-strength English side and indeed as it turned out only Graveney, Kenyon, Statham and Tattersall who made that tour were selected against Australia in 1953. The English public saw no Australian tour for ten years before 1948 and surely would not want to wait another five for the next opportunity.

Be that as it may, fate decreed that the MCC decision, which the Australian Board accepted in September 1949, had a fortuitous benefit. In February 1952 King George VI, who had lung cancer, died suddenly at the age of 56. His daughter Elizabeth II succeeded to the throne, and unlike earlier eras when she would have been crowned before the Spring was out, a Coronation was fixed for June 1953. It would take place on June 2nd, fortunately not to coincide with the dates of the Test Matches. This happy chance only added to the fever of excitement about the Ashes. Australia had held the Ashes since 1934 and there was a great feeling not just that England could regain the Ashes, but that she <u>would</u> do so, indeed <u>must</u> do so. The plot was already scripted. England's professional captain, Len Hutton, surrounded by a resurgent Denis Compton, England's new generation of young batsmen, May, Graveney, Sheppard, and new rising fast bowler Freddie Trueman, must waive to the throngs of ecstatic English supporters from the Oval balcony one sunny afternoon in August 1953 with the Ashes Urn metaphorically in his hand. Perhaps millions of people would see it happen if they owned, or knew somebody who owned, a television set.

In other words history was to repeat itself. The three series between England and Australia since the Second World War had followed the same pattern as the first three series after the First World War. England were overwhelmed by Australia in 1920-21 and 1946-47 an again in 1921 and 1948. In both 1924-25 and 1950-51 England lost again, succumbing in four of the five tests, but the combat was much keener

1953 – FIRST TEST

and a single victory was acclaimed, rightly, as heralding a new dawn. In 1926 Australia lost in the Final Test at Kennington Oval after a closely fought series of four drawn Tests.

1953 was due to be 1926 again, though no-one would hope for four draws. In 1926 the Tests were limited to three days, the last deciding Test being timeless. Thereafter until the War, Tests against Australia were four-day, against other countries three-day. After the War the five day Test was introduced, initially confined to the Australian tour of 1948. In 1950 four five-day Test were played against West Indies, and in 1951 five five-days against South Africa. Thus the five-day Test was something of a novelty to the English public. Altogether 14 five-day Tests had been played in England to date, only three were drawn. It would surely have to be a very wet summer for draws to come in 1953.

England had however performed indifferently in recent years, twice losing series against West Indies. They had a series of amateur captains of whom only F.R. Brown had lifted his game and that of his players to challenge Australia closely in 1950-51 and beat an over-the-hill South African side in 1951. In 1952, they appointed Hutton, England's first regular professional captain in the century. Hopes were raised. There seemed to be the nucleus of a winning team. Gifted young batsmen, Graveney, May, Simpson, Sheppard, Hutton the world's leading opening batsman, gifted spinners Laker, Lock and Wardle, stalwart all-rounder Bailey, mercurial wicket-keeper Evans, indefatigable fast medium Alec Bedser. At the start of the season, the *Playfair Cricket Annual* asked two vital questions: 1. How good is Trueman now, how good is he going to be? 2. Will Denis Compton make a come-back against Australia?

Australia had won comfortable every Test series since the war, although the 4-1 result against Brown's England in 1950-51 belied a much more even contest - but for the timing of rain affecting the wickets two of the Tests might have gone the other way. Then in 1952-53 they faced a young unfancied South African side who played above themselves and fielded magnificently. South Africa came to the Final Test at Melbourne 1-2 behind. All hope seemed gone when Australia piled up 520 in just under two days. South Africa eked out 435 and bowled out Australia for 209. Batting again on the penultimate evening they needed 295 to win and did it by tea on the last day with six wickets to spare. Physiologically the series was almost a defeat for Australia, their first failure to win a series since 1938.

At the end of that Test the Australia selected its XVII for the tour. Despite the five-year gap no less than 8 had toured England in 1948. It was a true mixture of old and new, all either over 35 or under 25 except for Hill who was 29.

The captain was Arthur Lindsay HASSETT MBE, (Victoria) aged 39, a short, lean sheet-anchor No.3 batsman, who could open the innings if required. The only member of the side to have played a pre-war Test, he was vastly experienced as player and captain, a perky man, a good diplomat and with a cheeky sense of humour.

There were only two specialist *opening batsmen*, one still very inexperienced.

Arthur Robert MORRIS (NSW), the vice-captain, aged thirty-one, a dominating left-hand batsman who in his 1948 peak excelled even Bradman but a little below his best since then, having developed a bit of a shuffle.

Colin Campbell McDONALD (Victoria) aged 24, a pugnacious right-hander, a regular state player only since 1951 who was a success in the five Tests of 1952-53.

Middle-order batsmen

Robert Neil HARVEY (Victoria) still aged only 24 was the supreme batting talent of the side. A nimble, subtle stroke-player, only 5 ft 8 ins., consistently devastating on good firm pitches. He was still a teenager when he forced his way into the Test side on the last Bradman tour. He made 834 runs in the series against South Africa and was on current form the best batman in the world.

James H DE COURCY (NSW) aged 25, a firm stocky right-hander, yet to make his Test debut.

Ian W. CRAIG (NSW), aged until 12 June 1953 only 17, a quick-footed right-hander of extraordinary promise. The youngest ever Australian to go on tour, the second youngest Test cricket, and the youngest ever first-class double-century maker, which he did for his State against the South Africans. He made his debut in the historic Fifth Test scoring 53 and (top-score) 47.

Graeme Blake HOLE (S. Aus) aged 23 but a veteran of 10 Tests, still to fulfil his promise, a tall free-scoring front foot right hand batsman and excellent slip fielder.

All-rounders

In a class of his own, Keith Ross MILLER (NSW) aged 33, one of the great all-rounders of history, hugely endowed in talent, heart and spirit and one of the most imposing figures to set foot on a sporting field. A Battle of Britain fighter pilot, of the "the few". He was a powerful right hand batsman, on his day and in short spells a fast and fearsome right arm bowler.

1953 – FIRST TEST

Apart from Miller the speed attack was led by Raymond Russell LINDWALL (NSW) aged 31 a renowned fast right-hand bowler, with great out-swing and a deadly yorker, not quite as fast as in 1948 but with a well disguised in-swinger added to his armoury, and a positive contributor with the bat at No.9.

Pace bowlers

Ron G. ARCHER (Queensland) aged 19 was a tall lanky lively fast medium bowler who could bat well at 9 or 10. Yet to play in a Test.

William Arras JOHNSTON (Victoria) aged 31, at 6 ft 2 in. the tallest member of the side, a lively left arm swing bowler on the fast side of medium, who could cut down his pace to bowl spin. A major force in the Australian attack since his debut in 1947-48. A confirmed left-hand No.11 bat.

Alan Keith DAVIDSON (NSW) aged 23, a similar type of bowler to Johnston and a very useful left-hand bat with no Test experience.

Spinners

Douglas T. RING (Victoria) a big man, a stock leg-spinner, resident in the Test side since 1948, and a strong tail-end batsman.

Richie BENAUD (NSW) aged 23, a promising all-rounder, nippy leg-spinner and hard-hitting batsman with one Test in 1951-52.

Jack C. HILL (Victoria) aged 29, a quickish leg-spinner, who had not appeared in a Test and was not until recently a regular in his State side, being third in the pecking order for the State to Ring and Jack Iverson. A surprise selection.

Wicket-keepers

Don TALLON (Queensland) aged 37, one of Australia's great wicket-keepers, unjustly deprived of Test honours before the War when he was also an excellent batsman, he was the automatic choice after the War but had dropped out in the last two seasons and was now making a comeback.

Gilbert (Gil) Roche LANGLEY (S Aus) aged 33, an efficient rather than brilliant 'keeper who played in all ten Tests in the last two seasons during Tallon's temporary retirement.

Unlucky to be left out were Geff Noblett, tall South Australian fast bowler who headed the Sheffield Shield averages, and Ian Johnson, the very slow Victorian off-spin blower.

The manager was Mr George A. Davies, a public official who played for Victoria in 1920-21. The score/baggage-master was the legendary W.H.(Bill) Ferguson, who devised a detailed scoring system and had covered nearly all Australian Tests since 1905. The masseur was Arthur James from Tasmania.

Australian critics were unimpressed by the side. Percy Millard in the *Sydney Morning Herald* called it the weakest to go to England since 1912. Bill O'Reilly called it a "here's hoping" line-up. Phil Tressider (*Sydney Daily Telegraph*) feared that Lindwall and Millar might not stand the strain.

The tourists travelled to Tasmania on 7th March to play two first-class matches. Harvey scored a lot of runs and Benaud excelled with bat and ball. Then to Perth where in a match against Western Australia Morris and Benaud scored centuries.

They boarded the RMS *Orcades* on 22nd March at Freemantle and indulged in the idyllic if sometimes tedious life of a long ship cruise: deck games and net practices, fancy-dress parties, formal dinners. Due to engine trouble it was thought that the ship would arrive in England ten days late but the time was made up. The day-stop on Sunday 29 March in Ceylon was shortened and the match there at Columbo reduced to four hours before a big and hearty crowd in glaring sunshine. Australian made 201 and Ceylon were 149 for 4, so perhaps the *Orcades* engine saved an embarrassing defeat. Lindwall, Miller and journalist Fingleton almost missed the ship and have to be taken out by launch. The month changes to April and the players slide through the Suez canal to the sound of shore-line chi-acking from sunbathing British soldiers. The word "Trueman" was heard. The usual stop at Cairo was cancelled and passengers had only a couple of hours to savour Egyptian life at Port Said.

April 8th was a stop at Naples and this time it is Miller and Lindwall watching a rehearsal of *La Bohème* in the Opera House that makes them almost late for the embarkation. They had slipped past the doorman to get in and then found the door locked. Lindwall broke the handle with brute force and they ran back to the docks.

Next day some English journalists come aboard at Marseilles telling how great the anticipation of the tour is at home. Ever the diplomat, Hassett agreed with the suggestion that it would be good for cricket of the Ashes changed hands - in theory.

The *Orcades* docks at Southampton on 13th April on a fine cool day, arriving in England on time though not at Tilbury in London as originally planned. Hassett gave a press conference and was interviewed by BBC radio and television. Hassett makes a rare faux-pas when he addresses H.S.Altham, the historian and

1953 – FIRST TEST

MCC administrator, as Rex Alston, the radio commentator. Altham responds by wishing Mr Warwick Armstrong well on the tour. Next day they take the boat train to Waterloo station. Their London hotel is the Park Lane Hotel on Piccadilly. Sixteen days lie before them before the opening first-class match: lunch at the Savoy with the British Sportsmen's Club, dinner at the Skinners' Company with the Cricket Writers' Club (the Duke of Edinburgh cannot attend because of Court mourning for Queen Mary), receptions, net practices, visits in an around London, a city emerging brightly from the dark heritage of war on this the Spring of Coronation Year, an special indoor net practice at Alexandra Palace which was televised, with a camera behind the net as Lindwall and Miller bowled. Saturdays at Wembley to watch England v Scotland soccer and Huddersfield v St. Helens Rugby League football. Lindwall and Archer had bad colds but recovered in time for the start of the tour.

When the tourists arrived in England, some embarrassment was caused by the publication of a book *Bumper* written by Keith Miller and journalist R.S.Whitington which contained a passage about Hassett's abilities as a captain, saying that he was too timid and cautious and does not think ahead, that England may in Hutton have the advantage in the leadership department. It made headlines in the English newspapers on the day of the Savoy Hotel lunch. Whatever his faults, Hassett knew how to diffuse a situation. He had to introduce each member of his team. He came to Keith Miller who stood rather sheepishly, and Hassett then said "I hear he has written a book".

On Sunday 26th April at East Molesey Cricket Club, beside the Thames near Hampton Court, over 10,000, including the Duke of Edinburgh watched 13-a-side East Molesey make 244 for 11 declared. The club team included Bernard Constable of Surrey, T.E. Bailey and Insole of Essex and Australian Tribe of Northants. Ten Australians bowled. John Arlott performed the loudspeaker duties. Having bowled 4 overs for one run and a wicket, Bill Johnston retired with a strained right knee: unfortunately it turned out to be a serious injury. Lunch lasted from 1.15 to 2.35. For Australians Morris scored 103 in 80 minutes. Miller hit a six which landed about ten feet short of Tagg Island in the river, a carry of 140 yards which would have earned him £600. Of the newcomers, Hole impressed, he reached the river twice. McDonald did not. 314 were scored in 44 overs. But the touring side were none too amused at Johnston's injury. Although some charity or benefit matches were played on Sundays, serious cricket was strictly 'verboten', and it was unusual for a touring side to play even as friendly a match as this on Sunday. Many of the Australians wondered why this club was singled out for this great honour. Funds were being raised for a new Pavilion (architect Basil Ward), and the club president Mr B.M.Turner had made several business trips to Australia, even set up branches of the cricket club in NSW, Victoria and Western Australia, and given the Freedom of the City of Melbourne. On one of his visits he persuaded the Australian Board of Control to play at East Molesey.

EAST MOLESEY 244-11dec (D.J.Insole (Essex) 52, T.E.Bailey (Essex) 40, R.Smith (Essex) 69, Lindwall 2-16, Ring 4-95) AUSTRALIANS 314-9 (Morris 103, Hassett 45, Miller 33, Hole 67, G.Tribe (Nhants) 6-112). *Australians won by 5 wickets.*

On Monday the Duke of Edinburgh opened the Imperial Cricket Memorial at Lord's, a museum behind the Pavilion, dedicated to the memory of cricketers who died in two world wars. Before the start of the season, the Chancellor, R.A.Butler, exempted cricket from entertainment tax. "In this country cricket occupies a special place among sports, not only as forming part of the English tradition but as a common interest helping to bind together the various countries of the Commonwealth. ... and as the total receipts of entertainments duty from cricket are so small, I propose to exempt it from duty altogether."

Spring chill: Worcester, April 29, 30, May 1.

The first-class season began with the Australians in the traditional opening game at Worcester, having come by train from Paddington the previous day. On a typical April day Lindwall peeled off two sweaters down to one sleeveless and bowled Peter Richardson fourth ball, but Worcestershire scored 246-3 in five hours. Benaud fielded with four sweaters. Don Kenyon, a contender to open the England batting with Hutton, made 117 not out by the close and the captain R.E Bird helped him to add 117. Lindwall and Miller did not bowl at full stretch, Archer was wayward and the fielding was almost lackadaisical. BBC television cameras were present.

Play started at 2pm on Thursday. Kenyon soon, against Benaud, played for leg-spin that was not there and was bowled, but Broadbent steered Worcestershire to the luxury of a declaration. Morris edged to gully. McDonald gave a slip chance and then was caught at short leg hooking, and Hassett glanced a catch to the leg trap. The Australians were 28-3, all falling to John Whitehead, a fast medium mechanical engineer specially registered from Yorkshire. But Miller and Hole counter-attacked to reach 119-3 at the close. On a better wicket and in better weather on the final day, the tourists batted through the day, scoring

1953 – FIRST TEST

323 in 280 minutes. Miller's 220 not out in 375 minutes was his highest score to date. Hole, Benaud and Archer also batted well but de Courcy was lbw to Whitehead to his first ball. Archer's 100 took only 87 minutes.

WORCESTERSHIRE 333-7dec (D.Kenyon 122, R.E Bird 76, R.G.Broadbent 52, Hill 3-57). AUSTRALIANS 542-7dec (Miller 220*, Hole 112, Benaud 44, Archer 108, J.P.Whitehead 5-89). *Drawn*.

Sun arrives: Leicester, May 2, 4, 5.

Sun and a good wicket made all the difference for the Australians. On the first day they scored 443 for 8. After 3 were out for 56 Harvey scored 202 in 285 minutes. After Miller was run out by Maurice Tompkin, Craig made his first appearance. He settled in well making 23 until he chopped onto his wicket cutting an in-swinger. Davidson hit a six and 11 fours. Wicket-keeper Firth injured his shoulder early in the day and kept wicket throughout, but was unfit to bat. Hassett declared overnight and Leicestershire fell to 84 for 7 at lunch. They followed on and the match was over by six o'clock in the second day. Leg-spinners Ring and Hill took the wickets.

AUSTRALIANS 443-8dec (Harvey 202*, Miller 42, Davidson 63) LEICESTERSHIRE 109 (C.T.Spencer 30, Davidson 2-23, Hill 4-57) and 180 (G.A. Smithson 30, C.H.Palmer 62*, J.E.Walsh 33, Ring 5-66, Hill 4-46). *Australians won by an innings and 154 runs.*

May 2nd was the first day of the County Championship, as it was also the day of great FA Cup Final at Wembley, where Blackpool 1-3 down to Bolton Wanderers with 20 minutes to go won 4-3 and England's most famous footballer Stanley Matthews got his first Cup-winners medal.. At Peterborough Middlesex were bowled out by humble Northants for 96 in 145 minutes, Clarke bowling unchanged for 5-31. In their second innings, thanks to 100 by Denis Compton (watched by the Chairman of the Test selectors) Middlesex left Northants 227 to win. They got to 225-7. Edrich bowled Clarke. Then with the scores level, Starkie was stumped off Young. Last man Fiddling survived the last three balls of the over. Now with only one run needed, Broderick, 80 not out, faced an over from Edrich, and incredibly it was a maiden. Off the first ball of the next over Young bowled Fiddling and the match was tied. Each side got six points.

Benaud's day: Bradford, May 6, 7, 8.

Yardley put the Australians in. Trueman is not playing, unable to get leave from the RAF. Hassett dropped out on the first morning when he found that he had an inflamed tendon on his right wrist. They made a moderate start but thanks to a Miller century reached 298-5 by the close. Miller was dropped twice, and he was largely responsible for the run out of young Craig, who was going well on 14, with a change of mind about going for a third run to long leg. Benaud was 3 not out at the close; next morning he overshadowed Miller and hit beautifully to reach 97 when he was caught at the wicket a few minutes before lunch. The members gave him a standing ovation. Wardle bowled a marathon 64-28-103-2, with no luck. After a lunch declaration, Yorkshire made only 145, Benaud completing a brilliant all-round day, but he cut open his spinning finger and bowled only 3 overs in the follow on. There was stony silence across the Park Avenue ground when Hutton walked back having had his defensive push blasted through by Lindwall on the fifth ball of the innings, possibly because his bat was caught in his pad. Hassett tried Davidson as an orthodox slow left arm spinner and he took 2 for 21 in 20 overs? With an hour to spare on the third day Yorkshire succumbed to an innings defeat, but Hutton played a solid 65, though troubled by Hill's flat leg-spin. Miller now had 421 runs for once out so far in the tour, but the run feast was to end there.

AUSTRALIANS 453-6dec (Morris 57, Harvey 37, Miller 159*, de Courcy 53, Benaud 97). YORKSHIRE 145 (N.W.D.Yardley 50*, Benaud 7-46) and 214 (L.Hutton 65, N.W.D.Yardley 56*, Hill 4-61). *Australians won by an innings and 94 runs.*

At Portsmouth A.E.Wilson of Gloucestershire became the first wicket-keeper to take 10 catches in a match (though other keepers had more victims including stumpings, and Walter Hammond had taken 10 catches in a match as fielder).

Champions overrun: the Oval, May 9, 11, 12

The county champions Surrey, with a near full-strength side including four likely members of the forthcoming England side, presented another innings win to the tourists. Again Lindwall started the rout with the fifth ball of the innings, Archer made a big impression and Surrey were all out in 100 minutes before lunch. May was caught behind second ball off a Lindwall special. The Australian batsmen went on the attack, but the Surrey bowlers held them to a reasonable total of 256 ending after 15 minutes on the second morning. Under a cloudless sky Surrey fared little better. David Fletcher was first in and last out for 61 in 175 minutes. May was again targeted by Lindwall and survived, without contact, a torrid over, one of the best he ever bowled, but after half an hour he was yorked by Archer's slower ball. The match finished by 3 o'clock on the second day, which helped the Australians to enjoy the dinner that evening at the

1953 – FIRST TEST

Armourers' and Braziers' Hall, with distinguished speakers Lord Tedder and Sir Walter Monckton. Two major English counties have now been beaten, deflating England's high hopes.

SURREY 58 (Archer 6-26) and 122 (D.G.W.Fletcher 61, Archer 5-35, Ring 3-31). AUSTRALIANS 256 (Hole 40, Harvey 66, Davidson 39, A.V. Bedser 4-60). *Australians won by an innings and 76 runs.*

Of the seven county championship matches, five produced close finishes. Worcestershire, needing 194 in 145 minutes to beat Glamorgan, and 55 in 30 minutes with 8 down, failed by one run with two balls left. Essex's last pair held out for 20 minutes to salvage a draw against Yorkshire. Gloucestershire, set 302 in 260 minutes, won with 15 minutes to spare. Middlesex needed 62 in 52 minutes to beat Hampshire and won with six minutes left. Lancashire went for a target of 244 in 125 minutes against Warwickshire, even though their opener Ikin was absent with a bad back, and just survived on 158-8.

Runs and horses: Fenner's Cambridge, May 13, 14

There is no lovelier place to be than Fenner's Ground, the home of Cambridge University on a sunny spring day, watching Australia pile up 385 in 305 minutes. Miller had his first failure, which enabled him to go off to Newmarket and lose money on the horses. Their wicket-keeper was a rugby player called Asquith who had been called up to play that morning and took two excellent catches. Marlar the Sussex off-spinner enhanced his reputation: if he were born ten years earlier or later he might have played for England. The weather broke overnight. Busby opened with an accomplished short innings, and the gifted future Test players, Subba Row and Gerry Alexander of West Indies offers some resistance as the University were rolled over twice amongst sunshine and showers on the second day.

AUSTRALIANS 383 (Morris 79, Craig 47, Davidson 71, Archer 63*, T.Hare 4-73, R.G.Marlar 5-139) CAMBRIDGE UNIVERSITY 130 (M.H.Bushby 34, F.C.M.Alexander 32, Ring 5-19) and 147 (R.Subba Row 41, Ring 4-57, Archer 4-31). *Australians won by an innings and 106 runs.*

The rain prevented results in all but two county matches. Glamorgan beat the weather by disposing of Kent in two days at Cardiff and with two wins in their two games were top of the championship table.

Bailey announces himself: MCC at Lord's, May 16, 18, 19

For the usual fixture against the touring team in May the MCC side was picked by the England selectors as a mixture of established Test players and future prospects and was regarded on both sides as an important trial of strength. This year the chairman of the selectors F.R. Brown played himself and led a team of which all but one, Alan Moss, were Test players and leading contenders for the Test series. Saturday was a fine sunny afternoon but due to saturation of the pitch not a single ball was bowled – raising an argument for covering pitches and a query about the rule that the umpires could not insist on play if both captains agreed not to. Hassett hoped to play but dropped out with a sore hand. On Monday MCC were put in by Morris and Lindwall soon had them 3 out for 9, bowling five overs downwind from the Nursery End. Simpson was beautifully caught by Davidson at 4th slip. David Sheppard edged another outswinger to Tallon. They make a quartet of England players, with Hutton and May, who have made ducks against the 1953 Australians. The rest were hypnotised by Ring, unable to read his flight, giving him 26 wickets so far, and were all out for 80 five minutes after lunch. On a dull still day, the Australians did not do much better. Sheppard started the rot with a spectacular diving catch at short leg. First Harvey and Benaud and then Lindwall, dropped before he scored, and Davidson salvaged the innings from 26 for 4. In the dark of the evening MCC lost both openers and May was hit on the shoulder by a Miller bumper, before Compton successfully appealed against the light, 19-2 at the close. Apparently the batsmen thought that the match regulations precluded them from appealing against the light, until Arthur Morris told them otherwise. Queen Sallotte of Tonga was present during the day.

MCC had requested the Australians to play an extra hour on the last day to compensate for the blank Saturday but they declined. MCC saved the game in what the *Times* correspondent called a miracle. Compton stayed from 11am to 1 pm and was lbw padding up to Davidson. Bailey was at the other end, taking 70 minutes to move his score from 7 to 8. At lunch MCC were 107 for 7, only two runs ahead, but Bailey was still there. Wardle stayed for half and hour till he gave Harvey a horrible skied catch, well taken running back from mid-on. 132 for 8, 31 ahead with 135 minutes left. Lindwall was not bowling due to leg strain. Tattersall stayed while 64 were added in 90 minutes. Tattersall was out and Moss quickly followed. Bailey was still there, 64 not out in 220 minutes. Australia needed 98 in only 30 minutes and sensibly declined the task. This same Bailey had not played for England since he was dropped in 1951

As it turned out the match became a prototype for what would happen in the Test series.

1953 – FIRST TEST

MCC (lost toss)

R.T.Simpson c Davidson b Lindwall	0	- lbw b Miller	5
D.S.Sheppard c Tallon b Lindwall	0	- b Miller	3
P.B.H.May lbw b Ring	16	- lbw b Lindwall	11
D.C.S.Compton lbw b Lindwall	2	- lbw b Davidson	45
T.W.Graveney c Davidson b Ring	12	- b Davidson	7
T.E.Bailey c Tallon b Davidson	1	- not out	64
*F.R.Brown c Harvey b Ring	9	- c Davidson b Miller	11
+T.G.Evans c Miller b Davidson	10	- b Miller	11
J.H.Wardle b Ring	6	- c Harvey b Davidson	16
R. Tattersall not out	7	- lbw b Ring	12
A.E.Moss c Benaud b Ring	12	- c Hole b Benaud	0
Extras (b 1, lb 4)	5	- (b 7, lb 4)	11
TOTAL (41.2 overs, 127 mins)	80	(109 overs, 309 mins)	196

WICKETS.- 1-0, 2-3, 3-9, 4-29, 5-30, 6-41, 7-41, 8-59, 9-65, 10-80.
BOWLING.- Lindwall 9-5-12-3; Miller 7-3-10-0; Ring 13.2-4-36-5; Davidson 12-5-17-2.

1-8, 2-15, 3-32, 4-55, 5-82, 6-93, 7-105, 8-131, 9-195, 10-196
Lindwall 12-8-17-1; Miller 24-8-47-4; Ring 13-6-16-1; Davidson 24-7-49-3; Hill 26-13-33-0; Hole 3-1-3-0; Benaud 7-1-20-0.

Australians

C.C.McDonald b Bailey	9	not out	8
*A.R.Morris c Sheppard b Moss	6	not out	4
R.N.Harvey c Compton b Wardle	33		
K.R.Miller b Bailey	0		
G.B.Hole lbw b Moss	0		
R. Benaud c Tattersall b Moss	35	c Tattersall b Moss	0
A.K.Davidson c Bailey b Tattersall	25		
R.R.Lindwall b Tattersall	33		
+D. Tallon c Evans b Tattersall	16	c May b Moss	1
D.T.Ring c Sheppard b Tattersall	11		
J.C.Hill not out	2		
Extras (b 6., lb 2, nb 1)	9		
TOTAL (47.2 overs, 162 mins)	179	For 2 wkts (8 overs, 30 mins)	13

WICKETS.- 1-15, 2-15, 3-15, 4-26, 5-72, 6-109, 7-126, 8-158, 9-174, 10-179.
BOWLING.-. Moss 14-1-70-3; Bailey 10-3-19-2; Tattersall 17.2-3-68-4; Wardle 6-1-13-1.

1-5, 2-9

Moss 4-2-7-2; Brown 4-1-6-0.

Match drawn
Umpires: D. Davies and Harold Elliott

Warwickshire embarrassed

Surrey began their Championship defence at last on May 16, at the Oval against Warwickshire. A wet pitch delayed the start until noon. Warwks were bowled out by 1.15. Alec Bedser achieved his best bowling figures to date, 8-18, helped by great catches in the leg-trap. Constable gave Surrey a reasonable start but they collapsed to 49 for 8. The captain Surridge hit 19 with 3 sixes in 4 balls of Hollies. Lock came in at 119 for 9. He scored 27 and when he retired hurt, hit above the eye and going to hospital, the Surrey innings ended for 146, a lead of 101. Warwks batted again at 5.30. With Lock absent Laker got his first bowl of the match, and promptly took a hat-trick. After shouting into the Pavilion to the Surrey Secretary to check that it could be done, Surridge invoked the extra-half hour. It could be claimed on any day if a finish looked possible. At 6.40 Warwks were all out for 52. Bedser took 12-35 in the match, Laker 5-29. The Warwickshire team could not even go home because they had an engagement with their MP at the House of Commons on Monday evening.

On Monday, Rev. E.T.Killick, of Cambridge University and Middlesex, who played for England against South Africa in 1929, now the Vicar at Bishop Stortford, collapsed at the wicket in a diocesan match at Northampton and died, aged 46.

1953 – FIRST TEST

Dinner with Mr.Jardine: Oxford, May 20, 21.

Australia were 2 down at lunch, after Oxford University had already made their first innings batting contribution. The tourist batting was tied down to be 136 for 6 at tea. But de Courcy made 142 in 220 minutes with 20 fours. An innings victory was achieved by tea on the second day. Dinner that night was hosted by Oxford Cricket Club President and former England captain Douglas Jardine.

OXFORD UNIVERSITY 70 (J.P.Fellows-Smith 21, Hill 3-11, Benaud 3-20, Miller 2-8) and 174 (H.B.Birrell 40, C.C.P.Williams 47, J.P.Fellows-Smith 50, Miller 3-19, Benaud 3-37). Australians 330 (Hole 47, de Courcy 142, Archer 45, Langley 40*, D.K.Fasken 5-108). *Australians won by an innings and 86 runs.*

There was a great third day at Gravesend. Kent were set to get 312 in nearly 5 hours. Godfrey Evans made 75 in an hour out of 105 with hard pulls and on-drives. Then he ran himself out when he called for an unwise sharp single. With half an hour left George Tribe took a grand running catch on the boundary and Northamptonshire won by 17 runs.

Whitsun controversy: Minor Counties at Stoke-on-Trent, May 23, 25

Odd that the Australians should be scheduled to play a Minor Counties conglomerate at Stoke on Whitsun holiday. The match was well attended, but any game against a county would have pulled in many more and 10,000 who came on Monday saw only 2 hours 10 minutes cricket as they wrapped up an innings victory. The Minor Counties championship consisted, as well as a few first-class county second XIs, of most of the English counties which were not first-class, Durham, Cornwall, Bedfordshire, Norfolk etc. Every year the best of its players were selected to meet the tourists, in a game which rarely extended them. The Counties' captain, Ben Barnett, a businessman now working England who was Australian wicket-keeper on two tours to England before the War, put the Australians in on a difficult wicket (rain having seeped through the covers). Harvey played what was in those circumstances one of his best innings of the tour, 109 in 150 minutes. The Australian Prime Minister Mr. Menzies, who happened to be visiting the local corporation was there after lunch. Without having to try too hard, the minor side were 27 for 6 at the Saturday close and Archer, bowling off-breaks, and Benaud disposed of them quickly on Monday. The match marked the return of Hassett, absent for five games with a strained arm, and the first appearance of Johnston since his injury at East Molesey, and an article by E.W.Swanton in the *Daily Telegraph* on Lindwall's drag. Before the front foot rule was introduced for no-balls in the 1960s, bowlers were supposed to have at least part of the back foot grounded behind the bowling crease at the moment of release of the ball. A fast bowler might land his back foot well behind the crease but his forward momentum would enable the back foot to slide forward and it would be impossible for an umpire to judge where the foot was at the moment of release. The *Telegraph* published a photograph showing his back foot well over and the ball still in his hand and no apparent signal from the umpire.

AUSTRALIANS 289 (Harvey 109, Hassett 32, de Courcy 40, F.Taylor 5-71). MINOR COUNTIES 56 (Lindwall 7-20, Johnston 3-20) and 62 (C.Lee 23, Archer 4-25, Benaud 5-13). *Australians won by an innings and 171 runs.*

On Saturday at Lord's, in lovely weather a large crowd saw Denis Compton return to form with 143 on his 35th birthday. At Old Trafford Trueman's rival as a young fast bowler, Brian Statham, bowled Hutton for 2, but Lancashire had to fight for a draw, being saved by Cyril Washbrook who came back to bat with stitches in his jaw after being struck earlier by Trueman. At Worcester on Monday 479 runs were scored for four wickets: Essex, moved from 13-2 to 359-4 dec and Worcs began their second innings with 133-0. Hampshire beat Kent and were top of the table.

1953 – FIRST TEST

Rain at Manchester, May 27, 28, 29

Atrocious weather which meant that no play was possible on the first day and the loss of 65 minutes on the third morning condemned this important fixture to a draw. Lancashire put up a good fight. On Thursday the Australians found the going hard on a sluggish pitch. Harvey took 2 hours to reach 50 but completed his 103 in a further 70 minutes. He was nearly stumped three times of Malcolm Hilton. Australian Ken Grieves took four catches at slip and the fielding was generally very tight. Hassett got in some careful match practice and even Miller was subdued. Lancashire had 20 minutes to bat, scoring 8 for 1. In the first over Umpire Corrall warned Lindwall for dragging his back foot over the crease and then no-balled him for it. At the end of the over Corrall consulted with Hassett about some remark made by Lindwall. Lindwall's second over was passed, and he bowled Winston Place playing no stroke. Next day, from 59 for 4, the captain Nigel Howard and Wharton saved the county with a stand of 81 in 70 minutes and in the end even the new ball could not secure the Australians a first innings lead. The 'drag' controversy blew over almost as quickly as it came; photographic evidence showed that others, such as Miller, Bedser and Trueman, were as guilty of drag as Lindwall.

AUSTRALIANS 298 (Hole 43, Hassett 34, Harvey 103, J.B. Statham 3-63, M.J.Hilton 4-117) LANCASHIRE 232-9 (N.D.Howard 78*, A.Wharton 57, Lindwall 4-41). *Match Drawn*

Test trial blues

At Birmingham an England XI were playing 'the Rest' in a Test trial match. This annual fixture seems always to have been marked by inclement weather, small crowds and unmemorable cricket, and 1953 was no exception. On the first day, with only 135 minutes play the England XI made 120 for 2. Hutton experimented with Trevor Bailey as his opening partner and the result was inconclusive. On the second day Compton and Simpson shared a cultured stand of 99. May looked out of touch, and so did David Sheppard who was on the Rest side. At the end the Rest were set 212 in 150 minutes and the match petered out to a meaningless draw. The match was memorable for two things: the appointment at the end of Len Hutton as England captain for the First Test, and what the *Times* correspondent called "the strange case of Trueman". England's new weapon bowled with little life and poor length and direction, and got a lambasting from Australian journalist Dick Whitington, who said that the only frightening thing about Trueman was his long, bandy-legged, pigeon-toed run-up. In Len Hutton's view, the only activity which makes a player fit for fast bowling is fast bowling, not physical jerks.

ENGLAND XI 269-6 dec (L.Hutton 49, R.T.Simpson 62, D.C.S.Compton 75, C.T.Spencer 3-51, F.R.Brown 2-18) and 116-2 dec (T.W.Graveney 39*). THE REST 174 (D.Kenyon 32, D.S.Sheppard 34, T.G.Evans 32, A.V.Bedser 3-36, A.E. Moss 3-53) and 118-0 (N.H.Rogers 53*, D.Kenyon 62*). *Match drawn.*

Leicestershire won a hard fought game against Gloucestershire. Surrey beat Somerset by 32 runs at Taunton, though Somerset made a good effort at making 297. Surridge dismissed centurion Gimblett and two others and held a slip catch to end the match.

C-day approaches: Nottingham, May 30, June 1

The Nottinghamshire club kindly agreed to play a two-day fixture of seven hours play so that the Australians would be free for Coronation day. The coach trip from Manchester deposited the tourists at their hotel just before midnight on Friday. Notts were 80 for 5 when Australian Bruce Dooland joined Simpson 40 minutes before lunch. Simpson batted stubbornly for 195 minutes. Dooland was more aggressive. When he hooked Archer for four he was treated to two head high beamers. Benaud cracked a bone in the finger of his left hand when attempting a return catch and took no further part in the match. The county only had half the opening attack because Butler was hit on the finger by a near-beamer from Miller when batting. In poor light the Australians lost both openers for 100 by the close. The crowd, whose county had given up a third day, were not pleased when Hole appealed unsuccessfully against the light. After McDonald was out Hassett came in and, in light which was if anything slightly better, persuaded the umpires to change their minds, much to the distaste of the crowd. Next morning Hassett and Miller, with two sixes into the pavilion, showed a welcome return to form. Adding 155 in 140 minutes, the tourists were 47 ahead at lunch, but churlishly decided to bat on rather than reward the county's gesture by going for a result. But hailstorms, rain and bad light allowed only two short spells of play after lunch so in the end it did not matter.

NOTTINGHAMSHIRE 208 (R.T.Simpson 65, B.Dooland 69, Hill 5-62) AUSTRALIANS 290-6 (Hole 69, Hassett 62, Miller 48, Davidson 38*). *Match drawn*

At Manchester Surrey achieved a fine win against Lancashire by eight wickets and joined Hampshire at the top of the table. Lock returned after his injury, he took 5 for 89 in the first innings and held in all seven catches at short leg. May hit a timely 75 as Surrey recovered from 49 for 5 in their first innings. Rain on the

1953 – FIRST TEST

third afternoon enabled all the players to watch the Coronation on a television in the Committee room. At Lord's the Middlesex-Northants match was ruined by weather. On Tuesday play was due to start at 2.30 because of the Coronation but persistent showers prevented any play at all.

Coronation day

The Australians stayed out of town on Monday night because there was no room in any London hotels. That day Jack Hobbs, and jockey Gordon Richards, were granted knighthoods. Tuesday dawned dull and rainy, but with news that New Zealander Edmund Hillary and Sherpa Tensing had conquered Mount Everest, the first known humans to do so. The rain relented slightly during the royal procession from Buckingham Place to St Paul's Cathedral and the sun blinked through on the return journey. The Australian had seats on the balcony of a club in Haymarket on the Coronation route, and they cheered loud enough for their Prime Minister Mr Menzies to hear them from his coach and return the greeting. And having seen the procession they then watched the ceremony at Westminster Abbey live in black-and-white on television. That night they travelled down to Brighton. Lights, flags, fireworks and bonfires were everywhere, and HMS *Eagle* was lit up in the English Channel.

Sir Donald arrives: Hove, June 3, 4, 5

From London down to the south coast to play Sussex. Recuperating from having organised the Coronation, as Earl Marshall of England, the Duke of Norfolk came to watch. Hassett tried himself as an opener and soon edged a catch to the slips. At last McDonald, plagued by bad form and injury, passed 20 for the first time. He was only 30 at lunch and made 106 after 230 minutes. Harvey excelled again, 82 in 126 minutes. Australia only just achieved a respectable total thanks to 20 byes conceded by Webb (though the all-round fielding was good) and a last wicket stand of 57 in 45 minutes between Hill and Johnston. In poor light Sheppard and John Langridge made 35 for 0, and next day took the opening stand to 112. Sheppard put himself in the Test reckoning with an assured 56, till he was deceived by Hill's slower ball. The last nine wickets fell for 106, helped by two run-outs. In the second innings Harvey was on top form, being 107 out of 173 for 1 at the close, and next day he was even overshadowed by Hassett, whose 108 took 3 hours, Harvey's 137 165 minutes. Sussex had a forbidding target of 367 in 260 minutes. They were 76 for 5 at lunch. James Langridge and Oakman added 81. The last pair held out for 20 minutes to save the game. This was James Langridge's last game for Sussex, ending a career of 31,706 runs and 1,530 wickets. On this day Sir Donald Bradman alighted at Croydon Airport, with his wife Lady Jesse. He is to write on the Test series for the *Daily Mail*.

AUSTRALIANS 325 (McDonald 106, Harvey 82, A.E.James 5-96) and 259-1 dec (Hassett 108*, Harvey 137*). SUSSEX 218 (D.S.Sheppard 56, John Langridge 74, Johnston 4-65, Hill 4-40) and 190-9 (G.H.G.Doggart 30, James Langridge 46, Johnston 3-49, Hill 4-38, Davidson 2-14). *Match drawn.*

Amongst the dismissals in Derbyshire's 106 on the first day, Revill took a blow from a vicious rising ball from Bedser on the knuckles; in pain he shook his glove off which dislodged a bail and the umpire ruled him out, hit wicket. In a low-scoring game Surrey won in two days and went 8 points clear of Glamorgan. Middlesex suffered a surprise defeat by ten wickets at home to Somerset.

Day's rest gained: Southampton, June 6, 8

The Australians had a welcome two-day win against Hampshire. Harvey reached a brilliant hundred in 135 minutes: it was his usual style, faultless and carefree until a careless shot got him caught at short leg. Then the last 8 wickets fell for 69 in 70 minutes. The county authority opened the gates to let in many queuing outside to sit on the grass, thus reducing the boundary by more than 10 yards. West Indian Test player, Roy Marshall, making his debut for the county whilst qualifying by residence for county cricket, took wickets with his off-breaks and hit 5 sixes and 5 fours in his second innings, 71 in 83 minutes. Morris, acting captain, gave Johnston an extended spell of bowling to test his fitness. With a day and a half left, Morris set Hampshire 307 to win and gambled on a quick finish, in preference to making the match safe and further batting practice. His enterprise was rewarded and the tourists got an extra day to prepare for the start of the Test series. At 109-2 the hope of a sensational Hampshire victory was blossoming, but then Marshall skied a catch to mid wicket.

AUSTRALIANS 268 (Morris 55, Harvey 109, R.E.Marshall 4-69) and 169 for 5 dec (Morris 50, de Courcy 54*) HAMPSHIRE 131 (Johnston 5-75, Archer 3-23) and 148 (R.E.Marshall 71, Johnston 4-21, Benaud 4-38). *Australians won by 158 runs.*

In a low-scoring game at Pontypridd, dominated by the seam bowlers Jackson and Gladwin of Derbyshire and Shepherd and Wooller of Glamorgan, Glamorgan won through by 13 runs. With the Test selection due next day, Peter May drove powerfully against Northamptonshire's attack (which included the chairman of the selectors) for 134 in 4 hours but Surrey could not bowl out Northants in the follow on,

1953 – FIRST TEST

dropping crucial catches. Graveney 'nudged the selectors' as well, when he made his highest career score, 211 in only 305 minutes in Gloucestershire's 505 for 5 in beating Kent at Gillingham. On Saturday at Lord's 20,000 people saw Compton's century against Yorkshire. Len Hutton was hit on the shoulder when fielding at short leg, and batted at No.8 for Yorkshire. A second match of the season was over in one day, the first game of the Bath Festival, on a new laid pitch, 30 wickets fell for 292 runs as Lancashire beat Somerset by an innings and 24 runs. Poor Bertie Buse, Somerset's veteran trouper, helped the financial catastrophe for his benefit match by taking 6 for 41.

1953 – FIRST TEST

FIRST TEST AT TRENT BRIDGE
Nottingham, June 11, 12, 13, 15, 16

In 1953 strictly no serious cricket or other cricketing business could be transacted on a Sunday, with the exception of the eagerly awaited England Test side for the coming Test. The selectors were F.R.Brown, N.W.D.Yardley, R.E.S.Wyatt (three former England amateur captains) and L.E.G.Ames (England professional wicket-keeper). The meeting lasted only half an hour. 12 names were solemnly announced on the lunchtime news, plus a designated 12th man:

Len HUTTON (Capt.) (Yorks) aged almost 37. England's established opening right-hand batsman and professional captain, first played for Yorkshire in 1934, England debut in 1937, scorer of the record Test score 364 at the Oval in 1938. His left arm was shortened after a training accident in the Army during the War. Since then he became the indispensable sheet-anchor of England's batting in the lean years from 1946 to 1951. He was senior professional, but never captain of Yorkshire. Very occasional leg-spin bowler and slip or leg slip fielder

Don KENYON (Worcs) aged 29. professional opening right-hand bat, consistent run-scorer since 1946, toured India in 1951-52.

Reg T. SIMPSON (Notts) aged 33 amateur. Opening or middle-order bat and excellent outfielder. Fairly regular Test player since 1949, scoring the decisive 150 in England's first Test victory against Australia in 1950-51.

Peter B.H. MAY (Surrey) aged 23. Amateur, (Charterhouse and Cambridge Univ) powerful and solid right-hand bat, likely to become England's premier batsman, century on Test debut in 1951. Good cover/mid-wicket fielder

Denis C.S. COMPTON (Middx) aged 35. Professional. Outstanding right-hand bat, slow left arm 'chinaman' bowler. Exact contemporary of Hutton but with a very different attitude and reputation, touched by a magical genius in the post-war years, professional footballer for Arsenal, which caused a knee injury which brought him down to earth in the 1950s. He failed spectacularly in the 1950-51 series but otherwise was a 'lucky' cricketer.

Tom W. GRAVENEY (Gloucs) Professional. aged almost 26. Stylish right-hand bat who could tear an attack apart with his effortless driving on a good day. County debut 1948, Test debut 1951

Trevor E. BAILEY (Essex) Amateur. (Dulwich and Cambridge Univ) Aged 29 Infuriatingly adhesive middle-order bat and right fast medium bowler with swing or cut, attacking or defensive as required. An excellent cricketing brain, potential England captain. Top-class close fielder

T. Godfrey EVANS (Kent) aged 32 Professional. Brilliant wicket-keeper and dashing low order bat. Automatic choice since his debut in 1946, he set new standards of wicket-keeping, diving for catches that others would not even consider, though occasionally he would drop a simple chance.

Alec V. BEDSER (Surrey) aged 34. Professional. outstanding right fast medium bowler, specialist in 'cutters' balls which swing one way then seam the other way off the pitch. Until now since the war he bore the brunt of England's pace bowling almost alone. Sound low order right hand bat.

G.A.R. (Tony) LOCK (Surrey) Professional aged 23. Aggressive slow left arm bowler, useful right hand bat and brilliant leg trap fielder. His quick ball pinged down at a fair speed, and his bent elbow caused some concern about the fairness of his delivery. He made his Test debut in 1952 and was already regarded as the foremost spin bowler.

Roy TATTERSALL (Lancs) Professional Aged 30. Tight slow medium off-break bowler. Left-handed bat. Test debut when flown out to Australia as a re-enforcement in 1950-51.

J. Brian STATHAM (Lancs) Professional Aged almost 23. Promising fast right-hand bowler, accurate, persistent, unflappable, relying mainly on cutting the ball of the seam; left-hand bat.

Designated 12th man C. Arthur MILTON (Gloucs) Aged 25 Professional. Fair-haired left-hand bat.

Lock damaged the forefinger of his left hand in the current championship match and had to withdraw. Having rested after his accident on 16 May, the skin on his spinning finger was soft and got torn when he started bowling again. So in came

John H. WARDLE (Yorks) Professional. Aged 30. Versatile slow left arm bowler who bowled only orthodox finger spin for Yorkshire but could also bowl 'chinamen', that is wrist spin off-breaks, and useful low order left hand bat.

Of the last England team to take the field at the Oval in 1952, Sheppard, Ikin, Watson, Laker, Lock and Trueman were replaced by Kenyon, Simpson, Compton, Bailey, Tattersall, Wardle and Statham.

Bedser was excused from bowling in the nets because of the view that he could do better with a rest, causing a rumour to start that he was unfit.

The touring side had several problems. Johnston was out of action since East Molesey, Hassett was recovering from a sore forearm, Benaud from torn skin on his spinning finger, Miller has back trouble and Langley a sore right hand. Lindwall strained his groin slightly in bowlers' footholds at Hove but expected to be fit enough to play. The Australian XIII, announced by Hassett after dinner at their hotel on Wednesday evening, was Morris, Hole, Hassett, Harvey, Miller, de Courcy, Benaud, Davidson, Archer Tallon, Lindwall, Hill and Johnston. Either Hole or Hassett would open the batting. Miller was unfit to bowl.

Umpires: D. Davies and Harold Elliott

1953 – FIRST TEST

Dour indecision - FIRST DAY, Thursday 11 June

11.05: England leave out Statham, giving only four bowlers.
11.10: Australia omit de Courcy (12th man) and Archer. Miller is to play after some massage on his strained left side.
11.12: Australia win toss. Pitch looks dry, hard and bare of grass. Hutton is disappointed not to bat on a near perfect wicket

Australia First Innings

Odd overs   ] →   from Pavilion End
Even overs   ] ←   from Radcliffe Road/City End

As usual Arthur Morris chooses to go to the non-striker's end.

#	Time	Bowler	Hole	Morris	Score	Notes
1	11.30	Bedser 1] →	- - - - -		0-0	Damp atmosphere ball swinging light poor
2		Bailey 1] ←		- - 2 - -	-2	
3	11.37 11.39	Bedser 2] →	W Hassett - - - -		1-2 -2	Hole bowled by full in-swinger, 0 in 7 mins 7 balls 0 fours. Crowd erupts. Delay while Hutton slowly sets field; further delay while Hassett takes guard again
4		Bailey 2] ←		- - 1 - -	-3	
5		Bedser 3] →	1	- 1 - - -	-5	
6		Bailey 3] ←	1	- - - 1 -	-7	
7		Bedser 4] →		- - - - -	-7	Morris almost put up a catch to Kenyon at mid-off
8		Bailey 4] ← off spell 4-1-5-0	- - - - -		-7	
9		Bedser 5] →		- - 4 (nb) - - -	-11	Morris drives no-ball straight for four
	12.00					

1953 – FIRST TEST

Over	Time	Bowler		Batsman 1	Batsman 2	Total	Notes
10		Wardle 1] ←		- - 1 - - -		-12	*Wardle accurate.* *Defensive field with one slip*
11		Bedser 6] →		- - - - 1		-13	
12		Wardle 2] ←		- - - 4 -		-17	*Hassett late cut for four*
13	12.15	Bedser 7] → off spell 7-3-7-1		- - - - -		-17	
14		Wardle 3] ←		- - - - -		-17	
15		Tattersall 1] →		- - - - 4		-21	*Tattersall has one leg slip but no slip*
16		Wardle 4] ←		- - - - -		-21	
17		Tattersall 2] → off spell 2-0-8-0		- - - 4 -		-25	*Morris snicks four through empty slip area*
18		Wardle 5] ←		- - - - -		-25	
19		Bailey 5] →		- - - 2 -		-27	*Bailey bowling outside off-stump*
20		Wardle 6] ←		- - - - 1		-28	*Hassett's first run for 25 balls*

1953 – FIRST TEST

21		Bailey 6] →	4 - - - -		-32	Hassett four to off-side
22		Wardle 7] ←		- - - - -	-32	
23		Bailey 7] →	- - - - (1 lb) -		-33	
24		Wardle 8] ←	- - - - -		-33	
25		Bailey 8] →		- - - - -	-33	
26	12.00	Wardle 9] ←	- - - 1 -	- -	-34	First run from the bat for 33 balls
27		Bailey 9] →	- 1 - - -		-35	
28		Wardle 10] ←	- - - - -		-35	
29		Bailey 10] →		- - - - -	-35	
30		Wardle 11] ←	- - - - -		-35	
31		Bailey 11] →	- 2 -	- - 1	-38	Morris first run for 28 balls

1953 – FIRST TEST

			Hassett	Morris	Total	
32		Wardle 12] ← off spell 12-7-9-0	1	- 1 - - -	-40	
33		Bailey 12] →	2 - 1 -	- - 1 -	-44	*Drizzle now on*
34		Bedser 8] ←	4 - - - -		-48	Long hop, Morris swings hard to leg for four Morris dropped by Hutton at backward short leg off softly hit hook
35	1.10	Bailey 13] → spell 9-3-17-0	- - 4 - - -		-	Hassett off-drive off back foot for four- Aus 52-1 in 100 mins
36	1.15	Bedser 9] ← spell 2-1-4-0		- (2 byes) - - - - -	-54	rain stops play *lunch taken 15 mins early*
		LUNCH First day	Hassett 25 98 mins 107 balls	Morris 26 105 mins 103 balls	1-54 105 mins 217 balls	

A dour indecisive morning.

West: batting secure but uninspiring. Good running between wickets. Fine throwing from the outfield by Graveney.

Fingleton: A dull opening session. Hutton set his fields well but mysteriously ended Bedser's first spell just as he was warming up. And England relapsed into negativity when Wardle came on. Bedser fielding beside Hutton in the slips seemed to be expressing dissatisfaction with the strategy.

Cardus wonders if it was a mistake to leave out Statham. So does Whitington.

Whitington: Hutton took Bedser and Bailey off too soon when the ball was swinging, and set ultra-defensive fields.

Bradman: Wardle bowled exceptionally well.

			Hassett 25	Morris 26	1-54	
37	2.20	Bailey 14] →	1 - - - -		-55	Re-start 10 mins late. Wicket appears dry.
38		Bedser 10] ←	- 1 - - -		-56	
39		Bailey 15] →	- 1 - 3 - -		-60	
40		Bedser 11] ←	- - - - (1 nb) - -		-61	Off no-ball Morris attempts sweep and 'dropped' by Hutton at short leg.

1953 – FIRST TEST

41		Bailey 16] → off spell since lunch 3-0-14-0	4 2 (nb) 3 - - -		-70	Hassett four through covers Hutton 2 to covers Hutton 3 driven firmly to on
42		Bedser 12] ←	- - - 1 -		-71	
43		Wardle 13] →	- - - - -		-71	
44		Bedser 13] ←	- - - - 1		-72	
45		Wardle 14] →	4 - - - -		-76	
46		Bedser 14] ←	- - - 1 -		-77	
47		Wardle 15] →	- - - 4 - -		-81	*Light now better* Hassett square cut 4, leaving May standing at third man.
48		Bedser 15] ← off spell since lunch 6-2-4-0	- - - - -		-81	Bedser so far 15-7-15-1
49		Wardle 16] →	- 1 4 - -		-86	
50		Tattersall 3] ←	- - - - -		-86	*Spinners put batsmen back on defensive*
51		Wardle 17] →	1 - - - -		-87	*Crowd slow handclap. Hassett stands aside till the noise subsides.*

1953 – FIRST TEST

52		Tattersall 4] ←	1	- 1 - - -	-89	
53		Wardle 18] →		- - - 1 -	-90	
54		Tattersall 5] ←		- - - - 1	-91	
55		Wardle 19] →		- - - - -	-91	*Continuing slight drizzle*
56		Tattersall 6] ←	1	4 - - 1 -	-97	
57		Wardle 20] →	1	- - - 1 -	-99	
58	3.18	Tattersall 7] ←		- 4 4 - 4	-111	2nd ball: Morris 50 in 163 mins 167 balls and Aus 103-1 in 163 mins. *3 good off-side fours, square cut and two off-drives*
59	3.21	Wardle 21] →	2	- - - -	-113	Hassett 51 in 157 mins off 174 balls
60		Tattersall 8] ←		1 - - - 1	-115	
61		Wardle 22] →		- - - - -	-115	
62		Tattersall 9] ←		4 - 1 - -	-120	Morris off-drive for his 11th four leaves Graveney standing. Hutton strengthens off-side field.

1953 – FIRST TEST

Over	Time	Bowler	Hassett	Morris	Score	Notes
63		Wardle 23] → off spell 11-3-20-0		- - - 1	- - - -121	
64	3.35	Tattersall 10] ← off spell 8-1-30-0		- - - - 2	- - - -123	Morris 2 on drive. Rain stops play 40 mins early
		TEA First day	Hassett 52 173 mins 194 balls	Morris 67 180 mins 186 balls	1-123 180 mins 387 balls	

SESSION 69-0 in 75 mins 170 balls
West: continual drizzle made ball greasy without livening the wicket
Fingleton: still poor entertainment for the large crowd.

Over	Time	Bowler	Hassett 52	Morris 67	1-123	Notes
		Evening				
65	4.35	Bedser 16] →	- - 1 - -		- - - - -124	
66		Bailey 17] ←	- - - - -		-124	*New ball taken during this over. Bailey bowling too wide*
67	4.43 4.45	Bedser 17] →		- - W Harvey -	2-124 -124	Morris lbw, shuffling across as usual 67 in 188 mins, 193 balls, 11 fours
68		Bailey 18] ←	- - - 1		-125	
69		Bedser 18] →	- 1	- - -	- 126	*Harvey looking confident.*
70		Bailey 19] ←	- - 1	- -	-127	
71	4.59 5.00	Bedser 19] →	- 1	W Miller - -	3-128 -128	Hassett calls for sharp single. Harvey c Compton, firm stroke to leg slip. 0 in 14 mins, 9 balls, 0 fours
72		Bailey 20] ←	1	- 2 -	-131	

1953 – FIRST TEST

73		Bedser 20] →		- - - - -	-131	
74		Bailey 21] ←		- 2 1 - -	-134	
75		Bedser 21] →		- - - - -	-134	
76		Bailey 22] ←	2	- - - -	-136	
77		Bedser 22] →		- - - - -	-136	
78		Bailey 23] ←	1	2 - - -	-139	
79		Bedser 23] → off spell 8-4-6-2	2 - 1	- -	-142	Bedser in innings 23-11-21-3
80		Bailey 24] ←		- - 2 - -	-144	
81		Wardle 24] →		- 1 - - -	-145	
82		Bailey .25] ←		- - 2 1 -	-145	*Bailey has beaten Miller several times*
83		Wardle .25] →		- - - - -	-145	

1953 – FIRST TEST

84		Bailey .26] ←		- - - 2 (nb) -	-147	
85		Wardle .26] →	- - - - -		-147	
86		Bailey .27] ←		- - - - -	-149	Appeal against the light refused at 5.45
87		Wardle .27] →	- - - - -		-147	
88		Bailey .28] ← off spell 12-3-18-0	- - - -	1	-148	*Bailey excellent spell of 80 mins*
89	5.55	Wardle .28] →	- - -	4 -	-152	Australians 152-3 in 260 mins
90		Bedser 24] ←	- - - -		-152	
91		Wardle .29] → spell 6-4-5-0	- - - -		-152	
92	6.05	Bedser 25] ← spell 2-1-5-0	- 1 - -	4 -	-157	Hassett stuck on 66 for 30 mins, 32 balls Hassett sharp single to covers- Miller has to dive to get in Miller four off inside edge Bad light appeal upheld, though light no worse. Close 25 mins early
		CLOSE First day	Hassett 66 261 mins 271 balls	Miller 19 65 mins 76 balls	3-157 270 mins 556 balls	

SESSION 34-2 in 90 mins, 169 balls

West: fine spell by Bailey with no luck.

Alston: uneventful day, honours even.

Arlott: Such advantage as there is lies with England

Fingleton: Evans kept magnificently in the poor light. The game is in no man's land.

Barnes: supine batting, negative bowling, sombre weather. The highest amusement for many of the crowd was to walk in front of the Press Box during the frequent stoppages and spot Sir Donald Bradman.

Times correspondent: England come out with their heads reasonably high. In effect they had three and a half bowlers, for Tattersall's rolled off-spin got minimal response

Bradman: honours are even

1953 – FIRST TEST

Two collapses: SECOND DAY, Friday 12 June

Overnight rain. Sky overcast. Ian Craig's 18th birthday. Team-mates cheer him at breakfast.

			Hassett 66	Miller 19	3-157	
93	11.30	Tattersall 11] → off spell 1-1-0-0	- - - - -		 -157	*Sawdust and towels.* *Ball slippery*
94		Bailey .29] ← 	- - - -	1	 -158	
95		Bedser .26] → 		- - - -	 - 158	
96		Bailey .30] ←	- 1 -	 2 1 	 -162	
97		Bedser .27] →		3 - - - -	 -166	
98		Bailey .31] ←		- - - - -	 -166	
99		Bedser .28] →		- 1 2 - -	 -169	
100		Bailey .32] ←		- - - - -	 -169	
101		Bedser .29] → off spell 4-1-13-0	4 - - - 2		 -175	Hassett sweetly-timed gentle straight drive for four
102		Bailey .33] ←		- - - 2 1	 -178	

1953 – FIRST TEST

Over	Time	Bowler			Score	Notes
103		Tattersall 12]→		1 - - 1 - -	-180	
104		Bailey .34]←	- - 1	2 - 1	-184	
105		Tattersall 13]→	1	- - 1 - -	-186	Score ticking along at good rate because of good running between wickets, especially in taking the first run quickly
106		Bailey .35]←		- - - - -	-186	
107		Tattersall 14]→		- - - 1 -	-187	
108		Bailey .36]←	1	- - - 3 -	-191	At 187 Bailey nearly bowled Miller, just missing off-stump.
109		Tattersall 15]→	1	- - 1 -	-193	
110		Bailey .37]←		- - - - -	-193	
111		Tattersall 16]→	1	- - - -	-194	
112		Bailey .38]← off spell 10-4-17-0	- - 1 - -		-195	End of another good spell by Bailey downwind
113	12.35	Tattersall 17]→	1	- - 1 - 1	-198	

1953 – FIRST TEST

Over	Time	Bowler	Batsman 1	Batsman 2	Score	Notes
114	12.41	Bedser 30] ←	- - 2 - -		-200	2 cover drive. 200 up in 345 mins
115		Tattersall 18] →		- - - - -	-200	
116		Bedser 31] ← off spell 2-0-10-0	3 - - - 2	- - 3 - -	-208	
117		Tattersall 19] →		- - - - -	-208	
118	12.55	Wardle 30] ←	- 4 4 - 1		-217	*Defensive field* Hassett hooks short ball and forces full-toss on the on-side for 4s. Hassett 101 on 346 mins, 344 balls
119		Tattersall 20] →		- - - - -	-217	
120		Wardle 31] ←	- - - 2	1	-220	*Wardle wayward in this spell*
121		Tattersall 21] →		- - - 1 -	-221	*With no sun, the ball stays wet*
122		Wardle 32] ←		- - - - -	-221	
123		Tattersall 22] →	3 - - - -	1	-225	*Tidy spell by Tattersall*
124	1.10	Wardle 33] ←	- 4 -	- - 3 -	-232	Miller glanced for 3. His 50 in 165 mins

1953 – FIRST TEST

#	Time	Bowler	Batsman 1	Batsman 2	Score	Notes
125		Tattersall 23] → off spell 12-3-21-1		4 - - - 1 -	-237	Miller drove over mid-off for 4
126	1.18 1.20	Wardle 34] ←		- - W Benaud 2 - -	4-237 -239	Miller c Bailey, running back from mid-wkt. Tattersall lets Bailey go for the catch. Batsmen crossed. 55 in 173 mins, 184 balls, 3 fours
127		Bedser 32] →		- - 3 - - -	- 242	
128		Wardle 35] ← off spell 6-2-21-1		- - - - - -	-242	
129		Bedser 33] →	1	- - - - -	-243	
	1.30	LUNCH 2nd day	Hassett 114 381 mins 371 balls	Benaud 3 10 mins 14 balls	4-243 390 mins 778 balls	

SESSION 86–1 in 120 mins, 222 balls

West: Miller played an assured innings though pinned down in the 40s, till he became too ambitious with lunch and the new ball imminent.

Fingleton: Miller committed his first indiscretion when he aimed a big hit towards Parr's tree.

Kilburn: a restless undistinguished innings by Miller

Being stiff Bedser bowled only 8 overs before lunch. He loosens up during the interval and feels ready for a big effort. Hutton hopes that the wicket will be drier and the atmosphere will stay the same.

#	Time	Bowler	Hassett 114	Benaud 3	Score	Notes
		Afternoon	Hassett 114	Benaud 3	4-243	
130	2.10	Bailey 39] ←	1	- - - -	-244	
131		Bedser 34] →		- - - - -	- 244	
132	2.17 2.19	Bailey 40] ←		W Davidson - - - -	5-244 -244	*New ball.* Benaud c Evans, diving 3 yards to catch leg-glance, great catch diving several feet sideways. Umpire raises finger. 3 in 17 mins, 20 balls, 0 fours Davidson appeal against light refused
133	2.23 2.25	Bedser 35] →	- W Tallon - - -		6-244 -244	Hassett bowled. Ball swings in pitches leg and fizzes away to hit top of off-stump. 115 in 394 mins, 380 balls, 9 fours

1953 – FIRST TEST

Ball	Time	Bowler/Batsman	Runs	Wicket	Score	Notes
134		Bailey 41] ←	- - - - -		-244	
135		Bedser 36] →	(1 lb) - - - 1 -		- 246	*England fielders now running to their places between overs*
136		Bailey 42] ←	- - - - -		-246	*Cheers for every maiden over*
137	 2.37 2.39	Bedser 37] →	- - W Lindwall -		 7-246 -246	Tallon bowled. Leg-cutter. 0 in 12 mins, 11 balls
138	 2.44 2.46	Bailey 43] ←	- - 1 W Hi'l -		 8 –247 -247	Lindwall c Evans. Edge outside off-stump, easy catch. 0 in 5 mins, 3 balls
139	 2.49	Bedser 38] →	1 - - - W Johnston		 9-248	Hill bowled, yorked by in-swinger. 0 in 3 mins, 6 balls
140	2.50	Bailey 44] ← Spell 6-3-3-2	- - - 1 -		 -249	
141	 2.55	Bedser 39] → Spell 7.3-4-6-4	- - W		 10 -249	Davidson bowled. Agricultural swipe. 4 in 36 mins, 32 balls, 0 fours
			Johnston 0 5 mins 2 balls		10-249 435 mins 847 balls	Bedser with the new ball 5.3-3-2-4. He equals SF Barnes' English Test record of 189 wickets

SESSION 6-6 in 45 mins, 69 balls
Australia lost 7 wickets for 12 runs
West: Evans' catch off Benaud was one of the finest of its kind. In fact he held it at second attempt in his right hand.
   Bedser got Hassett and Tallon with two magnificent leg-cutters. Hutton made Bedser lead England into the Pavilion.
Alston: the collapse was not so much bad batting as inspired bowling by Bedser supported by Bailey.
Fingleton: an extraordinary collapse on a true batting wicket. Bailey's contribution was important.
Kilburn: Hassett's innings was flawless, poised and unrelated to a game of cricket
The leading statistician Roy Webber says that, in proportion to the size of the innings, this is the greatest collapse in
   Test history.
There were five ducks in the innings.

1953 – FIRST TEST

Australia First innings

G.B.Hole	b Bedser	0	7 mins 7 balls 0 fours	1-2
A.R.Morris	lbw b Bedser	67	188 mins, 193 balls, 11 fours	2-124
A.L.Hassett	b Bedser	115	394 mins, 380 balls, 9 fours	6-244
R.N.Harvey	c Compton b Bedser	0	14 mins, 9 balls, 0 fours	3-128
K.R.Miller	c Bailey b Wardle	55	173 mins, 184 balls, 3 fours	4-237
R.Benaud	c Evans b Bailey	3	17 mins, 20 balls, 0 fours	5-244
A.K.Davidson	b Bedser	4	36 mins, 32 balls, 0 fours	10-249
D.Tallon	b Bedser	0	12 mins, 11 balls	7-246
R.R.Lindwall	c Evans b Bailey	0	5 mins, 3 balls	8-247
J.C.Hill	b Bedser	0	3 mins, 6 balls	9-248
W.A.Johnston	not out	0	5 mins, 2 balls	
EXTRAS	(b 2, lb 2, nb 1)	5		
TOTAL	(for 10 wkts)	249	435 mins, 847 balls, 140.3 overs	

BOWLING

Bedser	38.3	16	55	7	(2 nb)
Bailey	44	14	75	2	(2 nb)
Wardle	35	16	55	1	
Tattersall	23	5	59	0	

England First Innings

Odd overs → [.... from Radcliffe Road/City End
Even overs ← [..... from Pavilion End

			Hutton	Kenyon		Dim light
1	3.10	Lindwall 1 → [	- - 3 - 4	- 7		4 slips, gully, 3 short-legs Hutton 3 to long-leg Kenyon 4 edged past 4th slip
2		Johnston 1 ← [	- - - - -	- 7		Johnston bowling over the wicket to 4 short legs, 2 slips and gully. Hutton twice wrapped on pads
3		Lindwall 2 → [	- 1 - - 1	- 9		
4		Johnston 2 ← [	4 1 - 1 - -	-15		Hutton drives past cover for 4 Hutton almost gives catch to Lindwall at leg-slip
5		Lindwall 3 → [	- - - 2 - -	-17		
6		Johnston 3 ← [	- - - - -	-17		
7	3.32 3.34 3.35 3.37	Lindwall 4 → [		W Simpson - W Compton - - -	1-17 2-17 -17	Kenyon c Hill high at leg slip glancing, 8 in 22 mins, 13 balls, 1 four Simpson lbw, on back foot, no definite stroke, 0 in 1 min, 2 balls

1953 – FIRST TEST

8		Johnston 4 ← [		- - - - -	-17	
9	3.43 3.45	Lindwall 5 → [		- W Graveney - - - 1 (nb) -	3-17 -18	Compton c Morris, drove at wide ball, great catch swooping low to his right at gully, 0 in 6 mins, 5 balls Half-volley turned to leg
10		Johnston 5 ← [		- 1 - 2 - -	-21	
11		Lindwall 6 → [		- - - 4 - -	-25	Graveney 4 pulled to mid wkt
12		Johnston 6 ← [	- 1	- - - -	-26	
13		Lindwall 7 → [	1	- - (1 lb) - -	-28	
14		Johnston 7 ← [off spell 7-3-13-0	2 - 1 - -		-31	
15		Lindwall 8 → [	2	- - 3 - -	-36	
16		Hill 1 ← [		- 4 - - -	-40	Graveney cuts short ball to covers for 4
17		Lindwall 9 → [		- - - - 1	-41	

1953 – FIRST TEST

	4.15	TEA 2nd day	Hutton 16 65 mins 53 balls	Gravny 16 30 mins 30 balls	3-41 65 mins 103 balls	
		West: Compton drove at a ball he should have left alone in the circumstances				
		Evening	Hutton 16	Gravny 16	3-41	
18	4.35	Hill 2 ← [	- - - - -		-41	
19		Lindwall 10 → [	1	- - 1 - -	-43	
20		Hill 3 ← [	1	- - - - -	-44	
21		Lindwall 11 → [	1 1 -	- (1 bye) 1	-48	*In poor light Lindwall bowls a bouncer at Hutton and the crowd show its disapproval*
22	4.50	Hill 4 ← [		- - - (4 byes) - -	-52	4 byes from fierce leg-break which beat Tallon
23		Lindwall 12 → [off spell (incl. tea) 12-1-35-3	- 2 - 1	4 (nb) -	-59	Graveney cuts no-ball for 4 Graveney hit on shoulder by bumper
24		Hill 5 ← [	2 - - - 2		-63	
25		Davidson 1 → [		- - - - -	-63	
26		Hill 6 ← [	4 - - 2 4		-73	Hutton 4 past cover Lbw appeal Hutton 2 to cover Hutton cover drive for 4
27		Davidson 2 → [	2	- - (1 lb) - -	-76	

1953 – FIRST TEST

28	5.10 5.11	Hill 7 ← [		- - W May 2 - -	4-76 -78	Graveney c Benaud, swing to short fine leg, juggled catch, 22 in 65 mins, 63 balls, 3 fours
29		Davidson 3 → [		- - - 1 - -	 -79	*Light very poor, but no appeal*
30		Hill 8 ← [		- - - - -	 -79	
31		Davidson 4 → [		- - - - -	 -79	
32		Hill 9 ← [		- - - 1 -	 -80	
33	5.25 5.27	Davidson 5 → [		- 2 W Bailey 1 -	 5-82 -83	Hutton c Benaud, square drive to gully, ct on rebound from thigh, 43 in 115 mins, 101 balls, 3 fours *Bailey appeals against the light*
34		Hill 10 ← [		- - - - -	 - 83	
35		Davidson 6 → [		- - - - -	 -83	
36		Hill 11 ← [		- - - - -	 -83	
37		Davidson 7 → [		- - - - (1 lb) -	 - 84	
38		Hill 12 ← [		- - - 2 -	 -86	

1953 – FIRST TEST

Over	Time	Bowler	Bailey	Evans	Score	Notes
39		Davidson 8 → [off spell 8-4-11-0	- - 1 - - 4		-91	
40		Hill 13 ← [	- - - - -		-91	
41		Johnston 8 → [spell 1-1-0-0	1 - - - -		-92	
42	 5.55 5.57 5.58	Hill 14 ← [Spell (incl. Tea) 14-7-24-2		- - - W Evans - -	6 -92 -92	May c Tallon (wk), forward push, outside edge, 9 in 44 mins, 40 balls, 1 four *Bad light stops play*
		CLOSE 2nd day	Bailey 2 31 mins 28 balls	Evans 0 1 min 2 balls	6-92 148 mins 254 balls	

SESSION 51-3 in 83 mins, 151 balls
England need 8 runs to avoid follow on.

West: Graveney looked the part but got out to a ball he need not have played. Luck was with the Australian fielders. May out to a horrid ball. England now in deep trouble.

Alston: a wonderful two sessions after a dull morning.

Arlott: Bedser made us a chance and we have lost it. Even if England do not avoid the follow on, Hassett will probably bat again.

Bowes: when England appealed unsuccessfully against the light, it was 5 degrees worse than when the umpires came off for bad light yesterday. Today's splendid cricket was enhanced by the superb catches of Bailey, Compton, Evans, Morris and Benaud.

England claw back: THIRD DAY, Saturday 13 June

More rain during the night. But the wicket plays more easily.

Over	Time	Bowler	Bailey	Evans	Score	Notes
			Bailey 2	Evans 0	6-92	
43	11.30	Lindwall 13 → [	- - - 1 2		-95	*Poor light. Damp conditions. Overnight rain deadens the wicket. Ball gets wet.*
44		Johnston 9 ← [	1 - - - -		-96	
45		Lindwall 14 → [	- - 1 4 -		-101	Evans hooks bouncer for 4, saving follow on
46		Johnston 10 ← [	- 1 - - -		-102	

1953 – FIRST TEST

47		Lindwall 15 → [		- - - 1 - -	-103	
48		Johnston 11 ← [		- - - - -	-103	
49		Lindwall 16 → [		1 - - 1 -	-105	
50		Johnston 12 ← [		- - - - -	-105	Bailey ducks a bouncer
51		Lindwall 17 → [off spell 5-0-12-0		- - - 1 -	-106	Evans flashes at a bouncer
52	12.00	Johnston 13 ← [		- - - - -	-106	Evans ducks out of the way of two successive bouncers
53		Davidson 9 → [		- - 1 - -	-107	
54		Johnston 14 ← [		- - - - -	-107	
55	12.09 12.10	Davidson 10 → [		W Wardle - 2 1 - -	7-107 -110	Evans c Tallon (wk) snicked wide half-volley, walks as soon as he played the shot, head high catch, 8 in 40mins, 32 balls
56		Johnston 15 ← [off spell 7-4-3-0		- - - 1 - -	-111	
57		Davidson 11 → [		- - - - -	-111	Wardle plays defensively with 'soft hands'

1953 – FIRST TEST

58		Hill 15 ← [		- - - 1 - -	-112	
59		Davidson 12 → [		- - - - -	-112	
60		Hill 16 ← [		- 4 - - -	-116	Wardle snicks 4 uppishly through slips
61		Davidson 13 → [		- 2 1 1 -	-120	
62		Hill 17 ← [		- 1 - - -	-121	*Hill bowls outside leg to Bailey*
63		Davidson 14 → [		- - - - -	-121	
64	12.38 12.40	Hill 18 ← [	W Bedser	- - - - -	8-121 -121	Bailey lbw, playing back to top-spinner, 13 in 99 mins, 95 balls
65		Davidson 15 → [off spell 7-2-11-1		- 1 2 - -	-124	
66		Hill 19 ← [off spell 5-1-11-0		- - - 4 1 -	-129	Wardle drives straight, first bounce for 4 to pavilion rails
67	 12.55 12.57	Lindwall 18 → [	 W Tattersall	4 2 - 1 -	 9 -136	*New ball taken.* Wardle 4 and 2 to square leg. Wardle 1 edged past leg stump Bedser lbw, 2 in 15 mins, 12 balls, yorker, painful blow on foot
68		Johnston 16 ← [		- - 1 - -	-137	*Entertaining last wicket stand, Wardle constantly threatening to go for impossible singles*

1953 – FIRST TEST

Over	Time	Bowler		Batsman	Score	
69		Lindwall 19 → [		1 - - 1 - 1	-140	
70		Johnston 17 ← [		- 1 - (nb) 1 - -	-142	*Wardle dropped at leg-slip off Johnston* *Tattersall displays his famous 'dab' stroke*
71		Lindwall 20 → [		- - - - -	-142	*Tattersall middles the ball throughout this over*
72		Johnston 18 ← [spell 3-0-4-0		2 - - - -	-144	
73	1.15	Lindwall 21 → [spell 3.4-1-10-2		- - - W	10 -144	Tattersall bowled, 2 in 18 mins, 19 balls
				Wardle 29 65 mins 57 balls 3 fours	10-144 253 mins 439 balls	

SESSION 4-52 runs, 185 balls, 105 mins

ENGLAND FIRST INNINGS

L.Hutton	c Benaud b Davidson	43	115 mins, 101 balls, 3 fours	5-82
D.Kenyon	c Hill b Lindwall	8	22 mins, 13 balls, 1 four	1-17
R.T.Simpson	lbw b Lindwall	0	1 min, 2 balls	2-17
D.C.S.Compton	c Morris b Lindwall	0	6 mins, 4 balls	3-17
T.W.Graveney	c Benaud b Hill	22	65 mins, 63 balls, 3 fours	4-76
P.B.H.May	c Tallon b Hill	9	44 mins, 40 balls, 1 four	6-92
T.E.Bailey	lbw b Hill	13	99 mins, 95 balls	8-121
T.G.Evans	c Tallon b Davidson	8	40 mins, 32 balls	7-107
J.H.Wardle	not out	29	65 mins, 57 balls, 3 fours	
A.V.Bedser	Lbw b Lindwall	2	15 mins, 12 balls	9-136
R.Tattersall	b Lindwall	2	18 mins, 19 balls	10-144
Extras	(b 5, lb 3)	8		
TOTAL	(for 10 wkts)	144	253 mins, 439 balls	

BOWLING

Lindwall	20.4	2	57	5	(2 nb)
Johnston	18	7	22	0	(1 nb)
Hill	19	8	35	3	
Davidson	15	7	22	2	

1953 – FIRST TEST

AUSTRALIA Second Innings

Hassett takes the light roller
Odd overs] → ... from Pavilion End
Even overs] ← ... from Radcliffe Road/City End
Bedser has a sore foot, but he has kept walking around to stop it from stiffening

		Third day	Hole	Morris		Openers walk out slowly
1	1.26	Bedser 1] →	4 - - - -		-4	Hole 4 to long leg, uppishly through leg trap
	1.30	LUNCH	Hole 4 4 mins 6 balls	Morris 0 4 mins 0 balls	0 -4 4 mins 6 balls	

SESSION (BOTH SIDES) 4-56 RUNS, 191 BALLS, 109 MINS
During the interval the teams are presented to Mr. R.G.Menzies, the Australian Prime Minister, on the pitch

			Hole 4	Morris 0	0 -4	
2	2.10	Bailey 1] ←		- - 2 4 -	-10	Morris hooks for four
3		Bedser 2] →	(2 lb) - - - - -		- 12	
4		Bailey 2] ←		- 4 1 1 - 3	-21	Morris hooks 4 Morris off-drives for 3
5		Bedser 3] →	2 - - - 1 -		-24	
6		Bailey 3] ←		- - 2 1 -	-27	
7		Bedser 4] →	- W Hassett - 1	- 1	1 -28 -29	Hole bowled, off-stump, plays inside ball of full length, 5 in 21 mins, 11 balls, 1 four
	2.27					
	2.29					
8		Bailey 4] ←	- - - - - -		-29	Hassett gives stumping chance *Thunder-clouds looming*
9		Bedser 5] →		1 - - 4 -	-34	Hassett hit on chest. He pats the spot while Hutton and Compton watch intently Hassett edges 4 past 2nd slip

1953 – FIRST TEST

10		Bailey 5] ← off spell 5-1-28-0		2 2 - - 2 4	-44	*Morris in scintillating form*
11		Bedser 6] →		- - - - -	-44	
12		Wardle 1] ←		- - - - -	-44	
13	2.50 2.52	Bedser 7] →	W Harvey - - - -		2 -44 -44	Hassett c Hutton, fended short lifter to bkwd short leg, dolly catch, 5 in 31 mins, 21 balls, 1 four. Hutton's 50th catch in Test cricket *Close set field for Harvey, 3 slips 3 short legs*
14		Wardle 2] ←		- - - - 4	-48	
15	 2.57	Bedser 8] →		- - - 2 - -	-50	*No appeal despite poor light* Harvey 2 pushed past mid-off
16		Wardle 3] ←		- - - - -	-50	
17	 3.04 3.05	Bedser 9] →	- - - W Miller -		 3 -50 -50	Harvey c Graveney, hooks straight to bkwd short leg, 2 in 12 mins, 16 balls
18		Wardle 4] ←		- 4 - - -	-54	
19		Bedser 10] →		2 3 1 - -	-60	*England put out Kenyon at wide mid-on and Hutton square leg for Miller*
20		Wardle 5] ←		- - 4 - -	-64	*Morris stumping chance to Evans*

1953 – FIRST TEST

21		Bedser 11] →	-			
	3.17		- - -			
			W Benaud		4 -64	Miller c Kenyon at deep mid on, slow full pitch, hit too soon, 5 in 12 mins, 11 balls
	3.19		-		-64	
22		Wardle 6] ←		- 4 - - -	-68	Morris soaring 4 over mid-on *Wardle aiming to keep Morris at that end*
23	3.24 3.26	Bedser 12] →	W Davidson - - -		5 -68 -68	Benaud bld, through legs by big leg-cutter, (Umpire had to give him out) 0 in 5 mins, 2 balls
24	3.30	Wardle 7] ←		- - - 1 -	-69	Morris 50 in 84 mins, 70 balls
25		Bedser 13] →		- - 1 - 2	-72	Morris hooks hard just past Wardle's outstretched hand at fine leg for 1 Davidson does the same and Wardle gets a hand to it
26		Wardle 8] ←		- - - 1 -	-73	
27		Bedser 14] →		- - - 3 -	-76	
28		Wardle 9] ←		- - - - 1	-77	
29		Bedser 15] → off spell (incl. lunch) 15-7-28-5		- - - - -	-77	Bedser 14-7-24-5 in 95-minute spell since lunch, walks slowly to the slips
30		Wardle 10] ←	- - - - -		-77	Hutton consults with Compton, then brings on Tattersall
31		Tattersall 1] →		- - 3 - -	-80	

1953 – FIRST TEST

32		Wardle 11] ←		- 1 - - -	-81	
33	3.55 3.57	Tattersall 2] →		W Tallon 2 - 1 -	6-81 -84	Morris bowled behind legs, shuffling across, 60 in 109 mins, 100 balls, 7 fours
34		Wardle 12] ← off spell 12-3-24-0		- - 4 - - -	-88	*Light getting worse*
35	4.05 4.07	Tattersall 3] →		- 4 - W Lindwall 1	7-92 -93	Davidson drives 4 over mid-off Davidson c Graveney, run from midwkt behind sq leg (high hit against the spin) 6 in 39 mins, 33 balls, 1 four (batsmen crossed)
36	4.10	Bedser 16] ←		1 - 2 - 4 -	-100	Lindwall 2 over bowler's head Lindwall 4 through covers
37	4.15	Tattersall 4] →		4 2 - W	8-106	Tallon cut for 4 Tallon c Simpson, runs at full tilt from midwkt behind sq leg to catch sweep with right hand, 15 in 18 mins, 15 balls, 2 fours (batsmen crossed)
		TEA 3rd day	Lindwall 6 8 mins 5 balls		8-106 129 mins 220 balls	

SESSION 102-8 in 125 mins, 214 balls

West: When he bowled Hole Bedser took his 190th Test wicket, beating the record of S.F.Barnes, who is present at this match. The ball that bowled Hassett was a turning point; it put tremors in the Australian batting.

Alston: The Australian bating was surprisingly spineless.

In taking the great running catch off Tallon, Simpson decided he had to run as fast as possible and could not stare up at the ball.

It turns out that 'Deafy' Tallon, who is notoriously hard of hearing, misunderstood his instructions from Hassett. Hassett had been talking about appealing against the light and when Tallon became due to go in, Hassett said: "Don't forget Don, give it a go". Tallon heard only the ultimate utterance and one can imagine the look on Hassett's face when he went out and started flaying the bowling, then told Davidson to do the same. When Tallon was out Hassett asked him what the xxxx he was up to, and the misunderstanding came to light.

		Evening	Lindwall 6	Hill	8-106	
37 ctd	4.35	Tattersall 4 Ctd	(3 lb) -	-	-109	
38	4.37 4.39	Bedser 17] ←	4 2 W Johnston - - -		9-115 -115	Lindwall 4 through covers Lindwall c Tattersall, high catch to mid wicket, 12 in 10 mins, 10 balls, 2 fours
39		Tattersall 5] → Spell 5-0-22-3	1 - - - 4		-120	

1953 -- FIRST TEST

40	4.47	Bedser 18] ← Spell 2.2-0-16-2	3	W	10 - 123	Hill c Tattersall, even higher catch at mid wicket, 4 in 12 mins, 9 balls, 1 fours
			Johnston 4 8 mins 2 balls		10-123 141 mins 236 balls	

SESSION 2- 17 in 12 mins, 16 balls

AUSTRALIA SECOND INNINGS

G.B.Hole	b Bedser	5	21 mins, 11 balls, 1 four	1-28
A.R.Morris	b Tattersall	60	109 mins, 100 balls, 7 fours	6-81
A.L.Hassett	c Hutton b Bedser	5	31 mins, 21 balls, 1 four	2-44
R.N.Harvey	c Graveney b Bedser	2	12 mins, 16 balls	3-50
K.R.Miller	c Kenyon b Bedser	5	12 mins, 11 balls	4-64
R.Benaud	b Bedser	0	5 mins, 2 balls	5-68
A.K.Davidson	c Graveney b Tattersall	6	39 mins, 33 balls, 1 four	7-92
D.Tallon	c Simpson b Tattersall	15	18 mins, 15 balls, 2 fours	8-106
R.R.Lindwall	c Tattersall b Bedser	12	10 mins, 10 balls, 2 fours	9-115
J.C.Hill	c Tattersall b Bedser	4	12 mins, 9 balls, 1 fours	10-123
W.A.Johnston	not out	4	8 mins, 2 balls	
Extras	(lb 5)	5		
Total	(for 10 wkts)	123	141 mins, 236 balls, 39.2 overs	

Bowling

Bedser	17.2	7	44	7
Bailey	5	1	28	0
Wardle	12	3	24	0
Tattersall	5	0	22	3

Great ovation for Bedser. Even the Australians applauded him from their balcony.
Bowes: Apart from Hassett, none of the Australians could blame the wicket for their dismissals.

ENGLAND Second Innings

England need 227 to win, with more than two days to go. Hutton orders the heavy roller and the wicket behaves. The light is poor. England face a nail-biting hour and a half.
Odd overs → [... from Radcliffe Rd (City) end
Even overs ← [... from Pavilion end

			Hutton	Kenyon		
1	4.57	Lindwall 1 → [	-			*Big appeal for lbw against Hutton*
			-			
				1		
	5.00			-	-1	Bad light stops play for 15 mins

The umpires took some time to decide about going off. The light was no worse than at several times during the Australian innings.

1 ctd	5.15	Lindwall 1 Ctd	-	-	-1	
2		Johnston 1 ← [	- - (1 bye) - - -	3 (nb) -5		Kenyon 3 lifted into the deep
3		Lindwall 2 → [	- 1 - 2	-8		
4		Johnston 2 ← [	- - 1 (nb) - -	-9		Kenyon hooks single to Morris at long leg

1953 – FIRST TEST

5		Lindwall 3 → [		- - - - -	-9	
6		Johnston 3 ← [		- - - - -	-9	
7		Lindwall 4 → [		- - - - -	-9	*Kenyon misses three successive out-swingers*
8		Johnston 4 ← [	1	- - - (1 nb) - -	-11	*Lights on in England dressing room*
9		Lindwall 5 → [	3	- - - - 4	-18	
10		Johnston 5 ← [off spell 5-2-5-0		- - - - -	-18	
11		Lindwall 6 → [		- - - 3 -	-21	
12	5.55 5.57	Hill 1 ← [		. (1 wide) - 4 W Simpson - 4 -	1 -26 -30	Kenyon hits long hop to covers for 4 Kenyon c Hassett, full toss hit to wide mid-on, 16 in 43 mins, 39 balls, 2 fours Simpson edges his 2nd ball past slip for 4. Hole goes to right in anticipation then sticks out left hand. Ball did not carry.
13		Lindwall 7 → [	(1 nb) -	- - - - -	-31	
14		Hill 2 ← [	1	- 1 - - -	-33	

1953 – FIRST TEST

15		Lindwall 8 → [	1 1	1 - - (4 lb) 1	-41	
16		Hill 3 ← [spell 3-0-11-1		- - - 1 - -	-42	
17		Lindwall 9 → [spell 9-3-18-0		- - - - -	-42	
	6.15					Bad light stops play
		Close	Hutton 10 63 mins 45 balls	Simpson 8 18 mins 22 balls	1 –42 63 mins 107 balls*	* including 1 wide

If a wicket had fallen after six o'clock, Bailey, rather than Compton would have gone in next.

West: Kenyon appeared to play and miss a lot but mostly he was withdrawing from a stroke at the last moment.

Cardus: With Hutton still in the odds are definitely in favour of England

Fingleton: England should win. The day's turning point was the ball that hit Hassett on the chest. Australia do not have bowlers who can exploit the wicket as Bedser can.

Barnes: England should win if their batsmen concentrate on getting forward to the ball and scoring runs in front of the wicket. Johnston has been disappointing in this match and Keith Miller will have to be persuaded to try a few overs.

Swanton: if the wicket remains true and placid, the prospects for England are favourable.

Bradman: England have the chance of a lifetime, but rain will make the job harder.

Arlott: "the most exciting day I have ever known in a Test match"

Sunday

The sun shone on Sunday. There was a thunderstorm in the late afternoon but the worst of it missed Trent Bridge. Then came more rain

Cruel frustration: FOURTH DAY, Monday 15 June

No play. It rained solidly from Sunday night and kept on raining. Nearly 10,000 waited outside. After a short beak in the drizzle the captains inspected the wicket at 2.45 and play was abandoned for the day. The curator, Frank Dalling, tells the press that unless the rain stops soon there is a 3 to 1 chance against any play tomorrow. But the rain did stop and there was a light breeze and a little sunshine.

Times correspondent: Heartbreak house. It is perhaps fortunate for England that the rain did not give way to sunshine.

Bradman: This shows the need for complete covering of wickets. If the wicket gets sticky, my money is on Australia

Cruel anti-climax: FIFTH DAY, Tuesday 16 June

Wet pitch . Puddles at 11am inspection. It would suit England to play as soon as possible, for a sodden wicket would not suit the Australian attack. Sun comes out after lunch. England would not mind if the umpires had power to call upon the captains to play, but Hutton was wary of taking upon himself the decision to ask the umpires to make a ruling. As the day goes on, the desire to play shifts from England to Australia. Hutton decides not to ask the umpires to inspect at 3.00. Inspection at 4.00 when captains disagree. No play till 4.30. Sun disappears.

			Hutton 10	Simpson 8	1-42	
18	4.30	Johnston 6 ← [	- - - - (4 byes) - -		-46	*Crowd 5,000* *Johnston bowling round the wicket*
19		Hill 4 → [		- - - - -	-46	

1953 – FIRST TEST

#		Bowler				Score	Notes
20		Johnston 7 ← [		- - - - -		-46	*Johnston got some lift at the start*
21		Hill 5 → [			- - - - -	-46	
22		Johnston 8 ← [		- - - - -		-46	
23		Hill 6 → [			- - 4 - -	-50	
24		Johnston 9 ← [	1		- - - -	-51	
25		Hill 7 → [off spell 4-2-9-1			- 4 - - 1	-56	
26		Johnston 10 ← [	1		1 - - -	-58	
27		Benaud 1 → [			- - - - 1	-59	
28		Johnston 11 ← [			- - - - -	-59	
29		Benaud 2 → [off spell 2-0-6-0		- 4 - 1 -		-64	Hutton a regal 4 through extra cover
30		Johnston 12 ← [			- - - - -	-64	

1953 – FIRST TEST

#		Bowler		Balls	Score	Notes
31		Lindwall 10 →[		- - - 1 -	-65	*Lindwall inhibited by wet ground, not at full pace. Bowls in-swingers to 3 short legs.*
32		Johnston 13 ←[		- - - - -	-65	
33		Lindwall 11 →[	- - - - 1		-66	
34		Johnston 14 ←[	1	- - - -	-67	*Crowd very quiet. Match drifting nowhere.*
35		Lindwall 12 →[	2 4 - - -		-73	
36		Johnston 15 ←[		- - - 1 -	-74	
37		Lindwall 13 →[		- 1 - - 4	-79	Hutton late cut for 4
38		Johnston 16 ←[		- - - - -	-79	
39		Lindwall 14 →[	- 1 - (1 bye) - -		-81	
40		Johnston 17 ←[		- 1 - - 1	-83	
41		Lindwall 15 →[	4 - - - -		-87	Hutton late cut for 4

1953 – FIRST TEST

42		Johnston 18 ←[off spell 13-7-9-0		- - - - 2	-89	
43		Lindwall 16 →[off spell 7-0-19-0	- 1 - - -		-90	
44		Hill 8 ←[	- 2 - - -		-92	
45		Davidson 1 →[		- - - - -	-92	
46		Hill 9 ←[	- - - - 1		-93	
47		Davidson 2 →[	- 1	- - - - (1 bye)	-95	
48		Hill 10 ←[	- (1 bye) - - -	1	-97	
49		Davidson 3 →[	- - 1 (1 wide) -	1	-100	
50		Hill 11 ←[		- - - - 2	-100	
51		Davidson 4 →[	- 1	- - -	-101	
52		Hill 12 ←[off spell 5-1-6-0	1 - 1 - -		-103	

1953 – FIRST TEST

53		Davidson 5 → [off spell 5-1-7-0	2	- - - 1	-106	
54		Benaud 3 ← [		2 - - - -	-108	
55		Morris 1 → [	1 1	- - 1	-111	
56		Benaud 4 ← [		- - 2 - -	-113	
57		Morris 2 → [spell 2-0-5-0	1	- 1 - -	-115	
58	6.30	Benaud 5 ← [spell 3-0-9-0	4 - - - 1		-120	
		CLOSE	Hutton 60 183 mins 165 balls 6 fours	Simpson 28 138 mins 148 balls 2 fours	1-120 183 mins 354 balls*	* including 2 wides

SESSION 78 –0 in 120 mins, 247 balls (including 2 wides)

ENGLAND SECOND INNINGS

L.Hutton	not out		60	183 mins, 165 balls, 6 fours
D Kenyon	c Hassett b Hill		16	43 mins, 39 balls, 2 fours 1-26
R.T.Simpson	not out		28	138 mins, 148 balls, 2 fours
Extras	(b 8, lb 4, w 2, nb 2)		16	
Total	(for one wkt)		120	183 mins, 354 balls (incl. 2 wides), 58 overs

Bowling

Lindwall	16	4	37	0	(nb 1)
Johnston	18	9	14	0	(nb 3)
Hill	12	3	26	1	(w 1)
Benaud	5	0	15	0	
Davidson	5	1	7	0	(w 1)
Morris	2	0	5	0	

MATCH DRAWN

Match attendance: 86,000 (61,760 paying), receipts £29,261

   England had Evans padded up to go in for an innings of gay abandon to see if England might get in a position to go for the runs, but it soon became clear that Hutton and Simpson did not find conditions easy enough to take any risks. Hutton says that he and Simpson were keen to go for the runs and that he launched an attack on Hill, signalling that Evans, Compton and Wardle should be the next batsmen; after a few hefty blows, Hill was replaced by Johnston bowling to a completely defensive field, and the chase was called off. However this version of events is at odds with the scorers' record. Hill conceded only 9 runs in 4 overs and he was replaced by Benaud.

   Miller thinks that Hutton's signal for Evans to come in next was purely to tantalise the crowd, for the chance of victory had long gone. Lindwall thinks that Hutton wanted to have a go but Simpson held things up with his defensive attitude.

1953 – FIRST TEST

A huge anti-climax to what should have been a classic Test finish. Hutton never looked in any trouble. Lindwall never bowled at full pace and Johnston soon settled into his slow-medium style. There was a sepulchral silence from the crowd.

The general opinion is that the weather deprived England of a likely victory, with 187 need to win and nine wickets and two days available to get them. One partly discounts the position at the close on Tuesday since the England batting for the two hours play was to achieve a draw. West was fairly sure that England would have won. Fingleton "honours alone to England". F.R.Brown: "We certainly ought to have won". Barnes says that they "beat the ears off the Australians." Cardus says that England should go to Lord's with a moral ascendancy. Swanton thinks that England suffered from having only four bowlers, and that a useful addition would be an all-rounder: he suggests F.R.Brown, former England captain and chairman of the Test selectors. So does the *Times* correspondent Bailey thinks that the rain of the last two days removed the chance of an England win, but recalls that rain on the first day also handicapped Australia in getting a big first innings total. Bradman thinks that England won on points, but would have settled for a draw after the first innings. Arlott says that for all their nearness to victory, England have many selection problems: only Hutton, Bedser and Evans carried the show, with credit marks for Graveney and Tattersall. Cutler says that England could not be sure of victory, but the match has exposed Australian vulnerability, showing their county victories to be misleading

So ended a Test in which, says Barnes, the sun did not make itself visible at all for five days

If the policy of leaving wickets uncovered had not applied, there would have been a start more or less on time.

Hutton is re-appointed England captain, but only for the next Test.

There were no man of the match awards in 1953. Fifty years later, an adjudicator would praise the efforts of Hassett, Lindwall and Hutton, but the clear favourite would undoubtedly be Bedser. Indeed the match has been called Bedser's match. (Not bad for a man with a sore foot.)

While the Test was on there were two rounds of first-class cricket.

June 10,11,12

A blank Thursday at Brentwood deprived Surrey of a chance of a result against Essex, and the weather caused a stalemate at Bradford between Yorkshire and Notts. At Lord's Middlesex beat Leicestershire by an innings and Edrich made a cautious 127. At the Bath Festival, after the one-day finish in the previous match, the county groundsman was called into give emergency first aid to the wicket; he raked off acorns and gravel, put down liberal doses of liquid marl and cow-dung, spread cut grass over it and gave a good roll. 17-year-old off-spinner Brian Langford, in his second first-class match, took 14 for 156 to beat Kent. Somerset's leading all-rounder, Maurice Tremlett, was hit on the forehead at silly mid-off, his sinus bone splintered and his eye slightly dislodged; his season was over. But for a rain-stopped last day Oxford University would probably have beaten Derbyshire, the county having been bowled out for 95, with Cowdrey (yes, Colin) taking 4 or 30 with leg spin.

June 13,15,16

The Bath Festival ended with a two-day defeat for Somerset by Leicestershire, though Langford took another 11 wickets. At the Oval Surrey beat Kent by an innings and 256 with 30 minutes to spare. And Middlesex won comfortably at Worcester. There was no play at all on Monday and Tuesday at Manchester. Surrey now lead the championship table, played 9, points 68; Middlesex second with 66 from 10.

After the Test:

More rain: Chesterfield, June 17, 18,19

From Nottingham the Australians had the short pleasant journey to Chesterfield, and rested six of the XI who played in the First Test. Although the wicket had been covered some of the voluminous rain had seeped through and on a damp pitch and very slow outfield. When play began after lunch, G.L.Willatt the Derbyshire captain put them into bat. They struggled through to 191 for 9 at the close. Benaud provided the only relief when he came in at 85 for 5 and scored 70 in only 86 minutes. Craig stayed with him and his 17 in 90 minutes was more important than it looked. On Thursday the wicket took some spin. Derbyshire batted feebly for 69 all out, bamboozled by Ring's flight, and sacrificing two men to run outs. Australia again disappointed with the bat and made their lowest total against a county side to date. McDonald stuck in to make his second fifty of the tour. Hole, batting at his natural position of number 4, shone through with an assured 73 being last out. Edwin Smith, a coal mine fitter when not playing cricket, aged 19 and looking younger, impressed with his easy accurate off-spin. Needing 275 to win Derbyshire were 17-1 in the last half hour of the day. Overnight rain prevented any play on the last day and deprived the Australians of a likely victory.

1953 – FIRST TEST

AUSTRALIANS 197 (Hole 32, Benaud 70, C.Gladwin 5-84) and 146 (McDonald 51, Hole 73, C.Gladwin 4-59, E.Smith 5-36). DERBYSHIRE 69 (D.B.Carr 29, Ring 4-19 in 17 overs, Benaud 2-10) and 17-1. *Match drawn*

Surrey lost out in the Championship race when their home game against Essex was reduced to two days playing time. 51 behind on the first innings, Essex collapsed to 51 for 8 with 40 minutes play available. In his fourth over Alec Bedser took the first hat-trick of his career. Laker was on a hat-trick twice. Bailey and Preston saw out time whilst spectators sheltered under umbrellas, with the rain forcing an end with 20 minutes left. The Surrey batsmen should have forced the pace more quickly earlier in the day. On the other side of the Thames at Lord's, Middlesex got a gambler's win over Notts. Notts declared 72 behind in first innings, at lunch on the last day. Middlesex made 63 for 4 and declared setting Notts only 136 in two hours, a difficult enough task on a damp turning wicket and slow outfield, and dismissed them for 115 in 110 minutes. Middlesex now go to the top of the Table, 78 from 11 games, Surrey 72 from 10.

On Friday the death occurred of W.Findlay, who was Secretary of MCC when England last won the Ashes at home, in 1926. The Soviets declare a state of emergency in Communist East Berlin where workers have been demonstrating.

Manpower shortage: Sheffield, June 20, 22, 23

Hassett went to London for treatment in his arm. Morris rested and Miller led the side. Yorkshire batted steadily on Saturday for 251 for 5, Hutton escaped a stumping by Tallon when 34, and on Monday morning added 125 in 105 minutes. McDonald had twisted a knee in the field and did not bat. Tallon and Craig opened the innings. Hole at no.3 made another impressive 71 in 2 hours. Miller, captaining the side, was twice dropped early in his innings, partnered Harvey in a stand of 68 in an hour before Harvey fell 12 short of his 1000 runs for the tour. At 209 for 6, the target for avoiding the follow on (228) was at issue, but Miller was dropped again at slip off Foord at 215, and no further wicket fell before the close at 243 for 6. There was no collapse on the third morning and it was soon clear that the game was drifting towards a draw. Helped by Hill in a stand of 76 Miller was finally out after 190 minutes in which he gave five catch chances and one for run out. In the second innings Hutton batted faultlessly for 150 minutes and after he was caught at cover, the crowd of 9,000 drifted away while the non-regulars Hole, Harvey, de Courcy and Craig bowled. Only 12 Australians were in Sheffield, the rest staying in London, and when Langley fielded substitute for McDonald there was no-one to come out when Harvey was injured. The match attendance was 62,000. During this match the Australians stayed at the village of Grindleford, only a few miles away but in the completely different landscape of the Peak District. On Monday Miller and Lindwall slept in and got to the ground just before the start of play in the local undertaker's limousine.

YORKSHIRE 377 (L.Hutton 67, J.V.Wilson 39, W.Watson 61, W.H.H.Sutcliffe 57, R.Illingworth 40, J.H.Wardle 36, Lindwall 4-54) and 220-3 (L.Hutton 84, J.V.Wilson 56*, W.H.H.Sutcliffe 39*). AUSTRALIANS 323 (Hole 71, Harvey 69, Miller 86, J.H.Wardle 5-117). *Match drawn.*

At Bristol Middlesex captain Edrich declared twice, the first time successfully as young Fred Titmus with 8-53 bowled unchanged to bowl out Gloucestershire for 104. The second declaration was less fortuitous: he set Gloucs 274 in 215 minutes and their established batsmen Emmett, Graveney and Crapp saw them home in 76.1 overs, 195 minutes. Spinners Young and Titmus bowled 66 of the overs. At Derby, Surrey were all out for 81, Gladwin and Jackson bowling unchanged, and lost by an innings in two days. Glamorgan beat Somerset in two days. Sussex beat Kent and David Sheppard the captain.

SECOND TEST AT LORD'S
June 25, 26, 27, 29, 30

For the Second Test England's selectors met on Saturday evening at 10.pm at the Three Swans Hotel, Market Harborough and did not break up until 2am. They dropped Simpson, May and Tattersall. The team was Hutton (capt), Kenyon, Graveney, Compton, W.Watson (Yorks), Bailey, F.R.Brown (Northants), Evans (wk), Wardle, G.A.R.Lock (Surrey), Bedser and Statham. Lock withdrew on Monday and Tattersall (Lancashire) was recalled to replace him.

Willie WATSON (Yorkshire), aged 33, a solid left-handed middle-order batsman who made his Test debut in 1951. England international footballer.

Freddie R. BROWN (Northants) an all-round right hand-batsman, leg-break or medium pace bowler, aged 42 an occasional England player who was in the MCC side on the bodyline tour 1932-33. In 1949 he moved from Surrey to captain Northants. Third choice as England captain to tour Australia in 1950-51 he proved an inspiration as leader and as all-rounder. Now chairman of the England selectors. Unusually, Hutton made a press statement that he was happy to have his immediate boss in his side. During the Test Hutton could not stop himself from calling Brown "Skipper".

The selectors wanted a leg-spinner for Lord's and decided that Brown was the best available. Hutton took it upon himself to ask Brown, and to his surprise Brown said yes. The idea was first mooted at the end of the First Test, when Hutton was appointed captain for Lord's. Brown's selection was both welcomed and criticised. Bill Edrich was playing in a Sunday charity match at Badminton with Test selector Wyatt. On being told the team, he said "You've left out one of the best young cricketers in England [May] to bring back a man who is past his peak."

Umpires: F.S. Lee and H.G. Baldwin

10,000 locked out: FIRST DAY, Thursday 25 June

Hassett sees a specialist for treatment on his arm before start of play
 A warm humid cloudy morning.
England leave out Tattersall. Australia bring in Langley for Tallon and, surprisingly, Ring for Hill. Ring turns his leg-
 break more sharply than Hill, who relies mainly on the top-spinner, but Hill bowled well at Nottingham.
Australia win the toss
Gates closed before start of play at 11.00. 10,000 outside.

Australia First Innings

Odd overs   ] → from Pavilion End
Even overs   ] ← from Nursery End

		Bowler	Hassett	Morris		Ground full, att: 32,000, 30,905 paid
1	11.30	Bedser 1] →	- 2 - 1	- -	-3	Pleasant hazy morning *Hassett has a bandage on his right arm*
2		Statham 1] ←	- 4 1	- - 2	-10	
3		Bedser 2] →	- 1	- - - 4	-15	Morris checked drive past cover for 4
4		Statham 2] ←	- - - 1	-	-16	
5		Bedser 3] →	- 1	- - -	-17	*Bedser sluggish. Pitch easy paced and ball has stopped swinging.*

1953 – SECOND TEST

6		Statham 3] ←		1 - - - - 1	-19	
7		Bedser 4] →		- - 1 - -	-20	
8		Statham 4] ← off 4-0-12-0	1 - 1	- 1 - -	-22	
9		Bedser 5] →	- (nb) 4 1	- - -	-27	Hassett dropped at leg slip by Compton who moves the wrong way
10		Brown 1] ←	1	- - - -	-28	*Brown bowling medium pace seamers*
11		Bedser 6] →	- 1	- - -	-29	
12		Brown 2] ←	1	- 3 - -	-33	
13		Bedser 7] → off spell 7-1-16-0		- - - - -	-33	
14		Brown 3] ←	1	- - 1 -	-35	
15		Bailey 1] →	1 4 - - -		-40	*Sun now shining*
16		Brown 4] ←		- - - - -	-40	

1953 – SECOND TEST

Over	Time	Bowler	Batsman 1	Batsman 2	Wicket	Score	Notes
17		Bailey 2] →	4 1 1 - -	- (1 lb)		-47	*Unexplained change of ends during this over; surmised that 4th ball was run two but called one short.*
18		Brown 5] ←		- - - - -		-47	
19		Bailey 3] →	1	- 4 - - -		-52	Morris drive for 4 through extra cover
20		Brown 6] ← off spell 6-3-7-0	- - - - -			-52	
21		Bailey 4] →		- 2 - 4 -		-58	*Bailey beats Morris outside off and Evans takes ball above shoulder height*
22		Bedser 8] ←	1	2 1 - -		-62	
23		Bailey 5] →		- - - 2 1		-65	
24	12.52 12.54	Bedser 9] ←		- - - - W Harvey 1	1 –65	-66	Morris st Evans, pushing out, ball flicks pad, 30 in 82 mins, 90 balls, 3 fours
25		Bailey 6] →		- - 1 1 1		-69	
26		Bedser 10] ←		- 1 - - 4 1		-75	
27		Bailey 7] → off spell 7-0-31-0	- - - 2 - 1			-78	

1953 – SECOND TEST

28		Bedser 11] ←	- 1	2 - 2	-83	
29		Statham 5] →	- - 1 - -		-84	
30		Bedser 12] ←	- - - - 1		-85	
31		Statham 6] → off spell 2-1-1-0	- - .. - -		-85	
32		Bedser 13] ←		- - 1 - -	-86	
33		Wardle 1] → spell 1-0-1-0	- -	- - 1	-87	
34		Bedser 14] ← spell 7-0-19-1	- -	- - 1	-88	
	1.30	LUNCH	Hassett 46 120 mins 92 balls	Harvey 11 36 mins 23 balls	1-88 120 mins 205 balls	
		Afternoon	Hassett 46	Harvey 11	1-88	
35	2.10	Statham 7] →	- -	- - 1	- 89	Harvey 1,000 runs on the tour
36		Brown 7] ←	-	- - - 1	-90	*Brown bowls leg theory with six fielders on leg side*
37		Statham 8] →	1	- - 1 - -	-92	

1953 – SECOND TEST

38		Brown 8] ←		- 1 1 - 1	-95	
39	2.30	Statham 9] →		- - - - 2	-97	Hassett cuts for 2, 51 in 140 mins
40		Brown 9] ←	(1 lb) -	- - 1 - -	-99	
41	2.35	Statham 10] →	(2 lb) -	- - - - -	-101	
42		Brown 10] ←		- - - - -	-101	
43		Statham 11] → off spell 5-2-5-0		- - - - -	-101	
44		Brown 11] ←		1 4 - - -	-106	*3 of Hassett's five fours have been leg-side snicks* *Hassett dropped by Hutton at 2nd slip, despite seeming to grasp it firmly*
45		Bailey 8] →		4 - - 1 -	-111	
46		Brown 12] ←		1 - - 4 -	-116	Hassett hooks for 4
47		Bailey 9] →		- - - - -	-116	
48		Brown 13] ← off spell 7-1-14-0		1 - - - -	-117	

1953 – SECOND TEST

49		Bailey 10] →	4 - - 2 - -		-123	
50	3.00	Wardle 2] ←		- - 4 - -	-127	Harvey punches a 4 straight
51		Bailey 11] →	- 1 - - - 4		-132	
52		Wardle 3] ←		- 1 4 - - -	-137	
53		Bailey 12] →	- - 1 - -		-138	
54		Wardle 4] ←		- - - - (4 byes) -	-142	
55		Bailey 13] →		- - - - -	-142	
56		Wardle 5] ←		- - 4 - - -	-146	
57		Bailey 14] →	1 - 1 - 1 -		-149	*Unexplained change of ends in this over. Surmised that they ran two off third ball but was called one short*
58		Wardle 6] ←		4 - - - -	-153	
59		Bailey 15] →	1 - - 1 - -		-155	

1953 – SECOND TEST

60		Wardle 7] ←		- - - - -	-155	
61		Bailey 16] → off spell 9-1-24-0	1	- - - 1 -	-157	
62		Wardle 8] ← off spell 7-2-18-0		- 1 - - -	-158	
63		Statham 12] →		- - 2 - -	-160	
64		Bedser 15] ←	1	- - 1 - 2	-164	
65		Statham 13] →		- - 2 - -	-166	*New ball taken*
66		Bedser 16] ←	1	1 - 1 - -	-169	
67		Statham 14] →		- 1 - - -	-170	
68		Bedser 17] ←		- - - 2 3 -	-175	
69	4.08	Statham 15] →		- 1 - - -	-176	Harvey 50 in 154 mins
70		Bedser 18] ←		- - 2 - -	-178	

1953 – SECOND TEST

			Hassett 90	Harvey 52	1-180	
71		Statham 16] →	- - 2 - -			
	4.15		-		-180	
		TEA	Hassett 90 245 mins 214 balls	Harvey 52 161 mins 123 balls	1-180 245 mins 427 balls	

SESSION **92 runs in 125 mins, 222 balls**

		Evening	Hassett 90	Harvey 52	1-180	
72	4.35	Bedser 19] ←	- 1 - - -	1 - - - 1	-183	
73		Statham 17] →	- 2 - 1 -	- - - - -	-186	
74		Bedser 20] ←	1 - - - -	1 - - - -	-188	
75		Statham 18] →	- - - 1 -	- - - - 1	-190	
76	4.53 4.55	Bedser 21] ←		- W Miller - - -	2-190 -190	Harvey lbw, pushing to leg, ball straightened on leg stump, 59 in 179 mins, 139 balls, 4 fours
77		Statham 19] → off spell (incl. Tea) 8-0-17-0	- - 4 - - -		-194	*Hassett has cramp in both legs*
78	5.03 5.05	Bedser 22] ←	- - 4 - Hole -	- 2 (nb) - 1 - -	-201 -201	Hassett late cuts 4 for 101 Hassett retires hurt 101 in 273 mins, 232 balls, 12 fours
79		Brown 14] →	- - - -	1 - - -	-202	
80		Bedser 23] ←	- - - -	- - 1 -	-203	

1953 – SECOND TEST

81		Brown 15] →		- - - - 4	-207
82		Bedser 24] ←		- - - - -	-207
83		Brown 16] →		- - - - -	-207
84		Bedser 25] ←	- 1 - - -		-208
85		Brown 17] →	- - - 2 -		-210
86		Bedser 26] ← off spell (incl. Tea) 12-2-32-1		- 4 - - -	-214
87		Brown 18] →	- - 4 1	- 1	-220
88		Wardle 9] ←		- - - - -	-220
89		Brown 19] →		- - - - 1 -	-221
90		Wardle 10] ←	- - - - -		-221
91		Brown 20] →		- - - - -	-221

1953 – SECOND TEST

#	Time	Bowler	Runs	Wicket	Score	Notes
92		Wardle 11] ←	4 - - - - W	Benaud	3-225	Hole c Compton, edged drive to slip, 13 in 45 mins, 43 balls, 2 fours
	5.50					
93	5.52	Brown 21] →	4 - - - -		-229	
94		Wardle 12] ←	- - - - W	Davidson	4 -229	Benaud lbw, googly, cross bat swish to leg side, 0 in 5 mins, 6 balls
	5.57					
95	5.59	Brown 22] → off spell 9-2-18-0	- 1 - 4 - -		-234	Davidson dropped by Brown, hard c & b chance
96	6.05	Wardle 13] ←	- 6 W - -	Ring	5 -240 -240	Miller pulls 6 into Grandstand tier Miller bld, playing back, over and across, 25 in 70 mins, 61 balls, 3 fours 1 six Wardle 3 for 6 in 10 balls
	6.07					
97		Bedser 27] →	4 - - - -		-244	
98		Wardle 14] ←	- - - 4 1		-249	
99		Bedser 28] →	- - - - -		-249	
100		Wardle 15] ←	- - - 4 -		-253	
101		Bedser 29] →	- - - - -		-253	
102		Wardle 16] ←	- - 4 - -		-257	Davidson's 4th four, all through covers

1953 – SECOND TEST

103		Bedser 30] → spell 4-2-10-0		4 - 1 - - 1	 -263	
104	6.30	Wardle 17] ← spell 9-4-23-3		- - - - -	 -263	
		CLOSE First day	Davdsn 17 31 mins 32 balls	Ring 10 23 mins 23 balls	5-263 360 mins 626 balls	Attendance: 30,905.

SESSION 4-69 in 120 mins, 199 balls

   Three vital moments during the day: Hutton dropping Hassett on 55, Hassett retiring at 201-5; and Wardle's three-wickets in 10 balls. Wardle describes his dismissal of Miller: under orders to bowl tight, he tempted fate by tossing up a slower ball which was dropped by a spectator on the Grandstand balcony; avoiding any glance at his captain, he really pushed his luck by bowling a second flighted ball which deceived Miller and bowled him off his pads.

Whitington: Australia showed that trait of modern batsmen, lack of concentration. As a captain on trial with the chairman of the selectors on the field with him Hutton was obviously uncomfortable

Times correspondent: a day of steady consistent progress by Australia, till the fun started at ten to six.

Arlott: A disturbing feature was the unwillingness of Brown to bowl more than the occasional leg-break – he does not like bowling it against left-handers – and his medium pace swing was merely economical.

Some of the crowd leaving the ground joined the queue for tomorrow.

Despair and triumph for Hutton: SECOND DAY, Friday 26 June

Streets round Lord's covered in litter. Touts are asking £5 for a £1 seat.

		Morning	Davdsn 17	Ring 10	5-263	
105	11.30	Bedser 31] →		- - 2 - -	 -265	*Fine and warm*
106		Wardle 18] ←	- - - - -		 -265	
107		Bedser 32] →	 1	1 - - - -	 -267	
108		Wardle 19] ←	2 - - 1	- - - 4	 -274	Davidson drove knee high to Bedser at mid-off. He got both hands to it- it was deflected by Wardle's fingertips. Ring cut fine for 4
109		Bedser 33] → off spell (to-day) 3-0-8-0	4 - - - -		 -278	Davidson square cut for 4
110		Wardle 20] ←		- 1 - - -	 -279	Ring edged past Compton at 1st slip, who got one hand to it

1953 – SECOND TEST

111		Statham 20] →		- - - - -	-279	
112	11.52 11.54	Wardle 21] ←	1	W Hassett 1 - -	6 -280 -281	*Wardle bowling round the wicket* Ring lbw, playing back with crooked bat, 18 in 45 mins, 45 balls, 3 fours Hassett returns, cheered in all the way, hits ball which gives Hutton a nasty blow on left forearm
113		Statham 21] →		- - 1 - -	-282	
114		Wardle 22] ←		- - - - -	-282	*Hassett gives sharp chance wide to Compton at slip, who loses it on impact with ground*
115		Statham 22] → off spell 3-2-1-0	- - - - -		-282	
116		Wardle 23] ←		- - 1 4 - -	-287	Davidson uppish cover drive for 4
117		Bedser 34] →		- - - - -	-287	
118		Wardle 24] ←	- - 4 - -		-291	
119	12.17 12.19	Bedser 35] →		W Lindwall - - -	7 -291 -291	Hassett c Bailey at gully, diving forward; ball popped, came off shoulder of bat, 104 in 296 mins, 253 balls, 12 fours
120		Wardle 25] ←	- - - - 4		-295	
121	12.25	Bedser 36] →	4	- - - 1 -	-300	

1953 – SECOND TEST

122		Wardle 26] ←		- - - - -	-300	
123		Bedser 37] → off spell 4-2-7-1	(nb) 2	- - - - -	-302	
124		Wardle 27] ←		- 1 - -	-303	
125		Brown 23] →		- - - 4	-307	
126	12.40	Wardle 28] ←	6 4	- - - -	-317	Davidson drives 6 into Mound Stand for his 50, then 4 through covers
127		Brown 24] →		- - - - -	-317	
128		Wardle 29] ← off spell (to-day) 12-3-35-1	1	- - - -	-318	
129		Brown 25] → off spell 3-1-7-0	3	- - - -	-321	
130		Statham 23] ←		- - - -	-321	
131		Bedser 38] →		- 2 - - 1 -	-324	New ball taken. Lindwall dropped by Hutton at short leg, chest high. Hutton hurt on thumb, moves himself to cover.
132		Statham 24] ←		- - - - -	-324	

1953 – SECOND TEST

133		Bedser 39] →	2 - - 4 - -		-330	Davidson dropped by Hutton at cover. Hutton goes off with bruised hand. Tattersall sub. Brown takes over captaincy.
134	1.10 1.12	Statham 25] ←		- - W Langley - 1	8 -330 -331	Lindwall bld middle stump, 9 in 51 mins, 46 balls, 1 four. Statham's first Test wicket against Australia
135	1.15 1.17	Bedser 40] →		- W Johnston - 2 -	9-331 -333	Langley c Watson at square leg, left-handed, 1 in 3 mins, 5 balls. Bedser's 200th Test wicket
136		Statham 26] ←	- 2 - - -		-335	Hutton leaves the field for repairs- in stony silence. Brown takes over as captain.
137		Bedser 41] →		- - - - -	-335	
138	1.30	Statham 27] ←	- - 1 - -		-336	
		LUNCH	Davdsn 66 151 mins 131 balls	Johnston 2 13 mins 12 balls	9-336 480 mins 831 balls	

SESSION. 73-4 in 120mins, 205 balls

Fingleton: Ring looked unhappy with his decision. Hassett's innings a typically sound affair. Wardle did well. Statham commendable. Bailey expensive. Brown very negative.

		Afternoon	Davdsn 66	Johnston 2	9-336	
139	2.10	Bedser 42] →	- - 1 - -		-337	
140		Statham 28] ← spell (incl. lunch) 6-2-12-1	- 4 - 4 - -		-345	
141	2.20	Bedser 43] → spell (incl. lunch) 5.4-1-13-2	- - W	1	10 -346	Davidson c Statham at deep mid-off, high catch, 76 in 161 mins, 144 balls, 13 fours, 1 six
		All out		Johnston 3 23 mins 15 balls	10-346 490 mins 847 balls	

SESSION 10-1 in 10 mins, 16 balls

1953 – SECOND TEST

AUSTRALIA FIRST INNINGS

A.L. Hassett	c Bailey b Bedser	104	296 mins, 253 balls, 12 fours	7-291
A.R. Morris	st Evans b Bedser	30	82 mins, 90 balls, 3 fours	1-65
R.N. Harvey	lbw b Bedser	59	179 mins, 139 balls, 4 fours	2-190
K.R. Miller	b Wardle	25	70 mins, 61 balls, 3 fours 1 six	5-220
G.B. Hole	c Compton b Wardle	13	45 mins, 43 balls, 2 fours	3-225
R. Benaud	lbw b Wardle	0	5 mins, 6 balls	4-229
A.K. Davidson	c Statham b Bedser	76	161 mins, 144 balls, 13 fours, 1 six	10-346
D.T. Ring	lbw b Wardle	18	45 mins, 45 balls, 3 fours	6-280
R.R. Lindwall	b Statham	9	51 mins, 46 balls, 1 four	8-330
G.R. Langley	c Watson b Bedser	1	3 mins, 5 balls	9-331
W.A. Johnston	not out	3	23 mins, 15 balls	
Extras	(b 4, lb 4)	8		
TOTAL	(10 wkts)	346	490 mins, 847 balls, 140.4 overs	

At 201-2, Hassett retired hurt 101 and returned at 280-6

BOWLING

Bedser	42.4	8	105	5	(3 nb)
Statham	28	7	48	1	
Brown	25	7	53	0	
Bailey	16	2	55	0	
Wardle	29	9	77	4	

England's close catching inadequate. Watson was England's best fielder.
Fingleton: Bedser did not bowl as well as at Nottingham, bowled to wide.

ENGLAND – First Innings

Odd overs →] from Nursery end
Even overs ← [from Pavilion end

			Hutton	Kenyon		Breeze from Nursery end
1	2.35	Lindwall 1 → [	- 1 - 3 - 2	1 	-7	Lindwall's field: only 2 in front of the wicket (cover and mid-on) Hutton 3 to extra cover Kenyon 2 to mid wicket
2		Miller 1 ← [	- 1 - - -	 	-8	Miller's first over of the Test series
3	2.45	Lindwall 2 → [	- - - 1 W Graveney	 1	-9	Kenyon c Davidson back defensive shot of glove to close short leg, nobody appeals. Some doubt but Kenyon walks, 3 in 10 mins, 7 balls
4	2.47	Miller 2 ← [	- - 4 - 1 1		-15	Hutton off-drive for 4 Graveney straight drive, meanders single thinking it is going for four
5		Lindwall 3 → [	- - 4 - - -		-19	Graveney 4 turned to leg
6		Miller 3 ← [off spell 3-0-7-0	- - - - 1 -		-20	

1953 – SECOND TEST

7		Lindwall 4 → [		1 1 - -	-23	
8		Johnston 1 ← [	1 - - 1 - -		-25	
9		Lindwall 5 → [		1 - 2 - -	-28	
10		Johnston 2 ← [		- 4 - 4 - -	-36	Graveney two straight drives for fours to pavilion rails
11		Lindwall 6 → [	- - - - -		-36	
12		Johnston 3 ← [	1 1 - - -		-38	
13		Lindwall 7 → [off spell 7-1-25-1	1 - 4 - 1	1	-45	Hutton cover-drive for 4
14		Johnston 4 ← [	- - - - -		-45	
15		Ring 1 → [		- - - - 4 -	-49	Graveney flat-bats wide half volley to square cover for 4, feet not near the ball
16	3.35	Johnston 5 ← [	- - - - (nb) 2 -		-51	
17		Ring 2 → [		- 1 - 1 -	-53	

1953 – SECOND TEST

18		Johnston 6 ← [		- - - - -	-53	
19		Ring 3 → [		- - - - -	-53	
20		Johnston 7 ← [	1 -	- - - -	-54	
21		Ring 4 → [	 1	- - - -	-55	
22		Johnston 8 ← [	- (nb) 3 1	 1 - - -	-60	
23		Ring 5 → [off spell 5-1-14-0	4 3	 - - - -	-67	
24		Johnston 9 ← [	1	 - - 4 - -	-72	
25		Benaud 1 → [	- - 1	 - - -	-73	*Benaud two lbw appeals against Graveney*
26		Johnston 10 ← [	1 4	- - - 	-78	
27		Benaud 2 → [	- - - - -		-78	
28		Johnston 11 ← [	- - - - -		-78	

1953 – SECOND TEST

29		Benaud 3 → [		- 4 - - 1	1	-84
30	4.15	Johnston 12 ← [	1	1 - 4 - -		-90
		TEA	Hutton 46 100 mins 97 balls	Gravny 38 88 mins 78 balls	1-90 100 mins 182 balls	

SESSION (BOTH SIDES) 100-2 in 110 mins, 198 balls
Kenyon says: "If I touch the ball and it's caught, then I'm out."
Graveney in dominant mood. In the 15th over when he square drove a wide half volley for 4 with his foot straight down the wicket, a completely improvised stroke that went like a bullet for 4, he laughed. Hutton was not amused; "Shut up and get on with the game".

		Evening	Hutton 46	Gravny 38	1-90	
31	4.35	Benaud 4 → [	1	- - 1 1		-93
32		Ring 6 ← [	1	- - 4 -		-98
33	4.45	Benaud 5 → [	- - 1	- -		-99	Hutton 50 in 110 mins, 105 balls
34	4.50	Ring 7 ← [	- - - 1		-100	
35		Benaud 6 → [	- - 1	- -		-101
36		Ring 8 ← [off spell 3-0-13-0	4 - - 1	- 2		-108
37	5.00	Benaud 7 → [	- - 1	4 2 4		-119	Graveney 50 in 114 mins, 94 balls
38		Miller 4 ← [	- - - -			-119

1953 – SECOND TEST

#		Bowler				Notes
39		Benaud 8 → [off spell 5-0-22-0		- - 4 1 1	-125	
40		Miller 5 ← [		- - - - 1 -	-126	
41		Johnston 13 → [	1	- - - 1 -	-128	
42		Miller 6 ← [		- - - - -	-128	
43		Johnston 14 → [	- - (1 nb) - - - -		-129	
44		Miller 7 ← [		- 1 - 2 - -	-132	
45		Johnston 15 → [		- - - - -	-132	
46		Miller 8 ← [off spell 5-2-8-0	4 - - - -		-136	
47		Johnston 16 → [off spell 4-2-6-0		- (4 byes) - - 4 -	-144	
48		Lindwall 8 ← [	1	- - - - -	-145	*Lindwall bowling with one slip*
49		Davidson 1 → [	- 1	- - - -	-146	

1953 – SECOND TEST

50		Lindwall 9 ← [	- - - - -		-146	
51		Davidson 2 → [	1	- - - 1	-148	
52		Lindwall 10 ← [	- - - - 1		-149	
53		Davidson 3 → [	- 1	- - - (4 lb) 2	-156	
54		Lindwall 11 ← [off spell 4-1-5-0	- 1 1	- 1 -	-159	
55		Davidson 4 → [off spell 5-2-10-0	1 - - 1	1 -	-162	
56		Johnston 17 ← [	- - - - -		-162	
57		Benaud 9 → [		1 - - - -	-163	
58		Johnston 18 ← [	- - (nb) 4 -	- - 1	-168	
59		Benaud 10 → [		- - - - -	-168	
60		Johnston 19 ← [	- - - - -		-168	

1953 – SECOND TEST

61		Benaud 11 → [		- - - - -	-168	
62		Johnston 20 ← [	- 1	- - (1 nb) - -	-170	
63		Ring 9 → [	1	- - - - 1	-172	
64		Johnston 21 ← [		- - - 1 -	-173	
65		Ring 10 → [spell 2-0-3-0		- - - - 1	-174	
66	6.30	Johnston 22 ← [spell 5-2-10-0	1 - 1 -	1 1 -	-177	
		CLOSE	Hutton 83 215 mins 208 balls	Gravny 78 203 mins 186 balls	1-177 215 mins 401 balls	

SESSION 87-0 in 115 mins, 219 balls

Excellent day seen by 31,104 people.

Hutton and Graveney had the bowlers at their mercy but failed to press home their superiority in the last hour. Only 33 scored in the last 19 overs. At about 5.25 Hutton said to Graveney "See it out. Mustn't lose a wicket tonight".

Bowes: "I have never seen a more convincing, better or more enjoyable partnership for England since the War."

Times correspondent: What a difference a day makes! How much better it could have been if England held their catches.

Cardus: It is a long time since Australian bowlers had to struggle so hard on a long hot afternoon.

Bradman: England's batsmen have a chance to put them in a dominant position.

There were storms in the Midlands today.

Arlott saw Hutton at close of play. Wearily Hutton looked at the bruising on his hand and said: "I have played in over sixty Tests and I have dropped more catches to-day than in all those other games put together." He did not mention that the pain from fibrositis in his back restricted his movements.

1953 – SECOND TEST

England miss the boat: THIRD DAY, Saturday 27 June

15,000 queuing at 6 am. Gates closed at 10 am. Lindwall and Miller had a chat last night about Graveney's high backlift.

		Morning	Hutton 83	Gravny 78	1-177	
67	11.30	Lindwall 12 →[		- - -		New ball taken after 3rd ball
	11.35			W Compton	2-177	Graveney bld, yorked, played on, 78 in 208 mins, 190 balls, 12 fours
	11.37			- -	-177	
68		Miller 9 ←[	- - - - 3		-180	Hutton steers 3 to third man
69		Lindwall 13 →[	4 - 2 1 -		-187	Hutton 4 square drive to Tavern Hutton 2 glances to long leg
70		Miller 10 ←[	- - - - -		-187	Miller two short fast balls in succession A very fast over
71		Lindwall 14 →[		2 - - - 4	-193	Compton 2 steered past gully, lifting ball Compton 4 edged, dropping just short of Davidson on leg-side
72		Miller 11 ←[	- - 1 - -		-194	
73		Lindwall 15 →[		- - 2 - -	-196	Weather now cloudy
74	11.59	Miller 12 ←[		4 - - 4 -	-204	Compton 4 to long leg Compton nearly yorked Compton chance to leg trap Compton hooks for 4
75	12.02	Lindwall 16 →[	- 4 - - 3		-211	Hutton glances short ball for 4, misfield at fine leg, 100 in 247 mins, 236 balls. 117th century of his career
76		Miller 13 ←[	1	- - - 1 -	-213	

1953 – SECOND TEST

77		Lindwall 17 → [off spell 6-1-24-1	1 - - - 1 -		-215	
78	12.15	Miller 14 ← [off spell 6-2-14-0	- - - - - -		-215	
79		Johnston 23 → [	- - - 2 - -		-217	
80		Ring 11 ← [	- - - - -		-217	
81		Johnston 24 → [	- - - - -		-217	
	Drinks interval. Then Compton complained about pigeons who were convened behind bowler. Hassett scattered them					
82		Ring 12 ← [	- - - 2 -		-219	Hutton 2 to long leg, almost run out
83		Johnston 25 → [	- - - - 4		-223	Compton hooks for 4
84		Ring 13 ← [	- 1 4 - -	1	-229	Hutton 4 pull to mid wicket
85		Johnston 26 → [off spell 4-1-10-0	- - - - 4 -		-233	Compton 4 past cover off full toss
86		Ring 14 ← [off spell 4-1-13-0	1 - - - - 4		-238	Compton 4 straight drive to Pavilion
87		Miller 15 → [	- - 4 - - 4		-246	*Hutton beaten outside off stump, then survives lbw appeal* Hutton 4 cover drive Hutton 4 glanced to square leg

1953 – SECOND TEST

Over	Time	Bowler				Score	Notes
88		Davidson 5 ← [		- - - - -		-246	
89		Miller 16 → [		- - - 1	-	-247	
90		Davidson 6 ← [		- - - 1	-	-248	
91		Miller 17 → [	1	- - - -		-249	
92		Davidson 7 ← [	- - 1	- 2 1		-253	
93		Miller 18 → [off spell 4-0-13-0	- - 1	1 - - 1		-256	
94		Davidson 8 ← [		- - - - -		-256	
95		Benaud 12 → [	- 4 - - -			-260	*Hutton (130) chops a ball down onto Langley's pad, narrowly missing the wicket*
96		Davidson 9 ← [off spell 5-2-10-0	- - - 2 -	- 3		-265	
97		Benaud 13 → [	4 - 4 1	- (1 lb) -		-275	
98	1.20	Johnston 27 ← [	- - 4 - W Watson			3 -279	Hutton hooks 4, reaching 2,000 runs in Tests against Australia Hutton c Hole at short sq leg, pushing forward, 145 in 325 mins, 312 balls, 16 fours

1953 – SECOND TEST

99	1.21	Benaud 14 → [off spell 3-0-21-0		- 4 - - 4	-287	
100		Johnston 28 ← [		- - - - -	-287	
101	1.30	Miller 19 → [		- - - - -	-287	
		LUNCH	Watson 0 9 mins 6 balls	Comptn 47 113 mins 96 balls	3-287 335 mins 611 balls	

SESSION 110-2 in 120 mins, 210 balls

Graveney's dismissal when Lindwall was warming up for the new ball was a disappointment. It fuelled suggestions that he lacked total concentration. Cardus said he should set his alarm clock an hour earlier. Graveney says he stopped the yorker with his full bat but it still got through.

Compton says that the first spell by Miller this morning was the fastest he ever faced from Miller.

The legs of the crowd on the grass are covering the boundary rope. Police unable to get them back. Loudspeaker appeals during lunch to spectators in front of grandstand to get back over the rope.

Fingleton: Ring, Benaud, Johnston and Davidson have bowled a lot of loose stuff.

		Afternoon	Watson 0	Comptn 47	3-287	
102	2.10 2.15	Johnston 29 ← [	W Bailey	- - 4 -	4 -291	Watson sweeps for 4 to square leg Watson st Langley on leg-side off wk's pads, 4 in 14 mins, 12 balls, 1 four
103	2.17	Benaud 15 → [		- - - - 1	-292	
104		Johnston 30 ← [	-	- - - 3 -	-295	Compton 3 through leg trap. If Miller had not taken evasive action, it was an easy catch, 51 off 106 balls
105		Benaud 16 → [		- 2 - - -	-297	*Benaud bowling good length with some turn*
106		Johnston 31 ← [	-	- - - -	-297	
107	2.30	Benaud 17 → [	W Brown	- - 4 -	5 -301	Compton c Hole, playing forward, edged to slip, 57 in 113 mins, 118 balls, 9 fours

1953 – SECOND TEST

#	Time	Bowler			Total	Notes
108	2.32	Johnston 32 ← [	- - - - -		-301	
109		Benaud 18 → [	- - - - -	- (1 bye)	-302	*Bailey almost c & b*
110		Johnston 33 ← [	(1 nb) - - -	- 4 3	-310	Brown 4 to long leg Brown 3 cut
111		Benaud 19 → [off spell 5-1-19-1		- 4 - - 4 4	-322	Brown 4 to mid wkt Brown 4 first bounce to long off Brown 4 steered past gully
112		Miller 20 ← [	- - 1 - 3	- (2 byes)	-328	
113	2.50 2.52 2.53 2.54	Lindwall 18 → [		W Evans W Wardle - 1 -	6-328 7-328 -329	Brown c Langley, tickled low down leg side, 22 in 18 mins, 14 balls, 4 fours Evans bld 0 in 1 min, 1 ball
114		Miller 21 ← [		- - - - -	-329	*Wardle played and missed three times*
115		Lindwall 19 → [	- 1 - 1 -		-331	
116	3.06 3.08	Miller 22 ← [	W Bedser -	- 1 -	8-332 -332	Bailey c and b, spooned up slower ball, juggled with left hand, 2 in 49 mins, 34 balls. Miller's first of the series.
117		Lindwall 20 → [		- 2 - - 4 -	-338	Wardle 4 over mid-off

1953 – SECOND TEST

#	Time	Bowler	Balls	W	Score	Notes
118		Miller 23 ← [	1 - - - -	1	-340	
119	3.16 3.17	Lindwall 21 → [	1 W Statham - - -		9-341 -342	Bedser bld yorker, 1 in 8 mins, 7 balls
120		Miller 24 ← [	- 2 - 4 - -		-347	Wardle cut 2 Wardle off-drive 4. Big cheer for first innings lead.
121		Lindwall 22 → [	- 1 - 1 - -		-349	
122	3.22	Miller 25 ← [off spell 6-1-14-1	- 1 (1 wide) - - - -		-351	
123		Lindwall 23 → [off spell 6-1-12-3	- - - - - -		-351	
124		Johnston 34 ← [	- - - - 4		-355	Statham cuts for 4
125		Davidson 10 → [	2 - - 1 -		-358	
126		Johnston 35 ← [spell 2-0-14-0	- 1 (1 nb) - 4 4 1 -		-369	Statham 2 fours to long on
127	3.47	Davidson 11 → [spell 1.5-0-6-1	- - 2 1	W	10-372	Wardle bld 23 in 53 mins, 45 balls, 2 fours
		All out	Statham 17 30 mins 28 balls 3 fours		10-372 432 mins 768 balls	

SESSION **7-85 in 97 mins, 157 balls**

1953 – SECOND TEST

ENGLAND FIRST INNINGS

L.Hutton	c Hole b Johnston	145	325 mins, 312 balls, 16 fours	3-279
D.Kenyon	c Davidson b Lindwall	3	10 mins, 7 balls	1-9
T.W.Graveney	b Lindwall	78	208 mins, 190 balls, 12 fours	2-177
D.C.S.Compton	c Hole b Benaud	57	113 mins, 118 balls, 9 fours	5-301
W.Watson	st Langley b Johnston	4	14 mins, 12 balls, 1 four	4-291
T.E.Bailey	c and b Miller	2	49 mins, 34 balls	8-332
F.R.Brown	c Langley b Lindwall	22	18 mins, 14 balls, 4 fours	6-328
T.G.Evans	b Lindwall	0	1 min, 1 ball	7-328
J.H.Wardle	b Davidson	23	53 mins, 45 balls, 2 fours	10-372
A.V.Bedser	b Lindwall	1	8 mins, 7 balls	9-342
J.B.Statham	not out	17	30 mins, 28 balls, 3 fours	
Extras	(b 11, lb 1, w 1, nb 7)	20		
Total	(for 10 wkts)	372	432 mins, 768 balls, 126.5 overs	

BOWLING

Lindwall	23	4	66	5	
Miller	25	6	57	1	(1 w)
Johnston	35	11	91	2	(7 nb)
Ring	14	2	43	0	
Benaud	19	4	70	1	
Davidson	10.5	2	25	1	

England restricted to a lead of 26, thanks to Lindwall's devastating spell.

Cardus: Benaud looked dangerous on the few occasions when he dropped on a good length. It is possible that the Australians allowed the last pair a little indulgence so as to deny England a burst of bowling before a tea interval

Bowes: Davidson's fielding at short leg was worth about 40 runs to Australia

Australia Second Innings

Odd overs] →   from Pavilion End
Even overs] ←   from Nursery End

			Hassett	Morris		
1	4.10	Bedser 1] →	- 2 - 1	- -3		*Wind from Nursery End*
2	4.18 4.20	Statham 1] ←	- W Miller - - -	1 -3 -3		Hassett c Evans down leg side, Hassett surprised, controversial decision, 3 in 8 mins, 7 balls
3		Bedser 2] →		- - - 4 -	-7	
4		Statham 2] ←		- - - - 1	-8	*Miller hit twice on thigh; first hurt so much that he throws the bat down*
5		Bedser 3] →		- - 1 - 3	-12	
6		Statham 3] ←		- - - - -	-12	

1953 – SECOND TEST

7		Bedser 4] →		- - - 4 - -	-16	
8		Statham 4] ←		- - - 1 - -	-17	
9		Bedser 5] →		- - - - - -	-17	
10		Statham 5] ←		- - - 1 - 1	-19	
11		Bedser 6] → off spell 6-1-19-0	4	4 - - - - -	-23	
12		Statham 6] ←	1	- - - - 2	-26	
13		Wardle 1] →		- - - - -	-26	
14		Statham 7] ← off 7-2-11-1		- - - - 4	-30	Aust take lead at about 4.55
15		Wardle 2] →		- - - - 1	-31	
16		Brown 1] ←		- - - - -	-31	Brown bowls one over of medium pace
17		Wardle 3] →		- - - - -	-31	

1953 – SECOND TEST

Over	Time	Bowler			Score	Notes
18		Brown 2]←	- - - - -		-31	Brown switches to leg breaks
19		Wardle 4]→		- - - - 2	-33	
20		Brown 3]←	- 4 - - -		-37	
21		Wardle 5]→		2 - - - -	-39	
22		Brown 4]←	1 - - 4 - -		-44	
23		Wardle 6]→ off spell 6-3-5-0		- - - - -	-44	
24		Brown 5]← off spell 5-2-14-0	- 4 - -	- 1	-49	
25	5.35	Bailey 1]→		1 - (nb) 4 - -	-54	
26		Wardle 7]←		- - - - -	-54	
27		Bailey 2]→	- - 4 2 -		-60	Miller 4 to long off
28		Wardle 8]←		- - - 1 2	-63	

1953 – SECOND TEST

29		Bailey 3] →		- - 1 1 - -	-65	
30		Wardle 9] ←		- 6 - - -	-71	Miller hooks 6 onto Grandstand balcony
31		Bailey 4] →		- - - - -	-71	
32		Bedser 7] ←		2 - 1 - -	-74	
33		Bailey 5] →		- - (nb) 4 2 - 2	-82	
34		Bedser 8] ←		1 - - 1 -	-84	
35	6.10	Bailey 6] → off spell 6-1-23-0		- - - 2 -	-86	Miller 51 in 110 mins, 106 balls
36		Bedser 9] ←		- - - - -	-86	
37		Statham 8] →		- - - - -	-86	
38		Bedser 10] ←		1 - - 1 -	-88	
39		Statham 9] → off spell 2-0-6-0		- - - 2 4 -	-94	

1953 – SECOND TEST

40		Bedser 11] ← off spell 5-1-8-0		- - - 1 -	-95	
41	6.30	Wardle 10] → spell 1-0-1-0		- - 1 - -	-96	
		CLOSE 3rd day	Miller 58 130 mins 127 balls	Morris 35 140 mins 114 balls	1-96 140 mins 248 balls	

Fingleton: it transpires that the decision against Hassett was wrong. Miller, having been booed by the crowd, settled in with determination.

West: It was a marginal decision.

Barnes and Whitington: the ball appeared to hit Hassett's pad not his bat. Hassett said on his return to the dressing room when asked that it was off his hip. Evans heard a snick but was not sure and his appeal was more hesitant that the appeal of the other close fielders. At the close he asked Hassett if he hit the ball and Hassett replied "No I didn't and what's more you know I didn't".

Times correspondent: Australia's cautious response, which took the gloss off the day, was conditioned by Hassett's early departure and England's resort to defence.

Bradman: England are in danger of defeat.

Miller was so tired that he went straight back to his hotel for a sleep.

The Australian team, some former England captains, members of the Press corps and others such as Sir A.P.Herbert, Sir Pelham Warner and D.R.Jardine, dined at the Savoy, with steaks that the host Mr Menzies has brought over from Australia. F.R.Brown said that it was his First Test against Australia in England. Another England captain remarks: "I wondered why you were so keen to play."

Sir Winston Churchill has been taken ill and a summit conference in Bermuda has been postponed. In fact, unknown to the public he has suffered a near-fatal stroke. His long-expectant successor, Sir Anthony Eden is at this very time in Boston USA undergoing major surgery.

Aussies' night on the town: FOURTH DAY: Monday 29 June

Ground full, but gates do not have to be locked. Strong wind from Nursery End

		Morning	Miller 58	Morris 35	1-96	
42	11.30 11.32	Brown 6] ←		- - 4 4 - 1	-105	Morris 2 fours to leg off short balls. 101 stand in 142 mins
43		Statham 10] →		1 - 1 - -	-107	Statham bowling against breeze
44		Brown 7] ←		- - - - -	-107	
45	11.45	Statham 11] → off spell 2-0-7-0		- - 4 - 1 -	-112	*Morris tells Hutton that Statham is running onto the pitch* Morris edges 4 through gully Morris 50 in 155 mins, 128 balls Hutton takes Statham off.

1953 – SECOND TEST

#		Bowler		Balls	Score	Notes
46		Brown 8] ←		- - - - - (1 bye)	-113	*Brown nearly yorks Morris with slow flighted leg break*
47		Wardle 11] →		4 - - - -	-117	Morris cover drive for 4 Last ball, Morris lobs up on off side; Wardle runs for it
48		Brown 9] ←	- - 2 - -		-119	
49		Wardle 12] →		2 - - - -	-121	*Wardle bowling defensively*
50		Brown 10] ←	- - - 1 - -		-122	
51		Wardle 13] →	- - - - -		-122	
52		Brown 11] ←		- 1 - 1 4 -	-128	
53		Wardle 14] →	- - - 1	2 2	-133	
54		Brown 12] ←	1	- 4 - - 1	-139	
55		Wardle 15] →		- - - 4 - 1	-144	
56		Brown 13] ← off spell 8-2-29-0		4 - - - - 1	-149	*Morris (79) survives a plumb lbw because of faint tickle on bat*

1953 – SECOND TEST

57		Wardle 16] →		- - - - -	-149	
58	12.22	Statham 12] ←		- 4 - - -	-153	Miller perfectly timed late cut for 4, 150 stand in 180 mins
59		Wardle 17] →		- - 1 - -	-152	
60		Statham 13] ← off spell 2-0-5-0		- - - - 1 -	-155	
61		Wardle 18] →		- - 1 - -	-156	Morris dropped at 1st slip, easy chance waist-high. Hutton's 4th chance. Hutton's face turns white
62		Compton 1] ←		1 - 1 4 1 -	-163	
63		Wardle 19] →		- - - (3 byes) - 2	- 168	
64	12.40	Compton 2] ← off spell 2-0-10-1		- W Harvey 1 1 -	2-168 -171	Morris c Statham, hooking long hop, Statham running back from square leg, dives, hurts his head, batsmen crossed, 89 in 210 mins, 196 balls, 13 fours
65		Wardle 20] → off spell 10-3-20-0	- - - - -		-171	
66		Bailey 7] ←		- - - - -	-171	*New ball taken*
67		Bedser 12] →	2 - - - -		-173	

1953 – SECOND TEST

68		Bailey 8] ←		- - - - -	-173	
69		Bedser 13] →	- 1	- (4 lb) - - -	-178	
70		Bailey 9] ←		- - - - -	-178	
71		Bedser 14] →		- - - 2 - -	-180	Harvey violent hook for 2, very sharp chance to Bailey at short sq leg, who shakes his left hand for several minutes
72		Bailey 10] ← off spell 3-2-1-0	- - 1	- - - - -	-181	
73		Bedser 15] → off spell 4-0-9-0	- - 4 - -		-185	
74		Statham 14] ←	- 3	- - - -	-188	
75		Wardle 21] →		- - - - -	-188	
76		Statham 15] ←	- - - 4 4 -		-196	
77		Wardle 22] →	1 - - - 1		-198	

88

1953 – SECOND TEST

78		Compton 3] ← spell 1-0-11-0	1 1	4 4 1 - -209		
	1.30	Lunch	Miller 93 250 mins 228 balls	Harvey 16 48 mins 39 balls	2 –209 260 mins 470 balls	

SESSION 113-1 in 120 mins, 222 balls

West: surprised that Hutton did not give Bedser a spell at the start of the day.

Alston: Miller was a master of self-control.

Barnes: Hutton went on the defensive far too soon. He had pace bowler Statham bowling into the wind and leg-spinner Brown bowling with the wind.

Cardus "I have seldom seen attack so torpid and amiable as this of England's in a crucial moment at the beginning of the day."

On this very hot day, Bradman noticed that several spectators were stripped to the waist (male presumably)

		Afternoon	Miller 93	Harvey 16	2 –209	
79	2.10	Wardle 23] →	- 4 - 1	- -	-214	
80	2.18	Bedser 16] ←	- - 4 - -		-218	*Bedser reduces pace, as one slip and gully* Miller 4 off full-toss to mid wicket, 102 in 258 mins, 236 balls
81		Wardle 24] →	 4	- - - 1 -	-223	
82		Bedser 17] ←		- 4 - - -	-227	Harvey 4 snicked off inside edge
83		Wardle 25] →	- - - - -		-227	
84	2.29	Bedser 18] ←		- - - W Hole -	3-227 -227	Harvey bld, swinging in to hit middle stump, through bat and pad, 21 in 67 mins, 55 balls, 3 fours
85		Wardle 26] →	- - - - -		-227	
86		Bedser 19] ←		- - - - -	-227	*Bedser has 2 slips, 2 gullys, 2 short legs for Hole*

1953 – SECOND TEST

87		Wardle 27] →	- 1 - - 4 -		-232	Hole sweeps for 4
88		Bedser 20] ←	1 - 1 - - -		-234	
89		Wardle 28] →	- - - - -		-234	
90		Bedser 21] ←	- - - - -		-234	
91		Wardle 29] →	- - - - -		-234	
92		Bedser 22] ←	- - 1 - - -		-235	
93	2.52 2.54	Wardle 30] →	- - W Benaud - - -		4-235 -235	Miller bld, arm ball, played on, inside edge cutting, 109 in 292 mins, 271 balls, 14 fours 1 six. With a laugh he picks up the bails and chucks them to Evans
94		Bedser 23] ←	- - - - -		-235	
95		Wardle 31] →	- - - - -		-235	
96		Bedser 24] ←	2 - 4 - -		-241	Hole square cuts for 4
97		Wardle 32] →	1 - 1 - 4 -		-247	Benaud off the mark, nearly run out by Watson from mid wicket Benaud 4 high to long on

1953 – SECOND TEST

98		Bedser 25] ←		- - - - -	-247	
99		Wardle 33] →	(1 lb) -	- - - - -	-248	
100	3.14 3.16	Bedser 26] ←	W Davidson 1	 1 - - -	5-248 -250	Benaud c Graveney at mid on, pushing too soon at slower ball, 5 in 20 mins, 18 balls, 1 four
101		Wardle 34] →		4 - - - 1	-255	
102		Bedser 27] ←		- - 2 - 1 -	-258	
103		Wardle 35] →	4	1 - - -	-263	
104		Bedser 28] ← off spell 13-5-23-2		- - - - 1	-264	
105		Wardle 36] →		- - - 4 -	-268	
106		Brown 14] ←	(2 lb) -	- - - - 1	-271	
107		Wardle 37] →		- - - 4 -	-275	
108		Brown 15] ←		4 4 1 - -	-284	*Brown bowling slow to Hole, medium pace to Davidson*

1953 – SECOND TEST

Over	Time	Bowler			Score	Notes
109		Wardle 38]→		- - - - -	-284	
110		Brown 16]←	- 1 - 1 -		-286	
111		Wardle 39]→		- - - 1 -	-287	
112		Brown 17]←	- - - 3 -		-290	
113		Wardle 40]→		- - 2 - -	-292	
114	4.00 4.02	Brown 18]←	- - 4 W Ring -		6-296 -296	Davidson c & b, off googly, playing too soon, high catch to right hand, 15 in 44 mins, 34 balls, 3 fours
115		Wardle 41]→		- - - - -	-296	
116		Brown 19]←	- - - 4 -		-300	
117		Wardle 42]→		- - - 4 -	-304	
118	4.15	Brown 20]←	- - - 1 W		7-305	Hole lbw, 47 in 104 mins, 116 balls, 7 fours
		TEA	Ring 5 13 mins 13 balls		7-305 385 mins 710 balls	

SESSION 96-5 in 125 mins, 240 balls
A very good session for England, but they are still very vulnerable. Australia lead by 279

		Evening	Ring 5	Lindwall	7-305	
119	4.35	Wardle 43]→	- - - - - -		-305	
120	4.42	Brown 21]←	- 2 W Langley	- - 1	8- 308	Ring lbw, no stroke, 7 in 20 mins, 22 balls, 1 four
121	4.44	Wardle 44]→	- - - -	4 1	-313	
122		Brown 22]←	- - -	- - 1	-314	
123		Wardle 45]→		4 6 4 - - -	-328	Lindwall 4 over long on, Statham not standing on ropes; 6 to midwicket; 4 to square leg
124		Brown 23]←	1 - - -	- 1	-330	
125		Wardle 46]→ off spell (incl. lunch and tea) 26-11-76-1	4	- 4 - - 1	-339	
126		Brown 24]←		- - 2 - - -	-341	*Brown reverts to medium pace*
127		Bedser 29]→	- - - - - -		-341	
128		Brown 25]←	4 - - -	1 -	-346	
129		Bedser 30]→	-	- (2 lb) 4 - 2 6 (nb) 1	-361	Lindwall 6 off no-ball to mid wkt into Grandstand

1953 – SECOND TEST

130		Brown 26] ←		1		
	5.13		W Johnston	- - -	9-362	Langley bld, played on, 9 in 39 mins, 26 balls, 2 fours
	5.15			- -	-362	
131		Bedser 31] →		- - - 4 1 -	-367	
132		Brown 27] ← spell 7-0-15-2		- - -		
	5.21			1 - -	-368	Lindwall 50 in 46 mins, 45 balls
133		Bedser 32] → spell 3.5-0-18-1		- - - -		Lindwall bld 50 in 50 mins, 50 balls, 6 fours, 2 sixes
	5.25			W	10- 368	
		All out	Johnston 0 10 mins 5 balls		10-368 435 mins 801 balls	

SESSION 63-3 in 50 mins, 90 balls

AUSTRALIA SECOND INNINGS

A.L.Hassett	c Evans b Statham	3	8 mins, 7 balls	1-3
A.R.Morris	c Statham b Compton	89	210 mins, 196 balls, 13 fours	2-168
K.R.Miller	b Wardle	109	292 mins, 271 balls, 14 fours 1 six	4-235
R.N.Harvey	b Bedser	21	67 mins, 55 balls, 3 fours	3-227
G.B.Hole	lbw b Brown	47	104 mins, 116 balls, 7 fours	7-305
R.Benaud	c Graveney b Bedser	5	20 mins, 18 balls, 1 four	5-248
A.K.Davidson	c & b Brown	15	44 mins, 34 balls, 3 fours	6-296
D.T. Ring	lbw b Brown	7	20 mins, 22 balls, 1 four	8-308
R.R.Lindwall	b Bedser	50	50 mins, 50 balls, 6 fours, 2 sixes	10-368
G.R.Langley	b Brown	9	39 mins, 26 balls, 2 fours	9-362
W.A.Johnston	not out	0	10 mins, 5 balls	
Extras	(b 8, lb 5)	13		
TOTAL	(10 wkts)	368	435 mins, 801 balls, 132.5 overs	

BOWLING

Bedser	31.5	8	77	3	(1 nb)
Statham	15	3	40	1	
Wardle	46	18	111	1	
Brown	27	4	82	4	
Bailey	10	4	24	0	
Compton	3	0	21	1	

Times correspondent: Bedser should have put on earlier to deal with Lindwall.

Cutler: Wardle was tired and leg weary when he conceded 23 runs in his last two overs. When Lindwall came in he had figures of 34-14-73-1. Bailey and Statham should have come on after tea.

Arlott: Brown took 3 wickets in 15 balls when he turned to leg-spin for the first time in the match.

1953 – SECOND TEST

England Second Innings

Odd overs → [from Nursery End
Even overs ← [from Pavilion End
Pitch is taking spin. England need 343 in 413 minutes.

#	Time	Bowler	Hutton	Kenyon		Notes
1	5.37	Lindwall 1 → [	- - - 1	1	-2	*Lindwall bowling with five slips, three short legs*
2		Johnston 1 ← [	(1 wide) 1	- - 1 - -	-5	
3	5.47 5.49	Lindwall 2 → [	1 - -	W Graveney 1	1-6 -7	Kenyon c Hassett, short mid on, prodding at inswinging half volley off back foot, 2 in 10 mins, 5 balls Graveney 1 to leg side
4		Johnston 2 ← [		- - (1 nb) - - - -	-8	
5	5.57 5.59	Lindwall 3 → [	- - 2 W Compton - -		2-10 -10	Hutton c Hole, edged low to 2nd slip, 5 in 20 mins, 16 balls
6	6.02 6.04	Johnston 3 ← [	1	- 1 W Watson 1 -	3-12 -13	Graveney c Langley, trying to withdraw, deflected down, wk diving in front of slip, ct so low that Grvny waits for an appeal, 2 in 13 mins, 11 balls
7		Lindwall 4 → [	- - - - -		-13	
8		Johnston 4 ← [off spell 4-1-6-1	- - 1 - - -	- (1 nb) -	-15	
9		Lindwall 5 → [off spell 5-1-7-2	- - - - - 1		-16	

1953 – SECOND TEST

10		Ring 1 ← [		- - - 1 - -	-17	
11		Miller 1 → [		- - 1 - -	1 -19	
12		Ring 2 ← [		- - - - -	-19	
13		Miller 2 → [1-1-2-0		- - - - -	-19	Austrlns hurry to squeeze in extra over
14		Ring 3 ← [spell 3-1-2-0		- - - 1 -	-20	Watsn sharp chance to Lndwll, leg slip Watsn edge past Lndwll at catchable height, he moves the wrong way
	6.30	CLOSE	Compton 5 31 mins 29 balls	Watson 3 26 mins 25 balls	3-20 53 mins 86 balls	

Swanton: "Humanly speaking the game was lost and won in the final two hours tonight".
Times correspondent: The hand of defeat lies on England.
Cardus: England need a miracle or rain.
Bradman: "When Hutton went, so did England's chance of victory. Only an unexpected innings by some lesser player can now bring even the remotest possibility of a draw."
Bailey was deputed to come in as night watchman if a wicket fell after 6.00. In fact three wickets fell before 6.00.
When Graveney sent the ball down off the middle of his bat well short of the gap between first and second slip, Langley's swallow dive to scoop the catch was so good it was almost unfair.
It has been an outstanding day for Lindwall – until the last over of the day. Tonight the Australians go off to see *Guys and Dolls* at the Coliseum, attend a back-stage party, then dine at the Café de Paris.
The receipts for this match, £50,000 already exceed the record for a match at Lord's, £43,000 in 1948.

Cricketing Dunkirk: FIFTH DAY, Tuesday 30 June

Ground half empty, 14,000 attendance. Another lovely day. The Duke of Edinburgh attends for a while, also visiting Wimbledon.

		5th DAY	Compton 5	Watson 3	3-20	
15	11.30	Lindwall 6 → [		- 2 1 - -	-23	Ground very quiet Watson 2 to long leg
16		Johnston 5 ← [		- - - 4 -	-27	
17		Lindwall 7 → [		- - 1 - -	-28	

1953 – SECOND TEST

18		Johnston 6 ← [		- - - - -	-28	
19		Lindwall 8 → [		- - - - -	-28	
20		Johnston 7 ← [		- - - - -	-28	*Compton dropped off glove on leg side of Johnston*
21		Lindwall 9 → [		- - - 1 2 -	-31	
22		Johnston 8 ← [		- - 4 - -	-35	Watson 4 high to leg
23		Lindwall 10 → [	1	1 - - -	-37	
24		Johnston 9 ← [off spell 5-2-10-0		2 - - - -	-39	
25		Lindwall 11 → [off spell 6-1-12-0	(1 bye) - 1	- 1 1	-43	
26		Ring 4 ← [		- 2 - - -	-45	Watson pulls short ball for 2
27	12.12	Benaud 1 → [	2 2 - 1	- -	-50	*Benaud erratic in length*
28		Ring 5 ← [		- - 2 1 -	-53	

1953 – SECOND TEST

29		Benaud 2 → [	4 - 4 - - 4		-65	Compton back-cut for 4 Compton on-drive for 4 Compton cover drive past Harvey for 4
30		Ring 6 ← [	- - - - -		-65	
31		Benaud 3 → [off spell 3-0-22-0	- - 1 4 -		-70	Watson hooks long hop for 4
32		Ring 7 ← [	- - - 1	1	-72	52 scored in first hour *Hassett refuses break for drinks at 12.30*
33		Johnston 10 → [	- - - - -		-72	*Johnston bowling over the wicket*
34		Ring 8 ← [	1 - - - -		-73	*Watson nearly played on – had to kick the ball away*
35	12.40 12.42	Johnston 11 → [	- - - - W Bailey -		4-73 -73	Compton lbw, faster ball skidded through, 33 in 101 mins, 85 balls, 3 fours
36		Ring 9 ← [	- - - - -		-73	
37		Johnston 12 → [	- - - - -		-73	
38		Ring 10 ← [	4 - 1 (2 byes) - 4 -		-84	Watson cover drive for 4 Bailey 4 to leg
39		Johnston 13 → [	- - - 4 1 -		-89	Watson 4 to long leg

1953 – SECOND TEST

40		Ring 11 ← [		- - - 4 - -	-93	Watson hooks 4
41	12.59	Johnston 14 → [off spell 5-3-14-1	- - - 1	4 (nb) 4 -	-102	Watson hooks 4 to leg, then opens shoulders for four to midwicket, stand 29 in 17 mins
42		Ring 12 ← [off spell 9-2-22-0	- - - 1 - -		-103	Bailey hooks to leg for 1, stand reaches 30 in 20 mins
43	1.04	Miller 3 → [	(1 lb) - - - -	1	-105	Watson 50 in 120 mins, 120 balls
44		Benaud 4 ← [		- - - - - -	-105	Batsmen decide that Bailey should be kept away from the spinners because of the rough outside his off-stump.
45		Miller 4 → [	- - - - -		-105	
46		Benaud 5 ← [		- - 1 - -	-106	
47		Miller 5 → [	- - - - -		-106	
48		Benaud 6 ← [		- - - - -	-106	
49		Miller 6 → [off spell 4-3-1-0	- - - - -	- (1 lb)	-107	
50		Benaud 7 ← [		- 2 1 - - 4	-114	

1953 – SECOND TEST

51		Davidson 1 → [		- - - (2 lb) - -	- -116	
	1.30	LUNCH	Bailey 10 48 mins 42 balls	Watson 54 146 mins 150 balls	4-116 173 mins 309 balls	

SESSION 96-1 in 120 mins, 223 balls
There is now the faintest hope of a draw. Bailey had his usual hearty lunch. Watson had only a glass of milk.
Cardus: a limp indecisive morning, with everyone including the Australians waiting for the end.
Bradman: Compton looked in good form and was unlucky to get a ball that shot through.
Kilburn: No great sense of Australian urgency.

		Afternoon	Bailey 10	Watson 54	4-116	
52	2.10	Benaud 8 → [off spell (incl. Lunch) 5-3-8-0	- - - - -		-116	
53		Davidson 2 → [		- - 1 - -	-117	*Davidson at full pace*
54		Johnston 15 ← [		- 1 - - -	-118	
55		Davidson 3 → [		- - - - -	-118	
56		Johnston 16 ← [	- 1	- - -	-119	
57		Davidson 4 → [	1	- - - -	-120	
58		Johnston 17 ← [	- - - - -		-120	
59		Davidson 5 → [		- - - 1 -	-121	

1953 – SECOND TEST

#		Bowler			Score	Notes
60		Johnston 18 ← [		- - 4 - 1		
			(1 nb) - -		-127	
61		Davidson 6 → [off spell (incl. Lunch) 6-2-5-0	1	1 - - - -	-129	
62		Johnston 19 ← [		- - - - 1	-130	
63		Benaud 9 → [		- - 1 - 4	-135	
64		Johnston 20 ← [		- - - - -	-135	
65		Benaud 10 → [off spell 2-0-10-0	- - - 4 -	1	-140	
66		Johnston 21 ← [off spell 7-2-9-0	(nb) 4 1	- - - 1 1	-147	
67		Lindwall 12 → [		- - - - -	-147	*New ball taken*
68		Miller 7 ← [	- - 1	- - 1	-149	*Lindwall and Miller are bowling with plain hostility at top speed*
69		Lindwall 13 → [		- - - 1 -	-150	
70		Miller 8 ← [		- - - 1 - -	-151	

1953 – SECOND TEST

71		Lindwall 14 → [		- - - 1 - -	-152	
72		Miller 9 ← [		- - - - -	-152	
73		Lindwall 15 → [	- - 1	- - -	-153	
74		Miller 10 ← [	1	- - - -	-154	
75		Lindwall 16 → [	- - - 1	-	-155	
76		Miller 11 ← [	- 1	- - -	-156	
77		Lindwall 17 → [off spell 6-1-5-0	- - - 1	-	-157	
78		Miller 12 ← [	- 1	- - - 1	-159	12 runs off new ball in 40 mins, 12 overs
79		Davidson 7 → [		- (2 byes) - - - -	-161	
80		Miller 13 ← [		- - - - -	-161	
81		Davidson 8 → [		- - - - -	-161	

1953 – SECOND TEST

Over	Time	Bowler			Score	Notes
82		Ring 13 ← [	- - - 1	- -	-162	
83		Johnston 22 → [	- - 4 - (1 nb) - -		-167	
84		Ring 14 ← [		4 - - 1 -	-172	
85	4.00	Johnston 23 → [off spell 2-0-4-0		- - - - (1 nb) - (1 nb) - -	-174	100 stand in 158 mins
86		Ring 15 ← [off spell 3-0-11-0	1	- - - 4 -	-179	
87		Lindwall 18 → [	- - 1	- -	-180	
88		Hole 1 ← [spell 1-1-0-0	- - (1 lb) - - -		-181	
89	4.15	Lindwall 19 → [spell 2-0-2-0	- - 1 -	- - (1 lb) -	- 183	
		TEA	Bailey 39 173 mins 148 balls	Watson 84 271 mins 277 balls	4-183 298 mins 542 balls	

SESSION 67-0 in 125 mins, 233 balls

The massive new ball onslaught has been withstood, at the cost only of three painful blows on Bailey's hand. After the new ball was seen off, Watson suggested to Bailey that they might go for the runs to win; Bailey turned and walked away without a word. At tea Watson and Bailey slumped down in chairs and relaxed. The other players left them alone and went off for tea. Crowds are now streaming into Lord's and taxis block the roads. A marvellous session for England, but Australia can attack the last session with no fear of defeat. If England save the match it is three footballers who have done it: Watson of Sunderland, an England international with four caps, Compton of Arsenal, an FA Cup finalist and war-time England international, and Bailey an amateur international.

1953 – SECOND TEST

		Evening	Bailey 39	Watson 84	4-183	
90	4.35	Davidson 9 ← [		- 2 - - - -	-185	
91		Miller 14 → [	- - - - -		- 185	
92		Davidson 10 ← [		- - - - -	-185	
93		Miller 15 → [	- - - 4 - 2		-191	
94		Davidson 11 ← [		- - 1 - -	-192	
95		Miller 16 → [		- - - - -	-192	
96		Davidson 12 ← [	- - 2 - - -		-194	
97		Miller 17 → [off spell 4-2-7-0		- - - 1 - -	-195	
98		Davidson 13 ← [		- - 1 - - -	-196	
99	5.05	Ring 16 → [		- - - 4 - -	-200	
100		Davidson 14 ← [off spell 6-1-8-0	- - 1 - -	1	-202	

1953 – SECOND TEST

101		Ring 17 → [		- 1 - - -	-203	
102		Johnston 24 ← [		1 - - -	-204	
103		Ring 18 → [		- - - - -	-204	
104	5.20	Johnston 25 ← [		- - 4 - -	-208	Bailey 52 in 218 mins, 191 balls
105	5.25	Ring 19 → [		- - - 4 -	-212	*Watson edges between Hole's legs at 1st slip* Watson sweep for 4 to Tavern, nearly ct by Benaud who dived forward, 100 in 321 mins, 324 balls
106		Johnston 26 ← [		- - - -	-212	
107		Ring 20 → [		4 - - - -	-216	
108		Johnston 27 ← [	- - (nb) 4 1 - - 1		-222	
109		Ring 21 → [		- - - - -	-222	
110	5.40	Johnston 28 ← [	- - - (nb) 4 - -		-226	150 stand in 238 mins
111		Ring 22 → [		- - - 4 -	-230	

1953 – SECOND TEST

112		Johnston 29 ← [off spell 6-1-21-0		- - - 2 4	-236	
113	5.50 5.52	Ring 23 → [		- - W Brown 1 - -	5-236 -237	Watson c Hole, inside edge via pad to 1st slip, 109 in 346 mins, 351 balls, 16 fours
114		Benaud 11 ← [		- - - 1 - -	-238	*No Lindwall* !
115	5.59 6.00	Ring 24 → [	4 (1 wide) W Evans	- (2 byes) 1 - -	6-246 -246	Bailey c Benaud, at deep gully, loose shot to wide ball pitched in rough, 71 in 257 mins, 224 balls, 11 fours. Very annoyed Vehement appeal for stumping off Evans
116		Benaud 12 ← [		4 - - - -	-250	
117		Ring 25 → [		- - - - 1	-251	
118		Benaud 13 ← [		- - - - -	-251	
119		Ring 26 → [	4 - - 4 1	-	-260	
120		Benaud 14 ← [		- 3 - 2 -	-265	
121		Ring 27 → [	1	- 1 4 2 -	-273	
122		Benaud 15 ← [		- - - 1 -	-274	

1953 – SECOND TEST

123		Ring 28 →[	3	- 1 - - -	-278	
124		Benaud 16 ←[		- - - - -	-278	
125		Ring 29 →[spell 14-1-49-2	2 1	1 - - -	-282	
126	6.27 6.29 6.31	Benaud 17 ←[spell 7-3-11-1		- W Wardle - - - -	7-282 -282	Brown c Hole, slip, 28 in 35 mins, 37 balls, 4 fours
			Evans 11 31 mins 33 balls	Wardle 0 2 mins 4 balls	7-282 414 mins 766 balls	

SESSION 99-3 in 116 mins, 224 balls

England Second Innings

L.Hutton	c Hole b Lindwall	5	20 mins, 16 balls	2-10
D.Kenyon	c Hassett b Lindwall	2	10 mins, 5 balls	1-6
T.W.Graveney	c Langley b Johnston	2	13 mins, 11 balls	3-12
D.C.S.Compton	lbw b Johnston	33	101 mins, 85 balls, 3 fours	4-73
W.Watson	c Hole b Ring	109	346 mins, 351 balls, 16 fours	5-236
T.E.Bailey	c Benaud b Ring	71	257 mins, 224 balls, 11 fours	6-246
F.R.Brown	c Hole b Benaud	28	35 mins, 37 balls, 4 fours	7-282
T.G Evans	not out	11	31 mins, 33 balls, 0 fours	
J.H.Wardle	not out	0	2 mins, 4 balls	
Extras	(b 7, lb 6, w 2, nb 6)	21		
TOTAL	(for 7 wkts)	282	414 mins, 766 balls, 126 overs	

BOWLING

Lindwall	19	3	26	2	
Johnston	29	10	70	2	(10 nb, 1 w)
Ring	29	5	84	2	(1 w)
Miller	17	8	17	0	
Benaud	17	6	51	1	
Davidson	14	5	13	0	
Hole	1	1	0	0	

MATCH DRAWN

There were many notable performances in this Test of such a high quality of cricket. Ultimately the crucial innings of Watson stands out and has its niche in history.

Match attendance: 137,915 (126,909 paying). Receipts £57,716-15s. This is a record for any match anywhere in the world, beating £44,063 at Melbourne in 1946-47 and £43,000 at Leeds in 1948. The attendance record however is not as high as that Leeds match (158,000) nor as for several matches in Australia. 11,000 attended on the last day.

When Brown came in, he suggested that Bailey would face Lindwall if he came on. In the England dressing room they waited in dreadful anticipation for Lindwall and Miller to come on, but they never did. Brown decided to attack the spinners by hitting over the top of the close fielders. If he hit the ball for 4, there were no spectators on the grass today, time would be taken up by fetching the ball back.

In the innings Lindwall bowled only 19 of the 126 overs.

Fingleton: Australia were let down by spinners. Benaud has not had enough match practice, and Ring should not have replaced Hill. Hassett probably made a mistake in not bringing Lindwall on for last half hour. Neither side good enough to win. Possibly Hutton's dropped catches cost England the game.

Alston: A draw was the fairest result.

Cutler: Clearly Hassett kept the spinners on because they could bowl more overs. Australia lost their way in the morning and did not wake up until it was too late.

21 overs were bowled in the last hour, 11 in the last half hour.

1953 – SECOND TEST

Barnes: on this dust-heap England's batsmen did tremendous work and exposed the frailty of the Australian spin.
Bowes: Hassett appeared to be a trifle worried that England might get the runs. He never had an attacking field. The punishment of his spin bowlers worried him. The ball started to play some tricks when Brown and Evans were in. Brown decided to counter-attack. He hit the ball in the air, sometimes mis-hitting.
Lindwall thinks that with a little more adventure England could actually have won.
Swanton: the Australian fielding was not to blame; in the whole England innings only two half-chances were missed, both by Ring. Hassett should have given Lindwall a final fling.
Bradman: No match in history has been more gallantly saved. They ought to put Watson's effigy in the new Lord's War Memorial Gallery.

Brown spent the entire day apart from intervals on the same seat on the balcony with his pads on until he came in. He was the only player to see every ball bowled. Evans had his pads on all day and dozed on the couch in the dressing room. Hutton sat deep in the dressing room refusing to watch. Bedser moved around restlessly in the dressing room, holding newspapers and not reading them. The Duke of Edinburgh watched part of the play from the England balcony. Bailey went home with his wife Greta to Westcliff in Essex by train and found that some friends had brought round champagne. He is back at Lord's tomorrow for his county. Mrs Watson was at Lord's planning to go home to Sunderland whenever he was out. She missed three trains and they walked out of Lord's together, she to a hotel before going home tomorrow, he to catch the 7.45 down to Somerset.

While the Test was on there were two rounds of first-class cricket.

June 24, 25, 26

Yorkshire, without Hutton, Watson and Wardle lost to Northamptonshire for the first time since 1913, and Glamorgan suffered their first defeat of the season inflicted by Hampshire for whom Shackleton took 9 for 77 in the first innings. Needing 225 to win Notts were 88 short with 7 wickets left when a thunderstorm flooded Trent Bridge but Middlesex gained first innings points and stayed at the top of the Table. Surrey were beating Oxford University. Kent lost to Cambridge University by 134 runs. Essex played an entertaining game against a Commonwealth XI at Romford, containing the three Ws (Weekes, Worrell and Walcott), Roy Marshall, Bill Alley, Alf Valentine. Essex dismissed them for 84 in the first innings and a Walcott 115 in 150 minutes could not prevent a handsome Essex win.

June 27, 29, 30

Thursday was a memorable day for the Glamorgan off-spinner Jim McConnon He hit two sixes and 6 fours in 44 to give Glamorgan a lead of 59, then took all five Yorkshire wickets that fell for 49 by the close. On the last day they were all out for 99, McConnon 7-40, and were glad to need only 41 to win on a worn pitch. It was the Welsh county's first ever championship win against Yorkshire, who sank to 14th position.

Strange behaviour from the men of Middlesex: Lancashire declared overnight on 401 for 8, with a first innings lead of 55. With 5 ½ hours available on the last day they batted out time and when they made only 114 for 1 in 2 ½ hours before lunch, half the crowd decided they had better ways of spending the afternoon. Essex beat Kent for their first win of the season. Middlesex were still nominally top of the Table, 86 points from 14 games, Glamorgan 80 from 13. Surrey, who had a fallow week, 72 from 11, were still in best position.

Strange match for Harvey: Bristol, July 1, 2, 3

A deeply disappointed Australian team travelled to Bristol. Graveney showed his trademark style with 6 fours in 90 minutes. After an hour and a half break for rain, the last four wickets fell for 24, Lindwall taking 3 for 1 in 16 balls. Benaud was given a trial as opening partner for Morris and they put on 55 in good time. Then the Australia struggled against the tall off-spinner, on leave from the Army, Mortimore and closed at 71 for 4. On a sunny Thursday with the gates closed on 16,000, de Courcy averted a hat-trick for Mortimore off the first ball of the morning. He went on to make 97. Harvey made 141 in 165 minutes with 22 fours, a strange innings: he batted at number 9, gave three early chances and changed his bat twice. There was further entertainment for the crowd when Gloucestershire batted after tea. Veteran George Emmett and Graveney added 69 in 40 minutes and Emmett was 90 not out in 131 for 2 at the close, still 134 behind. The day saw 462 runs. Emmett carried on to add another 51 on the last morning. Harvey got a rare bowl, with his right-arm spin and got three wickets in his three overs. The Australians hit off 33 to win for the loss of Benaud who this time opened with Tallon. It was their first win since 8th June

GLOUCESTERSHIRE 137 (T.W.Graveney 52, Lindwall 4-18) and 297 (G.M.Emmett 141, D.M.Young 37, Miller 3-44, Harvey 3-9). AUSTRALIANS 402-9dec (Benaud 35, Miller 37, de Courcy 97, Harvey 141, J.B.Mortimore 4-104) and 33-1. *Australians won by nine wickets.*

1953 – SECOND TEST

The Australian manager was forced to issue a statement to the Press. The visit to "Guys and Dolls" had been arranged a month before. They had no time for a meal because the show started at 7.30 and were invited to supper at the Cafe Royal, and all the players "were well in bed before 1am."

Surrey struggled against Sussex at Guildford, though Lock returning after a month's injury, made his highest first-class score of 40. On Thursday Sussex captain David Sheppard scored 105. A good team effort and excellent fielding gave Sussex victory by seven wickets. At Lord's Bill Edrich made 211 on the first day against Essex. A standing ovation greeted Trevor Bailey's 84, during which he was hit on the elbow and went to hospital after he was out. In the fourth innings Bailey was unavailable to bat, and Essex were defeated, a fate which would surely have befallen England if he had been injured in the Test. McConnon bowled Glamorgan to another victory at Nottingham. Wimbledon tennis fortnight ends, a tournament dominated by Americans, winning four of the five finals.

Tyson's speed: Northampton, July 4, 6, 7

Put in by F.R.Brown, the tourists faced a very young and very fast bowler, a science graduate with a very long run-up called Tyson and after four balls McDonald and Hole were very back in the pavilion, both beaten by sheer pace, one lbw and sent off limping, the other bowled before he brought his bat down. Coming in at 10-3 Harvey punched him for three fours and was 96 at lunch. He made 118 out of a stand of 175 with Morris. Morris said later that Tyson's bouncer was the fastest thing he had ever seen. Later the Australian exile spinner Tribe took three wickets in an over. But Archer got enough support to enable 77 to be added for he last two wickets. Northants closed at 40-2 and on the second day, though the wicket was fully covered over the weekend, collapsed to 141-9 at lunch. In the second innings, Barrick and Livingston, another Australian, were making a fight of it, when Livingston drove hard to cover where Craig half stopped it. Harvey swooped on the ball from extra cover and threw the striker's wicket down before Barrick could make the single. The Australians secured an innings victory and a day off.

AUSTRALIANS 323 (Morris 80, Harvey 118, Archer 58, G.E.Tribe 5-97). NORTHAMPTONSHIRE 141 (Archer 7-56) and 120 (L.Livingston 30, Ring 5-46). *Australians won by an innings and 62 runs.*

Yorkshire came to the Oval and Hutton having been out with lumbago, was determined to pay in Alec Bedser's benefit match. Laker bowled well (6-38), and so did Lock though his spinning finger was not fully healed, in an innings of 137. When Surrey batted Trueman looked much better than earlier in the season. Thanks to May, Clarke, Laker and Alec Bedser, who scored 45 after avoiding a hat-trick, Surrey got a lead of 155. Hutton stayed for three hours to score 76 but after an hour on the last day Yorkshire had lost again, by 10 wickets. On the first day 21,000 spectators contributed £492 for Bedser. Middlesex also won at Birmingham.

Though the big match at the Oval affected the crowds, there was still much interest in the annual Oxford-Cambridge fixture at Lord's and they both had decent sides. Oxford had Cowdrey and an aggressive South African, J.P. Fellows-Smith. Cambridge had Subba Row of Surrey, Gerry Alexander, a future West Indies captain, Robin Marlar, Sussex spinner. On Saturday Cowdrey scored 116 in 165 minutes, when 8,000 attended. On the last day Cambridge need 238 to win in 320 minutes. At 186 for 8 with 37 minutes left, Marlar joined the opener Denis Silk and it seemed that Cambridge were aiming to save the game. Then Silk launched a burst of straight driving and they won the match with two wickets and seven balls to spare.

THIRD TEST AT OLD TRAFFORD
Manchester, July 9, 10, 11, 13, 14

On Sunday the England XII for the Third Test was chosen: Hutton, Edrich, Simpson, Graveney, Compton, Watson, Bailey, Evans, Laker, Wardle, Bedser, Trueman. From the XI who played at Lord's Kenyon was dropped for Simpson, Brown for Edrich, Statham (injured) for Trueman. And Tattersall, Lord's 12th man, was replaced by Laker. Lock's split spinning finger is still not healed. He was allowed to bowl (and bowled well) against Yorkshire with that finger strapped, but could not be risked for a Test. The problem of finding a good opening partner for Hutton was met by the selection of Edrich, who had not regularly opened the batting for Middlesex or England since the War. Simpson also had experience as an opener. David Sheppard, who was having a very good season as captain and opening batsman for Sussex, was overlooked again, apparently on the basis of his insecure batting in the Test Trial match

W.J.(Bill) EDRICH (Middlesex) aged 37, was a pugnacious and resolute right-hand batsman, specialist slip and in his prime a lively quick bowler. He nearly failed to fulfil the trust put in his tremendous promise before the War, but from 1946 to 1950 he was an indispensable member of the England side. He was not picked for the 1950-51 tour of Australia, and much missed, and had played no Test since then. Having become an amateur in 1947 he was now captain of Middlesex.

James C. LAKER (Surrey) aged 31, was a tight and classic action off-spin bowler, and useful low order right hand bat. He could run through any side on a pitch giving any help. He made his Test debut in West Indies in 1947-48, but was never a regular Test player. Even in 1953 the selectors preferred Tattersall, Wardle and (if available) Lock, and it was probably only the doubt about Lock's finger to last for a five-day match that gave him his chance.

Frederick S. TRUEMAN (Yorkshire) aged 22, was England's first really fast bowler since the war, and he burst on the scene against India in 1952 but was now conscripted for National Service and could make only occasional first-class appearances. Disappointing performances early in the season, especially in the Test Trial match, raised queries about his stamina and accuracy, but the whole country was dying to see him succeed and an improved outing in the recent match against Surrey prompted the selectors to bring him back.

On Tuesday it was announced that due to fibrositis in his shoulder the England captain Hutton might be unfit to play. His former Test partner Cyril Washbrook of Lancashire was to join the England party as a stand-in. But the problem arose as to who would captain the side of Hutton could not play. Brown might have to be re-selected. Arlott thinks that Washbrook would most likely take over. England's hotel was in the small market town of Lymm on the border between Lancashire and Cheshire. But Hutton does not join them until the morning of the Test.

With the long-range weather forecast being damp, England are optimistic for a good performance.

Umpires: D. Davies and H. Elliott

Evans' blunder: FIRST DAY, Thursday 9 July

Australia have omitted Ring and are forced to leave out Johnston, who has a return of his knee problem, in favour of young Archer.

England leave out Trueman, relying on four bowlers, because of the poor weather. Hutton announced fit to play at 10 am. Washbrook sent away. Edrich will open the batting.

Australia win toss. Benaud omitted. Test debut for de Courcy.

It has rained for most of Wednesday. Wet ground. Green pitch. At 1.30 the captains agree to start at 2.45 unless further rain falls.

Australia First Innings

Odd overs [↑ from Stretford End
Even overs [↓ from Manchester End

		Afternoon	Hassett	Morris		
1	2.50	Bedser 1 [↑	- - 1 - - -	- 1		Bedser bowling with the wind. Hassett batting like a man in a hurry
2		Bailey 1 [↓	1 - - - -	- 2		
3		Bedser 2 [↑	4 - - (4 byes) - 4	-14		Hassett cuts through slips for 4 byes down leg side missed by Evans Hassett glances over leg trap for 4

1953 – THIRD TEST

#	Time	Bowler				Score	Notes
4		Bailey 2 [↓			- 1 - - -	-15	Morris single to short leg, Laker slips on wet turf
5	3.04 3.06	Bedser 3 [↑		W Miller	1-15 - - 1 - 1	-17	Morris bld, back defensive shot, ball rolls back onto wicket, 1 in 14 mins, 11 balls
6		Bailey 3 [↓		- - - 1	 1	-19	Laker turns ankle in field. Trueman on as substitute
7		Bedser 4 [↑		- - 1 - -		-20	
8		Bailey 4 [↓ off spell 4-0-6-0		- - 2 - -		-22	
9		Bedser 5 [↑		- - - - 2		-24	Hassett appears to have sore right forearm
10		Wardle 1 [↓		- - - - -		-24	
11		Bedser 6 [↑ off spell 6-0-15-1		- - - 1 - -		-25	
12		Wardle 2 [↓		- - - 1 -	 1	-27	
13		Bailey 5 [↑		- 3 4 - - (nb) 4 -		-38	Hassett uppish 4 through leg trap *Bailey having trouble with footholds* Hassett square cuts 4 off no-ball
14		Wardle 3 [↓		- - 4 1 2 -		-45	Miller pulls to leg for 4 Sawdust put down

1953 – THIRD TEST

Over	Time	Bowler	Batsman 1	Batsman 2	Score	Notes
15	3.41 3.43	Bailey 6 [↑	- W Harvey - -	3	2-48 -48	Hassett bld off stump, playing late and across in-swinger, 26 in 51 mins, 48 balls, 4 fours
16	3.45 3.47	Bedser 7 [↓		W Hole - - -	3-48 -48	Miller plays on via pad and boot, 17 in 39 mins, 30 balls, 1 four
17	3.53	Bailey 7 [↑	- - 4 - -		 -52	Harvey flashes and misses Harvey 4 though point. Aust 52 up in 63 mins Harvey dropped by Evans, standing 15 yards back, two-handed catch in front of 1st slip
18		Bedser 8 [↓		2 4 - 1 -	 -59	Laker returns to field with strapped leg Hole square cuts for 4
19		Bailey 8 [↑	- 1 - -	- (1 lb)	 -61	
20		Bedser 9 [↓	- - - - 1		 -62	
21		Bailey 9 [↑	- - - 3	(1 nb)	 -66	
22		Bedser 10 [↓	- 1	- - 4 1	 -72	Hole on drive for 4
23		Bailey 10 [↑		1 - 3 2 -	 -78	
24	4.17	Bedser 11 [↓	- - 1 - 1	1	 -81	*Weather gusty and unpleasant*
		TEA	Harvey 15 34 mins 36 balls	Hole 16 30 mins 21 balls	3-81 87 mins 146 balls	

Cardus: second class cricket. The Australians seem to be psychologically afflicted if the pitch is not as dry as the Sahara. Evans' dropped catch off Harvey at 52 for 2 may go down in history.

1953 – THIRD TEST

The ball came higher and faster than Evans anticipated and as he jerked his gloves upwards the ball kicked out of base of his thumbs and deflected away off his chin. Many of the crowd got the impression that Evans was trying to throw the ball up in the air before he properly held it, but that is untrue.

			Harvey 15	Hole 16	3-81	
25	4.38	Bailey 11 [↑]	- - - 3	2	-86	
26		Bedser 12 [↓]	- - - - -		-86	
27		Bailey 12 [↑]		- - - - -	-86	
28		Bedser 13 [↓]	- - - 1	-	-87	
29		Bailey 13 [↑]		- - - - -	-87	*Harvey often flashes outside off-stump against Bailey*
30		Bedser 14 [↓] off spell (incl. tea) 8-2-24-1	1	- 1 - - 4	-93	Hole straight drive for 4
31		Bailey 14 [↑]	1	- - - - 1	-95	Laker goes off again with sore leg
32		Wardle 4 [↓]		- - - - -	-95	
33	5.05	Bailey 15 [↑]	- - -		-95	Rain. Aust 3-95 in 114 mins

STOPPAGE

1953 – THIRD TEST

#	Time	Bowler			Score	Notes
33	5.20	Bailey 15 ctd	-	-	-95	More sawdust put down
34		Wardle 5 [↓		- - - - -	-95	
35		Bailey 16 [↑	4 - - -	-	-99	Harvey 4 uppish past gully
36		Wardle 6 [↓		- - - - -	-99	
37	5.31	Bailey 17 [↑ off spell (incl. Tea & rain break) 13-3-44-1	4 1 - - -		-104	Harvey leg glance for 4. Aust 103 in 125 mins
38		Wardle 7 [↓	4 - 1	- -	-109	Harvey leg glance for 4
39		Bedser 15 [↑		- - 1 - - -	-110	
40		Wardle 8 [↓	- 1	- 4 - -	-115	
41		Bedser 16 [↑		- - - - -	-115	
42		Wardle 9 [↓		3 - - 4 - 1	-123	Harvey quick-footed straight drive for 4
43		Bedser 17 [↑	2 - 1	- -	-126	
44		Wardle 10 [↓		- - 3 - -	-129	

1953 – THIRD TEST

Over	Time	Bowler	Batsman 1	Batsman 2	Total	Notes
45		Bedser 18 [↑ off spell 4-1-5-0	- 1 - - -		-130	
46	6.00	Wardle 11 [↓	- - 1 - -		-131	Harvey edges to 3rd man for 1, his 50 in 101 mins, 104 balls
47		Bailey 18 [↑	- - 1 - -		-132	
48	6.03	Wardle 12 [↓	- - - - 1		-133	rain
RAIN STOPPAGE						
48	6.18	Wardle 12 ctd		-	-133	
49		Bailey 19 [↑	- - - - 2		-135	
50		Wardle 13 [↓		- - 4 - -	-139	
51		Bailey 20 [↑	1 - 2 2 - 1		-145	
52	6.30	Wardle 14 [↓		1 - - - 4 1	-151	Harvey drive for 4 well placed to left of mid on
			Harvey 60 118 mins 124 balls	Hole 41 114 mins 101 balls	3-151 171 mins 314 balls	Rain set in soon after close

SESSION 0- 70 in 84 mins, 168 balls

West: a poor day for England, missing the only catch offered. Australia have runs on the board and the wicket is likely to get worse.

Alston: an un-Test-like day with no big match atmosphere.

Times correspondent: Though it had its drawbacks and air of gloom the day was full of decision and incident.

Arlott: England are down to three bowlers and Edrich may have to bowl his defensive cutters.

Attendance about 15,000

1953 – THIRD TEST

Rain silences the Press: SECOND DAY, Friday 10 July

Play was about to start at 11.30 but rain drove players off. Another miserable day.

			Harvey 60	Hole 41	3-151	
53	11.55	Bailey 21 [↑	- - - - -		-151	*Turf slippery and slow*
54		Bedser 19 [↓	1	- - 1 - -	-153	
55		Bailey 22 [↑	- 4 - - 2		-159	Harvey off-drive for 4, all run, chased by Simpson
56		Bedser 20 [↓		- - - - -	-159	
57		Bailey 23 [↑ off spell 3-1-7-0		- 1 - - -	-160	
58		Bedser 21 [↓ off spell 3-1-3-0		- 1 - - -	-161	
59		Laker 1 [↑		- - 1 - -	-162	*Laker bowls over the wicket to Harvey*
60		Wardle 15 [↓	4 - - - -		-166	Harvey scorching drive past mid-off for 4
61		Laker 2 [↑		- 3 - 4 1 -	-174	Hole drives for 3, his first runs for 20 mins
62		Wardle 16 [↓	- - 1 - - -		-175	
63		Laker 3 [↑		- - 1 2 -	-178	*Drizzling rain*

1953 – THIRD TEST

Over	Time	Bowler		Runs	Score	Notes
64		Wardle 17 [↓		- - - -		
	12.33			-	-178	Rain

STOPPAGE

Over	Time	Bowler		Runs	Score	Notes
65	12.50	Laker 4 [↑		1 1 - - -	-180	Laker beats Hole with lifting ball
66		Wardle 18 [↓		- 1 - - 1	-182	
67		Laker 5 [↑		- - - - 1	-183	Hole almost bld, ball going over stumps Hole 50 in 160 mins, 143 balls
	12.58					
68		Wardle 19 [↓ off spell 5-1-11-0		- - 3 - 1 -	-187	
69		Laker 6 [↑		- - - - 2	-189	
70		Bedser 22 [↓		- - - - 1	-190	
71		Laker 7 [↑		- - - - -	-190	
72		Bedser 23 [↓		- - - - -	-190	
73		Laker 8 [↑ off spell 8-1-19-0		- - 1 - - 1	-192	
74		Bedser 24 [↓		- - - 3 1	-196	New ball taken Light rain starts to fall

1953 – THIRD TEST

75		Bailey 24 [↑		4 - 1		
			1		-202	
76		Bedser 25 [↓ spell 4-1-9-0	- 2 2 - -		-206	
77	1.30	Bailey 25 [↑ spell 2-0-14-0	2 4 1	- - 1	-214	Harvey 4 punched past cover. 101 in 194 mins, 205 balls
		Lunch	Harvey 102 196 mins 206 balls	Hole 66 204 mins 169 balls	3-214 249 mins 464 balls	

SESSION 0-63 in 78 mins, 150 balls
West: Harvey moved up a gear from yesterday, using his feet to attack the spinners.
More rain. Crowd show impatience when the rain stops and no sign of the umpires

		Afternoon	Harvey 102	Hole 66	3-214	
78	3.45	Bedser 26 [↓	1 - - -	- 1	-216	Cheers as Bedser runs up. Light very poor
79		Bailey 26 [↑ spell 1-0-3-0	1 -	- 1 - 1	-219	
80	3.57	Bedser 27 [↓ spell 2-0-4-0	- - 1 -	1	-221	Rain stopped play
			Harvey 105 208 mins 215 balls	Hole 66 204 mins 178 balls	3-221 261 mins 482 balls	

SESSION 0-7 in 12 mins, balls
Wicket soon under water and puddles cover most of the field. Rain floods a cable and cuts off all the telephones in the Press Box. Still out of order on Saturday morning
Arlott: slow sodden wicket, wet ball, slippery outfield, uniformly leaden sky, no day for cricket. Australia in virtually fool-proof position
Times correspondent: It looks already that only Australia can win this Test if weather permits.
Bradman: England can only lose or draw.
Hutton appointed England captain for last two Tests.
Ben Hogan of the USA has won the Open Golf at Carnoustie.
A hopeful sign today is that Lavrenty Beria, Stalin's bloody henchman, has been sacked as Soviet minister of internal affairs and expelled from the Communist Party.

Hair gets in your eyes: THIRD DAY, Saturday 11 July

No overnight rain. Sunshine arrives. Laker gets four more injections at Altringham Hospital.
Captains disagree, Hassett wanting to start, so umpires (in ordinary suits) inspect at 11.45. Crowd slow handclap. Hassett orders the heavy roller.

1953 – THIRD TEST

			Harvey 105	Hole 66	3-221	Crowd 25,000. Heavy roller used
81	12.00	Laker 9 [↑	- - - - -		-221	7 close fielders for Laker
82	12.05 12.07	Bedser 28 [↓		W De Courcy - - - 4	4-221 -225	Hole c Evans, chases a wide ball, Evans jumps high, 66 in 209 mins, 179 balls, 6 fours. De Courcy hit on hand by fast ball. De Courcy swings edgily over leg trap
83		Laker 10 [↑	- 1 - 2		-228	De Courcy nice on-drive for 2
84		Bedser 29 [↓	- - 1 -		-229	
85		Laker 11 [↑	- 1 - 4 -		-234	De Courcy square cuts a full toss for 4
86		Bedser 30 [↓	- 2 - 1 -		-237	Edrich at 1st slip fields ball for first time in match
87		Laker 12 [↑	1 - - - -		-238	
88		Bedser 31 [↓	4 1 - - 2	3	-248	Harvey 4, 1 and 2 with square drives
89	12.28	Laker 13 [↑	2 - - 1	4 1	-256	252 in 289 mins. Twice Harvey hits Laker uppishly through slips, once through empty 2nd slip area
90	12.32 12.33	Bedser 32 [↓	W Davidson - - - -		5-256 -256	Harvey c Evans, glancing down leg-side, 122 in 240 mins, 246 balls, 11 fours
91		Laker 14 [↑	- - - -	1	-257	Davidson dropped by Evans off thick edge, easy catch waist high, fielders already appealing

1953 – THIRD TEST

92		Bedser 33 [↓	- - 3 - - 1	-261	
93		Laker 15 [↑ off spell 7-1-22-0	- 4 - - -	-265	Davidson sweeps for 4
94		Bedser 34 [↓	- 2 - - 2 -	-269	
95		Wardle 20 [↑	4 - - 1 - -	-274	
96		Bedser 35 [↓	- - - - -	-274	
97		Wardle 21 [↑	- - - - -	-274	
98		Bedser 36 [↓	- - - - -	-274	
99		Wardle 22 [↑	- - - - -	-274	
100		Bedser 37 [↓	- - (2 bye) - - -	-276	
101		Wardle 23 [↑ off spell 4-2-9-0	- - 4 - - -	-280	
102		Bedser 38 [↓	4 - - - 1	-285	Davidson sweeps for 4 to fine leg, just short of diving Graveney

1953 – THIRD TEST

103	1.18 1.20	Laker 16 [↑	- - W Archer - 1		6-285 -286	Davidson st Evans, going down wicket for huge swipe, 15 in 45 mins, 51 balls, 3 fours
104		Bedser 39 [↓	- - - - -		-286	
105		Laker 17 [↑ spell 2-1-1-1		- - - - -	-286	
106	1.30	Bedser 40 [↓	- - 4 - -		-290	Archer 4 past point off slower ball
		Lunch	Archer 5 10 mins 14 balls	deCrcy 30 83 mins 59 balls	6-290 351 mins 638 balls	

SESSION 3-61 in 90 mins, 156 balls

Another easy catch dropped by Evans, off Davidson. Bradman thinks that Evans has an occasional habit of moving to take an off-side catch, then jerking his hands back as if to make a stumping. Such movement takes him across the line of flight.

		Afternoon	Archer 5	deCrcy 30	6-290	
107	2.10	Wardle 24 [↑		- - - - -	-290	
108	2.14 2.16	Bedser 41 [↓	- W Lindwall - 1 -		7-290 -291	Archer c Compton, 2nd slip, shaping to cut a riser, 5 in 14 mins, 16 balls, 1 four Lindwall 1 to cover
109	2.19 2.21	Wardle 25 [↑		- W Hill - - -	8-291 -291	Lindwall c Edrich, 2nd slip, low chance, 1 in 3 mins, 4 balls
110		Bedser 42 [↓	- - - 1 - -		-292	*Nearly every ball causes a divot in the pitch* De Courcy hit on hand, single past diving Compton at 2nd slip
111		Wardle 26 [↑		- - - 1 -	-293	

1953 – THIRD TEST

112		Bedser 43 [↓		- 2 - 4 - -	-299	de Courcy on-drive for 4
113		Wardle 27 [↑		- - - - -	-299	
114		Bedser 44 [↓		- - - 3 - -	-302	De Courcy cuts for 3
115	2.38 2.40	Wardle 28 [↑		- W Langley 2 1 -	9-302 -305	De Courcy lbw, on back foot swinging to leg, 41 in 111 mins, 87 balls, 4 fours
116		Bedser 45 [↓ spell (incl. Lunch) 18-5- 55-3		- 1 - - 4 4	 -314	Hill flicks to leg for 4 Hill cover drive for 4
117	2.47	Wardle 29 [↑ spell 5.3-3-8-3		- 4 W	10 -318	Langley swings to leg, almost 6 Langley c Edrich, high at slip, 8 in 7 mins, 7 balls, 1 four
			Hill 8 26 mins 22 balls 2 fours		10-318 388 mins 701 balls	

SESSION 4-24 in 37 mins, 63 balls

AUSTRALIA FIRST INNINGS

A.L. Hassett	b Bailey	26	51 mins, 48 balls, 4 fours	2-48
A.R. Morris	b Bedser	1	14 mins, 11 balls	1-15
K.R. Miller	b Bedser	17	39 mins, 30 balls, 1 four	3-48
R.N. Harvey	c Evans b Bedser	122	240 mins, 246 balls, 11 fours	5-256
G.B. Hole	c Evans b Bedser	66	209 mins, 179 balls, 6 fours	4-221
J.H. de Courcy	Lbw b Wardle	41	111 mins, 87 balls, 4 fours	9-302
A.K. Davidson	st Evans b Laker	15	45 mins, 51 balls, 3 fours	6-285
R.G. Archer	c Compton b Bedser	5	14 mins, 16 balls, 1 four	7-290
R.R. Lindwall	c Edrich b Wardle	1	3 mins, 4 balls	8- 291
G.RA. Langley	c Edrich b Wardle	8	7 mins, 7 balls, 1 four	10-318
J.C. Hill	not out	8	26 mins, 22 balls, 2 fours	
Extras	(b 4, lb 1, nb 1)	8		
TOTAL	(all out – 10 wkts)	318	388 mins, 701 balls, 116.3 overs	

BOWLING

Bedser	45	10	115	5	
Bailey	26	4	83	1	(2 nb)
Wardle	28.3	10	70	3	
Laker	17	3	42	1	

1953 – THIRD TEST

England – First Innings

Odd overs   [↑   from Stretford End
Even overs   [↓   from Manchester End

Hutton ordered heavy roller. Edrich plays his first innings against the 1953 Australians

#	Time	Bowler	Hutton	Edrich	Total	Notes
1	3.00	Lindwall 1 [↑	3	2 - - - -	- 5	Hutton 3 off full-toss to square leg Edrich 2 off full toss driven straight
2		Archer 1 [↓	1	- - - - -	- 6	
3		Lindwall 2 [↑	4 1	- - -	- 11	Hutton leg glances for 4
4		Archer 2 [↓	- - 1 - -	4 -	- 16	Edrich 4 snicked along ground through slips
5		Lindwall 3 [↑ off spell 3-1-10-0	- - - - -		- 16	
6		Archer 3 [↓		- - - - (1 lb) * 2 -	- 19	* leg bye not recorded, occurred somewhere in 5th or 6th over
7	3.23 3.25	Hill 1 [↑		- - W Graveney 4 - -	1-19 -23	Edrich c Hole, prod at leg-break edged to 1st slip, 6 in 23 mins, 24 balls, 1 four Graveney 4 off full-toss to long leg
8		Archer 4 [↓	- - - 1 - -		-24	
9		Hill 2 [↑	- - - - -		-24	
10		Archer 5 [↓ off spell 5-1-9-0		- - - - - -	-24	

1953 – THIRD TEST

#	Time	Bowler		Balls	Score	Comments
11		Hill 3 [↑		- - 2 - -	-26	
12		Miller 1 [↓		1 - 1 - -	-28	*Miller keeps his sweater on, bowls off-spin round the wicket, mixed with medium pace*
13		Hill 4 [↑		- - - - 4	-32	Hutton 4 imperious drive past cover
14	3.43 3.45	Miller 2 [↓		- - W Compton - -	2-32 -32	Graveney c de Courcy, arm ball, tying to hit over the top, easy catch to mid-off, 5 in 18 mins, 18 balls, 1 four Compton 'dropped' off bump ball at short leg by Hassett who takes off cap in pretended annoyance. Crowd laughs.
15		Hill 5 [↑		- - - 1 -	-33	
16		Miller 3 [↓		- - - - -	-33	
17		Hill 6 [↑		- - - 2 2 -	-37	Compton holdS up play when his hair blows in his eyes- a heckler suggests use of Brylcreem
18		Miller 4 [↓		- - - - -	-37	Hutton stops when piece of paper blows across. De Courcy takes three goes to catch it.
19		Hill 7 [↑		- - - - - -	-37	Appeal for catch behind down leg-side off Compton. Turned down by Umpire Elliott. Compton asks fielder to tuck in his pad strap.
20		Miller 5 [↓		- - - (1 lb) -	-38	
21		Hill 8 [↑		- - - - -	-40	

1953 – THIRD TEST

22		Miller 6 [↓ off spell 6-5-2-1		- - - - -	-40	
23		Hill 9 [↑ off spell 9-2-25-1	- - 4 - 4		-48	*Pitch seems to be easing*
24		Davidson 1 [↓ spell 1-0-1-0		- - 1 - -	-49	
25	4.15	Miller 7 [↑ spell 1-0-1-0		- - - 1 -	-50	Compton 1 pushed to long leg
		TEA	Hutton 31 75 mins 79 balls	Compton 6 30 mins 29 balls	2-50 75 mins 150 balls	

Compton's unruly and unbrylcreemed hair was blowing in his eyes, so during the tea interval Alec Bedser gives him an impromptu haircut

		Evening	Hutton 31	Compton 6	2-50	
26	4.35	Hill 10 [↓		- 2 1 - -	- 53	
27		Lindwall 4 [↑		- - - 2 - - (1 lb)	- 56	
28		Hill 11 [↓	4	- 1 - - -	- 61	
29		Lindwall 5 [↑	- 1	1 - -	- 63	
30		Hill 12 [↓	1 1	- - 1	- 66	
31		Lindwall 6 [↑	- - - - -		- 66	

1953 – THIRD TEST

32		Hill 13 [↓		- - - - -	- 66	
33		Lindwall 7 [↑		- - - - 4	- 70	
34		Hill 14 [↓ off spell 4-1-16-0		4 1 - - -	- 75	
35		Lindwall 8 [↑ off spell 5-1-9-0	- - - -	1	- 76	
36		Miller 8 [↓	1	- 1 - -	- 78	
37		Davidson 2 [↑	- - - 1 -		- 79	*Davidson bowling quick style*
38		Miller 9 [↓	- - - (1 lb) - -		- 80	
39		Davidson 3 [↑	- - - - -		- 80	
40	5.20	Miller 10 [↓		- - - - 4 -	- 84	50 stand in 77 mins
41		Davidson 4 [↑	- - - - 1		- 85	
42		Miller 11 [↓	- - - - -		- 85	

1953 – THIRD TEST

43		Davidson 5 [↑		2 6 - - -	- 93	Compton hooks bouncer just over de Courcy's head at long leg for 6
44		Miller 12 [↓		- - - - -	- 93	
45		Davidson 6 [↑		- - 1 2 -	- 96	
46		Miller 13 [↓		1 - - - 1	- 98	
47	5.33 5.40	Davidson 7 [↑ off spell 6-1-20-0		1 4 1 - - 1	- 105	103 up in 138 mins Hutton 50 in 140 mins
48		Miller 14 [↓		- - - 4 - -	- 109	
49		Harvey 1 [↑		- - - - -	- 109	*Harvey medium pace off-breaks*
50		Miller 15 [↓		- - - - -	- 109	
51		Harvey 2 [↑		- - - - -	- 109	
52		Miller 16 [↓ off spell 9-4-16-0		- - 4 - -	- 113	
53		Harvey 3 [↑ off spell 3-2-3-0		2 - - - -	- 115	

1953 – THIRD TEST

54		Archer 6 [↓	- - - - -		- 115	*Archer bowling off-breaks round the wicket*
55		Hill 15 [↑	4	- - 1 - -	- 120	
56		Archer 7 [↓		- 1 - - -	- 121	
57		Hill 16 [↑		- - - 1 -	- 122	
58		Archer 8 [↓		- - - - -	- 122	
59		Hill 17 [↑	- - 4 - -		- 126	
60	6.12 6.14	Archer 9 [↓		- W Wardle - - -	3-126 - 126	Compton c Langley (wk) pushing at arm ball, 45 in 127 mins, 115 balls, 3 fours
61		Hill 18 [↑ 4-1-10-0	- - - - -		- 126	
62		Archer 10 [↓		- - - - -	- 126	
63	6.22 6.24	Lindwall 9 [↑ spell 1-1-0-1	- - W Watson - -		4-126 - 126	Hutton lbw, ball nipped in off seam, 66 in 182 mins, 208 balls, 10 fours

1953 – THIRD TEST

64		Archer 11 [↓] spell 6-5-1-1		- - - -		
	6.30			-	- 126	
		CLOSE	Watson 0 6 mins 3 balls	Wardle 0 16 mins 16 balls	4-126 190 mins 384 balls	

Session 76-2 in 115 mins, 234 balls
England need 43 to avoid follow on.
Attendance for the first three days: 61,181 paying £25,000.
Cardus: Hutton and Compton played safely and well, but could have scored more runs. Mediocrity reigns supreme.
Arlott: Compton has done much to re-establish himself.
Bradman: England have fought back well. Compton's was one of his best innings.
Times correspondent: The only certainty is that Australia cannot lose. In retrospect, Hassett might have declared at lunch or even earlier.

Sunday
Persistent rain all day. Hutton spent the day quietly at home in Pudsey. Some England players played gold at Mere Country Club in Cheshire. The Press and Broadcasters match at Didsbury is washed out.

No hope: FOURTH DAY, Monday 13 July
No play. Only Hassett and Lindwall went to the ground. Play was called off at 10.45. Sun comes out at five o'clock. According to statistics the highest level of rainfall in the Manchester area falls in the last three weeks of July. Arlott met a man and his young son who had come down from Falkirk for the only day of Test cricket they could watch this year.
5,308 people have paid in advance; their tickets will give admission tomorrow..
Swanton: unless there is hot sun the wicket should stay too placid to give any hope of a result.
Arlott: Australia cannot lose. If the rain produces a freaky wicket, England may be in difficulties if they have to follow on.

Excitement comes too late: FIFTH DAY, Tuesday 14 July
Pitch almost dry enough for a start on time, and Umpires decide to start at 12.00, but more rain falls. England need 43 more runs to avoid the follow on, at which point the match will be dead. Hassett is in no hurry to lead his men out.

			Watson 0	Wardle 0	4-126	
65	2.10	Lindwall 10 [↑]	4 - - - -		- 130	Full toss, Watson cover drive for 4
66		Miller 17 [↓]		- - - - -	- 130	*Nearly every ball takes a piece out of the pitch.*
67		Lindwall 11 [↑]	- - - - (1 lb) -		- 131	
68		Miller 18 [↓]	- - - - -		-131	
69		Lindwall 12 [↑]		- - - - -	- 131	

1953 – THIRD TEST

Over	Time	Bowler	Batsman 1	Batsman 2	Score	Notes
70		Miller 19 [↓	- - - 1	-	- 132	
71		Lindwall 13 [↑	- - - -	-	- 132	
72		Miller 20 [↓		- - 4 - -	- 136	Wardle 4 high through covers
73		Lindwall 14 [↑	1	- - -	- 137	
74		Miller 21 [↓		- - 4 - 2 -	- 143	Watson hooks for 4 to long leg
75		Lindwall 15 [↑		- - - - -	- 143	
76		Miller 22 [↓ off spell 6-2-12-0	- - - - 1	-	- 144	
77		Lindwall 16 [↑	- - 3 - -		- 147	
78		Davidson 8 [↓	(1 lb) * - - 1 - -			* leg-bye not recorded occurring somewhere between 77.4 and 78.2
	2.55		W Simpson		5- 149	Watson bld, yorked, 16 in 51 mins, 51 balls, 2 fours
79	2.56	Lindwall 17 [↑	- - - - -			
	3.00		W Bailey		6- 149	Wardle bld, full length inswinger, 5 in 66 mins, 58 balls, 1 four
80	3.02	Davidson 9 [↓	- - - - -		- 149	

1953 – THIRD TEST

#	Time	Bowler			Score	Notes
81		Lindwall 18 [↑		- - - - -		
	3.05			1	- 150	150 up in 245 mins
82		Davidson 10 [↓		- - - - 1	- 151	
83		Lindwall 19 [↑		- - - - 1	- 152	
84		Davidson 11 [↓		- - 1 - -	- 153	
85		Lindwall 20 [↑ off spell 11-4-7-1	- -	- - - 1	- 154	
86		Davidson 12 [↓ off spell 5-1-9-1	1	- - 1 4 -	- 160	Bailey 4 cover drive
87		Hill 19 [↑	1	- - 4 - -	- 165	Bailey square cut for 4
88		Miller 23 [↓	- - 1	- -	- 166	
89		Hill 20 [↑	- - - - -		- 166	*Simpson dropped at Davidson at gully*
90	3.35	Miller 24 [↓ off spell 2-0-7-0		4 - - 2 -	- 172	Bailey fine off-drive for 4 to save the follow on
91		Hill 21 [↑	- - - 4 -		- 176	

1953 – THIRD TEST

92		Archer 12 [↓]		- - - - -	- 176	
93		Hill 22 [↑]		- 1 - - -	- 177	
94		Archer 13 [↓]		- - - - -	- 177	
95		Hill 23 [↑]		- 1 4 - -	- 182	*Simpson dropped again off Hill, by Archer at short leg*
96		Archer 14 [↓]		- (4 bye) 1 - - -	- 187	
97		Hill 24 [↑]		- - - - -	- 187	
98		Archer 15 [↓]	1	- - - -	- 188	
99		Hill 25 [↑]	(1 lb) -	- - - -	- 189	
100		Hole 1 [↓]	4 - 4 1	- -	- 198	
101		Hill 26 [↑]		- - - 1 -	- 199	
102	4.06	Hole 2 [↓] off spell 2-0-16-0	1 - 4 1	1 -	- 206	200 up in 306 mins

1953 – THIRD TEST

103		Hill 27 [↑	1 - - 1 -		- 208	
104		Davidson 13 [↓		- - - - -	- 208	
105	4.16	Hill 28 [↑	- 1 - - -		- 209	
		TEA	Simpson 31 80 mins 63 balls	Bailey 24 74 mins 93 balls	6- 209 316 mins 630 balls	

SESSION 83-2 in 126 mins, 246 balls
Swanton: Hill was an awkward proposition and England are lucky that Johnston is not playing.
Hutton has been appointed captain for the last two Tests.

			Simpson 31	Bailey 24	6- 209	
106	4.35 4.39 4 41	Davidson 14 [↓	- - W Evans 2 - 3		7- 209 -	Simpson c Langley (wk) 31 in 84 mins, 66 balls, 5 fours
107		Hill 29 [↑	- - 1	- -		
108		Davidson 15 [↓	- - 1 - -		-	
109		Hill 30 [↑	- - - 1	-		
110		Davidson 16 [↓	- - - - -		-	4 byes unrecorded, occurring somewhere between 106.4 and 113.1
111		Hill 31 [↑	- 1 - 6		-	
112		Davidson 17 [↓	- - 1 -	1 1	-	

1953 – THIRD TEST

113	4.57 4.59	Hill 32 [↑		W Laker - (1 lb) 2 -	8- 231 - 234	Bailey c Hole, at slip via wk's glove, 27 in 96 mins, 106 balls, 3 fours
114		Davidson 18 [↓		- - 1 - 4 -	- 239	
115	5.05 5.06	Hill 33 [↑		4 W Bedser - - - 4	9- 243 - 247	Laker cuts for 4 Laker lbw 5 in 6 mins, 7 balls, 1 four
116	5.10	Davidson 19 [↓		- - 3 - -	- 250	250 up in 351 mins
117		Hill 34 [↑	4	- - - 3	- 257	
118		Davidson 20 [↓ off spell 8-2-30-1	- 2 - 4 1	6	- 270	Bedser huge 6 over long-on
119		Hill 35 [↑ spell 17-3-46-2	- - 1	- -	- 271	
120	5.20	Morris 1 [↓ spell 1-0-5-1	- - 4 - 1	W	10- 276	Bedser bld by chinaman, 10 in 14 mins, 10 balls, 1 six, 1 four
			Evans 44 39 mins 57 balls		10- 276 361 mins 720 balls	Morris, 'Bedser's rabbit', has his revenge and leads off the Australia team, smiling broadly

SESSION 67-3 in 45 mins, 90 balls

ENGLAND FIRST INNINGS

L. Hutton	lbw b Lindwall	66	182 mins, 208 balls, 10 fours	4-126
W.J. Edrich	c Hole b Hill	6	23 mins, 24 balls, 1 four	1-19
T.W. Graveney	c de Courcy b Miller	5	18 mins, 18 balls, 1 four	2-32
D.C.S. Compton	c Langley b Archer	45	127 mins, 115 balls, 3 fours	3-126
J.H. Wardle	b Davidson	5	66 mins, 58 balls, 1 four	6-149
W. Watson	b Davidson	16	51 mins, 51 balls, 2 fours	5-149
R.T. Simpson	c Langley b Davidson	31	84 mins, 66 balls, 5 fours	7-209
T.E. Bailey	c Hole b Hill	27	96 mins, 106 balls, 3 fours	8-231
T.G. Evans	not out	44	39 mins, 57 balls, 1 six, 3 fours	
J.C. Laker	lbw b Hill	5	6 mins, 7 balls, 1 four	9-243
A.V. Bedser	b Morris	10	14 mins, 10 balls, 1 six, 1 four	10-276
Extras	(b 8, lb 8)	16		
TOTAL	(all out – 10 wkts)	276	361 mins, 720 balls, 120 overs	

1953 – THIRD TEST

BOWLING

Lindwall	20	8	30	2
Archer	15	8	12	1
Hill	35	7	97	3
Miller	24	11	38	1
Davidson	20	4	60	2
Harvey	3	2	2	0
Hole	2	0	16	0
Morris	1	0	5	1

Australia lead by 42 runs

Swanton: Bailey's 27 was as valuable in skill, courage and resource as his 71 at Lord's. Bailey himself says it was his best innings of the series.

Bradman: the match has been magnificently saved by England.

Australia – Second Innings

Harvey has fluid on the knee and is not expected to bat.

Odd overs	[↑	from Stretford End
Even overs	[↓	from Manchester End

			Hassett	Morris		
1	5.30	Bedser 1 [↑	- 4 4 - - -		- 8	*Eight close fielders* Two fours to leg by Hassett
2	 5.37 5.39	Laker 1 [↓	- - - -	- - - W Miller 1	 1- 8 - 9	Morris c Hutton, 2nd slip, defensive prod, off gloves, 0 in 7 mins, 4 balls
3	 5.40 5.42	Bedser 2 [↑	- W Hole - 1	3 -	 2- 12 - 13	Hassett c Bailey, diving forward at gully, off leg-cutter, 8 in 10 mins, 9 balls, 2 fours
4		Laker 2 [↓	(2 lb) - - - -		 - 15	
5		Bedser 3 [↑		- 2 - - -	 - 17	
6	 5.50 5.52	Laker 3 [↓	- 1	W de Courcy - - -	 3- 18 - 18	Miller st Evans, made no effort to get back, 6 in 11 mins, 10 balls
7	 5.55 5.57	Bedser 4 [↑ off spell 4-1-14-2	- - W Davidson -		 4-18 - 18	Hole c Evans (wk) off leg-cutter 2 in 13 mins, 14 balls. Bedser's 100th wicket of the season

1953 – THIRD TEST

8		Laker 4 [↓		- - - - -	- 18	
9	6.00	Wardle 1 [↑		- - - 2 -	- 20	Davidson 2 placed to leg
10		Laker 5 [↓	(1 lb) -	- - 6 - 1	- 28	
11		Wardle 2 [↑		- - - - -	- 28	
12		Laker 6 [↓		- 1 - - 1	- 30	
13	6.13	Wardle 3 [↑		- - - 1 W Harvey	5- 31	de Courcy st Evans, going down for huge swing, 8 in 13 mins, 17 balls, 1 six
14	6.15	Laker 7 [↓		- - - - -	- 31	
15	6.18 6.20 6.21	Wardle 4 [↑		- - - W Archer - W Lindwall	6- 31 7- 31	Harvey bld behind legs, 0 in 3 mins, 4 balls Archer lbw 0 in 1 min, 2 balls
16	6.23	Laker 8 [↓		- - - - -	- 31	
17	 6.26 6.28	Wardle 5 [↑ spell 5-2-7-4		- 4 - W Hill - -	 8- 35 - 35	Lindwall pushed to leg for 4 Lindwall bld, agricultural swing, off-stump sags, 4 in 3 mins, 4 balls

1953 – THIRD TEST

18	6.30	Laker 9 [↓ spell 9-5-11-2	- - - - -		- 35	*Davidson alone showed how to bat*
		CLOSE	Davidson 4 33 mins 42 balls	Hill 0 2 mins 2 balls	8- 35 60 mins 108 balls	Match attendance: 59,735. Receipts £27,904

AUSTRALIA – SECOND INNINGS

A.L. Hassett	c Bailey b Bedser	8	10 mins, 9 balls, 2 fours	2-12
A.R. Morris	c Hutton b Laker	0	7 mins, 4 balls	1-8
K.R. Miller	st Evans b Laker	6	11 mins, 10 ball	3-18
G.B. Hole	c Evans b Bedser	2	13 mins, 14 balls	4-18
J.H. de Courcy	st Evans b Wardle	8	13 mins, 17 balls, 1 six	5-31
A.K. Davidson	not out	4	33 mins, 42 balls	
R.N. Harvey	b Wardle	0	3 mins, 4 balls	6-31
R.G. Archer	lbw b Wardle	0	1 min, 2 balls	7-31
R.R. Lindwall	b Wardle	4	3 mins, 4 balls	8-35
J.C. Hill	not out	0	2 mins, 2 balls	
Extras	(lb 3)	3		
TOTAL	(for 8 wkts)	35	60 mins, 108 balls, 18 overs	

BOWLING

Bedser	4	1	14	2
Laker	9	5	11	2
Wardle	5	2	7	4

Hassett could have declared at 6.20 and ended the match then. Spectators booed Australian incoming batsmen for not hurrying to the wicket. Some of them had changed out of their cricket gear when the England innings ended.

England and Australia have not achieved a finish at Manchester since 1905. This was a dismal game for the patient Mancunians until the last gasp. Bruce Harris, the veteran cricket correspondent of the London *Evening Standard*, left towards the end of the England innings to catch the 5.50 train home, and missed the last hour. In fact there was a whole compartment-ful of journalists bound for London. Harris heard from a passenger who had been listening to the radio before joining the train that Australia were 31 for 8. He put his head through the compartment to tell the others and they all laughed.

Man of the match: in this miserable, and at the end almost farcical Test, the only outstanding performance was by Neil Harvey.

West: If Harvey had been caught when 4 on the first day, Australia could have been all out by tea, Australia might have needed to save an innings defeat on the last day. Hutton did well to inflict psychological blows on Australia but the collapse should not be taken too seriously. Miller, de Courcy and Lindwall virtually gave away their wickets.

Bradman: it is scarcely feasible that the collapse would have happened if the game had been alive. But instead of taking the chance to practice on a wet wicket, the Australians have given England a boost by their light-hearted display

Alston: The play was not wholly meaningless, it demonstrated that England had a much superior bowling attack on a wet drying wicket. It might have been a different day if Johnston had been in the Australian team. It was a disappointing Test, lacking tension, but England's reputation came out the better and Hutton was right to pack the batting.

Fingleton: this Test is best forgotten, but the Australian collapse cannot be ignored coming after their sudden crash at Nottingham. They showed again their tendency to try to hit out when in trouble against spin.

Whitington: the Australians light-hearted approach in the last hour is no guide to things to come. Once the collapse started they could not stop it.

Cutler: The batsmen had been told to relax and entertain; the collapse is no true reflection.

Swanton and Arlott: Lindwall, de Courcy and Miller made carefree shots, the pressure was off, but Australia showed a lack of conviction and fallibility against the turning ball and an inability to stop the rot. This will have a psychological effect if Australia are caught on a turning wicket at Leeds.

Barnes: England's challenge is becoming increasingly menacing and if Australia do not force a win at Leeds there is every chance of losing the Ashes at the Oval.

Cardus: The Australian batsmen did not surrender light-heartedly to cheer us up, and none showed the skill to cope with bowlers who can get flight and break on an encouraging wicket.

Brown: Miller, de Courcy and Lindwall obviously threw their wickets away, but Australia would hardly have been able to top 100 in the conditions if they had all played sensibly.

Lindwall: We played hit-and-miss cricket, rather than risk injury, and in the knowledge that a draw was inevitable.

Harvey: in some ways the collapse was due to lack of concentration, but the real reason was the magnificent bowling of Wardle, Laker and Bedser, unplayable on a soggy wicket.

The events of the last hour almost decided the fate of the Ashes, in a way that nobody could foresee at the time. The closing comments on the end of the Fourth Test explain why.

1953 – THIRD TEST

July 8, 9, 10

The weather that visited Manchester also made its mark in the county matches, especially in the north. It prevented first innings points in the matches between Derbyshire and Kent at Chesterfield, and between Worcestershire and Lancashire at Worcester. It ruined the third day at Nottingham. Yet there was a full three days play at Leicester where Somerset lost by seven wickets. A blank Thursday at Sheffield and more rain on the last day stopped Yorkshire from beating Gloucestershire. Early on Friday play was interrupted by spikes of ice 4 to 5 inches long falling from the heavens. They were thought to have fallen from high-flying aircraft. One fell on the open window of the Press Box. Sussex started their Worthing week with a two-day innings victory over Hampshire; Ian Thomson took nine wickets and was awarded his county cap. Surrey were bowled out for 99 chasing 240 against an undistinguished Warwickshire attack. Middlesex remain at top of the Table. Sussex jump over Glamorgan and Surrey into second place.

July 11, 13, 14

The rain moved south, without leaving the hapless Manchester: 11 hours lost at Colchester. No play after 2.30 on the second day at Gloucester versus Glamorgan. No play when Somerset set Hampshire 174 at Portsmouth. Yorkshire had the better of a draw against Middlesex at Bradford where Monday was a wash-out. But there was no excuse for wretched Surrey playing Kent at Blackheath. Peter Loader, filling in for Alec Bedser, took 13 for 113, 9 for 28 in Kent's first innings of 63. (He took 12 for 117 in the previous match.) Peter May, captaining in the absence of Surridge, made 116. Kent were 239 behind on first innings and by mid afternoon on Monday had fallen to 49 for 5. Enter E.G.Witherden in only his third match of the season. With help from the tail to shepherd Kent to 186 for 7 at the close, though May claimed the extra half hour to try to force a two-day finish. On Tuesday his 8th wicket stand with Murray-Wood was extended to 143. Surrey needed only 85 to win but rain prevented even a start to the task. Sussex were on top throughout against Worcestershire at Worthing, after the captain Sheppard made 129 in 225 minutes, his 5th century of the season, and won by five wickets. Middlesex still lead the Table with 110 points from 17 matches, but Sussex had 104 from only 14. Glamorgan still third, 92 from 15, Surrey 88 from 15. Yorkshire drop to 13th place.

Sheppard misses out: Gentlemen v Players at Lord's: July 15, 16, 17

Outside the Tests, this was the major representative match of every season, although throughout the century the pool from which the members of each team were drawn was unequal. The Gentlemen had won only twice since 1919. As usual they were short of pace bowling but had a good crop of fine young amateur batsmen: May, Insole, Sheppard, Cowdrey (who was selected but could not play) and sturdy all-rounders like Bailey, F.R.Brown and Wilf Wooller. The Players could pick a virtual Test XI from those eligible, but Hutton, Lock, Wardle, Statham and Laker had to drop out. The first day saw the completion of both first innings. At lunch the Gents were 89 for 3, but there was a heavy downpour during lunch followed by sunshine and by 3pm they were all out. Marlar's off-breaks from the Pavilion end worried the Players batsmen and they fell to 47 for 6, but Evans saved a rout by a bright 46. In the closing minutes Moss struck Brown over the Nursery stand into the practice ground for six.

On Thursday, Reg Simpson dominated a second wicket stand with Edrich. The Notts opener used his feet delightfully against the spinners and had no trouble against pace. At lunch he was 77 out of 123 for 1. He reached 100 out of 159 and was finally caught at deep mid-off for 117 in 165 minutes with a six and 15 fours. His rival for the Test place, David Sheppard who was in great form for Sussex, failed for the second time, edging a nasty ball from Bedser into the slips early on. May started promisingly but edged a sharp leg-break from the Australian Bruce Dooland. Edrich, who had stuck on 43 for half an hour, took charge and reached 98 not out in nearly four hours. At that point, ten minutes after tea, a deluge ended play for the day with the Gents 275 for 4, a lead of 281.

Friday was a day for the off-spinner. First Tattersall coming on at the Nursery End bowled Insole and had Edrich caught in the leg trap. As the Gentlemen were chasing quick runs he bowled Brown, Wooller and Brennan in one over to save them the bother of a declaration. The Players faced the hopeless target of 318 in five hours. The shower interruptions before lunch seemed to ease the wicket. In 55 minutes Washbrook and Emmett put on 62. The Sussex off-spinner Marlar came on from the Pavilion End after lunch. Washbrook was enticed forward, Graveney mishooked to short leg, Compton pushed to the leg trap, Wooller also mishooked and Emmett after a 2½ hour century drove in the air to deep mid on. Spots of rain were falling when the last man Moss was bowled by Palmer at 4.40 and heavy rain soon followed. But the Gentlemen had achieved their first win since 1938. Marlar bowled unchanged and took 7 for 79. He was as close as he would ever come to being considered for Test honours.

1953 – THIRD TEST

Gentleman (won toss)

R.T.Simpson (Notts) c Bedser b Tattersall	26	c Watson b Tattersall	117
D.S.Sheppard (Sussex) c Dooland b Tattersall	5	c Dooland b Bedser	6
W.J.Edrich (Middx) c Bedser b Tattersall	8	c Dooland b Tattersall	98
P.B.H.May (Surrey) c Compton b Bedser	32	c Evans b Dooland	11
C.H.Palmer (Leics) st Evans b Tattersall	18	lbw b Bedser	20
D.J.Insole (Essex) c Watson b Bedser	6	b Tattersall	4
T.E.Bailey (Essex) c Evans b Bedser	10	c Dooland b Bedser	16
*F.R.Brown (N'hants) not out	11	b Tattersall	17
W.Wooller (Glam) c Graveney b Bedser	0	b Tattersall	0
+D.V.Brennan (Yorks) b Bedser	0	b Tattersall	0
R.G.Marlar (Sussex) b Tattersall	0	not out	0
Extras (b 12, lb 1)	13	(b 10, lb 12)	22
Total (59.5 overs, 175 mins)	**129**	**(97.3 overs, 310 mins)**	**311**

WICKETS.- 1-17, 2-25, 3-52, 4-50, 5-104, 6-118, 7-118, 8-118, 9-120, 10-129

BOWLING.- Bedser 21-9-34-5; Moss 6-0-21-0; Tattersall 19.5-4-47-5; Dooland 13-6-14-0

1-22, 2-179, 3-207, 4-264, 5-275, 6-276, 7-307, 8-307, 9-307, 10-311

Bedser 30.3-9-74-3; Moss 14-3-34-0; Tattersall 21-2-83-6; Dooland 24-5-80-1; Compton 8-1-18-0.

Players

G.M.Emmett (Glos) c Bailey b Wooller	4	c Bailey b Marlar	82
*C.Washbrook (Lancs) c Brennan b Wooller	5	b Marlar	41
T.W.Graveney (Glos) c Wooller b Bailey	2	c Wooller b Marlar	2
D.C.S.Compton (Middx) b Marlar	13	c Sheppard b Marlar	0
W.Watson (Yorks) b Palmer	29	c Sheppard b Wooller	9
D.Barrick (N'hants) c Sheppard b Marlar	7	c Brennan b Palmer	17
B.Dooland (Notts) lbw b Wooller	0	c Insole b Marlar	31
+T.G.Evans (Kent) b Brown	46	c and b Marlar	7
R.Tattersall (Lancs) b Bailey	1	not out	15
A.V.Bedser (Surrey) b Bailey	3	b Marlar	9
A.E.Moss (Middx) not out	9	b Palmer	3
Extras (lb 4)	4	(b 5, lb 1)	6
Total (56.4 overs, 175 mins)	**123**	**(68 overs, 185 mins)**	**222**

WICKETS.- 1-6, 2-9, 3-11, 4-30, 5-46, 6-47, 7-84, 8-111, 9-113, 10-123

BOWLING.- Bailey 10.4-3-14-3; Wooller 17-3-30-3; Marlar 20-9-37-2; Brown 5-0-21-1; Palmer 4-0-17-1.

1-89, 2-112, 3-113, 4-136, 5-140, 6-180, 7-187, 8-196, 9-196, 10-219

Bailey 8-1-17-0; Wooller 15-1-47-1; Marlar 26-3-79-7; Brown 13-1-55-0; Palmer 6-0-18-2.

Gentlemen won by 95 runs
Umpires: W.F.Price and J.S.Buller

Surrey won at home to Worcestershire by an innings and 190 runs. Loader took 8-21 to bowl them out for 82 in the first innings. A storm prevented Middlesex from setting an interesting target at Derby. Rain also deprived Glamorgan of a chance against Notts, and Lancashire against North ants. Cowan took 11 wickets in Yorkshire's innings victory at Gloucester, their second win of the season. Sussex had no match.

The Hague, July 16

Yesterday the tourists flew to Holland, from London airport to Amsterdam. Each man was insured for £5,000. The Australians played a match for the first time in Holland, at the Hague. On the matting pitch surrounded by elm and willow trees, there were many unintended bouncers, even from the spinners. Fortunately Lindwall was not playing and Miller did not bowl. They hit freely, the Dutchmen fielded keenly, took all their catches, and 4,000 people watched

AUSTRALIANS 279 (Morris 70, McDonald 66, E.Vriens 4-84, Van der Luur 3-66) DUTCH XI 122 (P.van Arkel 3, Davidson 2-16, Ring 2-22). *Australians won by 157 runs*

On Friday the England Test XII for next Thursday was selected. From the XII at Manchester, Wardle and Trueman (who was 12th man there) made way for Lock and Statham, nether of whom were fully fit to play for the Players.

Royal visit: Middlesex at Lord's, July 18, 20, 21

The Australians came back to England to play Middlesex at Lord's, a fixture traditionally held at this time of year between two of the northern Tests. On Saturday there were 20,000 under a clear blue sky when Middlesex scored 71 for one in 85 minutes, Robertson out for a delightful 27 before hooking a bumper hard to the only fielder in front of square on the on-side, then torrential rain. On Monday, there was sun in the sky, though not in the cricket, to greet the visit of the Queen and Prince Philip. Normally the monarch makes an annual visit to Lord's during the Test, but this year her schedule was a bit crowded in June. Another 20,000 saw the presentation of the teams in front of the pavilion during the tea interval. When she asked Ian Craig if it was his first tour to England, he replied "Yes ma'am and if I don't do any better it will

1953 – THIRD TEST

be my last". Apart from that they saw 233 runs in six hours, on a pitch which took spin slowly. Edrich had lost his timing and took three hours for 49. The innings of 182 took 82 overs. The Australian batsmen were only moderately entertaining. After a bright start they sank to 99 for 3, when Hole joined Miller. On nought for half an hour Hole pulled the persistent Young for six.

On the hot last day, starting at 154-3, Miller showed some urgency. With the new ball Moss sent back Millar and Hole in successive overs, bringing de Courcy to make a classic 74 in an hour with six fours and five sixes. In 2½ hours before lunch 180 runs were added. The Australians now had a first innings lead of 184 and could well have declared for the chance of bowling Middlesex out in the remaining 170 minutes. Ostensibly to give Archer, Ring, Lindwall and Langley some batting practice, more probably to save any exertions for his bowlers and fielders, Hassett allowed the innings to run its natural course. When they were all out at 3 o'clock, and the Middlesex innings meandered pointlessly, and the match ended with Hassett Craig and de Courcy bowling an over each. 10,000 people thought that their 4 shillings would have been better spent elsewhere.

MIDDLESEX 150 (H.P.Sharp 36, W.J.Edrich 49, Lindwall 4-40, Hole 2-3) and 112-4 (H.P.Sharp 51, W.J.Edrich 32). AUSTRALIANS 416 (McDonald 43, Miller 71, Hole 41, de Courcy 74, Benaud 52, Archer 58*, Langley 46, A.E. Moss 4-103). *Match drawn*

Yorkshire lost by ten wickets at Derby. A blank third day at Swansea deprived Glamorgan of beating Gloucestershire. In a low scoring match at Bournemouth, Sheppard opened with 88, including 3 sixes and a four in one over off Shackleton, (who later in the match became the second bowler after Bedser to reach 100 wickets for the season) and Sussex won by 93 runs to go to the top of the Championship table for the first time since 1932, just beating the rain. Surrey beat Leicestershire by nine wickets to move into second place. Lock tested his fitness by playing for Surrey 2nd XI at Beddington and took 5 Wiltshire wickets for 25.

The Imperial Cricket Conference met at Lord's on Tuesday. The Australians match versus Nottinghamshire was given first-class status. England's Test series home and away until 1964-65 were arranged (and all the series took place exactly as stated).

1953 – FOURTH TEST

FOURTH TEST AT HEADINGLEY
Leeds, July 23, 24, 25, 27, 28

Headingley is a favoured ground for Australia. In nine Tests since 1899 there have been four Australian wins and none for England.

Umpires: F Chester and F.S.Lee

England reach new depths of dullness: FIRST DAY, Thursday 23 July

Alan Davidson arrives at breakfast this morning at the hotel in Harrogate with the news that he has become a father of either a boy or a girl. "Bet and baby both well", the cable said.

England leave out Statham, again playing only four bowlers. Australian 12th man Hill, unluckily yielding place to Benaud.

Australia win toss. Hutton threw the coin onto the ground. If that was a subterfuge to make Hassett think that he was desperately keen to bat, it failed. There was surprise when Hassett put England in. Arlott thought it unwise, a gamble on the hope that the wicket will be responsive to spin at the start and that the weather will settle and the wicket be firm and dry after that. Kilburn: Hassett unsure how the pitch will behave, preferred to find out by bowling rather than batting. Rain had seeped through the covers overnight. In the heavy atmosphere Hassett feared what Bedser might do.

35,000 crowd. A spatter of rain delayed the start

England - First Innings

Odd overs \ → from Football Stand End
Even overs \ ← from Kirkstall Lane End

			Hutton	Edrich		
1	11.50 11.51 11.53	Lindwall 1 \ →	- W Graveney 1 - - -		1- 0 - 1	Hutton plays confidently to mid-on Hutton bld, off stump, yorked by late inswinger, 0 in 1 min, 2 balls Graveney pushes to cover for single Field: 3 slips, gully, 2 short legs, long leg, cover
2		Miller 1 \ ←	- - - - -		- 1	Field: 3 slips, gully, 4 short legs, cover
3		Lindwall 2 \ →		- - - 2 -	- 3	Edrich near to lbw Edrich 2 past short leg
4		Miller 2 \ ←	- - 1 -	-	- 4	Graveney 1 to cover
5		Lindwall 3 \ →		- - - - 1	- 5	
6		Miller 3 \ ←	- - 1	- -	- 6	
7		Lindwall 4 \ →	- - - - -		- 6	

1953 – FOURTH TEST

8		Miller 4 \ ← off spell 4-2-2-0		- - - - -	- 6	
9	12.20	Lindwall 5 \ →		- - - - 1	- 7	
10		Davidson 1 \ ←		- - - - -	- 7	
11		Lindwall 6 \ →		- 4 - - -	- 11	Slow bouncer, Edrich sq cut for 4 Edrich hooks straight to de Courcy
12		Davidson 2 \ ←		- 2 - 1 -	- 14	
13		Lindwall 7 \ → off spell 7-2-9-1		- - - - -	- 14	
14		Davidson 3 \ ←		- - - 1 -	- 15	
15		Miller 5 \ →		- - - 1 1	- 17	
16		Davidson 4 \ ←		- - 1 - -	- 18	
17		Miller 6 \ →		- - - - -	- 18	
18		Davidson 5 \ ←		- - - 1 -	- 19	

1953 – FOURTH TEST

19		Miller 7 \ →		- (4 bye) - - -	- 23	4 byes, just missing leg stump
20		Davidson 6 \ ← off spell 6-1-11-0	- 4 - - 1	-	- 28	Graveney off-drive for 4 past Morris
21		Miller 8 \ →	- - - - -		- 28	Miller appeals loudly for lbw; as he walks back he grins and doffs Umpire Chester's hat
22		Lindwall 8 \ ←	- 2 - 1	- (1 lb) 1	- 33	
23	1.09 1.10	Miller 9 \ →		- - - W Compton -	2- 33 - 33	Edrich lbw, turning to off-side, half forward, 10 in 79 mins, 56 balls, 1 four
24		Lindwall 9 \ ←	- - - 1		- 34	
25		Miller 10 \ →	- - - 1	- -	- 35	Compton beaten by fast outswinger
26	1.20 1.22	Lindwall 10 \ ←	- 1	- W Watson - -	3- 35 - 35	Compton c Davidson, slower ball, steered to leg slip, 0 in 10 mins, 5 balls
27		Miller 11 \ →	- - - -		- 36	
28	1.30	Lindwall 11 \ ←		2 - - - -	- 38	
		LUNCH	Gravny 21 97 mins 97 balls	Watson 2 8 mins 8 balls	3-38 100 mins 168 balls	

Cardus: a timid start to the Test, glowering sky, subdued crowd, lack of any rhythm to the game, interruptions while boys walk behind the bowler's arm. There is apparently no room for sightscreens at Headingley.

1953 – FOURTH TEST

Arlott: Hutton's dismissal was met with stunned silence and a long delay before the formality of applause for the Australians. In the session Lindwall and Millar bowled as a pair better than at any time on the tour. No blame attaches to the wicket for England's poor position.

Hutton's wife and son Richard had just settled into their seats when he was out. Richard burst into tears.

			Gravny	Watson	3-38	
29	2.10	Miller 12 \ →	- - - - -		- 38	*Crowd near 40,000*
30		Lindwall 12 \ ←		- - - - -	- 38	
31		Miller 13 \ →	2 - 4 - -		- 44	Graveney 2 to extra cover Graveney 4 glanced
32		Lindwall 13 \ ←	- 1	- - 1 - -	- 46	*Interruption for movement in crowd, then a dog comes on chased by a policeman*
33	2.26	Miller 14 \ →	4 - - - -		- 50	Graveney 4 to long off off full-toss, 50 up in 116 mins
34		Lindwall 14 \ ←		- - - 1 -	- 51	
35		Miller 15 \ →		- - - - -	- 51	
36		Lindwall 15 \ ← off spell (incl. lunch) 8-1-14-1	- 3 - - -		- 54	Graveney 3 to long off, just stopped by Harvey
37		Miller 16 \ → off spell (incl. lunch) 12-7-16-1	- - - 2 - 1		- 57	
38		Archer 1 \ ←	- - 3 - -	- 1	- 61	Watson gives technical chance to Langley

1953 – FOURTH TEST

Over		Bowler		Runs		Total	Notes
39		Davidson 7 \ →		- - - - -		- 61	*Watson very defensive*
40		Archer 2 \ ←		- - - 1 -		- 62	Graveney mistimes a hook which lobs into empty space on leg side
41		Davidson 8 \ →		- - - 1 -		- 63	
42		Archer 3 \ ←		- - - - -		- 63	
43		Davidson 9 \ →		- - 2 - -		- 65	Watson turns to leg for 2
44		Archer 4 \ ←		- - - - -		- 65	
45		Davidson 10 \ →		- - 1 - -	1	- 67	
46		Archer 5 \ ←		- - - - -		- 67	
47		Davidson 11 \ →		- 1 - - -	(1 lb) -	- 69	
48		Archer 6 \ ←	1	- - 1 -		- 71	
49		Davidson 12 \ →		- - - - -		- 71	

145

1953 – FOURTH TEST

50		Archer 7 \ ← off spell 7-3-8-0	- 1 - - - (4 bye) -		- 76	4 byes off bouncer
51		Davidson 13 \ → off spell 7-2-9-0	- - - 1 - 2		- 79	
52		Benaud 1 \ ←	1 - - - - (1lb)		- 81	
53		Lindwall 16 \ →	- - 1 1 2 -		- 85	
54	3.37	Benaud 2 \ ←	- - - 1 - -		- 86	Graveney 50 in 184 mins, 178 balls
55		Lindwall 17 \ → off spell 2-0-6-0	2 - - - - -		- 88	
56		Benaud 3 \ ←	1 - - - -		- 89	
57		Archer 8 \ →	- 1 - - -		- 90	Graveney skies a hook just out of reach of three leg-side fielders
58		Benaud 4 \ ←	- - - - -		- 90	
59		Archer 9 \ → off spell 2-0-2-0	- - - 1 -		- 91	

1953 – FOURTH TEST

				Gravny 54	Watson 17	3-92	
60		Benaud 5 \ ←	- - 1 - -			- 92	Rain stops play. Tea taken
	3.59	TEA		Gravny 54 206 mins 200 balls	Watson 17 117 mins 97 balls	3-92 209 mins 360 balls	

SESSION 54-0 in 109 mins, 192 balls

Cardus: Short balls which were clamouring to be pulled or hooked or square cut went unpunished by Graveney and Watson. They made numerous errors of timing and footwork.

				Gravny 54	Watson 17	3-92	
61	4.25	Davidson 14 \ →		- - - - -		- 92	
62		Benaud 6 \ ←			- - 4 - -	- 96	
63		Davidson 15 \ →		- 1 - - -		- 97	
64		Lindwall 18 \ ←		- - - - -		- 97	New ball
65		Miller 17 \ →			- 1 - - -	- 98	
66		Lindwall 19 \ ←			- - - - -	- 98	
67	4.42 4.44	Miller 18 \ →		W <u>Simpson</u> - - - -		4- 98 - 98	Graveney c Benaud, 3rd slip, slash over slips, Benaud knocks it up and falls backwards to catch it, 55 in 223 mins, 219 balls, 3 fours
68		Lindwall 20 \ ←			- - - - -	- 98	
69		Miller 19 \ →			- - - 2 -	- 100	100 up in 236 mins 6th ball: Simpson loses sight of ball, makes no attempt to hit it, hit on left elbow
	4.52						

1953 – FOURTH TEST

70		Lindwall 21 \ ←		- - - - 1		
	4.56			rh - Bailey	- 101	Simpson retires hurt, 2 in 12 mins, 12 balls
71	4.58	Miller 20 \ →		- - - - -	- 101	
72		Lindwall 22 \ ←		- - - - 1	- 102	
73		Miller 21 \ →		- - 2 - -	- 104	
74	5.11	Lindwall 23 \ ←	3	- - 1 W Evans	5- 108	Watson bld via instep, 24 in 153 mins, 137 balls, 1 four
75	5.13	Miller 22 \ →		- - - - -	- 108	
76	5.19 5.21	Lindwall 24 \ ←	1 (ro) (w) Laker	1 - - - -	6-110 - 110	Evans gives technical chance to Archer at short leg. Evans hits to mid wkt. Bailey runs down and is sent back, Bailey run out (Hassett-Lindwall) 7 in 21 mins, 20 balls. Bailey hurt in diving back, and limps off the field.
77		Miller 23 \ →	2 1	4 - -	- 117	Evans 4 edged over slip
78		Lindwall 25 \ ←	2 - - - -		- 119	*Simpson stays at the ground in case he has to bat, just when he is about to go to hospital for an X-ray*
79		Miller 24 \ →	3	1 - 1 -	- 124	
80		Lindwall 26 \ ←		- - - - 1	- 125	

1953 – FOURTH TEST

81		Miller 25 \ →		- - 2 - -	- 127	
82		Lindwall 27 \ ←	- - - - -		- 127	
83		Miller 26 \ →	1 - - - -		- 128	
84		Lindwall 28 \ ← off spell 11-5-11-1	- - - - -		- 128	
85		Miller 27 \ → off spell 11-3-21-1	- - 1 - -		- 129	
86		Archer 10 \ ←	- - 1	2 -	- 132	
87		Davidson 16 \ →	- - - - -		- 132	
88	6.03 6.04	Archer 11 \ ←	W Lock - 1 - -	1	7-133 - 134	Laker c Lindwall, short ball hit to bkwd sq leg, 10 in 42 mins, 36 balls, 0 fours
89		Davidson 17 \ →	- - - - 1		- 135	
90		Archer 12 \ ←	- - - 1	1	- 137	
91		Davidson 18 \ →	- - - - -		- 137	

1953 – FOURTH TEST

92		Archer 13 \ ← off spell 4-1-7-1	- - - - -		- 137	
93		Davidson 19 \ → off spell 4-2-2-0	- - - -	1	- 138	
94		Benaud 7 \ ←	1 - -	1 1 -	- 141	
95		Miller 28 \ → spell 1-1-0-0	- - - - -		- 141	
96	6.30	Benaud 8 \ ← spell 2-0-4-0	- - - - 1		- 142	
		CLOSE	Lock 5 26 mins 32 balls	Evans 18 77 mins 57 balls	7- 142 334 mins 576 balls	

SESSION 50-4 in 125 mins, 216 balls

An unaccountably dismal and dour struggle by England's batsmen. They seemed to be mesmerised by Hutton's early departure. Fingleton says that, apart from the very occasional ball which lifted slowly, and the persistent swing through the air, there was nothing to give them any difficulty.

Alston: Though the batting was woeful, Lindwall and Miller gave a fine display of fast seam bowling.

Swanton: England were almost unbelievably bad.

Cardus: "Such cricket defies explanation and disperses the most charitable of excuses."

Times correspondent: The wicket was never truly difficult; it was just self-destructively poor batting.

Brown: "the worst display I have ever seen ... lamentably defensive." Graveney seised up after a couple of off-drives after lunch.

Bailey says he was run out because Evans instinctive movement forward misled him. He slipped when trying to get back and dived over the crease but had not grounded his bat when Hassett took off the bails. Evans says that Bailey called 'yes' and Evans said 'no'.

Bailey drove Simpson to the hospital and while Simpson was waiting to be X-rayed, Bailey noticed swelling on his own left knee and had treatment as well.

Arlott: England need some rain during the night.

Alan Davidson now ascertained the gender of his off-spring, and he was called Neil, after Neil Harvey.

SOS for Chelsea footballer: SECOND DAY, Friday 24 July

Simpson will bat, Bailey will bowl and Watson will field, but none are fully fit

				Lock 5	Evans 18	7- 142	
97	11.30	Lindwall 29 \ →		- - - - -		- 142	Lbw appeal against Lock first ball
98		Archer 14 \ ←			- 4 - - 2	- 148	Evans drives to midwkt for 4 Evans 2 square to off

1953 – FOURTH TEST

Over	Time	Bowler		Runs	Wicket	Score	Notes
99		Lindwall 30 \ →		- - - - -		- 148	
100		Archer 15 \ ←		- - - - 1		- 149	
101	11.46 11.48	Lindwall 31 \ →		- - - W Simpson - 1		8- 149 - 150	Evans lbw, pulling a short ball, kept low, 25 in 93 mins, 73 balls, 2 fours. Simpson returns, having had electric massage on his hand
102		Archer 16 \ ←		- - 1 - -		- 151	
103		Lindwall 32 \ →		- - 2 - 3		- 156	2nd: Simpson 2 to leg. 6th ball: Simpson attempts to get strike for shot past Hassett at mid-on, is nearly run out by Miller taking return at bowler's wicket. Chester says not out. Miller throws ball on ground. Crowd boo him.
104		Archer 17 \ ←		- - - 1 -		- 157	Miller is booed on going to his position at third man, he puts out hands in *Kamarad* fashion and starts conversation with spectators. *Slight drizzle*
105		Lindwall 33 \ →		- - 4 - -		- 161	Simpson 4 square cut
106		Archer 18 \ ← off spell 5-0-10-0	- 1 - - -			- 162	
107		Lindwall 34 \ →	1	- - (1 lb) - 1		- 165	
108		Davidson 20 \ ←		- - - - -		- 165	
109	12.17 12.19	Lindwall 35 \ → spell 7-2-14-2	1	1 - - W Bedser -		9- 167 - 167	Simpson c Langley (wk) diving in front of 1st slip, pushing at wide half-volley, 15 in 41 mins, 43 balls, 1 four

1953 – FOURTH TEST

110		Davidson 21	-			Lock bld, playing across full toss, 9 in 77 mins, 66 balls, 0 fours
		\ ←	-			
		spell	-		10- 167	
	12.21	1.4-1-0-1	W			
		ALL OUT		Bedser 0	10- 167	
				2 mins	385 mins	
				1 ball	658 balls	

SESSION 25-3 in 51 mins, 82 balls

England First Innings

L. Hutton	b Lindwall	0	1 min, 2 balls	1-0
W.J. Edrich	lbw b Edrich	10	79 mins, 56 balls, 1 four	2-33
T.W. Graveney	c Benaud b Miller	55	223 mins, 219 balls, 3 fours	4-98
D.C.S. Compton	c Davidson b Lindwall	0	10 mins, 5 balls	3-36
R.T.Simpson	c Langley b Lindwall	15	41 mins, 43 balls, 1 four	9-167
W. Watson	b Lindwall	24	153 mins, 137 balls, 1 four	5-108
T.E. Bailey	run out (Hassett-Lindwall)	7	21 mins, 20 balls	6-110
T.G. Evans	lbw b Lindwall	25	93 mins, 73 balls, 2 fours	8-149
J.C. Laker	c Lindwall b Archer	10	42 mins, 36 balls, 0 fours	7-133
G.A.R.Lock	b Davidson	9	77 mins, 66 balls, 0 fours	10-167
A.V.Bedser	not out	0	2 mins, 1 ball	
Extras	(b 8, lb 4)	12		
TOTAL	{for 10 wkts)	167	385 mins, 658 balls, 109.4 overs	

At 101-4 R.T. Simpson retired hurt, 2 and returned at 149-8

BOWLING

Lindwall	35	10	54	5
Miller	28	13	39	2
Davidson	20.4	7	23	1
Archer	18	4	27	1
Benaud	8	1	12	0

West and Whitington: Simpson appeared to be a yard short. Fingleton: he appeared hopelessly out. Umpire Chester later claimed that he was unsighted, though the batsmen were taking a third run. Miller says that the ball came one bounce straight into his hands; he broke the wicket with his back to Simpson but when he turned round Simpson was still several feet short; he appealed formally and quietly, and when the umpire shook his head he asked four more times.

England have dire problems about taking the field. Simpson will not field. Bailey has a swollen knee and will field and try to bowl. Watson, being treated for a swollen foot, hopes to field at least at the start. Dolding, the ex-Chelsea footballer on the Lord's staff, will be here tomorrow. Statham will be released tomorrow to go to play for Lancashire at Chesterfield. Lancashire will supply Peter Marner and Malcolm Hilton. 12th man today is Yorkshire colt Billy Bolt.

Australia First Innings

Odd overs \ → from Football Stand End
Even overs \ ← from Kirkstall Lane End

				Hassett	Morris		
1	12.35	Bedser 1		-			Simpson not fielding – Statham substitutes
		\ →		-			
				-			Sun breaks through briefly
				1			
					-	- 1	
2		Bailey 1		-			After trying his full run-up then stopping, Bailey bowls at half pace on half run-up, has noticeable limp
		\ ←		-			
				2			
				-			
				1			
					1	- 5	
3		Bedser 2		1			
		\ →		4			Hassett edges through 2nd slip area for 4
				-			
				1			
					- (4 bye)		4 byes, just missing Morris's off stump
					-	- 15	

1953 – FOURTH TEST

#	Time	Bowler			Total	Comments
4		Bailey 2 \ ←	- - - - -		- 15	
5		Bedser 3 \ →		2 - 2 - -	- 19	Morris 'Harrow glide' for 4, just missing leg stump Morris edges 2 through slips
6		Bailey 3 \ ← off spell 3-0-5-0	- - 1 - -		- 20	Hassett edges past Compton at leg slip, who gets a hand to it
7		Bedser 4 \ →	- 1 - - -		- 21	
8	1.00	Lock 1 \ ←	- 1 - - -	- - 4 -	- 26	Morris 4 to mid wicket 26-0 in 25 minutes
9		Bedser 5 \ →	1 - - - -		- 27	
10		Lock 2 \ ←	- - - - -		- 27	*Lock has 3 slips for Hassett*
11	1.10 1.12	Bedser 6 \ →		- - - W **Harvey** -	1- 27 - 27	Morris c Lock, turned low to leg slip, 10 in 35 mins, 30 balls, 1 four. Bedser's 30th wicket of the series
12		Lock 3 \ ←	- - - - 1		- 28	Ball turns and Hassett edges of shoulder of bat just short of Compton at gully. Hutton brings up two more slips
13		Bedser 7 \ →	- - - - 4		- 32	Hassett glances full length inswinger over leg trap for 4
14		Lock 4 \ ←		4 3 4 - -	- 43	Harvey edges 4 past Edrich at slip Harvey 3 to leg Hassett glances 4 to long leg

1953 – FOURTH TEST

Over	Time	Bowler	Hassett	Harvey	Total	Notes
15		Bedser 8 \ →		- 2 2 - -	- 47	*Bedser 3 slips and 3 leg slips*
16	1.30	Lock 5 \ ←		- - - 4 -	- 51	Harvey 4 square cut
		LUNCH	Hassett 26 55 mins 56 balls	Harvey 11 18 mins 10 balls	1- 51 55 mins 96 balls	

Alston: Hutton failed to post slips as well as leg-trap with the new ball.

Over	Time	Bowler	Hassett 26	Harvey 11	1- 51	Notes
17	2.10	Bedser 9 \ →	- 1 4 - -		- 56	Hassett 4 to square leg
18		Lock 6 \ ←		- - - 2 -	- 58	*Harvey dropped by Evans on 12*
19		Bedser 10 \ →	- - - - 3		- 61	
20		Lock 7 \ ←	- - - - -		- 61	
21		Bedser 11 \ →	- - - -	1	- 62	
22		Lock 8 \ ←	- - - - -		- 62	
23		Bedser 12 \ →	4 - - - -		- 66	Hassett edges 4 over Hutton's head at slip, missed catch
24		Lock 9 \ ←		- 4 - - -	- 70	

1953 – FOURTH TEST

25	2.35 2.37	Bedser 13 \ →	W Miller - 2 - 2 -		2- 70 - 74	Hassett c Lock, at bkwd short leg off inswinger, 37 in 80 mins, 83 balls, 5 fours
26		Lock 10 \ ←		- - 4 - - 1	- 79	
27		Bedser 14 \ → off spell (incl. lunch) 14-1-41-2		- - - 2 - 1	- 82	
28		Lock 11 \ ←		- 1 - - - -	- 83	
29	 2.53	Bailey 4 \ →		- - - - - -	- 83	Ball out of shape - replaced
30		Lock 12 \ ←	- - - - 1		- - 84	
31	 3.04	Bailey 5 \ →	- - - - - W Hole		3- 84	Miller c Edrich at slip, boot high catch, waited to be given out by Chester, 5 in 27 mins, 20 balls
32	3.06	Lock 13 \ ← off spell (incl. lunch) 13-3-39-0		1 - - - - 4	- 89	Hole edges first ball near to Edrich at slip
33		Bailey 6 \ →		2 2 - 1 -	- 94	
34		Bedser 15 \ ←		- - 4 - -	- 98	
35		Bailey 7 \ →	- - - 2 -		- 100	

1953 – FOURTH TEST

36		Bedser 16 \ ←		4 1 - - - -	- 105	
37		Bailey 8 \ → off spell 5-2-12-1	4	- - - - 1	- 110	
38		Laker 1 \ ←	1	- - 1 - 4	- 116	
39		Bedser 17 \ →	4	4 - - 1 1 -	- 122	
40		Laker 2 \ ←		- - - - -	- 122	
41		Bedser 18 \ → off spell 2-0-9-0	3	- - - - -	- 126	
42	3.36	Laker 3 \ ←	1	- - - 1 -	- 128	Harvey 50in 104 mins, 86 balls
43		Lock 14 \ →		- - - - -	- 128	
44		Laker 4 \ ←		- - - - -	- 128	
45		Lock 15 \ →	1	- 3 - - -	- 132	
46		Laker 5 \ ←		- - - 4 - -	- 136	

1953 – FOURTH TEST

47		Lock 16 \ →	- - - - -		- 136	
48		Laker 6 \ ←	1 1	1 1 - -	- 140	
49		Lock 17 \ →	- - - - -		- 140	
50		Laker 7 \ ←	- (1 wide) - 4 1	(1 wide) 4	- 151	Batsmen run for the wide
51		Lock 18 \ → spell 5-3-4-0	4 - - - -		- 155	
52	4.15	Laker 8 \ ←	1	- - 1 - -	- 157	
		TEA	Hole 29 69 mins 70 balls	Harvey 66 143 mins 109 balls	3- 157 180 mins 314 balls (incl.2 w)	

SESSION 106-2 in 125 mins, 218 balls

			Hole 29	Harvey 66	3- 157	
53	4.35	Bailey 9 \ →	- 4 1 - -	1	- 163	Statham and Hilton field as substitutes for Bailey and Watson
54		Laker 9 \ ← off spell (incl. tea) 9-1-33-0		- - - - 4 1	- 168	Australia take lead after 185 mins
55	4.44 4.46	Bailey 10 \ →		- W de Courcy - - 4 4	4- 168 - 176	Harvey lbw, straight ball, kept low, 71 in 152 mins, 118 balls, 9 fours de Courcy 2 fours to mid wicket
56		Lock 19 \ ←	- - 4 - -		- 180	Hole sweeps to long leg for 4

1953 – FOURTH TEST

Over	Time	Bowler			Score	Notes
57		Bailey 11 \\ →		- - - - 2	- 182	
58	4.56 4.58	Lock 20 \\ ←	1	- W Benaud 1 - -	5- 183 - 184	de Courcy lbw, ball straightened, 10 in 10 mins, 12 balls, 2 fours
59		Bailey 12 \\ →		- - - 1 2	- 187	
60		Lock 21 \\ ←		- 4 - - -	- 191	
61		Bailey 13 \\ → off spell 5-0-23-1	- 4 - - -		- 195	
62		Lock 22 \\ ←		- - - - -	- 195	
63		Bedser 19 \\ →	1	- 1 (nb) - -	- 197	
64		Lock 23 \\ ← off spell 5-2-10-1		- - - - -	- 197	
65		Bedser 20 \\ →	- 1	- -	- 198	Hole edges to slip, dropped by Edrich Edrich moves to cover with sore thumb
66	5.21	Bailey 14 \\ ←	4	- - - -	- 202	202 in 226 mins. Hole 51 in 114 mins, 99 balls
67		Bedser 21 \\ →		- - - - -	- 202	*New ball*

158

1953 – FOURTH TEST

Over	Time	Bowler	Batsman 1	Batsman 2	Wicket	Notes
68	5.28 5.30	Bailey 15 \ ←	- 1	W Davidson - - -	6- 203 - 203	Benaud bld, via edge and pad or thigh, 7 in 30 mins, 37 balls, 1 four
69	5.32 5.34	Bedser 22 \ →	W Archer 2 - - -		7- 203 - 205	Hole c Lock, low at bkwd short leg, 53 in 126 mins, 107 balls, 8 fours
70		Bailey 16 \ ←	- - 1 -	1 1	 - 208	
71	5.42 5.44	Bedser 23 \ →		- - W Lindwall - 1	8- 208 - 209	Davidson c Evans, thick edge driving, 2 in 12 mins, 8 balls
72		Bailey 17 \ ←		- 4 - - -	- 213	
73	5.50 5.52	Bedser 24 \ →	1	- 4 W Langley - 4	9- 218 - 222	Lindwall on-drive for 4 Lindwall bld, yorked, 9 in 6 mins, 12 balls, 2 fours
74		Bailey 18 \ ←	- - 2 - 1	4	- 229	
75		Bedser 25 \ →	2 1	1 (nb) - - 4 -	- 237	
76		Bailey 19 \ ←		- - - - -	- 237	
77		Bedser 26 \ →	- - 4 - - 1		- 242	

1953 – FOURTH TEST

78		Bailey 20 \ ←	1 1 - - -	1	- 245	
79		Bedser 27 \ →	- 1 2 - -	1	- 249	
80	6.17	Bailey 21 \ ←	1 - - 1	- (4 lb) 2	- 257	
81		Bedser 28 \ →	- - 1 -	1	- 259	
82		Bailey 22 \ ← spell 9-1-31-1	- - 4 -	- 1	- 264	
83	6.30	Bedser 29 \ → spell 10.5-1-36-4	- - 1 1	- - 1 W	10- 266	Langley c Hutton, low at short leg, 17 in 38 mins, 26 balls , 2 fours
			Archer 31 56 mins 46 balls		10- 266 295 mins 501 b*	* incl. 2 wides

SESSION 109-7 in 115 mins, 187 balls

AUSTRALIA FIRST INNINGS

A.L. Hassett	c Lock b Bedser	37	80 mins, 83 balls, 5 fours	2-70
A.R. Morris	c Lock b Bedser	10	35 mins, 30 balls, 1 four	1-27
R.N. Harvey	lbw b Bailey	71	152 mins, 118 balls, 9 fours	4-168
K.R. Miller	c Edrich b Bailey	5	27 mins, 20 balls	3-84
G.B. Hole	c Lock b Bedser	53	126 mins, 107 balls, 8 fours	7-203
J.H. de Courcy	lbw b Lock	10	10 mins, 12 balls, 2 fours	5-183
R. Benaud	b Bailey	7	30 mins, 37 balls, 1 four	6-203
A.K. Davidson	c Evans b Benaud	2	12 mins, 8 balls	8-218
R.G. Archer	not out	31	56 mins, 46 balls, 3 fours	
R.R. Lindwall	b Bedser	9	6 mins, 12 balls, 2 fours	9-218
G.R.A. Langley	c Hutton b Bedser	17	38 mins, 26 balls , 2 fours	10-266
Extras	(b 4, lb 8, w 2)	14		
TOTAL	(for 10 wkts)	266	295 mins, 501 balls (incl. 2 wides) 82.5 overs	

BOWLING

Bedser	28.5	2	95	6	(2 nb)
Bailey	22	4	71	3	
Lock	23	9	53	1	
Laker	9	1	33	0	(2 w)

Fingleton: a wonderful session for Bedser and for Evans who stands up at the wicket to take him.

Cardus: England achieved a resurrection.

Bailey, Alston and the *Times* correspondent: Hutton did not seem keen to get Australia all out before the close but in the process he gave away a lot of runs. Lock should have been tried against the last pair.

Arlott: The lead of 99 gives Australia wide margin if the atmosphere allows Lindwall and Millar to swing the ball tomorrow.

1953 – FOURTH TEST

Frustration for 40,000: THIRD DAY, Saturday 25 July

20,000 locked out.

England Second Innings

Odd overs [↑ from Football Stand End
Even overs \ ← from Kirkstall Lane End
Simpson's arm is improved. Watson's swelling down

			Hutton	Edrich		
1	11.30	Lindwall 1 \ →	- - - 2 1		- 3	*Sky dark, atmosphere damp.* *Field: 3 slips, gully, 2 short legs* Hutton 2 pushed to square leg. Crowd roar.
2		Miller 1 \ ←	- - 1 - -		- 4	Appeal for lbw against Edrich
3		Lindwall 2 \ →	- - - - 3		- 7	Hutton 3 pushed to off-side
4		Miller 2 \ ←	1 - - 1 -		- 9	
5		Lindwall 3 \ →	- - 4 - -		- 13	Edrich 4 edged through slips. No third man
6		Miller 3 \ ←	- - - - -		- 13	
7		Lindwall 4 \ →	- - 4 - -		- 17	Edrich 4 off full-toss through mid-off
8		Miller 4 \ ←	- - 1 - -		- 18	
9		Lindwall 5 \ →	- 2 - 3 -		- 23	Bumper, Hutton edges through slips
10		Miller 5 \ ← off spell 5-1-8-0	(1 lb) - - - - 4		- 28	Edrich fine hook for 4, crowd cheers

161

1953 – FOURTH TEST

11		Lindwall 6 \ →	- 1 - 4 -		- 33	England's best opening stand of the series Edrich pulls for 4
12		Archer 1 \ ←	- 2 - - -		- 35	6th ball: Benaud moves from gully to short leg, Archer bowls bumper, hitting Hutton on throat
13		Lindwall 7 \ → off spell 7-0-25-0	- 1 - - -		- 36	Bumper to Hutton
14		Archer 2 \ ←	- - - - -		- 36	
15		Davidson 1 \ →	- - - 4 -		- 40	Hutton majestic cover drive for 4
16		Archer 3 \ ←	- - - - -		- 40	
17	12.30	Davidson 2 \ → 2-0-9-0	- - 1 4 -		- 45	Edrich cuts 4 fine of gully
18		Archer 4 \ ←	- - - - -		- 45	
19		Miller 6 \ →	- - - - 1		- 46	
20		Archer 5 \ ←	- - 1 1 -	1	- 49	
21	12.40	Miller 7 \ →	- - 4 1 -		- 54	Edrich 4 square cut - 53 up in 70 mins

1953 – FOURTH TEST

Over	Time	Bowler				Score	Notes
22		Archer 6 \ ←		- - - - -		- 54	Hutton almost gives catch to Benaud at short leg off bumper
23		Miller 8 \ →	- - 2 - -			- 56	Hutton 2 square cut, diving stop by Lindwall
24	12.52 12.54	Archer 7 \ ←	W Graveney -	- - 1 -		1- 57 - 57	Drizzle. Hassett wants to come off. Umpires decide to play on Hutton c Langley (wk) ball moves away and lifts, 25 in 82 mins, 70 balls, 1 four
25		Miller 9 \ →	- - - - -			- 57	
26		Archer 8 \ ←	- - - - -			- 57	*Archer bowls two bouncers to Graveney*
27		Miller 10 \ →	- - - - 2			- 59	
28		Archer 9 \ ← spell 9-5-7-1	1 - - - -			- 60	Graveney turns 1 through leg trap
29	1.10	Miller 11 \ → 5.3-1-12-0	- - 2			- 62	Rain
			Gravny 3 16 mins 12 balls	Edrich 33 100 mins 89 balls		1- 62 100 mins 171 balls	

Just before Hutton was out, Hassett asked Hutton about the rain and Hutton said "It's alright for batting, Lindsay", the exact reverse of a conversation during the Nottingham Test. Hassett's look of disgust turned to delight as Hutton was out.

No further play. Of the 40,000 crowd, 4,000 are still here at 3 o'clock. They wait patently with no slow hand clapping. More rain in the evening. At a dance at Ilkley, Lindwall auctions a bat for Alec Bedser's Benefit and raises £22.

Sunday is dry and breezy with fitful sunshine.

England cling on: FOURTH DAY, Monday 27 July

The crowd overflow the boundary and in the course of the morning the boundary line has to be brought in. There are numerous stoppages for movement behind the bowler and pieces of paper blowing into the batsman's vision.

1953 – FOURTH TEST

				Gravny 3	Edrich 33	1- 62	
29 ctd	11.30	Miller 11 ctd \\→ Spell. 0.3-0-0-0		- - -		- 62	Two medium pace balls, then a leg-break
30		Archer 10			- - - - -	- 62	Field: 2 slips, gully, short mid-off, 2 short legs
31	11.35 11.37	Lindwall 8 \\→		W Compton - 2 1 -	-	2- 62 - 65	Graveney bld, full length, hit off-stump, 3 in 21 mins, 16 balls. Lost sight of ball against dark background. Compton pushes 2 to mid wkt off full toss *Light poor*
32		Archer 11 \\←		- - - - -		- 66	
33		Lindwall 9 \\→		- - 1 -	- (1 bye)	- 67	
34		Archer 12 \\←		- - 3 - -	-	- 70	
35		Lindwall 10 \\→		- - - 1 -		- 71	*Lbw appeal against Compton*
36		Archer 13 \\←		- - - - -		- 71	
37		Lindwall 11 \\→ off spell 4-0-9-1			- - - - 4	- 75	*Appeal against the light* Edrich pulls 4 to mid wkt off bouncer, his first runs today
38		Archer 14 \\← off spell 4-3-3-0		- - - -		- 75	Appeal against light after 2nd ball. turned down after long consultation
39		Miller 12 \\→			- - - 1 -	- 76	

1953 – FOURTH TEST

			Comptn	Edrich		
40		Davidson 3 \ ← spell 1-1-0-0		- - - -	- - - - - 76	Increasing drizzle, then thunderstorm
	12.11	LUNCH	Comptn 8 34 mins 33 balls	Edrich 38 141 mins 121 balls	2- 76 141 mins 240 balls	Rain stops at 1.30

SESSION 14-1 in 41 mins, 69 balls

			Comptn 8	Edrich 38	2- 76	
41	2.10	Miller 13 \ →	1 - - - -		- 77	Compton turns 1 to leg A flier – Edrich leaves it alone
42		Archer 15 \ ←	- - - - -		- 77	
43		Miller 14 \ →		- 2 - - -	- 79	Edrich hooks for 2. Davidson catches it up Edrich hit on chest
44		Archer 16 \ ← off spell 2-1-6-0	1 4 -	1 - -	- 85	Compton 1 to third man Edrich hard cut for 1 Compton hooks for 4 off his face
45		Miller 15 \ →		- - - - -	- 85	
46		Davidson 4 \ ←	- - - - -		- 85	
47		Miller 16 \ →		- - (4 lb) * - 2 -	- 91	* 4 leg byes at some point in this over to fine leg
48		Davidson 5 \ ←	- - 1 - -		-92	
49		Miller 17 \ →	- - - 3 -		- 95	Compton hooks straight to Davidson at short sq leg, ball canons off his wrist for 3

1953 – FOURTH TEST

50		Davidson 6 \ ←	- - 1 - -		- 96	
51	2.46	Miller 18 \ → off spell (incl. lunch) 7-1-14-0	- - - 1 - 4		- 101	Edrich cuts wide long hop for 4, 101 up in 175 mins
52		Davidson 7 \ ← off spell 4-1-8-0	4 1 - 1 - -		- 107	Compton 4 past cover off full-toss Compton 1 to fine leg
53		Lindwall 12 \ →	- - - - -		- 107	*Testing over for Edrich*
54		Hole 1 \ ←	- - 2 - -		- 109	*Hole bowls off-breaks, only one close fielder*
55	2.59	Lindwall 13 \ →	- - 4 - 4 -		- 117	Edrich flashes 4 through 3rd slip gap for his 52 in 190 mins, 163 balls
56		Hole 2 \ ←	- - - - -		- 117	Sun comes out
57		Lindwall 14 \ →	- - 2 1 4 1		- 125	
58		Hole 3 \ ← off spell 3-1-6-0	4 - - - - -		- 129	
59		Lindwall 15 \ → off spell 4-1-17-0	- - - 1 - -		- 130	
60		Archer 17 \ ←	1 1 - - - -		- 132	

166

1953 – FOURTH TEST

61		Benaud 1 \ →		- - - - -	- 132	
62		Archer 18 \ ←		- - - - 1	- 133	
63		Benaud 2 \ →		- - - - -	- 133	
64		Archer 19 \ ← off spell 3-0-4-0	1	- - - -	- 134	
65		Benaud 3 \ → off spell 3-2-1-0	- - 1	- - -	- 135	
66		Miller 19 \ ←		- - - - -	- 135	
67		Lindwall 16 \ →		1 2 - - -	- 138	New ball
68		Miller 20 \ ←		- - 1 - -	- 139	
69		Lindwall 17 \ →		- - - - -	- 139	
70		Miller 21 \ ←		- - - - -	- 139	
71	3.52 3.54	Lindwall 18 \ →		W Watson - - - -	3- 139 - 139	Edrich c de Courcy, drive to gully, reflex catch, 64 in 243 mins, 211 balls, 10 fours

1953 – FOURTH TEST

72		Miller 22 \ ← off spell 4-3-1-0	- - - - -		- 139	
73		Lindwall 19 \ →		2 - - - -	- 141	Watson pushes off-drive for 2
74		Archer 20 \ ←	- - 1 - -		- 142	
75		Lindwall 20 \ →	4 1 - - -		- 147	
76	4.15	Archer 21 \ ←	- - - - -		- 147	
		TEA	Comptn 47 159 mins 141 balls	Watson 2 21 mins 18 balls	3- 147 266 mins 456 balls	

Session 71-1 in 125 mins, 216 balls
England lead by 48 runs.

			Comptn 47	Watson 2	3- 147	
77	4.35	Lindwall 21 \ →		- - - - -	- 147	
78	4.42	Archer 22 \ ←	- 1 4 - -		- 152	Watson hooks bouncer for 4 - 152 up in 273 mins
79		Lindwall 22 \ →	1 - - - -		- 153	
80		Archer 23 \ ←	- - - - -		- 153	
81		Lindwall 23 \ →		- 4 - - -	- 157	

1953 – FOURTH TEST

82	4.54	Archer 24 \ ←	1 1	- - 1 -	- 160	Compton 50 in 178 mins, 151 balls
83		Lindwall 24 \ → off spell (incl. tea) 9-4-15-1	- - - - -		- 160	Compton hit on left hand, drops his bat and walks away. Resumes after a few minutes.
84		Archer 25 \ ← off spell (incl. tea) 6-2-11-0		- - - 2 -	- 162	
85		Miller 23 \ →	- 1	- - 1	- 164	
86		Benaud 4 \ ←		- - - - 1	- 165	
87		Miller 24 \ →		- - - - -	- 165	
88		Benaud 5 \ ←	- - - - -		- 165	
89	5.20	Miller 25 \ →		- - - -	- 165	Bad light
89 ctd	5.40	Miller 25 ctd \ →		- -	- 165	Miller bowls round the wicket to Watson
90		Benaud 6 \ ←	2 	- - - -	- 167	
9	5.46	Miller 26 \ →		- - - - W Simpson	4- 167	Watson c Davidson, off glove at gully, juggled catch running back, 15 in 72 mins, 77 balls, 2 fours
92	5.48	Benaud 7 \ ← off spell 4-1-7-0	- - - - 4		- 171	

1953 – FOURTH TEST

93	5.51 5.53 5.56	Miller 27 \ →		W Bailey - 4 - - -	5- 171 - 175	Simpson c de Courcy, at 3rd slip, nasty riser, 0 in 3 mins, 1 ball Miller on a hat-trick Bailey 4 past cover Rain
94	6.14	Lindwall 25 \ ←	1	- - - - -	 - 176	
95		Miller 28 \ →		- - - - -	 - 176	
96		Lindwall 26 \ ←		- - - - -	 - 176	
97		Miller 29 \ →		- - - - 1	 - 177	
98		Lindwall 27 \ ← spell 3-2-1-0		- - - - -	 - 177	
99	 6.30	Miller 30 \ → spell 8-5-7-2		- - - -	 - 177	Compton has injured hand
			Comptn 60 236 mins 197 balls	Bailey 4 19 mins 22 balls	5- 177 343 mins 594 balls	

SESSION 30-2 in 77 mins, 138 balls
England lead by 78 runs.
Miller to-day 19.3-9-22-2
In the final 16-minute session, nine fieldsmen crowded round the bat.
Edrich joins the list of hospital visitors, having his thumb X-rayed, but it is only a case of bad bruising.
Fingleton: another unchallenging display by England's batsmen, giving up any hope of victory.
Whitington: 117 runs in 4 hours requires some explanation beyond the state of the pitch, the weather interruptions and Compton's sore hand
Alston: No praise can be too high for Compton. He stood firm for four hours during frequent stoppages and kept the Ashes alive. But he and Watson could have taken the fight to the enemy. Then the rain stoppages revitalized the bowlers to put Australia back on top.
Arlott: England have a good chance if they can get another 100 runs.
 An armistice is signed in the Korean War.

1953 – FOURTH TEST

Six hours of suspense and agony: FIFTH DAY – Tuesday 28 July

A cloudy day. No queues outside the ground.
Compton does not resume. His hand is too painful to hold the bat. Archer takes the field but is unable to bowl due to stomach strain

			Evans	Bailey 4	5- 177	
100	11.30	Lindwall 28 \ ←	- - - - -		- 177	
101		Miller 31 \ →	- - - - 4		- 181	Bailey hooks for 4 to long leg
102		Lindwall 29 \ ←	- - 1 -		- 182	
103		Miller 32 \ →	- - - - -		- 182	
104		Lindwall 30 \ ←	- - - - -		- 182	
105	11.48 11.50	Miller 33 \ →	- - - W Laker 1		6- 182 - 183	Evans c Lindwall, square leg, slower ball from 23 yards, same shot as previous ball, 1 in 18 mins, 21 balls
106		Lindwall 31 \ ←	- - - - -		- 183	
107		Miller 34 \ →	- - - - -		- 183	
108		Lindwall 32 \ ← off spell 5-3-3-0	- - - 2 -		- 185	
109		Miller 35 \ → off spell 5-3-5-1	- - - - -		- 185	

1953 – FOURTH TEST

110		Benaud 8 \ ←	- - - - -		- 185	*Benaud gets turn and lift.* *Given 4 close fielders*
111		Davidson 8 \ →		- - - - -	- 185	*Davidson in faster style*
112		Benaud 9 \ ←	- - 2 - 1		- 188	Laker 2, misfield by Harvey at cover Laker 1-top edged sweep Lndwl ran for
113		Davidson 9 \ →	4 - - - -		- 192	Laker 4 cover drive, full toss
114		Benaud 10 \ ←		- - - - -	- 192	
115		Davidson 10 \ → off spell 3-1-6-0	- 1 - - 1		- 194	
116		Benaud 11 \ ←		- - - - -	- 194	
117		Lindwall 33 \ →	1 - 1 - -		- 196	
118		Benaud 12 \ ←		- - 1 - 1 -	- 198	Bailey hooks short ball for 1, stopped by de Courcy
119	12.28	Lindwall 34 \ →	4 - 1 - -		- 203	Laker places 4 between Hole and Benaud in slips. 202 up in 401 mins. England lead passes 100, with 5 hours left.
120		Benaud 13 \ ←		- - - - -	- 203	

1953 – FOURTH TEST

#		Bowler			Score	Notes
121		Lindwall 35 \ →		- - - - -	- 203	*Bailey nearly gives catch off pads to Miller at short leg*
122		Benaud 14 \ ← off spell 7-4-6-0	- - - 1 -	-	- 204	
123		Lindwall 36 \ →	1	- - - - -	- 205	
124		Davidson 11 \ ←-	- - - 2 - -		- 207	*Davidson in slow style, round the wicket*
125		Lindwall 37 \ → off spell 5-2-8-0		- - - - -	- 207	
126		Davidson 12 \ ←	- - - 1 -		- 208	
127		Benaud 15 \ →	- - - 1 -	1	- 210	
128		Davidson 13 \ ←	-	- - - - -	- 210	
129		Benaud 16 \ →	4 - - - 4 -		- 218	Laker 4 through covers Laker 4 through covers
130		Davidson 14 \ ←		- - - - -	- 218	
131		Benaud 17 \ → off spell 3-0-11-0	- - - - - 1		- 219	

1953 – FOURTH TEST

132		Davidson 15 \ ← off spell 5-2-4-0	- 1 - - -		- 220	
133	1.10	Lindwall 38 \ →	1 - 4 -	1	- 226	New ball Laker 4 square cover drive. Laker 39 out of 44 in 80 mins
134		Miller 36 \ ←	- - - - -		- 226	
135		Lindwall 39 \ →	4 - 1 - -	1	- 232	50 stand (Laker 44) in 88 mins
136		Miller 37 \ ←	- - - - 1		- 233	
137		Lindwall 40 \ →	- - - - -		- 233	
138	1.28 1.30	Miller 38 \ ← spell 3-1-3-0	1 - - - -	1	- 235	Appeal against the light
		LUNCH	Laker 45 100 mins 95 balls	Bailey 16 139 mins 140 balls	6- 235 463 mins 828 balls	

SESSION 58-1 in 120 mins, 234 balls

Cutler: Many think that Hassett relied too much on his pace bowlers whom Laker played well. But England have missed the boat- they should have gone for the runs this morning.

There is some doubt about the appeal against the light. West and Fingleton say that Bailey appealed in perfectly good light at 1.29 as the Australians hurried to change ends to get one more over in. Arlott says that a purple-black cloud appeared slowly from the south-west. While the umpires conferred, Miller took off the bails and presented them to the umpires and Hassett resignedly led his team off. Barnes says that Bailey appealed at 1.25, having frequently stopped the bowler in his run-up to pat down imaginary spots on the pitch. Harris says: "Bailey told me afterwards that he had made a tactical use of his right to appeal, though he would not have done so had the light been so bright that such an action would have been absurd." The incident was so close to the stroke of lunch that some commentators do not remark on it at all. Cutler saw only one of "those flamboyant umpire conferences that have irritated everyone throughout the series".

Bailey himself says: "At 1.28 I expended the one appeal a day against the light that a batting side is allowed. By the time the umpires had consulted it was time for lunch."

Slight rain during lunch interval. England lead by 136 with 4 hours left.

1953 – FOURTH TEST

			Laker 45	Bailey 16	6- 235	
139	2.10	Lindwall 41 \\→		- - - 1 -	- 236	Bailey 1 to fine leg
140		Davidson 16 \\←	- - - - -		- 236	
141		Lindwall 42 \\→	2 1	- - -	- 239	Laker 2 edged to third man
142	2.27	Davidson 17 \\←	- - - - W Compton		7- 239	Laker c Benaud, 2nd slip, 48 in 117 mins, 104 balls, 6 fours
143	2.29	Lindwall 43 \\→		- - - 1 -	- 240	Compton resumes, having had injection to kill pain. He removes hand from bat after every stroke.
144		Davidson 18 \\←	- - - - -		- 240	
145		Lindwall 44 \\→		- - - - - -	- 240	Compton edges to first slip where Hole claims catch. Umpire Lee says not out after conferring with Chester. Next ball appeal for catch behind turned down. Australians are annoyed
146		Davidson 19 \\←		- - 2 - -	- 242	
147		Lindwall 45 \\→	1	- - - - -	- 243	Compton 1 to leg
148		Davidson 20 \\←	- - - - -		- 243	
149		Lindwall 46 \\→		- - (1 lb) - - -	- 244	

1953 – FOURTH TEST

Over	Time	Bowler	Wicket	Batsman 1	Batsman 2	Score	Notes
150		Davidson 21 \ ←		- - - - -		- 244	
151	2.51 2.53	Lindwall 47 \ →	W Lock	- - - -		8- 244 - 244	Compton lbw, inswinger, 61 in 258 mins, 217 balls, 3 fours. England lead 145 with 197 mins left
152		Davidson 22 \ ←		- - - - -		- 244	
153		Lindwall 48 \ →		- - - - -		- 244	
154		Davidson 23 \ ←		- - 1 - -		- 245	
155		Lindwall 49 \ →		- 3 - -	1	- 249	Bailey 3 to long on Bailey 1 to fine leg
156		Davidson 24 \ ←		- - - - -		- 249	
157	3.10	Lindwall 50 \ →		1 - - -	1	- 251	250 up in 522 mins
158		Davidson 25 \ ← off spell 10-8-3-1		- - - - -		- 251	
159		Lindwall 51 \ → off spell (incl. lunch) 14-6-24-1		- - - - -		- 251	
160		Benaud 18 \ ←		- - - - 1		- 252	

1953 – FOURTH TEST

161		Miller 39 \ →	- - 1 - - 1		- 254	
162		Benaud 19 \ ← off spell 2-1-1-0	- .. - - -		- 254	
163	3.31	Miller 40 \ →	- - - 4 - W Bedser		9- 258	Lock 4 to mid wicket Lock c Morris running in from long leg, 8 in 38 mins, 44 balls, 1 four
164	3.33	Lindwall 52 \ ←	- - - - -		- 258	Batsmen crossed. England lead 159 with 157 mins left
165		Miller 41 \ →	- - - - 1		- 259	
166		Lindwall 53 \ ←	- - - 1 -		- 260	
167		Miller 42 \ →	- - - - -		- 260	
168		Lindwall 54 \ ← off spell 3-1-2-0	1 - - - -		- 261	
169		Miller 43 \ →	- - - - -		- 261	
170		Davidson 26 \ ←	- - - - -	- (2 lb)	- 263	
171		Miller 44 \ →	- - - - -		- 263	*Crowd getting noisy. Miller refuses to bowl until it subsides. Then Bailey adjusts his glove and Miller sits down.*

1953 – FOURTH TEST

172		Davidson 27 \ ←		- - - - -	- 263	
173		Miller 45 \ →	1 1 -	- - - -	- 265	
174		Davidson 28 \ ←		- - - - 1	- 266	*About 4.00 Bailey looks to the dressing room making sweeping gestures with the bat.*
175		Miller 46 \ →		- 4 - -	- 270	
176		Davidson 29 \ ←	1 - -	- - - - -	- 271	
177		Miller 47 \ → spell 9-4-13-1	- - - - -		- 271	
178	4.14	Davidson 30 \ ← spell 4.3-2-6-1	4 - W		10 -275	Bailey 4 off full toss Bailey c Hole, slip, 38 in 263 mins, 275 balls, 4 fours
			Bedser 3 41 mins 29 balls		10- 275 587 mins 1065 balls	

SESSION 40-4 in 124 mins, 237 balls

ENGLAND SECOND INNINGS

L. Hutton	c Langley b Archer	25	82 mins, 70 balls, 1 four	1-57
W.J. Edrich	c de Courcy b Lindwall	64	243 mins, 211 balls, 10 fours	3-139
T.W. Graveney	b Lindwall	3	21 mins, 16 balls	2-62
D.C.S. Compton	lbw b Lindwall	61	258 mins, 217 balls, 3 fours.	8-244
W. Watson	c Davidson b Miller	15	72 mins, 77 balls, 2 fours	4-167
R.T. Simpson	c de Courcy b Miller	0	3 mins, 1 ball	5-171
T.E. Bailey	c Hole b Davidson	38	263 mins, 275 balls, 4 fours	10-275
T.G. Evans	c Lindwall b Miller	1	18 mins, 21 balls	6-182
J.C. Laker	c Benaud b Davidson	48	117 mins, 104 balls, 6 fours	7-239
G.A.R. Lock	c Morris b Miller	8	38 mins, 44 balls, 1 four	9-258
A.V. Bedser	not out	3	41 mins, 29 balls	
Extras	(b 1, lb 8)	9		
TOTAL	(for 10 wkts)	275	587 mins, 1065 balls, 177.3 overs	

At 177-5 Compton retired hurt 60* and returned at 239-7

BOWLING

Lindwall	54	19	104	3
Miller	47	19	63	4
Archer	25	12	31	1
Davidson	29.3	15	36	2
Hole	3	1	6	0
Benaud	19	8	26	0

Going back to the Pavilion, Miller, who was thoroughly annoyed by Bailey, hears a derogatory remark about himself by a spectator and grabs a man in the crowd, then relents when the man says it was someone else who shouted.

1953 – FOURTH TEST

Fingleton: Neither captain seems to have wanted to press for victory today. By mid-afternoon Hassett started to give the impression that he did not want to bowl England out.

Alston said at one point to Australian listeners during the Bailey-Lock partnership, "I'll stop talking till something happens." He finds it a complete negation of cricket that such methods should be needed to save a Test Match.

Cardus: Before lunch England's tactics were sensible, but in the afternoon the stonewalling, so deliberate that it must have been done to orders, was a belittlement of cricket.

Whitington and Lindwall: Australians were annoyed because when Umpire Lee called to Chester about whether Hole had made a good catch off Compton, Chester seemed to be caught unawares, then came suddenly to life and ridiculed the appeal contemptuously, shouting a loud "Not out!" and turning on his heels back to his position. This encouraged the crowd to react against Hole. Miller, standing beside Hole at slip, thinks that it was a clean catch at least an inch above the ground. Hassett thinks that the ball was picked up "a clear six inches above the ground".

Davidson: Hole caught it, clean as a whistle. When he turned down the appeal, Chester turned to me saying gruffly "You Australians play it hard".

Compton says that he edged the ball very low to Hole; he looked at Hole waiting or a sign that he had or had not caught it. Hole hesitated then went into a huddle with the other fielders, then said firmly that it was a good catch. Compton said that because of the hesitation, the umpire should decide. Umpire Lee asked Chester, who snapped "No it was bloody well not out".

Australia Second Innings

Odd overs \ → from Football Stand End
Even overs \ ← from Kirkstall Lane End
Target 177 in 115 mins

West says on television that he thinks the Australian cannot make a serious effort at the target. Alston's view is that they will take the bold approach. Cutler judges that it would be an impossible task for England. Arlott thinks a draw the likeliest result; there will be enough turn to command respect from the batsmen. Bailey says that his team were confident Australia had no chance of winning and on a wicket responding to spin they should get into an amount of trouble.

Hutton gets Lock to bowl a few practice deliveries with the new ball before the Australian batsmen come out.

			Hassett	Morris		
1	4.35	Bedser 1	-			M. Hilton (Lancs) fielding substitute for Compton
		\ →	1			
				3		
			-			Morris drive for 3
			(2 bye) -		- 6	2 byes, cutter just missed stumps, well chased by Simpson
2		Lock 1		-		3 short legs. Lock bowls too short.
		\ ←		-		
				4		Morris cuts and hooks twice.
				4		
				4		Long leg and third man posted
	4.40			2	- 20	Target 157 in 110 mins
3		Bedser 2	-			
		\ →	1			
				4		Morris 4 square
				-		
				-	- 25	
4		Lock 2	2			
		\ ←	-			Hassett bld, draws away attempting cut, inside edge, 4 in 13 mins, 10 balls, 0 fours
	4.48		-			
			W		1- 27	
			Hole			
	4.49		-			Hole beaten by spin
				-	- 27	Target 152 in 101 mins
5		Bedser 3		-		
		\ →		-		
				-		
				-		
				-	- 27	
6		Lock 3	2			Morris cuts for 2, well fielded by Hilton at short third man
		\ ←	-			
			1			
				2		
				-		
				-	- 32	

1953 – FOURTH TEST

Over	Time	Bowler	Batsman 1	Batsman 2	Score	Notes
7		Bedser 4 \ →		- - - - 1	- 33	
8		Lock 4 \ ←	3 1	- - 1	- 38	
9		Bedser 5 \ →	- 1	- 1 -	- 40	Morris 1, well stopped by Watson at long leg
10		Lock 5 \ ← off spell 5-0-27-1		- 1 - - -	- 41	
11	5.10	Bedser 6 \ →	1	1 - - 3 -	- 46	Hole hooks for 1, well stopped by Simpson Target 131 in 80 mins
12	5.13 5.15	Laker 1 \ ←		- 4 4 W Harvey - 1	2- 54 - 55	Morris hooks 4 just over Bailey's finger tips at square leg Morris st Evans, stranded on off-side, 38 in 38 mins, 38 balls, 6 fours Target 123 in 75 mins
13		Bedser 7 \ →	4	- - - 1	- 60	Hole hooks to long leg for 4 almost 6
14		Laker 2 \ ← off spell 2-0-17-1	1	4 - 3 - -	- 68	*Hutton puts*
15		Bedser 8 \ →	1	- - - - - (1 lb)	- 70	*two,* *then three,* *then four*
16		Lock 6 \ ←		- - - 1 -	- 71	*men in the deep*
17		Bedser 9 \ →	2	1 - - - -	- 74	

1953 – FOURTH TEST

#	Time	Bowler	Wicket	Runs	Score	Comments
18		Lock 7 \ ←		4 - 1 - - 2	- 81	
19		Bedser 10 \ →		- 2 1 - 4 4	- 92	
20	5.39	Lock 8 \ ← off spell 3-0-21-0		- 4 4 4 - 1	- 105	Harvey fine off-drive for 4. 102 up in 64 mins. Target 75 in 51 mins
21	5.44	Bedser 11 \ →	W Davidson	- 1 1 1 3	3- 111	Harvey lbw, playing across straight ball, on leg stump, goes for leg bye, 34 in 29 mins, 39 balls, 5 fours
22	5.45	Bailey 1 \ ←		- (1 wide) . 1 - (1 lb) - 1 -	- 115	Target 66 in 45 mins, about 6 per over. Bailey consults with Hutton and comes on to bowl. Batsmen run for wide down leg side to Evans *Bailey off long run, bowling leg side to 6 leg fielders, fine 3rd man, cover, mid-off* Sharp leg-bye, ball bounces off Hole's pad
23		Bedser 12 \ →		- 1 - - - 1	- 117	
24	5.56 5.57	Bailey 2 \ ←	W de Courcy	- 1 - - -	4- 117 - 118	Hole c Graveney on ropes at deep square leg, 33 in 67 mins, 48 balls, 3 fours. Batsmen crossed. Would have been six. Target 60 in 33 mins
25	6.00	Bedser 13		1 - - 1 -	- 120	59 needed in 30 mins, about 7 per over
26		Bailey 3 \ ←		- - - 1 -	- 121	
27		Bedser 14 \ →		- 6 - - 1	- 128	de Courcy hooks 6 to square leg
28		Bailey 4 \ ←		1 - (1 lb) - - -	- 130	

1953 – FOURTH TEST

Over		Bowler		Batsman	Batsman	Score	Notes
29		Bedser 15 \ →		1 / - / 1 / - / 2 / -		- 134	
30		Bailey 5 \ ←		- / - / - / - / -		- 134	
31		Bedser 16 \ →		- / - / - (1 lb) / 1 / 1 / -		- 137	
32		Bailey 6 \ ← spell 6-1-9-0	1	1 / - / 2 / - / - (1 bye)		- 142	
33	6.30	Bedser 17 \ → spell 17-1-65-1		4 / - / - / - / - / 1		- 147	Davidson cover drive for 4 *Bedser bowled unchanged*
			de Crcy 13 33 mins 35 balls	Dvdsn 17 45 mins 28 balls	4- 147 115 mins 199 balls (inc.1 w)		

Bailey walks off slowly, exhausted, the last one off the field

AUSTRALIA – SECOND INNINGS

A.L. Hassett	b Lock	4	13 mins, 10 balls, 0 fours	1-27
A.R. Morris	st Evans b Laker	38	38 mins, 38 balls, 6 fours	2-54
G.B. Hole	c Graveney b Bailey	33	67 mins, 48 balls, 3 fours	4-117
R.N. Harvey	lbw b Bedser	34	29 mins, 39 balls, 5 fours	3-111
A.K. Davidson	not out	17	45 mins, 28 balls, 1 four	
J.H de Courcy	not out	13	33 mins, 35 balls, 1 six	
Extras	(b 3, lb 4, w 1)	8		
TOTAL	(for 4 wkts)	147	115 mins, 199 balls (incl. 1 wide), 33 overs	

BOWLING

Bedser	17	1	65	1	
Lock	8	0	48	1	
Laker	2	0	17	1	
Bailey	6	1	9	1	(1 w)

MATCH DRAWN

England nearly lost this match because of what happened in the last hour of the Manchester Test. Hutton thought that there was a good chance of his spinners Lock and Laker running through the batsmen as Wardle and Laker had done there. It was a fair judgement, but he clung on to the hope for too long. Only just in the nick of time was he persuaded to give up all hope of victory and it required the questionable tactic of leg-side bowling by Bailey, coupled with some slowing in the over-rate to salvage the draw.

Although Australia morally won this Test hands down and were by far the more positive side, no one player made an outstanding contribution. Because of his courageous and in the decisive batting and bowling on the last day, entirely negative in character, the man of the match award must go to Trevor Bailey. But for him Ashes would have gone.

West: Apart from a couple of balls by Lock that turned and lifted sharply, the pitch was gently paced and utterly lifeless. The failure to send in Miller and even Lindwall, instead of de Courcy and Davidson may have cost Australia the match. de Courcy seemed in unable to decide what tactic to adopt. Australia were in charge of this Test throughout the five days and achieved a clear moral victory. In the match England scored 442 for 20 in 972 minutes, Australia 413 for 14 in 407 minutes.

Whitington: Hutton's tactics were just right. He took the risk to win by trying Lock and Laker with attacking fields, knowing that he had Bailey and his leg-theory to call upon when all chance of bowling then out had gone

Cutler: Hutton should have opened with Bailey and forced Australia on the defensive and then tried the spinners.

Brown agrees: four or five wickets might have fallen if Australia had to make the running against tight off-side bowling to a 5-4 field, then Hutton could have switched to all out attack. "I do not pretend to like the method by which

1953 – FOURTH TEST

England saved the match, but there was nothing new about it." England were helped by Hassett's choice of batting order; having a left- and right-hander at the crease caused time consuming field changes. And it was great relief not to see Miller or Lindwall come in.

Fingleton: Hassett had no pre-conceived notion about whether to go for victory. The catch by Graveney could well have been taken on or over the line and the umpires might well have inspected it. Hassett sent Davidson with instructions to go for the runs but he was unable to do it. Some thought that the more experienced Miller should have gone in, but he had tired legs having bowled 75 overs in the match

Swanton: If England had batted sensibly on the first day, they might have won this match. But E.W. makes no criticism of Bailey's bowling tactics, which cured the previous tactic of bowling straight to a split 5-4 field which left too many gaps in the field.

Arlott: The spinners beat Hassett's bat several times. Perhaps Morris and Harvey bluffed Lock and Laker out of their accuracy and flight. Bedser also was not at his best. Australian morale must be boosted. But England have come from behind the save the game. The Headingley crowd's biggest cheer was for Bailey.

Cardus: Australia won on points and on the value of pleasure given. But the last cheer is for Bailey, a plucky cricketer.

Alston: In two minds, grateful that the door was not closed on the Ashes but sorry that England had used such dreary tactics to stay in the match. England were outplayed in everything but stubbornness.

Hutton says he based his hopes in Lock on what Davidson had done in the England innings. He bowled several good balls that deserved a wicket, but he tried too hard to spin the ball and bowled too fast and lost his length. He should have slowed down and flighted the ball. Bedser could not find his length for the first time in the series. When 66 were needed in 45 minutes "my answer was to put on Trevor Bailey, who because of his knee injury had not to that point been used in the innings. I asked Trevor to bowl down the leg-side without the aid of a slip fieldsman." The entirely negative tactic is bad for the game but Australia have used it, through Johnston on the last day at Nottingham, and through Ernie Toshack in 1946-47 and 1948. If one side uses the tactic the other cannot afford to avoid it. Legislation should be introduced which will inhibit this and other defensive bowling tactics.

Bowes: If Lock could have got lift and turn as Davidson had done, no team could have got the runs to win.

Bailey says that Australia started with no intention of going for the runs; with memories of the last hour of Old Trafford, England were too slow in realising that they could lose. On Harvey's dismissal Bailey asked to be put on instead of Lock and he came on immediately. After a 'huddle', Hutton decided to bring Bailey on and suggested that he try his full run up. He decided to bowl leg theory, with all fielders on the leg side, except fine third man, short cover and wide mid off. "I do not advocate this type of bowling but in the circumstances there was nothing else to do." Bailey told Lindwall's biographer (1995): "I went to Len and said 'Give me the ball and I'll bowl leg theory' ".

Compton was off the field throughout, with his injured hand, watching from the pavilion. "Hutton's judgement seemed to desert him. ... I had the impression that momentarily he had lost his head. ...He kept on bowling Lock, and the Australian batsmen kept on driving the score along. It was Bailey who took action. He and Bill Edrich went across the field to Hutton and told him in effect that he'd got to do something to save the game. Eventually Hutton made a decision and Bailey took the ball. ... If it hadn't been for Trevor Bailey, Hutton's tactics would have thrown away the game. Not that I can agree with what Bailey did; I think it was unfair and should never have been done, though I can fully understand why he did it."

Laker agrees. He thinks that Lock was a bad choice to open the bowling. Edrich, at slip, kept urging him to bring on Bailey. Hutton was too dazed to accept the obvious facts. Finally Edrich and Bailey persuaded him to take the right course.

Lock himself thinks that the pitch was not helpful enough for his spin and that Hutton should have given Bailey a few overs with the new ball.

Evans, writing in 1956, makes no criticism of Hutton. He suggests that Australia could have taken more chances to force the runs. In his 1960 autobiography he says that Bailey came up to him and said: "This is all wrong Godfrey. If we keep Lock on we'll lose the match". Evans did not support him but as the runs kept flowing he agreed that Bailey was right and they both approached Hutton, who accepted their advice at once. Hutton's initial tactic was right but he reacted too slowly to the changing situation.

Edrich says that he went up to Hutton and said: "Len, for God's sake, put Trevor on." Bailey approached them at that moment. Hutton looked vacant, muttered "Trevor, Trevor" and put Bailey on.

Lindwall thinks that Hutton was justified in his initial tactic. He could not know that Bedser and Lock would bowl badly. And the rolling of the pitch between innings eased the pitch more than expected.

Graveney thinks that leg theory makes a travesty of the game, but this was one of those exceptional cases where it was justified. Hutton could have closed up the game from the start, but he took a gamble for a result and he could fairly take every step to save the game when the risk of defeat was looming.

Harvey: "Hutton should never have condoned such deplorable tactics and he was as much to blame as Bailey".

Hassett says: "My instructions were to risk all in an effort to win". Not only did Bailey bowl leg theory that was impossible to score off, but "the rate of overs slowed down to an extent which to my mind infringed the spirit of and the rule governing fair play."

Bradman, on the other hand, has high praise for Bailey's batting and bowling, and commends England for not using any delaying tactics. Hutton should have given Bailey the new ball. England never had a chance of winning. Miller should have been sent in to bat.

1953 – FOURTH TEST

Some suggest that Bailey also slowed down the over rate. Before Bailey came on England bowled 21 overs in 70 minutes (3.33 minutes per over). After that they bowled 12 in 45 minutes (3.75 minutes per over). Bedser was bowling at one end throughout the innings. Of course Bailey would take a longer run and naturally take longer to bowl an over than the spinners Lock and Laker who partnered Bedser until Bailey came on.

This was Lock's first Test against Australia and at the end of the match Hutton presented him with one of the stumps and a toy lion which had been England's dressing room mascot throughout the Test.

Match attendance: 151,000 (£112,697 paying) receipts £48,313. Today: £22,000.

The Australians are objecting to Chester officiating in the Final Test, because of his general attitude to them and two specific incidents, the ruling that Simpson was not run out and the disallowance of Hole's catch off Compton. Later it was announced that Chester would not stand for the rest of the season due to illness. Chester, a very promising cricketer until he lost his right arm below the elbow in the First World War, turned to umpiring and was the most famous and highly regarded umpire in the world. During the summer he appeared to develop a dislike of the Australians, perhaps of their over-enthusiastic appealing. He often responded to an appeal with a contemptuous "Not out". This particularly annoyed Miller, who previously got on well with Chester and exchanged racing tips with him on the field.

July 22, 23, 24

Glamorgan won by four wickets at Ebbw Vale against Warwickshire. Wilfred Wooller took 8-45 in the first innings and when Glamorgan needed 245 to win in 235 minutes he made 67 not out. Lancashire beat Somerset in two days. At Lord's Middlesex were struggling at 84 –5 when Doug Wright went off with a strained muscle. They recovered to 191, then Moss and Warr bowled Kent out for 43- the lowest score of the season- and Middlesex won in two days. At Horsham, Sussex bowled out Yorkshire for 226, made 387 for 3 declared (Sheppard 187 not out, adding 279 with veteran George Cox) but despite the best efforts of Marlar could not force a win. Surrey were not playing. Middlesex were back on top, Sussex two points behind with two games in hand.

July 25, 27, 28

While the Test worked up to its unexpected conclusion, Sussex did all they could to beat Kent but in the last two hours could only get eight of them out, having to be satisfied with four points for first innings lead. That was enough to put them back at the top of the Table because rain ruined the first two days of Middlesex's contest so that it became a battle for first innings points which Glamorgan's last wicket pair secured. Yorkshire suffered a rather cruel defeat at Nottingham: having followed on they recovered well in the second innings to be able to secure a draw but Sutcliffe gambled on a declaration setting Notts 110 to win in 67 minutes and Notts won by four wickets. Yorkshire sank to 14th position. Surrey lost to Gloucestershire, when 17-year-old David Allen an off-spinner destined to play for England, took 6 for 13 to bowl them out for 111.

Because of the stalemate in the Test series, Mr. Ronald Aird, Secretary of MCC, announced that the Board of Control would ask Australia to agree to a 6th day in the Final Test at the Oval, because of the unprecedented weather in previous Tests, though 30 hours is ample time to decide a Test.

Night train to King's Cross: The Oval: July 29, 30, 31

The Australian plans did not cater for the possibility that the Leeds Test might run its full course. When the Test ended at 6.30 on Tuesday the team were due to start pay against Surrey at the Oval at 11.30 on Wednesday. They had booked a 6.40 train, but even the players who were not in the Test side came just too late to the station, held up by autograph hunters in the Headingley car park. They had to wait for the 10.30 train on which no sleeper berths were available, and arrived at King's Cross station at 5am. They managed to reserve some first-class carriages in which they could lie down on the seats. Some lay on the floor. Lindwall was among those whose bed was a mat in the corridor. A stranger (who turned out to be a journalist) occupied one of the seats and refused to move. Hassett complained at one station and at the next stop two policemen came on and removed the trespasser. England players were luckier. Bedser, who was taking a rest, Bailey and Laker were in the same train but had booked sleepers in the first-class compartments. Fingleton shared a four-man sleeper with three other Australian journalists in third-class.

To make things worse Hassett lost the toss and a listless Lindwall opened the bowling. At the other end was Johnston, returning for his first game since the end of June. Fletcher and May added 128 for the second wicket. Rain stopped play for an hour before tea. On the restart Lindwall and Johnston had the new ball and the score changed from 154-1 to 168-5. May played some masterful shots in his 56 after a sticky start. After tea he took 45 minutes to move from 55 to 56 until Lindwall had him lbw. Subba Row and McIntyre stayed to the close when Surrey were 202 for 5. Thursday saw Harvey's ninth century of the summer in front of 25,000 people. He came in at 120-2 after Morris hit a six off Surridge and was caught off a leading edge at mid-off next ball. Harvey and Hassett put on 117 in 70 minutes. Harvey reached 100 in 125 minutes with 10 fours and a six. A break for rain and the new ball changed the position and Australia slumped to 327 for 9 at the close. Craig got to 16 when he was run out by his partner Ring. On Friday morning the ground was under water and the match was abandoned even before 11.30.

SURREY 209-8dec (D.G.W.Fletcher 78, P.B.H.May 56, Lindwall 3-58, Johnston 4-51). AUSTRALIANS 327-9 (Morris 67, McDonald 30, Hassett 67, Harvey 113, P.J.Loader 3-74, W.S.Surridge 3-49). *Match drawn*

In response to Mr Aird, the Australian Board sent a cable: "Australian Board agrees to your suggestion that duration be increased to six days." On 29 July the selectors announced the first ten names invited to tour the West Indies next winter: Hutton (captain), May, Graveney, Compton, Watson, Bailey, Evans, Lock, Laker, Trueman. It was announced that Alec Bedser had agreed to take a winter's rest. With the addition of an opening batsman, this could very well be the XII players summoned for the Oval Test.

Having saved England with bat and ball at Leeds, Bailey was on show next day at Chelmsford. He made 68 not out in Essex's 392 for 6 declared and took 4-38 and 6-39 as Somerset fell to an innings defeat in two days. Middlesex beat Hampshire easily at Southampton. Sussex got no points due to a blank third day at Northampton. Northants made 330-1 dec, Sussex 300-6. Yorkshire gained their third championship win of the season, trouncing Kent by 152 runs. Trueman took 10-136 in the match. Lancashire set Worcestershire 337 to win at Blackpool despite several dropped catches won by 18 runs. Bob Berry, a slow left armer who toured Australia in 1950-51, took all ten for 102.

At the end of July, the championship seems to lie between Middlesex and Sussex. The top positions are: Middlesex 134 points from 21 games; Sussex 124 from 19; Glamorgan 116 from 20; Surrey 112 from 18; Lancashire 108 from 19; Leicestershire 104 from 20.

Harvey's tenth century: Swansea, August 1, 3, 4

The sun shone for the big seaside crowds at Swansea, and Harvey obliged again. Glamorgan staged a reasonable recovery after losing two wickets for nought to Johnston. Watkins, a left-hander who played for England in 1948, relished the short ball and hit 12 fours and a six. The selectors might well consider him to replace Watson for the Final Test. At the close Australia were 93-1, Harvey 20 not out. On Monday, he scored 132 in two hours before lunch. In all he made 180 out of 240 in 167 minutes with 3 sixes and 28 fours. This was his 10th century, with a further 11 matches, if he wanted to play in all of them, to pass Bradman's record of 13 centuries on an England tour, or conceivably threaten Denis Compton's 1947 record of 18, and all this in a wet season. For Haydn Davies, it was the best innings he had ever seen from behind the wicket. Then Craig got his first 50 of the tour. Glamorgan lost 6 for 62 by the close. But on Tuesday rain delayed the start to 1.45, and Wooller and Muncer had a match-saving stand of 125. The departure from Swansea is delayed when a window in the tourists' coach is broken by the swarm of autograph hunters.

GLAMORGAN 201 (W.G.A.Parkhouse 33, A.J.Watkins 76, Johnston 6-63, Davidson 2-32) and 188-7 (W.Wooller 71*, B.L.Muncer 56, Davidson 3-32). AUSTRALIANS 386 (Morris 48, McDonald 56, Harvey 180, Craig 50, J.E.McConnon 6-175). *Match drawn.*

The Bank holiday meant traditional county fixtures (which is why Glamorgan, the youngest first-class county) were lucky enough to get to play the touring team). At Hove, Middlesex put Sussex out for 118 but batted too slowly before a record 15,000 crowd on Monday. Sussex led by Doggart who made 104 in 280 minutes ensured at Middlesex got only four points. At the Oval, Surrey, who declared twice with three wickets down, set Notts 209 in 135 minutes. John Clay made 58 in 68 minutes. Wickets and runs came. The last wicket pair needed seven off the last over bowled by Lock, but off the first ball Rowe went for a sharp single, was sent back and could not beat Subba Row's throw to the wicketkeeper. Leicestershire made 311 for 2 to beat the hitherto undefeated Northants. The Roses match at Sheffield attracted 62,000. Lancashire elected not to enforce the follow on and set Yorkshire 356 in five hours. Yorkshire showed no interest in that unenterprising target. With two hours to go a storm saved Yorkshire when four wickets were left to fall. Trueman was now taking wickets and at the end of this match he learned that the selectors had secured from the Air Ministry a special extension of his leave for two more matches. Middlesex stayed top, Surrey displaced Sussex.

With some hindsight one might have been tempted to go to Lord's to see the Public Schools representative games, to see a certain E.R.Dexter, captain of Radley, bat, though he scored only 3 and 23 for Southern Schools v the Rest and 2 and 0 for the Public Schools v Combined Services.

1953 – FOURTH TEST

Hassett's duel with the Warwickshire crowd: Birmingham: August 5, 6, 7

The Australians, though fielding strong bowling side, had a poor day on Wednesday when Warwickshire made 225 for 4 in 250 minutes on a sluggish pitch. When Doug Ring was marking his run-up to bowl, the square leg umpire said the Ray Lindwall: "Is this Lindwall?"-"No"-"Who's Lindwall then?"-"I am", "Sorry, I thought you were bigger". The normally stodgy openers Gardner and Horner made 143 in 140 minutes, interrupted by a 105 minute break for rain. Gardner reached his century - the first ever for Warwickshire against Australia - but added only six on Thursday. Lindwall took 3 for 12 and then Dollery declared. Hassett and McDonald opened with 104 in nearly 1½ hours. Hassett lofted a catch to deep mid-off, then Hollies who changed ends had McDonald stumped, Hole lbw sweeping and Miller stumped yards out. In worsening light de Courcy was out and it was left to Craig and Benaud to take Australia coolly to 162 for 5 at the close.

On the final morning, they were all out after 40 minutes. Dollery soon declared the county second innings closed and Australia were set 166 in 170 minutes, of the face of it a generous gesture. But it was inspired. Dollery had spotted that the wicket was starting to take considerable spin at one end. Hollies opened the bowling, with three slips and it became obvious at once that the tourists would make no attempt at the target. Hassett and McDonald started with 12 in 55 minutes, Hassett and Hole 12 in 50, Hassett and Miller 15 in 30, Hassett and de Courcy 13 in 25 minutes. Craig was out first ball then Benaud stayed with Hassett for the last few minutes. Hassett gave a masterly display of concentrated defence against the turning ball on a variable pitch. He bore the brunt of Hollies' bowling, despite him changing ends more than once. But the crowd of 20,000 booed and slow handclapped. Cries of "Mind you don't hurt yourself", "Wakey, wakey!", "Oh, he's hit it". Twice play was stopped because of the noise. BBC Radio commentator Rex Alston told his audience that it was a travesty of cricket and advised them to switch off. Hollies told Hassett that the crowd were on the verge of invading; Hassett said ""The first one that comes near me gets my bat around his ear", But, said Hollies, "it's not the first one you'll have to worry about". The booing continued as Dollery shook hands with Hassett and the players walked off, separated by police from the crowd. Hassett was his phlegmatic self. He raised his cap the booers. And when the team coach left the ground to the accompaniment of more booers, Hassett booed back at them, causing momentary laughter.

The events of the day brought down an avalanche of criticism on Hassett and his men from the English Press. During the winter dust from the car park had been used to make the wicket faster. Fingleton backed them to the hilt: the pitch had small pebbles and sundry extraneous matter in it, Hollies was probably the best leg-spinner in England; and on true Test pitches at Lord's and Headingley Bailey's defensive marathons had been universally praised. But Barnes accused Australia of a travesty of sportsmanship, deriving from an obsession with avoiding defeat on the tour and thought that they could have won a thrilling victory if they had taken on the attack. Alston could see the justification for Hassett's attitude in terms of saving defeat and admired his wonderful performance, but thought that he should have made some effort, however slight, to go for victory before putting up the shutters. It was, he thought, a travesty of the game attributable the fetish for an unbeaten record.

Warwickshire (won toss)

F.C.Gardner lbw b Lindwall	110	not out	33
N.F.Horner lbw b Miller	61	hit wkt b Miller	12
J.R.Thompson c and b Miller	0	run out	16
J.S.Ord b Johnston	15	not out	1
*H.E.Dollery b Lindwall	18		
A.Townsend lbw b Lindwall	11		
+R.T.Spooner not out	21		
A.V.Wolton b Lindwall	4		
T.L.Pritchard b Miller	2	b Miller	2
Extras (b 15, lb 13)	28	(b 4, lb 4)	8
Total (for 8 wkts dec) (97.4 overs, 277 mins)	270	(3 wkts dec) (31 overs, 100 mins)	76

K.R.Dollery and W.E.Hollies did not bat
WICKETS.- 1-143, 2-143, 3-176, 4-217, 5-232, 6-255, 7-259, 8-270

1-20, 2-61, 3-71

BOWLING.- Lindwall 18-3-47-4; Johnston 27-6-84-1; Ring 15-5-25-0; Benaud 8-2-28-0; Hole 8-3-10-0; Miller 21.4-7-48-3

Lindwall 9-2-13-0; Johnston 7-3-21-0; Miller 15-4-34-2

1953 – FOURTH TEST

Australians

*A.L.Hassett c Hollies b Pritchard	60	not out	20
C.C.McDonald st Spooner b Hollies	46	c Townsend b Hollies	5
I.D.Craig c Gardner b Wolton	29	(6) lbw b Wolton	0
G.B.Hole lbw b Hollies	12	(3) c Townsend b Hollies	4
K.R.Miller st Spooner b Hollies	0	(4) b K Dollery	10
J.H.de Courcy lbw b Wolton	13	(5) c and b Wolton	11
R Benaud c Gardner b Hollies	7	not out	0
R.R.Lindwall b Wolton	1		
D. Ring c and b Pritchard	5		
W.A. Johnston not out	1		
+D.Tallon c Gardner b Hollies	1		
Extras (b 4, lb 1, nb 1)	6	(lb 2)	2
Total (97.3 overs, 288 mins)	**181**	**(58 overs, 170 mins)**	**53**

WICKETS.- 1-104, 2-112, 3-132, 4-143, 5-157, 6-166, 7-170, 8-179, 9-179, 10-181.
1-12, 2-24, 3-39, 4-52, 5-52

BOWLING.- Pritchard 32-11-60-2; K.Dollery 15-3-32-0; Hollies 33.3-15-45-5; Townsend 5-2-18-0; Wolton 12-2-20-3.

Pritchard 12-6-9-0; K.Dollery 6-0-16-1; Hollies 22-16-14-2; Townsend 3-1-2-0; Wolton 15-8-10-2.

Umpires: E.Cooke and A.E.Boulton-Carter

Middlesex won at Canterbury thanks to the spin bowling of Titmus and Young. At the end of Canterbury week, Kent's 13th defeat, the Kent players mutinied against their captain, Murray-Wood, and Douglas Wright was appointed for the rest of the season. Lancashire won at Nottingham. Glamorgan eschewed the challenge of scoring 302 in 3 hours set by Somerset. Surrey, for whom Lock was resting to save his finger, beat Hampshire by 105 runs at the Oval. At Hove Sussex followed on 241 behind Derbyshire; but with centuries by Suttle and Jim Parks junior, Sussex made 325; Derbyshire needing 85 in 55 minutes, were 82 for 7 at the close, losing one wicket for one run in the last over. Sussex emulated England's leg-theory tactics and the Derbyshire batsmen hit at everything. In an enthralling and absorbing three days at Leicester, Yorkshire declared with a three-run first innings lead at the end of the second day; Leicestershire batted boldly but Wardle took 7 for 74 and Yorkshire needed only 179 to win. Wardle joined Watson in a third wicket stand of 67 in half an hour. When last man Foord joined Trueman, 25 were needed in 22 minutes, and Trueman hit three successive fours but went out of his crease and was stumped, and Leicestershire won by six runs with 15 minutes to spare. The fox county moved up to third place, pushing Sussex down to fifth.

Unbroken sunshine: Manchester, August 8, 10,11

Morris got the innings off to a brilliant start, hitting 20 in one over in Statham's opening spell, which knocked the England pace bowler out of kilter. The lunch score was 106 for 4. But the spinners put on the brake and the innings subsided to 167-7, then Davidson, thrice dropped, and Ring put on 143 in 75 minutes. Of the eventual total of 372 in 310 minutes, 252 came in boundaries. On Monday, Lancashire opener Winston Place ducked into a short unrising ball from Miller and retired hurt with a crack above his ear. The county did better in the follow on. The Australian Ken Grieves and Geoffrey Edrich took their overnight stand to 104. Tallon conceded 18 byes in the innings. Needing 105 in under 2½ hours, the tourists won with over an hour left. The match was blessed with unbroken sunshine.

AUSTRALIANS 372 (Morris 64, Miler 30, Davidson 95, Ring 88, Lindwall 32, R.Tattersall 5-80, K.J.Grieves 3-23) and 106-3 (Morris 38, R.Tattersall 3-45). LANCASHIRE 184 (9 out) (W.Place ret hurt 38, K.J.Grieves 36, Miller 3-37) and 292 (9 out) (J.T.Ikin 56, G.A.Edrich 59, K.J.Grieves 80, Archer 3-45). *Australians won by three wickets.*

The championship leaders met at Lord's. Crowds of 25,000, 28,000 and 15,000 attended. Peter May picked the ideal occasion to make 159 in four hours on Saturday. On Monday Edrich became the first to 2,000 runs, Compton hit 113, but after tea Middlesex collapsed from 227-5 to 248 all out, with Laker taking 4 wickets in 10 balls. Surridge delayed his declaration until 3.45 on the last day. Middlesex were set 287 in 145 minutes and neither side showed any interest in a result. "Surrey and Middlesex spent a whole sunny day denying each other anything.... A Chinese puzzle beyond comprehension" wrote the *Times* correspondent. The crowd showed their lack of appreciation.

Again Sussex followed on and recovered in the second innings; needing 169 to win, Gloucestershire were 154 for 6 with 15 minutes left. Sheppard had instructed his bowlers to bowl leg theory to a leg-side field, Bailey-fashion, and the Cheltenham crowd slow handclapped. Gloucs captain Jack Crapp walked out and suggested that the match might as well be abandoned as a draw. Sheppard switched back to orthodox attack and Ian Thomson took three wickets in four balls, but Andy Wilson stood firm in the last over bowled by Marlar. Leicestershire won easily at home to Kent. Glamorgan got four points in a high scoring draw at Worcester.

On Saturday England's Test XII is announced. Simpson and, unluckily, Watson are dropped. May and Trueman come in. Lock remains a doubtful starter, the skin of his spinning finger having shown some wear, will not play again for Surrey before the Test starts. Wardle will play if Lock is unfit.

1948 revisited: Southend, August 12, 13

On this ground in 1948 Bradman's team made 721 all out on the first day and bowled Essex out twice on the second day. This year they made 477 for 7 on the first day in six hours, 102 overs, and bowled Essex out twice on the second day. Morris won the toss and set the tone with a quick 33. De Courcy hit four sixes over long on and one four to leg in one over of Greensmith's leg breaks. His 164 took 145 minutes. Even Trevor Bailey conceded 71 in 18 overs. On Thursday Ring and – good news for Australia – Johnston wrapped up victory on a wicket which had turned nasty. It was more like the nearby beach than a cricket pitch and the ball spun so much that four men were bowled behind their legs. In February this ground had been under four feet of Thames estuary water.

AUSTRALIANS 477-7dec (Hole 89, Morris 33, de Courcy 164, Davidson 58, Benaud 67). Essex 129 (R.Horsfall 26, Ring 5-47) and 136 (W.T.Greensmith 31, Johnston 6-39). *Australians won by an innings and 212 runs.*

Surrey led by 183 on first innings, centuries by Subba Row and Eric Bedser, and despite falling to 37-3 Leicestershire survived. At Portsmouth Glamorgan needed 224 in 140 minutes but shut up shop at 55-2. Sussex followed on again, this time at Birmingham, and just survived, their seventh draw in seven matches. Lancashire lost by one wickets to Northants. Yorkshire achieved their second victory in succession.

Trueman, back in the Test squad, took 4-65 and 6-47 for the Royal Air Force against the Royal Navy. (The match was played at Lord's which might be described as neutral territory.)

As thoughts turned away from the counties to the greater battle at hand, the last lap of the championship looked like this:

	Played	*W*	*L*	*D*	*Pts*	*Max poss*
Middlesex	24	10	2	10	150	198
Surrey	22	10	4	8	144	216
Leicestershire	24	9	5	10	140	188
Lancashire	22	8	3	8	124	196
Sussex	23	8	3	11	124	184
Glamorgan	23	8	2	11	120	180
Gloucestershire	23	8	4	9	120	180
Warwickshire	24	5	6	12	104	152
Derbyshire	23	6	7	8	96	156

Of the rest only Hampshire had a mathematical possibility of winning.

1953 – FIFTH TEST

FIFTH TEST AT THE OVAL
Kennington, August 15, 17, 18, 19

Six days should be ample time to decide this Test and the fate of the Ashes. The last fortnight has been the best weather of the summer and there are rumours of a heat-wave. As Arlott says, the two teams are so evenly balanced yet so dissimilar in make-up. Peter May, Jim Laker and Alec Bedser drove from Loughborough in Leicestershire on Friday evening. On the radio they heard the Australian team, and stopping at a village pub in Bedfordshire they discussed the astonishing news that the team contained no spinner. Lock, who has been resting from Surrey games bowls for an hour in the nets at Lords to the MCC Secretary R.Aird, watched by the chairman of the selectors, and his precious finger passes the test. Bradman says that if Australia win the toss, Australia will win the match. Queues started at noon on Friday. 2,000 queue overnight.

Umpires: F.S.Lee and D.Davies

Even contest: FIRST DAY, Saturday 15 August

The forecast is dull and overcast with scattered showers later. 22,000 queuing at 9am when gates open. But fear of a full house kept many away. In fact the ground is never full and the attendance was 26,300. Outside the ground was a teeming market-place for ticket touts, sellers of seats in flats outside the ground, purveyors of food, newspapers and souvenirs. England leave out Wardle. Lock is fit. At 10.45 he is told that he is playing. Australia go in to the Test without a spinner.

Australia win toss at 11am, Hassett calling heads again for the fifth time, though he says he makes up his mind as the coin is in the air. The crowd fall silent when informed. The wicket was shorn of grass and looks flat and true. Hassett has also won the 'dummy toss' done for Press photographers in the first four Tests, but now at last the dummy toss came down tails and Hassett has called wrongly for the first time. Hutton displayed such pleasure at this notional win that the England team in the dressing room prepared to bat.

Australia First Innings

Odd overs] ← from Vauxhall Road End
Even overs] → from Pavilion End

			Hassett	Morris		
1	11.30	Bedser 1] ←	- 4 1 - - -		 - 5	2 slips, gully, 2 short legs Hassett 4 to fine leg off full toss Hassett 1 to mid on Bailey moved to long leg Big cheer as Trueman takes the ball
2		Trueman 1] →	1 - - - - 1		 - 7	Hassett 1 to cover Bouncer to Morris. More cheers *Trueman's field 2 slips, gully, 2 short legs.* *Runs up off 25 yards* Appeal for catch behind Morris dropped by Cmptn at sht fine leg
3		Bedser 2] ←		- - 2 - 2 -	 - 11	
4		Trueman 2] →	- - - - - 1		 - 12	*Fast accurate over*
5		Bedser 3] ←	1	- - - - -	 - 13	

1953 – FIFTH TEST

6		Trueman 3] →	4 - - (1 nb) - 2 -		- 20	Hassett leg glance for 4 between Evans and Compton *Appeal for catch behind down leg side*
7		Bedser 4] ←		- - - 1 -	- 21	
8		Trueman 4] →		- - - - -	- 21	
9	12.00	Bedser 5] ←	3 - 1 -	1 1	- 27	*Slight drizzle*
10		Trueman 5] → off spell 5-1-12-0		- - - 2 1	- 30	Morris almost bowled Morris evades bouncer Morris almost yorked
11		Bedser 6] ←		- 1 - 1 -	- 32	*Still a few spots of rain*
12		Bailey 1] →	- - 1 - -		- 33	
13		Bedser 7] ←	- - - 1 -		- 34	
14		Bailey 2] →	- - - - -		- 34	*Bailey's first two overs too much wide of off stump*
15	12.25 12.27	Bedser 8] ←		- - 4 - W Miller -	1- 38 - 38	Morris 4 uppish through leg trap Morris lbw, no stroke to in-dipper, 16 in 55 mins, 49 balls, 1 four

1953 – FIFTH TEST

16		Bailey 3] →	1 1	- - - 1 (nb) 1		Miller 1 to covers, well stopped by Trueman
	12.31			W Harvey	2- 41	Miller lbw, in-dipper, 1 in 4 mins, 6 balls
17	12.33	Bedser 9] ←	1 	- - - -	- 42	
18		Bailey 4] →	2 - - 1	- - - 2	- 47	
19	12.43	Bedser 10] ← off spell 10-0-30-1	1 	- - 4 - -	- 52	Harvey 4 off-drive. 52 up in 73 mins
20		Bailey 5] →	- - - - 1		- 53	
21		Trueman 6] ←	4 - - - -		- 57	Hassett 4 to leg off full toss
22		Bailey 6] →		- 2 - - -	- 59	
23		Trueman 7] ←	- - - 4 3	-	- 66	Hassett swings 4 Hassett on-drive for 3
24		Bailey 7] → off spell 7-1-16-1	- - - 1	- - - - 3	- 70	
25		Trueman 8] ← off spell 3-0-21-0	 3	2 - 1 - 4	- 80	
26		Bedser 11] →	2 - - 2 1	-	- 85	

1953 – FIFTH TEST

27	1.15	Lock 1] ←	- - 1 - -		 - 86	Hassett 50 in 105 mins, 81 balls, then asks for new bat
28		Bedser 12] →	- - - - -		 - 86	
29		Lock 2] ←	- - 2 1 - -		 - 89	
30		Bedser 13] → off spell 3-1-6-0	- - - 1 - -		 - 90	
31		Lock 3] ← spell 3-0-8-0	- - 4 - - -		 - 94	Harvey square cut for 4 past cover
32	1.30	Trueman 9] →	1 2 - 1 - -		 - 98	Hassett pulls back due to sparrow on pitch, dead ball Bouncer
		LUNCH	Hassett 51 120 mins 94 balls	Harvey 29 57 mins 45 balls	2- 98 120 mins 194 balls	

A fair morning for Australia. Morris has fallen to Bedser once in each of the five Tests. Light rain for 20 minutes during lunch. This gives the pitch some extra life.

			Hassett 51	Harvey 29	2- 98	
33	2.10	Bedser 14] ←	 1 	- - 1 1	 - 101	
34		Trueman 10] →	 1 	- - 1 1	 - 104	
35	2.25 2.27	Bedser 15] ←	 W Hole - - -	- 3 (nb) 	 3- 107 - 107	Hassett c Evans (wk) standing up, ball moved away late, 53 in 135 min, 99 balls, 4 fours

192

1953 – FIFTH TEST

Over	Time	Bowler	Batsman 1	Batsman 2	W/Score	Notes
36		Trueman 11] →		- - W de Courcy 2 (nb) 2 -	4- 107 - 111	Harvey c Hutton, running back from mid wkt, late hook, 36 in 77 mins, 60 balls, 3 fours Rain
	2.30					
	2.32					
	2.35					

A short shower drives the players off, then bright sunshine appears for the first time. The crowd are impatient for a re-start.

Over	Time	Bowler	Batsman 1	Batsman 2	Score	Notes
37	2.44	Bedser 16] ←		4 (nb) - 1 - - 1 -	- 117	de Courcy 4 to long on over bowler's head Hole dropped at leg slip by Lock, sharp chance
38	2.50 2.52	Trueman 12] →	1 2 2	- W Archer 1	5- 118 - 123	de Courcy c Evans (wk), following an away-dipper, 5 in 9 mins, 6 balls, 1 four
39		Bedser 17] ←	4 1	1 - -	- 129	Hole 4 on-drive
40		Trueman 13] →	4 1	 - - -	- 134	Hole 4, intended hook edged over slips *Six slips for Archer*
41		Bedser 18] ←	1 1	- - - 	- 136	
42		Trueman 14] → off spell (incl. lunch) 6-0-25-2	 - - 2 -	- 1 	- 139	
43		Bedser 19] ←	 1	- - 1 -	- 141	
44		Bailey 8] →	2 - 1	 - (1 nb) - -	- 145	
45		Bedser 20] ← off spell 7-0-25-1	- 1 1	- - 1 	- 148	

1953 – FIFTH TEST

46	3.22	Bailey 9] →	1	- 1 - - -	- 150	150 up in 183 mins
47		Lock 4] ←		- - - - -	- 150	
48		Bailey 10] → off spell 3-0-9-0	- - - 2 2		- 154	
49		Lock 5] ←		- - - - 1	- 155	
50		Trueman 15] →	1	- - - 1	- 157	
51		Lock 6] ← off spell 3-1-4-0	1 1	1 - - -	- 160	
52	3.40 3.42	Trueman 16] →	-	W Davidson - - -	6- 160 - 160	Hole c Evans (wk) chasing wide out-swinger, 37 in 64 mins, 47 balls, 2 fours *Trueman clutches his side, apparently having a 'stitch'*
53	3.46 3.48	Bedser 21] ←		W Lindwall - - - -	7- 160 - 160	Archer c & b, driving at slower ball, 10 in 54 mins, 48 balls, 0 fours. Bedser's 39th wicket in the series- a new record for Ashes series
54		Trueman 17] →	1	- 1 - -	- 162	
55		Bedser 22] ←		- - - - -	- 162	
56		Trueman 18] → off spell 5-1-8-1	1	- - 2 1 -	- 166	

194

1953 – FIFTH TEST

57		Bedser 23] ←		- - 1 - -	- 167	
58		Bailey 11] →		- - - - -	- 167	
59		Bedser 24] ← spell 4-2-12-1	1 1 1	4 1 - 4	- 178	Lindwall 4 through covers Lindwall 4 through covers
60	4.15	Bailey 12] →	- - - - -		- 178	
		TEA	Dvdsn 4 33 mins 21 balls	Lindwl 14 27 mins 30 balls	7- 178 236 mins 367 balls	Hot and sultry

SESSION 80-5 in 116 mins, 173 balls. Yet again the Australian middle order fails.

		Evening	Dvdsn 4	Lindwll 14	7- 178	
61	4.35	Laker 1] ←		1 - - - 1	- 180	*Davidson dropped by Edrich at slip, one-handed chance*
62		Bailey 13] →	4 - - 4 - 4		- 192	Davidson 4 to square cover Davidson 4 to extra cover Davidson 4 to long leg
63		Laker 2] ←		- - - - 4 2	- 198	Laker 4 swung fine to long leg
64	4.47	Bailey 14] → off spell (incl. tea) 4-2-17-0	1	- - 2 - 2	- 203	201 up in 248 mins
65	4.50 4.52	Laker 3] ← off spell 3-0-15-1	4 W Langley 1 - 2 -		8- 207 - 210	Davidson 4 square cut Davidson c Edrich, edged off back foot to slip diving low to right, 22 in 48 mins, 35 balls, 4 fours Lindwall slices over extra cover, between Bdsr & Grvny who gets to it but drops it
66		Trueman 19] →	- - - - -		- 210	New ball taken

1953 – FIFTH TEST

#	Time	Bowler			Total	Notes
67		Bedser 25] ←		- - - 1 - -	- 211	
68		Trueman 20] →	4 4 - -	1	- 220	Langley hooks bumper for 4
69		Bedser 26] ←		- - 1 - 1	- 222	
70		Trueman 21] →	- 1	- 2 - 1	- 226	
71		Bedser 27] ← off spell 3-0-5-0	1	- - - 1 - (4 bye)	- 232	
72		Trueman 22] → off spell 4-1-15-0	- 1	- 1 - -	- 234	
73		Lock 7] ←		- 4 - - -	- 238	
74		Laker 4] →	2 - 3	- - 2	- 245	
75	5.30 5.32	Lock 8] ←	- W Johnston - - -		9- 245 - 245	Langley c Edrich, outside edge to slip, 18 in 38 mins, 29 balls, 2 fours
76	 5.38	Laker 5] → off spell 2-0-19-0		- 2 2 - 4 4	- 257	Lindwall cover-drive Lindwall cover-drive, 53 in 90m 79 b
77		Lock 9] ← off spell 3-1-7-1	- - - 3 -	- -	- 260	Johnston off-drive for 3

1953 – FIFTH TEST

Over	Time	Bowler	Runs	Balls	Score	Notes
78		Trueman 23] →	- - 1 - -		- 261	Johnston dropped by Bedser at 3rd slip
79		Bedser 28] ←	1 - - 4 - -		- 266	
80		Trueman 24] →	- - 4 - -		- 270	Johnston 4 through covers
81		Bedser 29] ← spell 2-0-10-0	- - - 4 (nb) - 1	-	- 275	
82	6.00	Trueman 25] → spell 2.3-0-5-1	- - W			Lindwall c Evans (wk) 62 in 112 mins, 97 balls, 8 fours
			Johnstn 9 28 mins 20 balls		10- 275 321 mins 496 balls	

SESSION 97-3 in 85 mins, 129 balls

Australia First innings

A.L. Hassett	c Evans b Bedser	53	135 min, 99 balls, 4 fours	3-107
A.R. Morris	lbw b Bedser	16	55 mins, 49 balls, 1 four	1-38
K.R. Miller	lbw b Bailey	1	4 mins, 6 balls	2-41
R.N. Harvey	c Hutton b Trueman	36	77 mins, 60 balls, 3 fours	4-107
G.B. Hole	c Evans b Trueman	37	64 mins, 47 balls, 2 fours	6-160
J.H. de Courcy	c Evans b Trueman	5	9 mins, 6 balls, 1 four	5-118
R.G. Archer	c & b Bedser	10	54 mins, 48 balls, 0 fours	7-160
A.K. Davidson	c Edrich b Laker	22	48 mins, 35 balls, 4 fours	8-207
R.R. Lindwall	c Evans b Trueman	62	112 mins, 97 balls, 8 fours	10-275
G.R. Langley	c Edrich b Lock	18	38 mins, 29 balls, 2 fours	9-245
W.A. Johnston	not out	9	28 mins, 20 balls, 1 four	
Extras	(b 4, nb 2)	6		
TOTAL	(for 10 wkts)	275	321 mins, 496 balls, 81.3 overs	

BOWLING

	O	M	R	W	
Bedser	29	3	88	3	(3 nb)
Trueman	24.3	3	86	4	(2 nb)
Bailey	14	3	42	1	(2 nb)
Lock	9	2	19	1	
Laker	5	0	34	1	

Johnston now has a tour average of 64. Trueman leads the England side off.

Alston: England missed a glorious chance to press home the advantage after tea. Lindwall's innings had incalculable value. The gamble with Trueman paid off. His pace made the batsmen play too late.

Cardus: the play was largely commonplace and anonymous, except for the gusto of young Trueman and the acrobatics of Evans in keeping to him.

Brown is impressed by Trueman's away-swing, his aggressive attitude, and his good use of the bouncer.

Bailey thinks that England were lucky not to be batting first; Lindwall and Miller would have made much of the enlivened wicket after lunch. So also says Bedser.

Arlott: despite four dropped catches, England's fielding was probably its best of the series, Trueman being superb. But Cutler says that the fielding was village green standard.

Graveney takes the blame for dropping Lindwall in the 65th over. He left the catch for the man behind him, then suddenly remembered it was Alec Bedser, tired from bowling, and turned back for the catch, got there in time only for it to pop out of his hands.

Bowes: When he lost the toss Hutton would have settled gladly for an Australian score of 275 or more.

1953 – FIFTH TEST

England First Innings

Odd overs → [from Vauxhall Road End
Even overs ← [from Pavilion End

			Hutton	Edrich		
1	6.10	Lindwall 1 → [spell 1-1-0-0	- - - - -		- 0	Bouncer Ball goes of shoulder of bat, just short of slip, Hutton's cap falls close to stumps
2		Miller 1 ← [spell 1-0-1-0		- - - - 1	- 1	Edrich pulls for 1. Bad light
	6.17					
		CLOSE	Hutton 0 7 mins 6 balls	Edrich 1 7mins 6 balls	0- 1 7mins 12 balls	

Hutton was wearing his lucky cap, the one he wore at the Oval in 1938.

Sunday

Bailey was billed to play in a match at the home of Southend Club of which he was president, upon the opening of new Pavilion. Unwilling to play in the middle of the Test, but loathe to disappoint the local supporters, he opened the Pavilion and batted for a short time.

England despondent: SECOND DAY, Monday 17 August

Thousands of people locked out. Mounted police are there to hold them at bay. A bright sunny day with patches of very thin cloud.

			Hutton 0	Edrich 1	0- 1	
3	11.30	Lindwall 2 → [		- - - - -	- 1	*5 slips, 2 leg slips* Edrich plays and misses
4		Miller 2 ← [	- - - - -		- 1	*One bouncer*
5		Lindwall 3 → [	- - 2 4	- 1 -	- 8	Edrich 1 pushed to mid on Hutton 2 snicked to leg Hutton 4 leg glanced
6		Miller 3 ← [	- - - 4 -	- 1	- 13	Hutton 4 to long leg off bumper
7		Lindwall 4 → [	2 - - -	3	- 18	Edrich on-drive for 3
8		Miller 4 ← [	- - - 4 1		- 23	Edrich 4 guided to third man

1953 – FIFTH TEST

9		Lindwall 5 → [		1 - - - 2	- 26	
10		Miller 5 ← [		4 4 - 1 1	- 36	Edrich hooks 4 square Edrich soft hook for 4 through Lindwall's hands at fine leg
11	12.01	Lindwall 6 → [		- - 1 - - W May	1 – 37	Edrich almost plays on off pads Edrich lbw, forcing full-toss to on, only bowler appealed, 21 in 38 mins, 33 balls, 3 fours
12	12.02	Miller 6 ← [		- - 1 - -	- 38	May beaten first ball by yorker
13		Lindwall 7 → [off spell 6-1-19-1	1 1 - 1 -		- 41	
14		Miller 7 ← [	- - 1 - -		- 42	
15		Johnston 1 → [	1 - 1 - -		- 44	*Johnston bowling at medium pace*
16		Miller 8 ← [off spell 7-1-26-0		- - 4 - -	- 48	Attempted leg break, May 4 off full toss past point. Next ball a bouncer
17	12.20	Johnston 2 → [	- 2 - 1 -		- 51	50 up in 57 mins
18		Davidson 1 ← [	(1 wide) . - - 1 1		- 54	*Davidson left arm over fast medium*
19		Johnston 3 → [		- - 2 - -	- 56	

1953 – FIFTH TEST

20		Davidson 2 ← [	- - 1 - - -		- 57	May flashes and misses
21		Johnston 4 → [	- - - 4 - -		- 61	*Johnston switches to spin over the wicket* Hutton 4 over the wicket
22		Davidson 3 ← [	- 1 - 1 - -		- 63	
23		Johnston 5 → [	- - - 4 - -		- 67	
24		Davidson 4 ← [off spell 4-0-7-0	- - 1 - - 1		- 69	
25		Johnston 6 → [	- - - - - -		- 69	
26		Archer 1 ← [	- - 4 (nb) - - -		- 73	May 4 slashed over slips
27		Johnston 7 → [	- - - - - -		- 73	
28		Archer 2 ← [off spell 2-0-8-0	4 - - - - -		- 77	May 4 forced off toes
29		Johnston 8 → [	- - - - - -		- 77	
30		Lindwall 8 ← [	- - - 1 - -		- 78	

200

1953 – FIFTH TEST

31		Johnston 9 → [		- - - - -	- 78	
32		Lindwall 9 ← [	1	- - - -	- 79	Hutton's first run for 7 overs
33		Johnston 10 → [off spell 10-4-16-0	- - 1 - -		- 80	Hutton 1 pushed into covers
34		Lindwall 10 ← [off spell 3-0-5-0	- 1 1	1 -	- 83	
35		Davidson 5 → [	- - 2 - -		- 85	
36		Miller 9 ← [		- - - -	- 85	
37		Davidson 6 → [spell 2-0-6-0	- - 4 - -		- 89	Hutton hits wide full toss over slips for 4
38	1.30	Miller 10 ← [		- - - - -	- 89	
		LUNCH	Hutton 46 127 mins 115 balls	May 21 88 mins 81 balls	1- 89 127 mins 229 balls (and 1 w)	

SESSION **88-1 in 120 mins, 217 balls**
Times correspondent: The Australian attack is not only innocuous but also monotone.
Arlott: The batsmen have prodded the pitch with curiosity. Johnston may hold the key.
BOYS are perched on the top of the outside wall. Buses filled with faces at the windows crawl slowly round the Harleyford Road.

1953 – FIFTH TEST

		Afternoon	Hutton 46	May 21	1- 89	
39	2.10	Archer 3 → [	- 2 1 - - -		- 92	Delay while spectators sit down
40	2.17	Miller 11 ← [	- - 1 - - -		- 93	Hutton 50 in 134 mins, 121 balls, sharp single on off-side, Miller throws at wicket and May might have been run out if stumps hit
41		Archer 4 → [	- 1 - - - -		- 94	
42	2.25	Miller 12 ← [	- - 4 - - 4		- 102	Hutton 4 through covers Hutton 4 leg glance. 102 up in 142 mins
43		Archer 5 → [		- - 4 - - -	- 106	May 4 through covers. May hit to mid wkt and Hutton runs; Hsstt throws to Archer who breaks wkt without ball, Hutton stranded
44		Miller 13 ← [	- - - - 2		- 108	
45		Archer 6 → [off spell 3-0-12-0		4 - - - - -	- 112	May 4 through covers
46		Miller 14 ← [off spell (incl. lunch) 6-2-12-0	1	- - - - -	- 113	
47		Johnston 11 → [	- 1	- - - 4	- 118	May 4 swung high to sq leg, almost six
48		Lindwall 11 ← [	- - - - -		- 118	
49		Johnston 12 → [off spell 2-0-9-0		- - - - 4	- 122	*May almost bowled* May square cover drive for 4

1953 – FIFTH TEST

#	Time	Bowler			Score	Notes
50		Lindwall 12 ← [	- - - 1	- -	- 123	
51		Davidson 7 → [	- 1	1	- 125	
52		Lindwall 13 ← [		- - - 1	- 126	*Surrey Secretary B.K.Castor shoos away the pigeons over the loudspeaker*
53		Davidson 8 → [		- - - -	- 126	
54		Lindwall 14 ← [off spell 4-1-7-0	- 2 - - 2 1		- 131	
55		Davidson 9 → [off spell 3-1-7-0	- 4 - - - 1		- 136	Hutton straight drive off full toss
56	3.10 3.12	Johnston 13 ← [	1	- W Compton - - -	2- 137 - 137	May c Archer, turns ball to bkwd short leg, 39 in 148 mins, 134 balls, 7 fours
57		Hole 1 → [	- - - - -		- 137	
58		Johnston 14 ← [		- - - - -	- 137	
59		Hole 2 → [	1	- - - -	- 138	
60		Johnston 15 ← [	- 3 - - - 1		- 142	Hutton 3 edged uppishly through gully 6th ball: Comptn calls Hutton for risky single to get off mark, de Crcy's throw from cover misses stumps

1953 – FIFTH TEST

61	3.28	Hole 3 → [		4 - (4 bye) - 1 - -	- 151	Compton off-drive for 4 of full toss Compton almost bowled, ball goes for byes, 150 up n 205 mins
62		Johnston 16 ← [		- - - - -	- 151	
63		Hole 4 → [		- - 2 - -	- 153	
64		Johnston 17 ← [		- - - - 1	- 155	
65		Hole 5 → [		- - - - -	- 155	Hutton only 6 runs in last half hour
66	3.41 3.43	Johnston 18 ← [	W Graveney	- - - -	3- 154 - 154	Hutton bld, off-stump, playing around yorker, 82 in 218 mins, 185 balls, 8 fours. First bowled victim of the match *New ball now available*
67		Hole 6 → [		- - - - -	- 154	
68		Johnston 19 ← [	2	- - - -	- 156	Graveney 2 past cover
69		Hole 7 → [off spell 7-4-8-0		- - - - -	- 156	
70		Johnston 20 ← [		- - - - -	- 156	
71		Archer 7 → [		- - - 2 (nb) 1 -	- 159	

1953 – FIFTH TEST

Over	Time	Bowler	Batsman A	Batsman B	Score	Notes
72		Johnston 21 ← [		- - 2 - 4 -	- 165	Compton hook for 4
73		Archer 8 → [spell 2-1-3-0	- - - - -		- 165	Graveney goes for run to mid-on; sent back by Compton, he has to dive for crease as Hassett's throw hits wicket
74	4.15	Johnston 22 ← [off spell 10-5-14-2		- - - - -	- 165	
		TEA	Gravny 2 32 mins 25 balls	Comptn 16 63 mins 69 balls	3- 165 252 mins 446 balls	

SESSION 76-2 in 125 mins, 217 balls

For about three overs before he was out, Hutton could not see the ball after it left the bowler's hand. He did not see three balls that he missed outside the off-stump from Johnston and did not see the ball that bowled him.

England, and especially Compton surrendered the initiative in the last hour before tea when only 28 runs were scored.

Alston: the inept batting of Compton and Graveney is threatening to undo the good work of the first three batsmen.

Arlott: In county cricket Graveney and Compton would get enough bad balls to keep the score moving even when in defensive mode, but Hassett's team bowl no rubbish.

Times correspondent: Putting Johnston on from the Pavilion End at 3.10 was the turning point.

Over	Time	Bowler	Batsman A	Batsman B	Score	Notes
			Gravny 2	Comptn 16	3- 165	
75	4.35	Miller 15 → [	- - 2 - -		- 167	
76	4.40 4.42	Lindwall 15 ← [		W Bailey 2 1 - -	4- 167 - 170	Compton c Langley (wk) down leg-side, lifting ball, 16 in 68 min, 70 balls, 2 fours
77		Miller 16 → [		- - - - -	- 170	
78	4.49 4.50	Lindwall 16 ← [	- W Evans 1 - 4 -	1 (nb)	5- 170 - 176	New ball taken Graveney c Miller, 1st slip, outside edge, flings himself downward to take boot high catch, 4 in 46 mins, 36 balls, 0 fours Evans 4 slashed through Davidson's hands at slip
79		Miller 17 → [		- - - - -	- 176	*Five slips for Miller*

1953 – FIFTH TEST

80		Lindwall 17 ← [	- - 1 - -		- 177	
81		Miller 18 → [	- - 3 - - 1		- 181	
82		Lindwall 18 ← [	- - 1 1 - -		- 183	
83		Miller 19 → [	- 4 - - 2 -		- 189	Evans 4 glanced to long leg
84		Lindwall 19 ← [off spell 5-022-2	1 - 4 4 1 -		- 199	Evans 4 hooked square Evans 4 fine glance
85	5.15	Miller 20 → [	1 - - -	1	- 201	200 up in 292 mins
86		Johnston 23 ← [	- - - - -		- 201	
87		Miller 21 → [	1 - - -	1	- 203	
88		Johnston 24 ← [	- - - - 1		- 204	
89		Miller 22 → [	- - - - -		- 204	
90		Johnston 25 ← [	1 - - W Laker	4 (nb) 1	- 210	Evans hooks long hop almost for six Evans run out, goes for run to Dvdsn fine leg, sent back by Bailey, falls in turning, gets up and dives back one foot short, 28 in 45 mins, 34 balls, 4 fours
	5.35					

1953 – FIFTH TEST

91	5.37	Miller 23 → [		- 1 - 1		
				1	- 213	
92		Johnston 26 ← [		- 4 - 2 4 1	- 224	Bailey 4 off-drive Bailey 4 off-drive
93		Miller 24 → [		- - 1		
	5.46		W Lock		7- 225	Laker c Langley (wk) ball lifts and moves away, 1 in 9 mins, 3 balls
	5.48			- -	- 225	
94		Johnston 27 ← [		- 1 - - -	- 226	
95		Miller 25 → [		- - - - -	- 226	
96		Johnston 28 ← [	- 1	- 1 - -	- 228	*Lock dropped by Davidson at bkwd square leg*
97		Miller 26 → [off spell 12-4-21-1		- - - 1 - -	- 229	
98		Johnston 29 ← [		1 - - - -	- 230	
99		Lindwall 20 → [		- - - - -	- 230	
100		Johnston 30 ← [	- - - - -		- 230	
101		Lindwall 21 → [		1 - - - -	- 231	

1953 – FIFTH TEST

102		Johnston 31 ← [off spell 9-3-22-0		- - - - -	- 231	
103		Lindwall 22 → [	- 2 - - -		- 233	
104		Miller 27 ← [spell 1-1-0-0		- - - - -	- 233	
105	6.30	Lindwall 23 → [spell 4-1-5-0	1	1 - - -	- 235	
		CLOSE	Lock 4 42 mins 39 balls	Bailey 35 108 mins 100 balls	7- 235 367 mins 634 balls	

SESSION 70-4 in 115 mins, 188 balls

A disappointing final session for England. They are 40 behind with three wickets left and will have to bat last, though there is consolation in the absence of an Australian spinner.

Evans run out: Evans thought that Davidson at fine leg was fielding deeper. Davidson was supposed to be deep when Evans was facing and up to save one for Bailey. But when Bailey took a single, Davidson forgot to drop back and Evans did not appreciate that.

West: "In common with many others, I cannot help felling that the Ashes are likely to stay in Australia's keeping."

Alston: England to-day achieved a scoring rate of 38 runs per hour, on a sunny day. Yesterday in poor light and a humid atmosphere, Australia scored at 51 per hour.

Swanton: Evans' run out was a breach of the basic rules of calling; Evans should not have run unless called by Bailey.

Arlott: This was by far the unhappiest innings I have ever seen Compton play. His spark has gone, at least temporarily. Miller has bowled as fast as ever to-day and deserves better figures. The match seems to be within Australia's compass. England will not get the lead of 100 which they really need, but their ability to fight in adversity always gives some hope.

The decisive shift: THIRD DAY, Tuesday 18 August

Light rain at 6 am. Heavy roller applied. Pitch easy-paced. Ground almost full when play starts.

			Lock 4	Bailey 35	7- 235	
106	11.30	Miller 28 ← [		- - - - -	- 235	*Miller bowls round the wicket to Bailey*
107		Lindwall 24 → [	(1 bye) -	- - 1 -	- 237	Bailey glances for 1 to long leg
108		Miller 29 ← [		- - - - -	- 237	

1953 – FIFTH TEST

109	11.40 11.42	Lindwall 25 → [	W Trueman - - - -		8- 237 - 237	Lock c Davidson, bkwd short leg, ct off gloves fending off lifting ball, 4 in 52 mins, 43 balls, 0 fours
110		Miller 30 ← [		2 - - - -	- 239	
111		Lindwall 26 → [	(1 lb) - - - - -		- 240	
112		Miller 31 ← [off spell 4-2-3-0	- 1 - - -		- 241	
113		Lindwall 27 → [	1 4 - - -		- 246	Bailey 4 to square leg off full toss
114	12.00	Johnston 32 ← [	- 4 (2 bye) - - 1	1	- 254	Trueman off-side 4:- 250 up in 397 mins Trueman scoop stroke, Hole from 1st slip to short leg almost catches it
115		Lindwall 28 → [	- 1 - - -		- 255	de Courcy saves 4 runing from fine leg and throws fast and flat to Langley
116		Johnston 33 ← [	- - 1 - -		- 256	
117		Lindwall 29 → [	- - - - -		- 256	*Lindwall bowls bumpers to Bailey*
118		Johnston 34 ← [	- 3 - - -		- 259	Trueman 3, misfield by Harvey at cover
119		Lindwall 30 → [	(1 lb) - - - 2 -		- 262	

1953 – FIFTH TEST

120	12.17 12.19	Johnston 35 ← [	W Bedser - - 2 - -		9- 262 - 264	Trueman bld round his legs, 10 in 35 mins, 24 balls, 1 four Bedser tells Bailey: don't farm the bowling, let's take every run we can get Bedser 2 to leg
121		Lindwall 31 → [	1 - - 1 - -		 - 266	Bedser 1 edging bumper over gully's head
122	12.28	Johnston 36 ← [	- 1 4 - -		 - 271	Bailey late cut for 4, 52 in 166 mins, 161 balls
123		Lindwall 32 → [off spell 9-3-12-1	- 1 - - -		 - 272	
124		Johnston 37 ← [	- - - - -		 - 272	*Johnston bowls round the wicket with five close fielders, getting some turn and lift.*
125		Miller 32 → [	- - - - -		 - 272	
126	12.40	Johnston 38 ← [	- - - - 4 -		 - 276	Bedser 4 all run, lofted shot bounces in front of Miller at mid-off; he does not bother to chase it. England take lead.
127		Miller 33 → [	- - - - -		 - 276	
128		Johnston 39 ← [	- - 1 - 1 -		 - 278	
129		Miller 34 → [off spell 3-2-2-0	- 1 - 1 -		 - 280	
130		Johnston 40 ← [	- (3 bye) - - - -		 - 283	

1953 – FIFTH TEST

131		Hole 8 → [	- - - - -		- 283	
132		Johnston 41 ← [		- - - - -	- 283	
133		Hole 9 → [	- - - - -		- 283	
134		Johnston 42 ← [		- - - - 4	- 287	Bailey hook to long leg for 4
135		Hole 10 → [	1 - - - -		- 288	
136		Johnston 43 ← [		- - - - -	- 288	
137		Hole 11 → [off spell 4-2-3-0	2 - - - -		- 290	
138		Johnston 44 ← [		- - 1 - -	- 291	
139		Archer 9 → [	(2 byes) - - - - -		- 293	
140		Johnston 45 ← [off spell 14-4-33-1		1 - 4 - - -	-298	Bedser back-foot cover-drive for 4
141		Archer 10 → [	1 - - - -		- 299	

1953 – FIFTH TEST

142		Davidson 10 ← [1-0-6-0		1 - 1 - 1 3	- 305	Bailey places to cover for 1 – 300 up Bailey 1 to third man
143	1.30	Archer 11 → [spell 2.3-2-1		1 - W	10 – 306	Bailey bld leg stump, playing forward, 64 in 228 mins, 222 balls, 6 fours
		LUNCH	Bedser 22 71 mins 75 balls		10-306 487 mins 859 balls	

SESSION 71-3 in 120 mins, 225 balls

ENGLAND FIRST INNINGS

L. Hutton	b Johnston	82	218 mins, 185 balls, 8 fours	3-154
W.J. Edrich	lbw b Lindwall	21	38 mins, 33 balls, 3 fours	1-37
P.B.H. May	c Archer b Johnston	39	148 mins, 134 balls, 7 fours	2-137
D.C.S. Compton	c Langley b Lindwall	16	68 min, 70 balls, 2 fours	4-167
T.W. Graveney	c Miller b Lindwall	4	46 mins, 36 balls, 0 fours	5-170
T.E. Bailey	b Archer	64	228 mins, 222 balls, 6 fours	10-306
T.G. Evans	run out (Davidson/Langley)	28	45 mins, 34 balls, 4 fours	6-210
J.C. Laker	c Langley b Miller	1	9 mins, 3 balls	7-225
G.A.R. Lock	c Davidson b Lindwall	4	52 mins, 43 balls, 0 fours	8-237
F.S. Trueman	b Johnston	10	35 mins, 24 balls, 1 four	9-262
A.V. Bedser	not out	22	71 mins, 75 balls, 2 fours	
Extras	(b 9, lb 5, w 1)	15		
TOTAL	(for 10 wkts)	306	487 mins, 859 balls, 142.3 overs	

BOWLING

Lindwall	32	7	70	4	(1 nb)
Miller	34	12	65	1	
Johnston	45	16	94	3	(1 nb)
Davidson	10	1	26	1	(1 w)
Archer	10.3	2	25	1	(2 nb)
Hole	11	6	11	0	

Once again England have been 'baileyed-out'. The pitch remains benign and Australia have a chance to forge ahead.
Cardus: Bailey's batting was not merely monumental but geological. He bats, if not for eternity, at least for posterity.
Arlott: It is anyone's guess what will happen next.
Bailey says that he was bowled by a ball that pitched well outside the off-stump. The turn achieved by Johnston makes Bailey think that England have the match in their grasp.
England lead by 31

Australia Second Innings

Odd overs:] → from Pavilion End
Even overs:] ← from Vauxhall Road End

			Hassett	Morris		
1	2.10	Bedser 1] →	2 (2 byes) - 2 - - 2		- 8	Hassett drive to mid on for 2 2 byes, fumble by Evans
2		Trueman 1] ←	- - - 4 - -		- 12	Morris hooks 4 to mid wkt. No-one moves
3		Bedser 2] →	- 1 - - - 2		- 15	Morris 2 past cover

1953 – FIFTH TEST

4		Trueman 2] ← Off Spell 2-1-4-0	- - - - -		- 15	
5		Bedser 3] → off spell 3-0-13-0	- - 4 - - -		- 19	
6	2.35	Laker 1] ←	1 - 2 W Hole	- 1	1- 23	Laker rubs ball on ground. 1 slip, 2 short legs, bowling round the wicket Hassett play and misses Hassett 2 to fine leg Hassett lbw, playing back and across, 10 in 25 mins, 18 balls, 0 fours
7	2.37	Lock 1] →	- - - - -		- 23	*Lock bowls over the wicket to left-handers*
8		Laker 2] ←	2 - - 1 4	1	- 31	Hole cuts for 2 Hole sweeps for 4
9		Lock 2] →	- - - -	1	- 32	Australia go ahead
10		Laker 3] ←	- - - - -		- 32	*Laker has only one slip for Morris*
11		Lock 3] →	- - - - -		- 32	
12		Laker 4] ←	- 2 - 4 -		- 38	Morris cuts 2 through point Morris 4 cover drive
13		Lock 4] →	- - - - -		- 38	
14		Laker 5] ←	- 4 - - -		- 42	

1953 – FIFTH TEST

15		Lock 5] →	- - 2 - 2 -		- 46	
16		Laker 6] ←	- - - - - -		- 46	
17	3.05	Lock 6] →	1 1 - (1 bye) - -		- 50	50 up in 55 mins
18		Laker 7] ←	1 (2 bye) - - - -		- 53	
19		Lock 7] →	- - - (2 lb) - -		- 55	
20	3.14 3.15	Laker 8] ←	- 4 W Harvey - 1 -		2- 59 - 60	Hole sweeps 4. Laker puts out a deep extra cover and a long on Hole lbw, on back foot, 17 in 37 mins, 40 balls, 2 fours Harvey short single to extra cover
21	3.19 3.21	Lock 8] →	W Miller - - - -		3- 60 - 60	Harvey bld, plays over ball on-driving, 1 in 4 mins, 3 balls . The crowds, inside and outside the ground, erupt. Buses have now brought Harleyford Road to a standstill.
22	3.25 3.26	Laker 9] ←	1 - - W de Courcy -		4- 61 - 61	Miller c Trueman at short square leg, 0 in 4 mins, 8 balls
23	3.28 3.30	Lock 9] →	W Archer - - 2 1		5- 61 - 64	Morris lbw, ball fizzes in, 26 in 78 mins, 62 balls, 4 fours Archer 2 just over cover – Graveney has run in too quickly
24		Laker 10] ←	4 2 4 - - 1		- 75	Archer cuts for 4 Drives 2 uppishly to Bedser at mid-off Inside edge to leg for 4

1953 – FIFTH TEST

#	Time	Bowler		Runs	Score	Notes
25		Lock 10] →		- - - 1 -	- 76	
26		Laker 11] ←		1 - - 4 -	- 81	de Courcy sweeps for 4
27	3.42 3.44	Lock 11] →	(W) Davidson	- 4 - - 6 -	6- 85 - 91	Archer off-drives for 4 de Courcy run out, backs up too far on Archer's shot to mid wkt, Bailey throw to Lock, 4 in 16 mins, 8 balls, 1 four Archer 6 to long on into members' stand.
28		Laker 12] ←		- - - 2 - -	- 93	
29		Lock 12] →	(1 lb) -	- 1 - - -	- 95	
30	3.53	Laker 13] ← off spell 13-2-57-3		- - 4 6 - -	- 105	Davidson hooks to long leg for 4 Davidson sweeps to mid wicket for 6 into the gasometer crowd
31		Lock 13] →		- 2 - - 4 -	- 111	Archer off drives for 4
32		Bedser 4] ←		- - - 1 -	- 112	
33		Lock 14] → Off spell 14-5-33-2		3 1 - 1 - -	- 117	
34		Bedser 5] ←		- - - - -	- 117	
35		Laker 14] →		- - - 1 - -	- 118	

1953 – FIFTH TEST

36		Bedser 6] ← Spell 3-1-3-0		- 1 - - -	- - 120	
37	 4.15	Laker 15] → Spell 2-0-12-0	3	- 4 - 4 -	 - 131	Archer almost bowled. Archer 4 off short ball past cover Archer off-drive for 4
		TEA	Davdsn 21 31 mins 34 balls	Archer 44 45 mins 49 balls	6- 131 125 mins 222 balls	

A tremendous session: a major collapse and a brave fightback.
Arlott: 70 runs in 45 minutes since Morris was out: the game is back in the balance.
Kilburn: Hole's dismissal probably reprieved the spin pair from being taken off.

		Evening	Davdsn 21	Archer 44	6- 131	
38	4.35	Lock 15] ←	- - - - -		 - 131	Ball lifts and hits Davidson on face. *Lock bowls off-theory to six off-side fielders*
39		Bedser 7] →		- - 4 - -	 - 135	*Archer almost bowled off pads* Archer 4 through extra cover
40	 4.44 4.45	Lock 16] ←	- - W Lindwall - (2 byes) -		 7- 135 - 137	Davidson bld, ball spins sharply between bat and pad to hit off stump, 21 in 40 mins, 44 balls, 1 six 1 four
41		Bedser 8] → Off Spell 2-0-5-0	(2 byes) -	- - - 1	 - 140	
42	 4.50 4.52	Lock 17] ←		- - - W Langley -	 8- 140 - 140	Archer c Edrich at slip, ball spins sharply, 49 in 60 mins, 65 balls, 1 six 7 fours
43		Laker 16] → Off Spell 1-0-3-0	1	- - 2 - -	 - 143	Langley cuts for 2
44	 5.00 5.02	Lock 18] ←	- - 1	 W Johnston - - (2 bye)	 9- 144 - 146	Langley c Trueman at 2nd slip, 2 in 8 mins, 7 balls

1953 – FIFTH TEST

45		Bedser 9] →	- - - 1	- -	- 147	
46	5.10	Lock 19] ←	- - 6 - -		- 153	Lindwall 6 to square leg
47		Bedser 10] →	- - - - -		- 153	
48		Lock 20] ←	- - 1 - 3 -		- 157	Johnston 3 over mid-off's head
49		Bedser 11] → Off Spell 3-1-3-0	- - - 2 -		- 159	
50		Lock 21] ← Spell 7-4-11-3	- - - - -		- 159	*Lindwall dropped by Edrich at slip*
51	5.27	Laker 17] → Spell 0.5-0-3-1	- 1 - 2 W		10- 162	Lindwall c Compton, almost a six, ct high above head at long off, 12 in 42 mins, 30 balls, 1 six
				Johnston 6 25 mins 20 balls	10- 162 177 mins 305 balls	

SESSION **31-4 in 52 mins, 83 balls**

AUSTRALIA SECOND INNINGS

A.L. Hassett	lbw b Laker	10	25 mins, 18 balls, 0 fours	1-23
A.R. Morris	lbw b Lock	26	78 mins, 62 balls, 4 fours	5-61
G.B. Hole	lbw b Laker	17	37 mins, 40 balls, 2 fours	2-59
R.N. Harvey	b Lock	1	4 mins, 3 balls	3-60
K.R. Miller	c Trueman b Laker	0	4 mins, 8 balls	4-61
J.H. de Courcy	run out (Bailey/Lock)	4	16 mins, 8 balls, 1 four	6-85
R.G. Archer	c Edrich b Lock	49	60 mins, 65 balls, 1 six 7 fours	8-140
A.K. Davidson	b Lock	21	40 mins, 44 balls, 1 six 1 four	7-135
R.R. Lindwall	c Compton b Laker	12	42 mins, 30 balls, 1 six	10-162
G.R. Langley	c Trueman b Lock	2	8 mins, 7 balls	9-144
W.A. Johnston	not out	6	25 mins, 20 balls, 0 fours	
Extras	(b 11, lb 3)	14		
TOTAL	(for 10 wkts)	162	177 mins, 305 balls, 50.5 overs	

BOWLING

Bedser	11	2	24	0
Trueman	2	1	4	0
Laker	16.5	2	75	4
Lock	21	9	45	5

1953 – FIFTH TEST

This was the realisation of what had been foreshadowed in the last hour at Manchester. The young Australian batsmen, thinks Fingleton, are paying the price for inexperience on uncovered wickets responsive to spin.

England need 132 to win in 18 hours 53 minutes. Bailey is confident that England can win because Australia have only one bowler who is useful in the conditions.

Lock and Laker were the ideal combination to bowl Australia out, but they were not helped by the very casual attitude in the field.

Bowes: The spinners were successful because they bowled to a plan: Lock bowled off theory with only three leg side fielders; Laker bowled leg theory with three on the off side.

Arlott: the pitch suited the spinners better than Bedser's cutters, which is good news for England

Brown: A good county side would have made about 230. The wicket did not give especially quick turn, the light was good, and the bowling of Lock and Laker was not quite as good as it appeared

England Second Innings

Odd overs → [from Vauxhall Road End
Even overs ← [from Pavilion End

			Hutton	Edrich		
1	5.37	Lindwall 1 → [	2 - - 2 - 1		- 5	
2		Miller 1 ← [	1 - - - -		- 6	
3		Lindwall 2 → [off spell 2-0-8-0	1	2 - - - -	- 9	Edrich 2 over slips
4		Miller 2 ← [	1	- 4 - - -	- 14	Edrich hooks for 4
5		Johnston 1 → [	- - 2 - -		- 16	
6		Miller 3 ← [		- - - - -	- 16	
7		Johnston 2 → [	2 - - 4 - -		- 22	
8		Miller 4 ← [		- - - - -	- 22	

1953 – FIFTH TEST

9		Johnston 3 → [	- - - - -		- 22	
10	6.10 6.12	Miller 5 ← [	1- W May - -	1	1- 24 - 24	Hutton run out, turns to square leg, goes for 2nd run, beaten by de Courcy's throw to Langley, 17 in 33 mins, 30 balls, 2 fours
11		Johnston 4 → [	- 4 - -		- 28	
12		Miller 6 ← [off spell 6-2-14-0	2 - - - 4		- 34	May 2 off legs May 4 on-drive
13		Johnston 5 → [	- - 4 - -		- 38	Edrich 4 to extra cover off full toss
14		Archer 1 ← [spell 1-1-0-0	- - - -		- 38	
15	6.30	Johnston 6 → [spell 6-2-16-0	- - - - -		- 38	
		CLOSE	May 6 18 mins 14 balls	Edrich 15 53 mins 46 balls	1- 38 53 mins 90 balls	

The end of a day when England took a giant step towards victory.
A big lapse of concentration by Hutton; there was never a second run.
Alston: one of the greatest and most dramatic days in Test history.
Cardus: we may get the bellringers ready without tempting providence, for Hassett does not have the right bowling to exploit the wicket
Arlott: Australia's bowlers will fight but the pitch is of no help to fast bowling
Today BBC cancelled Children's Hour to show the evening session. The BBC Light Programme has cancelled its programmes tomorrow to give ball-by-ball commentary of Rex Alston and John Arlott, and Bernard Kerr's commentary to Australia. After an initial refusal MCC has allowed BBC television to broadcast the match from 11.25.
Let us now take a break from the tension and apprehension of the Test poised for its climax, and go back to the county scene.

August 15, 17, 18

On the other side of the Thames from the goings on at the Oval, Middlesex were put out for 155 on a good pitch on a dull day by Worcestershire for 155; Worcs made 399-9dec in which six men passed 30. Middlesex did better at second attempt but left the visitors only 27 to win. Yorkshire made 323-4 dec at Leeds and then rain washed out all play after lunch on Monday. Surrey had nearly five hours to go for four points but lost both openers in 20 minutes and idled thereafter. Yorkshire claimed the extra half hour but could not bowl out Surrey, so no points to either side. Leicestershire succumbed to the pace bowling of Jackson and Gladwin at Derby and took no points, losing with twenty minutes left. Rain interfered at

1953 – FIFTH TEST

Cardiff where Sussex gained first innings points, after five pointless games. In the Cheltenham Festival Lancashire beat Gloucestershire in two days even after 2½ hours was lost on the first day. The left arm spin of Berry (5-17) bowled them out in the second innings for 49 in 81 minutes. The first nine places in the Table were unchanged.

Five more selections were announced for the tour to West Indies to complete the side: A.E.Moss, Middlesex pace bowler, R.T.Spooner, Warwickshire wicket-keeper, K.G.Suttle, young Sussex batsman, Statham and Wardle. Bill Edrich, 15 not out in the final Test, was not among them.

The final countdown: FOURTH DAY, Wednesday 19 August

The England XII are photographed as a team in front of the Pavilion.
94 runs more to win. 25,000 people are present. Many more watch on television or listen to the radio.

	11.30		May 6	Edrich 15	1-38	
16		Lindwall 3 ← [	- - - -		 - 38	
17		Johnston 7 → [		- - - -	 - 38	*Johnston has 2 slips, gully and six saving single.* *Harvey stops a fierce square cut by Edrich*
18		Lindwall 4 ← [	- - 3 2 -	 - 43		May 3 to long off, well chased by de Courcy Edrich cuts a flier for 2
19		Johnston 8 → [	1 - - 1 -	 - 45		
20		Lindwall 5 ← [	- - - -	 - 45		
21	11.48	Johnston 9 → [	- - 4 1 -	 - 50		May cover drive for 4 50 up in 71 mins
22		Lindwall 6 ← [	- - 1 - -	 - 51		
23		Johnston 10 → [	- - - - -	 - 51		
24		Lindwall 7 ← [	- - - 1 -	 - 52		

1953 — FIFTH TEST

25		Johnston 11 → [		- - - - -	- 52	
26		Lindwall 8 ← [	(1 lb) -	2 - - -	- 55	Edrich 2 to mid on
27		Johnston 12 → [	4	- - -	- 59	May edges flighted ball between wk and slip
28		Lindwall 9 ← [		- - - 1 -	- 60	
29		Johnston 13 → [		- - - - -	- 60	
30		Lindwall 10 ← [	- - - - 2		- 62	*For May Lindwall has 3 short legs*
31		Johnston 14 → [		- - - - -	- 62	
32		Lindwall 11 ← [	- - - - -		- 62	
33		Johnston 15 → [		1 - - - -	- 63	
34		Lindwall 12 ← [		- - - - -	- 63	Drinks interval
35		Johnston 16 → [	- 4 - 3 -		-70	May edges 4 between wk and Miller at slip- Miller is standing too wide May 3 high to mid-on

1953 – FIFTH TEST

Over	Time	Bowler	Runs	Total	Notes
36		Lindwall 13 ← [off spell 11-4-23-0	1 - - 4 4 1	- 80	Lindwall bowls two head-high bumpers, his first of this spell. both pulled for 4 by Edrich
37		Johnston 17 → [	- - - - - -	- 80	
38		Miller 7 ← [	- - 1 - - -	- 81	
39		Johnston 18 → [	- - 2 - - -	- 83	
40		Miller 8 ← [	- - - - - 1	- 84	
41		Johnston 19 → [	- - - - - -	- 84	*Edrich edges to 2nd slip were Hole grasps the ball but cannot hold it as he falls to the ground*
42		Miller 9 ← [	- - - - -	- 84	*Miller bowls off-spin with five leg-side fielders for May*
43		Johnston 20 → [	- - - - - -	- 84	*Edrich dropped again by Hole at 2nd slip*
44	1.05 1.07	Miller 10 ← [	4 - W <u>Compton</u> - -	2- 88 - 88	May square drive for 4 May c Davidson at leg slip, inswinger, 37 in 113 mins, 89 balls, 5 fours
45		Johnston 21 → [	- - - - - -	- 88	
46		Miller 11 ← [off spell 5-1-10-1	- 2 - 1 1 -	- 92	Compton 2 to leg Compton 1 to leg

1953 – FIFTH TEST

47		Johnston 22 →[		3 - - - -	- 95	Edrich jabs to onside for 3
48	1.20	Lindwall 14 ←[	1	1 - 3 -	- 100	Edrich steers through slips for 3
49		Johnston 23 →[		- - - - -	- 100	
50		Lindwall 15 ←[	- - 1 -		- 101	
51	1.30	Johnston 24 →[	- - - - -		- 101	
		LUNCH	Comptn 5 23 mins 25 balls	Edrich 41 173 mins 162 balls	2- 101 173 mins 306 balls	

SESSION 63-1 in 120 mins, 216 balls

Johnston has bowled unchanged all morning from the Vauxhall End, 18-11-24-0. Fingleton thinks that he should have been tried from the Pavilion End. 18 overs 31 to win

Alston: Australia gave nothing away and England could not wear them down. May has shown that he will be England's No.3.

Cardus: Every run has had to be worked for. Johnston has missed taking wickets by inches for several mishits off him have just eluded the field

			Comptn 5	Edrich 41	2- 101	
52	2.10	Lindwall 16 ←[		- - - - -	- 101	
53		Johnston 25 →[	1	- - - -	- 102	
54		Lindwall 17 ←[	- - 2 - -		- 104	Compton 2 to leg
55		Johnston 26 →[		3 - 1 - - 4	- 112	Edrich cuts for 3 through Hole's legs

Edrich 4 to fine leg |

1953 – FIFTH TEST

Over	Time	Bowler	Batsman 1	Batsman 2	Score	Notes
56		Lindwall 18 ← [	- - 3 - -	-	- 115	*4 men in leg trap for Compton*
57		Johnston 27 → [	2 - - - -		- 117	
58		Lindwall 19 ← [	- - - - -	1	- 118	Outside off-stump, no stroke Glance to long leg To Hassett at mid-on, who misfields Well stopped by Archer bkwd shot leg Slower ball down leg side, no stroke Full toss, Compton miscues
59		Johnston 28 → [		- - - -	- 118	Edrich back defensive Well stopped by Dvdsn, shot leg Edged to Hole at 2nd slip Pads up
60	2.40	Lindwall 20 ← [	1 - - -	2	- 121	Compton glances to long leg Edrich 2 betwn wkt and mid on, 50 in 203 mins, 189 mins
61		Johnston 29 → [off spell (incl. lunch) 23-11-36-0	1 - - -	-	- 122	Compton cut to 3rd man To mid-off
62		Lindwall 21 ← [off spell 6-1-10-0	- - - -	1	- 123	Push to mid wkt Pushed past Johnston at midwkt Well stopped by Archer at leg slip
63		Hassett 1 → [spell 1-0-4-0	- 1 - 2 - 1		- 127	Smiles all round Compton 1 to long leg, de Courcy To Archer at short leg Edrich 2 via Langley's boot to fine leg Edrich nearly stumped, Langley fumbles Edrich 1 to long leg, de Courcy
64	2.50	Morris ← [spell 0.5-0-5-0	- 1 - 4		- 132	Buses are stationary Edrich sweeps for 1, sharp single Cmptn hooks, Dvdsn fields brilliantly Cmptn hooks square for 4. The ball is swallowed up in advancing crowd
			Comptn 22 63 mins 57 balls	Edrich 55 213 mins 207 balls	2- 132 213 mins 383 balls	On BBC Television, Brian Johnston says: "Is it the Ashes? Yes England have won the Ashes!"

The players run off but are caught up in the great hordes on the pitch.

SESSION 31-0 in 40 mins, 77 balls

ENGLAND SECOND INNINGS

L. Hutton	run out (de Courcy/Langley)	17	33 mins, 30 balls, 2 fours	1-38
W.J. Edrich	not out	55	213 mins, 207 balls, 6 fours	
P.B.H. May	c Davidson b Miller	37	113 mins, 89 balls, 5 fours	2-88
D.C.S. Compton	not out	22	63 mins, 57 balls, 1 four	
Extras (lb 1)		1		
TOTAL	(for 2 wkts)	132	213 mins, 383 balls, 63.5 overs	

1953 – FIFTH TEST

BOWLING
Lindwall	21	5	46	0
Miller	11	3	24	1
Johnston	29	14	52	0
Archer	1	1	0	0
Hassett	1	0	4	0
Morris	0.5	0	5	0

England win by eight wickets.

Attendance today: 25,000 paying £5,300

Match attendance: 115,000 (98,812 paying) receipts £37,000.

This Test was won on Tuesday afternoon. Lock has a slight edge over Laker and gets the man of the match award.

Cardus: Edrich's innings is worth framing in gold. With the sides so evenly balanced the merest straw of chance would sway the scales. England have won because in Lock and Laker they have bowlers suitable to the wicket. As long as wickets are covered in Australia, so England will beat them in this country where rain and sun or wearing turf require batsmen experienced against the spinning ball.

Near the end the next man in Graveney suggested that it would be fitting for Bailey to go in for the winning run if a wicket should fall, but Bailey declined the honour.

England's win has been seen by Jack Hobbs, Herbert Sutcliffe, Patsy Hendren and Herbert Strudwick who played in the side who won the Ashes here in 1926.

Hutton comes out onto the Pavilion balcony, in his shirt and tie, cigarette in hand. He addresses the crowd though a loudspeaker: "I am happy and thrilled that England have won this series and especially on this ground – which has always been a happy hunting ground for me. I feel a bit sorry for my friend Lindsay who has had a very hard season and he has been a wonderful opposition captain. I hope Australia continues to produce cricketers of the quality of Hassett, who has done so much for the game, not only in Australia, but in all parts of the world. Thank you for this most wonderful reception."

Then Hassett: "I would just like to offer my congratulations to Len and the English team. They have earned this victory from the very first ball, to the second last over anyway. Len was quite right when he spoke of our difficulties – especially as I have been suffering from an injured right forearm. I would like to pay tribute to this great Oval crowd for their sporting behaviour throughout the match. There has not been one incident out of place. If you could see how friendly all the members of the Australian team were with the English team you could hardly understand how they can look so hostile to one another on the field. I feel rather proud of the way the Australian boys played and I think you also enjoyed the way we played. We shall be waiting for you in Australia in a couple of years' time. I hope the cricket then will be just as enjoyable and as close as this series."

Hutton then moved into a Press Conference in the Office of the Surrey Secretary. He paid tribute to Lindwall and Miler, the finest opening pair he faced he said, singled out Bedser, Bailey and Evans on the England side, said that he did want to win the toss and bat on the first day, that the wicket on which Australia were bowled out for 162 was a good wicket, and agreed that Trueman was a good prospect though still a colt, and promised a magnificent side to tour Australia in 1954-55.

Hassett did not speak to the Press. He merely issued a statement.

Later the England team went up onto the flat TV and radio roof on the Pavilion above the England dressing room.

The two teams partied together with bottles of champagne and iced cake. Both sides were delighted that the unbearable tension was over. Lindwall singled out Bailey and told him how much he had done to win the Ashes. Bedser went into the Australian dressing room and they all shook his hand. He had a glass of beer. The champagne ran out but Hassett managed to get another case from somewhere. Keith Miller picked up an empty bottle and threw it out the window. The Australian team were soon throwing them at the wall, using the clock as a target. Bedser and Morris went off together for a quiet talk. The party broke up about six o'clock. Everybody had a two days of rest before they need step on a cricket field again. Bedser drove Morris back to his hotel in Piccadilly. Bailey met his wife and some friends at the Connaught Club in London. Edrich and Compton went out on the town and ended the night at a friend's flat. Graveney arrived home at 2.30am. Hutton was driven by a friend up the A1 to his home in Kingsmead, near Pudsey his birthplace and was greeted by his wife and two young sons and the Mayor of Pudsey. The damaged clock and marks on the dressing room wall were left for the Surrey authorities to observe. Hassett apologised the next day; no action was taken, presumably the authorities thought that the damage was a price worth paying for winning the Ashes.

On Monday Freddie Trueman's 83-year-old grandmother fell ill and died, but at her wish he was not told anything until the match was over.

In Thursday's *Times* the day's play makes the main news page column 7: ENGLAND REGAIN THE ASHES – Memories of 1926" alongside column 6 "Fluctuations in Egg Prices".

Lindwall says: "England just about deserved to win the Ashes". That was the general opinion. Bradman says "Congratulations, England, you have won a notable victory in glorious fashion against incalculable odds".

1926 was the last time when any English crowd saw England win a series against Australia

WINDING DOWN

August 19, 20, 21

While the Middlesex batsman were bringing the Ashes home at the Oval, their colleagues suffered in the field at Lord's where Gloucestershire made 344 for 9 and Middlesex followed on 201 behind and surrendered meekly after 85 minutes on the third day. For Surrey the Cambridge Blue Raman Subba Row continued to impress with 125 but they could not force a win against Northants. Sheppard steered Sussex to their first victory in a month. There was rain at Swansea, but Lancashire bowled out Glamorgan for 88 and a blank third day. Needing 242 in a day and a half, Leicestershire got home by two wickets against Essex just before a storm broke. Leicestershire go to the top of the table for the first time ever.

	Played	W	L	D	Pts	Max poss
Leicestershire	26	10	6	10	152	176
Middlesex	26	10	4	10	150	174
Surrey	24	10	4	9	148	196
Lancashire	24	9	3	9	140	188
Sussex	25	9	3	12	140	176
Gloucestershire	25	9	5	9	132	168
Derbyshire	25	8	7	8	120	156
Glamorgan	25	8	2	13	120	156

Four weeks anti-climax: Taunton, August 22, 24, 25

Now begins the phase of the tour which many of the Australians thoroughly dislike. They have left their homes, their wives and concubines in the middle of March. They have played almost continuous six days a week first class cricket before large crowds who demand their best at all times. The climax has come and gone, the Ashes decided in five nerve-racking Tests. A two-week boat journey home lies ahead. Yet before that they have eight more games, four more weeks of cricket and travel. Festival matches of little intrinsic worth to entertain crowds in the dying days of summer and attract more cash in an already very profitable venture.

First it was Somerset, the certain wooden-spooners. After two days rest (apart from the journey from London to Somerset) they picked themselves up and made 486 in 5½ hours against wayward bowling and fielding after being put in by the captain Ben Brocklehurst. Hassett and McDonald opened with 120 in 90 minutes, later Davidson and Lindwall passed 100 together in 90 minutes. Davidson needed the assistance of last man Hill to make the last 21 runs of his first century of the tour. Somerset were reduced to 11-2 by Lindwall at the close. Somerset were 68-6 when Smith was joined by 18-year-old Pakistani Yawaar Saeed on his first-class debut, and they added 89. On Tuesday rain prevented play until 2 pm when there were only two hours available. British Guianaian Peter Wight saved the game hitting 20 fours in 109 not out in 2 hours, made out of 149 while he was at the wicket.

AUSTRALIANS 486 (Hassett 148, McDonald 53, de Courcy 53, Davidson 104*, Lindwall 45). SOMERSET 187 (R.Smith 77*, Yawaar Saeed 48, Lindwall 2-12, Ring 4-88) and 156-2 (P.B.Wight 109*). *Match drawn.*

Surrey and Middlesex met again, at the Oval. Surrey scored 236, May, 59, completing his 2,000 runs. On Monday Compton made 63 out of 77 in a stand with Edrich, but the last seven wickets fell for 66 for 155 all out, Lock 6-28. Surrey scored enough to set Middlesex 256 to win, who collapsed to 38 for 5 on Monday evening and Laker and Lock bowled them out for 120 before lunch. Leicestershire lost by ten wickets at Nottingham where Dooland took 4-25, in a total of 92, and 6-57. At Eastbourne, Marlar bowled out Gloucestershire for 84. Sheppard made another century and Sussex were 181-1dec by Saturday close; with no play until 3.30 on Monday, Sheppard courageously declared and Gloucestershire fell for 113 so that Sussex gained a creditable win by ten wickets, allowing Sheppard to pass 2,000 runs for the season. At Manchester there was only two hours play in all between Lancashire and Kent. Derbyshire v Essex at Buxton had no play at all, the only game of 1953 so to suffer.

Surrey are at the top for the first time since 11th June: 160 points from 25 games, Sussex 152 from 26, Leics 152 from 27, Middlesex 150 from 27.

Johnston inches towards century: Gentlemen at Lord's, August 26, 27, 28

The Australians came back to London for their Lord's farewell match, against the Gentlemen. Sixteen wickets fell on the first day of undistinguished batting. It was a good day for two young players who might well have been considered to tour West Indies; Cowdrey and Marlar. On Thursday Bill Johnston with 27 not out took his batting aggregate and average for the season to 97. "Class will out" he said. By tea the Gentlemen had raced to 150 for 2, May having hit 13 and 14 in an over off Archer and Benaud respectively. The day ended with Cowdrey serenely resisting 3 bouncers by Miller in one over, done to keep him at the striker's end at the close, and a possibility of the Gentlemen beating the Australians for the first time since 1878. An MCC member expressed his disapproval of the bumpers to Morris as the team entered the Pavilion. On Friday Australia needed 253 to win in 280 minutes, and as many as 10,000 people were there to see them do it with an hour to spare. Morris made his first hundred of the tour, adding 111 in even time with Miller despite a spell of six successive maiden overs.

GENTLEMEN OF ENGLAND 157 (D.S.Sheppard 39, M.C.Cowdrey 50, Benaud 4-20) and 249 (D.S.Sheppard 34, W.J.Edrich 75, P.B.H.May 50, M.C.Cowdrey 57, Lindwall 5-68). AUSTRALIANS 154 (R.Benaud 25, W.A.Johnston 27*, R.G.Marlar 5-41) and 253-2 (Morris 126*, Miller 67, Harvey 30*). *Australians won by eight wickets.*

Surrey beat Glamorgan by 172 runs at the Oval, declaring twice for only 8 wickets. Clark made his highest ever score, 186. Middlesex and Sussex were not playing. Lancashire beat Notts in two days on a tricky pitch at Old Trafford. 27 wickets fell on the first day. Notts made 110 and 105, Lancashire 90 and 126-0. Tattersall took 9-40 (including 7-0 in 19 balls and a hat-trick) and 5-33. At Worcester Lowson scored 259 not out for Yorkshire and Kenyon 238 not out for Worcestershire (who were 33-4 soon after the start of the second day) and, Worcestershire declared one run ahead, and Yorkshire did not bother to set a target. 17 wickets fell in three full days. Essex scored 331-2 to beat Gloucs on a wearing wicket at Clacton

The championship position is now:

	Played	W	L	D	Pts	Max poss
Surrey	26	12	4	9	172	196
Lancashire	26	10	3	9	152	176
Sussex	26	10	3	12	152	176
Leicestershire	27	10	7	10	152	164
Middlesex	27	10	5	10	150	162

If Surrey win at Hove or if they draw there and Lancashire fail to win, the Title will stay at the Oval.

Evans' benefit: Canterbury: August 29, 31, September 1

For the last county game, among the tents, flags and the lime tree at St Lawrence Canterbury, Kent made 167 for 9 in a first day restricted to 235 minutes of drizzle and cold. The Australians dropped six catches, four off Phebey. A collection was made and on Saturday night a dance was held for Godfrey Evans' benefit. Hassett did the raffle draw and a woman from Maidstone who owned a café won a car. Hassett and Evans were imbibing together until 3am. Monday, with a crowd of 16,500, saw the Australians make 465 for 8 in 325 minutes. Hassett declared before Johnston came in. Even Tallon got some runs, recalling the batting of his youth in Australia before the War, adding 101 with Hill in less than an hour. On Tuesday Kent could resist the hostile bowling of Davidson and Johnston for only 110 minutes. Ridgeway and Mallett hit 46 in 13 minutes. Benaud had four catches dropped off him in his five overs. After a poor season in which they changed captains from Murray-Wood to Wright, Kent much needed the cash boost of £3206 from the gate money

KENT 181 (A.H.Phebey 85*, Johnston 5-35) and 108 (Johnston 6-38, Davidson 3-10). AUSTRALIANS 465-8dec (Hassett 65, Hole 78, Miller 68, Benaud 45, Tallon 83*, Hill 51*). *Australians won by an innings and 176 runs.*

Championship deciders

There was no play on Saturday in six matches. Only south of the Thames saw any cricket. Surrey, who could clinch the title with a win at Hove lost 3 for 49 to Sussex when play started at 2.30, but recovered to 134 for 4 at the close.

On Monday the last six wickets fell for 86 in 90 minutes. Then Sussex damped the spirits of the large holiday crowd on the sunshine with a pedestrian 189 for 7 by the close, tied down by the accurate Surrey bowling, and many of those runs came off the edge of the bat. Lancashire bowled out Middlesex for 174 and made 132 for 3 at the close.

On Tuesday Lancashire secured a first innings lead in half an hour and at once declared. Middlesex meandered up to lunch, then showed some purpose afterwards, eventually declaring at 167 for 8 to set Lancashire 167 in 81 minutes. Ikin was bowled second ball and after that Lancashire could make only a token effort. At 62 for four, neither side claimed the extra half hour. At Hove Sussex made their initial objective the securing of a first innings lead and on doing so, Sheppard declared. Surrey were 62 for two at lunch. Afterwards May reached a handsome 100 in 2½ hours. Not seeking a result the Surrey second innings went to 244 for 2. As they walked off the field the news from Lancashire meant that Surrey had won the championship for the second year in succession. No points from the match was enough. The three top teams had one match to play, Surrey were 16 points ahead of both Sussex and Lancashire. It was a sadly unglamorous way to win the title and it could hardly be said that Surrey has bestrode the season like a colossus. The only excitement of the day was at Clacton where Essex, needing 197 in 145 minutes, beat Warwickshire off the last ball of the day by two wickets. Horsfall reached 100 in 85 minutes, the fastest in the 1953 championship.

Johnston's hundred: South at Hastings, September 2, 3, 4

All that remained of the season were the last round of championship matches and the Festivals. Quite a strong South of England side were easily beaten. The Australians scored 564 for 9dec in 357 minutes, off 111.3 overs. Johnston came in and was given two legside long hops. He swiped and missed the first then tucked the second away for 4 and took his aggregate and average to 102, whereupon Hassett declared.

SOUTH OF ENGLAND 198 (D.C.S.Compton 81, Johnston 6-77) and 203 (P.E.Richardson 90, Hill 4-76). AUSTRALIANS 564-9dec (Hassett 106, McDonald 125, de Courcy 118, Davidson 85*, Langley 39). *Australians won by an innings and 163 runs.*

Surrey rounded off their season with a convincing win at Southampton. Lock (8-26 and 5-43) bowled out Hampshire for 82 and 127 and though they only made 151 Surrey won by nine wickets in two days – a nine-wicket win when the top score for Surrey was May's first innings 35! The only other county match was at Hove where Sussex, 340-5, beat the rivals for second place Lancashire by an innings and 12 runs.

The final County Championship Table reads:

		Plyd	W	L	D	Tied	No decn	First Inns lead in Match Lost	Drawn	Pts
1.	Surrey	28	13	4	10	0	1	0	7	184
2	Sussex	28	11	3	13	0	1	1	8	168
3.	{ Lancashire	28	10	4	10	0	4	1	8	156
	{ Leicestershire	28	10	7	10	0	0	3	6	156
5.	Middlesex	28	10	5	10	1	1	1	5	150
6.	{ Derbyshire	28	9	7	9	0	3	2	5	136
	{ Gloucestershire	28	9	7	10	0	0	2	5	136
8.	Nottinghamshire	28	9	10	8	0	0	4	1	128
9.	Warwickshire	28	6	7	14	0	0	2	11	124
10.	Glamorgan	28	8	4	14	0	0	0	6	120
11.	Northamptonshire	28	6	3	15	1	1	2	7	114
12	{ Essex	28	6	7	13	0	0	1	6	100
	{ Yorkshire	28	6	6	13	0	0	1	4	100
14.	Hampshire	28	6	11	11	0	0	2	4	96
15.	Worcestershire	28	5	12	10	0	0	1	2	72
16.	Kent	28	4	14	8	0	0	1	3	64
17.	Somerset	28	2	19	6	0	0	0	3	36

Points: Win 12, First inns lead in match drawn or lost 4, Tie 6

Craig's consolation: Combined Services at Kingston, September 5, 7

In the first match of the Kingston Festival, the Australians won easily against the Combined Services. Because of National Service, the Armed Forces in this era contain some leading players. In this match, Trueman, Ingelby-Mackenzie, Horton, Shirreff, Spencer and Wells who are or will be regular first-class cricketers. Miller, in his final match of the tour, and de Courcy added 377 for the fourth wicket in 205 minutes and Craig got a decent score at last. Miller and de Courcy set out to deal with Trueman, who conceded 95 runs in 14 overs and retired with a bruised heel. Morris was able to declare at the overnight score and the Services were put out twice on the second day. The attendance was disappointing considering the lovely weather.

AUSTRALIANS 592-4 dec (Miller 262*, de Courcy 204, Craig 71*). COMBINED SERVICES 161 (A/c M.J.Horton 45, Miller 3-17, Ring 3-40) and 170 (Mdn.A.C.D.Ingelby-Mackenzie 66, Hill 6-34). *Australians won by an innings and 261 runs.*

In the Scarborough Festival, the Gentlemen v Players match, Len Hutton signed off his most memorable season with a century before lunch, and 241 in 225 minutes. For the Gentlemen Peter May and Colin Cowdrey made the first of many large partnerships they would have together in the 1950s. May made 157 and Cowdrey 100. At one stage Evans bowled while Wardle kept wicket. The three days produced 532, 380 and 484 runs, and the Gentlemen won by five wickets with five minutes to spare. At Hastings the South of England played the Rest in another light-hearted affair. When on Monday it appeared that the

South might win in two days they put on their part-time bowlers, George Tribe, the Northamptonshire Australian, hit the fastest century of the season in 75 minutes and in the end the South lost by 27 runs.

Festival cricket: Pearce's XI at Scarborough, September 9, 10, 11

These were the last three days of first-class cricket in England in 1953. The Scarborough Festival match was regarded as a kind of sixth Test against Australia, and the team comprised eleven Test cricketers, ten of whom had played in the current series, and the other was Norman Yardley England captain a few years before. But the match was played in a very un-Test like spirit. Pearce's XI made 320 with 10 sixes and 31 fours and Australia made 57-1 by the close. On Thursday their innings closed for 317 in 250 minutes, containing 4 sixes and 39 fours. Bedser took the last two wickets in successive balls and this protected Johnston from facing a ball. When he arrived at the wicket Johnston handed to Yardley a note from Lindsay Hassett asking him to protect the bearer. Hutton then scored a stylish century being stumped off his opposing captain off the last ball of the day making Pearce's XI 167-2. On Friday the visitors were set 320 to win in 220 minutes. Benaud, tried in this match as an opener, and Morris started slowly, so slowly that they might be declining the challenge. The bowling of Tattersall and Wardle brought a change. The 100 came up in 75 minutes, the next 100 in only 38 minutes. When Benaud was caught on the boundary he had made 135 out of 209 in 110 minutes with 11 sixes and 9 fours. Four of the sixes came from successive balls by Tattersall in an over that cost 25 runs. Wickets fell cheaply and with 23 minutes left 33 were needed with three wickets to go. Langley was caught at point, 11 needed in five minutes. Five needed off the last over bowled by Bedser. No run, single to Hill, two to Davidson, one leg-bye, scores level. The field closed in and Hill swung a lofty six. Again Johnston's average was not exposed to any risk. The total match attendance was 55,000

T.N.PEARCE'S XI 320 (L.Hutton 49, R.T.Simpson 86, T.E.Bailey 35, A.V.Bedser 40, Hill 4-65) and 316-8dec (L.Hutton 102, T.W.Graveney 66, P.B.H.May 43, W.J.Edrich 33). AUSTRALIANS 317 (Hole 52, Hassett 74, Harvey 41, Davidson 39, A.V.Bedser 4-66) and 325-8 (Benaud 135, Morris 70, A.V.Bedser 5-86). *Australians won by two wickets*

The only other match was the second game of the Kingston Festival. A not terribly distinguished 'Commonwealth XI' beat an England XI comfortably. The crowds were disappointing.

The end of the road: Scotland, September 15, 16, and 18, 19

There remained two two-day games at Paisley and Raeburn Place Edinburgh. The first day at Paisley was blank. Five hours were lost at Edinburgh.

Paisley. AUSTRALIANS 377-9dec (Morris 101, Hole 56, Benaud 89, Johnston 35) SCOTLAND 100-3 (R.H.E.Chisholm 55*). *Drawn*

Edinburgh. SCOTLAND 101 (R.H.E.Chisholm 43, Lindwall 4-31, Hassett 3-2) and 88-2 (R.H.E.Chisholm 41, I.M.Anderson 40*). AUSTRALIANS 308 (McDonald 35, Archer 63, Davidson 60, R.J.Nichol 5-99). *Drawn*

Summing up
Rain favours the brave

Wisden has recently devised an algebraic calculation for assessing how good or bad a summer was in terms of weather, taking into account the average daily maximum temperature, hours of sunshine, total rainfall and number of dry days in England and Wales during the four main months, producing a figure ranging theoretically from 0 to 1,000. An average summer would be 550-600. The best in the 20th century was 812 in 1976, the worst 394 in 1954. The reading for 1953 was 551. Not a particularly bad summer but it is perceived as wet because of bad weather on important occasions, such as the 25 days of Test cricket and Coronation day. Outside the two Tests in London, the weather was terrible.

When rain was not falling it was an absorbing, tense and sometimes agonisingly slow contest. It was the batting which mostly failed to achieve. No innings total reached 400, a feature of no other Ashes series between 1920 and 1971. Neither captain ever declared his innings closed, nor even was in a position to consider doing so. (This has occurred in no other Ashes series in England between 1920 and 1971, nor in Australia between 1946 and 1975. It is extremely rare in any Test series apart from those in Australia before the Second World War, which were all timeless). Heralded as the weakest side to tour England since 1912 (an accolade accorded to every Australian team thereafter until 1972) the Australian tourists were not much weaker than in 1948, and set new standards in fielding. Graveney says that it was the best Australian side he played against, which covers 1953 to 1968.

Langley did not have Evans' reputation, nor his athletic style, but he could cover any snick between backward short leg and second slip infallibly. He dropped nothing in his four Tests.

There was much criticism of the manager of the side. George Davies was according to Whitington rather over fond of alcohol. He did not set a good example the younger men in the side and made some embarrassing errors. When the Duke of Edinburgh was opening the Lord's museum he told Davies that he would like to meet the touring team in the Long Room afterwards. Davies forgot and only Miller, who had overheard the conversation, was there.

Hutton goes down in history as one of England's great captains, and on performance none could better him. Those who played under him, notably Compton, Graveney and Laker, are comparatively uneffusive on their assessment of his captaincy in this series. Over-rigid, uncommunicative, unhelpful to younger players with a more adventurous attitude, unimaginative, too reliant on fast bowling? No-one doubts his absolute determination to achieve the Ashes, and it must have been a huge lifting of a burden of anxiety from his shoulders when he did it. He presented to everyone who appeared for England in the Tests a Ronson table cigarette lighter inscribed "In honour of regaining the Ashes"

For Bailey 1953 made him typecast for ever as the barnacle, the stonewaller, but in this year at least it made him a national hero.

The fair result?

Did England deserve to win? In terms of natural talent, positive attitude and entertainment value, they fell far short of Australia. In doggedness, determination, guts and courage, they lead. If it had been a dry warm summer like 1947 or 1955, Australia would have won. In a wet summer, with uncovered wickets, England had the batsmen and the spinners able to make the best of the conditions. Australian batsmen foundered and Australian spinners could not take advantage. There are two reasons for this: one, for the last two years wickets in Australia had been completely protected from the rain; second, even before that rain in Australia followed by hot sun made wickets so dangerous that it was pot luck for batsmen and bowlers needed only to bowl accurately to get wickets. Of the 1953 side, really only Hassett, with two previous tours of England, could be relied on to bat skilfully in a drying or wearing wicket. If he struggled and got out the psychological effect on the others was disastrous.

On the other hand, the advantage to England in wet weather is given in one hand then taken away with the other, because the rain often reduced the playing time so much that the match can only be a draw.

England lost all five tosses. A great disadvantage, but at Trent Bridge, Old Trafford and Headingley, it was a good toss to lose. At Lord's the toss was vital and batting first was a big benefit. At the Oval, as it turned out, England would have wanted to bat but the short light showers that came during this match meant that Australia got the worse of the batting conditions.

Epitome of the Tests
(6-ball overs)

In the following Test statistics, for the purposes of balls received by an individual, no-balls are included (since the batsman can score off them) but not wides. For the purposes of balls received by the team, no-balls and wides are included (since they accrue runs to the innings total). Aggregates of overs bowled exclude no-balls and wides.

ENGLAND

TEST	Wkts	Runs	Mins	Balls	Overs	Wides
1st	10	144	253	439	72.4	0
	1	120	183	354	58	2
2nd	10	372	432	768	126.5	1
	7	282	414	766	126	2
3rd	10	276	361	720	120	0
4th	10	167	385	658	109.4	0
	10	275	587	1065	177.3	0
5th	10	306	487	859	142.3	1
	2	132	213	383	63.5	0
Totals	**70**	**2074**	**3315**	**6012**	**997**	**6**

England scored 29.63 runs per wkt, 37.54 runs per hour, 34.50 runs per 100 balls, 2.08 runs per over.

Australia bowled 108.81 balls per hour, 18.05 overs per hour, 47.35 mins per wkt, 85.89 balls per wkt, 14.24 overs per wkt.

1953

AUSTRALIA

TEST	Wkts	Runs	Mins	Balls	Overs	Wides
1st	10	249	435	847	140.3	0
	10	123	141	236	39.2	0
2nd	10	346	490	847	140.4	0
	10	368	435	800	132.5	0
3rd	10	318	388	701	116.3	0
	8	35	60	108	18	0
4th	10	266	295	501	82.5	2
	4	147	115	199	33	1
5th	10	275	321	496	81.3	0
	10	162	177	305	50.5	0
Totals	**92**	**2289**	**2857**	**5040**	**836**	**3**

Australia scored 24.88 runs per wkt, 48.07 runs per hour, 45.41 runs per 100 balls, 2.74 runs per over.
England bowled 105.85 balls per hour, 17.56 overs per hour, 31.05 mins per wkt, 54.78 balls per wkt, 9.09 overs per wkt.

Man of the Match

(as selected by B. Valentine)
1st Test: Alec Bedser
2nd Test: Willie Watson
3rd Test: Neil Harvey
4th Test: Trevor Bailey
5th Test: Tony Lock

AVERAGES

ENGLAND – batting and fielding

	M	I	NO	Runs	HS	Avge	100s -50s	Runs per hour	Runs per 100 balls	Ct
L.Hutton	5	9	1	443	145	55.37	1-3	22.93	40.68	4
W.J.Edrich	3	5	1	156	64	39.00	2	15.70	29.38	6
W.Watson	3	5	0	168	109	33.60	1-0	15.85	26.75	1
D.C.S.Compton	5	8	1	234	61	33.42	2	18.82	34.87	4
T.E.Bailey	5	7	0	222	71	31.71	2	13.15	22.75	3
J.H.Wardle	3	4	2	57	29*	28.50	0	18.39	34.76	0
P.B.H.May	2	3	0	85	39	28.33	0	16.72	32.31	0
T.W.Graveney	5	7	0	169	78	24.14	2	17.07	30.56	4
F.R.Brown	1	2	0	50	28	25.00	0	56.60	98.04	1
T.G.Evans	5	7	2	117	44*	23.40	0	26.29	46.61	11+5st
R.T.Simpson	3	5	1	74	31	18.50	0	16.63	28.46	1
J.C.Laker	3	4	0	64	48	16.00	0	22.07	42.67	0
A.V.Bedser	5	6	3	38	22*	12.67	0	13.91	28.36	1
F.S.Trueman	1	1	0	10	10	10.00	0	17.14	41.67	2
D.Kenyon	2	4	0	29	16	7.25	0	20.47	45.31	1
G.A.R.Lock	2	3	0	21	9	7.00	0	7.54	13.73	3
R.Tattersall	1	1	0	2	2	2.00	0	6.67	10.53	2
J.B.Statham	1	1	1	17	17*	--	0	34.00	60.71	2

Wicket-keepers: Evans conceded 42 byes for 16 dismissals.

ENGLAND bowling

	Overs	Mdns	Runs	Wkts	Avge	10wM-5wI	Balls per wkt	Runs per 100 balls
A.V.Bedser	265.1	58	682	39	17.48	1-5	40.8	42.9
G.A.R.Lock	61	20	165	8	20.62	1	45.7	45.1
D.C.S.Compton	3	0	21	1	21.00	0	18.0	116.7
F.S.Trueman	26.3	4	90	4	22.50	0	39.7	56.6
J.C.Laker	58.5	11	212	9	23.55	0	39.2	60.1
J.H.Wardle	155.3	58	344	13	26.46	0	71.5	37.0
R.Tattersall	28	5	81	3	27.00	0	56.0	48.2
F.R.Brown	52	11	135	4	33.75	0	78.0	43.7
J.B.Statham	43	10	88	2	44.00	0	129.0	34.2
T.E.Bailey	143	33	387	8	48.37	0	107.2	45.1

AUSTRALIA – batting and fielding

	M	I	NO	Runs	HS	Avge	100s-50s	Runs per hour	Runs per 100 balls	Ct
A.L.Hassett	5	10	0	365	115	36.50	2-1	21.00	39.33	2
R.N.Harvey	5	10	0	346	122	34.60	1-2	26.72	50.22	0
A.R.Morris	5	10	0	337	89	33.70	3	24.78	43.60	2
G.B.Hole	5	10	0	273	66	27.30	2	23.64	44.61	8
K.R.Miller	5	9	0	223	109	24.78	1-1	21.17	37.10	2
R.G.Archer	3	5	1	95	49	23.75	0	30.81	53.67	1
A.K.Davidson	5	10	2	182	76	22.75	1	21.71	40.35	5
R.R.Lindwall	5	9	0	159	62	17.67	2	33.83	62.11	2
J.H. de Courcy	3	6	1	81	41	16.20	0	25.31	49.09	3
D.T.Ring	1	2	0	25	18	12.50	0	23.08	37.31	0
G.R. Langley	4	6	0	55	18	9.17	0	24.81	55.00	8 + 1 st
D.Tallon	1	2	0	15	15	7.50	0	30.00	57.70	2
J.C.Hill	2	4	2	12	8*	6.00	0	16.74	30.77	1
R.Benaud	3	5	0	15	7	3.00	0	11.69	18.07	
W.A.Johnston	3	6	6	22	9*	--	0	13.33	34.37	0

Wicket-keepers: Tallon conceded 13 byes for 2 dismissals. Langley conceded 44 byes for 9 dismissals.

AUSTRALIA bowling

	Overs	Mdns	Runs	Wkts	Avge	10wM-5wI	Balls per wkt	Runs per 100 balls
A.R.Morris	3.5	0	15	1	15.00	0	23.0	65.2
R.R.Lindwall	240.4	62	490	26	18.84	0-3	55.5	33.9
J.C.Hill	66	18	158	7	22.57	0	56.6	39.9
R.G.Archer	69.3	27	95	4	23.75	0	104.2	22.8
A.K.Davidson	125	42	212	8	26.50	0	93.7	28.3
K.R.Miller	186	72	303	10	30.30	0	111.6	27.1
W.A.Johnston	174	67	343	7	49.00	0	149.1	32.9
D.T.Ring	43	7	127	2	63.50	0	129.0	49.2
R.Benaud	68	19	174	2	87.00	0	204.0	42.6
R.N.Harvey	3	2	2	0	--	0	--	11.1
A.L.Hassett	1	0	4	0	--	0	--	66.7
G.B.Hole	17	8	33	0	--	0	--	32.3

Australians tour record

	Australians						Home team				
Result	Runs	W	Mins	Balls	w/nb	Opponent	Runs	W	Mins	Balls	w/nb
D	542	7	423	876	3	Worcs	333	7	411	804	2
W	443	8	360	732	7	Leics	109	9	141	258	0
	0	0	0	0	0		180	9	197	377	1
W	453	6	478	978	5	Yorks	145	10	195	372	6
	0	0	0	0	0		214	10	297	617	0
w	256	10	263	494	0	Surrey	58	10	100	157	0
	0	0	0	0	0		122	10	175	310	1
w	383	10	305	647	0	Cambr U	130	10	173	324	0
	0	0	0	0	0		147	10	150	282	0
d	179	10	162	284	1	MCC	80	10	127	248	0
	13	2	30	48	0		196	10	303	109	0
w	330	10	286	618	0	Oxford U	70	10	90	175	0
	0	0	0	0	0		174	10	215	472	0
w	289	10	280	594	0	Minor Cs	56	10	98	148	3
	0	0	0	0	0		62	10	85	144	0
d	298	10	335	637	2	Lancs	232	9	255	85	2
d	290	6	266	550	0	Notts	208	10	255	504	3
d	325	10	313	624	1	Sussex	218	10	260	496	5
	259	1	185	384	0		190	9	255	564	3
w	268	10	235	427	2	Hants	131	10	155	307	0
	169	5	120	216	0		148	10	148	289	0

1953

d	249	10	435	843	1	Eng 1st	144	10	253	436	0
	123	10	141	236	0		120	1	183	348	4
	197	10	251	480	0	Derbys	69	10	139	278	0
	146	10	148	267	0		17	1	32	72	0
d	323	9	312	656	2	Yorks	377	10	458	891	8
	0	0	0	0	0		220	3	210	486	6
d	346	10	490	844	0	Eng 2nd	372	10	432	761	8
	368	10	435	797	0		282	7	414	756	8
w	402	9	332	634	0	Gloucs	137	10	187	352	2
	33	1	19	35	0		297	10	268	505	2
w	323	10	310	525	2	Northants	141	10	162	286	0
	0	0	0	0	0		120	10	173	345	1
d	318	10	388	699	1	Eng 3rd	276	10	361	726	0
	35	8	60	108	0		0	0	0	0	0
d	416	10	382	813	0	Middlesex	150	10	242	492	1
	0	0	0	0	0		112	4	110	234	0
d	266	10	295	497	2	Eng 4th	167	10	385	658	0
	147	4	115	198	1		275	10	587	1065	0
d	327	9	312	558	1	Surrey	209	8	319	605	1
d	386	10	316	608	2	Glamorgan	201	10	272	491	1
	0	0	0	0	0		188	7	272	525	2
d	181	10	288	585	1	Warwks	270	8	277	586	0
	53	5	170	348	0		76	3	100	186	0
w	372	10	308	609	0	Lancs	184	9	225	448	0
	106	3	81	167	0		292	9	299	590	0
w	477	7	360	612	0	Essex	129	10	133	264	0
	0	0	0	0	0		136	10	149	305	0
L	275	10	321	489	2	Eng 5th	306	10	487	855	1
	162	10	177	305	0		132	2	213	383	0
d	486	10	315	567	2	Somerset	187	10	189	396	1
	0	0	0	0	0		156	2	160	360	0
w	154	10	190	364	0	Gents	157	10	225	442	1
	253	2	217	464	0		249	10	325	600	0
w	465	8	325	582	0	Kent	181	10	255	490	0
	0	0	0	0	0		108	10	110	181	0
w	564	9	357	669	1	South	198	10	213	405	0
	0	0	0	0	0		203	9	157	345	0
w	592	4	355	714	1	Comb Serv	161	10	165	312	0
	0	0	0	0	0		170	10	162	334	0
w	317	10	248	503	0	Pearce'sXI	320	10	257	494	0
	325	8	216	419	1		316	8	215	399	0
	13684	381	12710	24304	41		11008	534	13860	25729	73

Australians scored	*Opponents scored*
35.92 runs per wkt	20.61 runs per wkt
64.60 runs per hour	47.66 runs per hour
56.30 runs per 100 balls	42.78 runs per 100 balls
(56.13 adjusted to exclude w/nb from runs	(42.50 adjusted to exclude w/nb from runs)
(56.20 adjusted to add w/nb to balls)	(42.66 adjusted to add w/nb to balls)
Opponents bowled	*Australians bowled*
114.73 balls per hour (excl w/nb)	111.38 balls per hour (excl w/nb)
63.79 balls per wkt (excl w/nb)	48.18 balls per wkt (excl w/nb)

INDEX

Archer, R.G. 7	Kent 225
Australia 6	Kenyon, D. 16
Australians tour record 230	Knighthoods 14
Bailey, T.E. 16	Laker, J.C. 108
BBC 217	Lancashire 13, 185
Bedser, A.V. 16	Langley, G.R. 7
Benaud, R. 7	Leicestershire 9
Bibliography 4	Lindwall, R.R. 7
Brown, F.R. 6, 16, 52	Lock, G.A.R. 16
Bumper, Miller and Whitington 8	Lord's Test 52
Cambridge University 10	May, P.B.H. 16
Chester, Umpire Frank 182	MCC 10
Combined Services 226	McDonald, C.C. 6
Compton, D.C.S. 16	Menzies, R.G. 12, 14
Coronation 5, 14	Middlesex 137
County Championship 9	Miller, K.R. 6
County Championship Table 226	Minor Counties 12
Craig, I.W. 6	Morris, A.R. 6
Davidson, A.K. 7	Mount Everest 14
Davies, George 7, 228	Northamptonshire 106
de Courcy, J.H. 6	Nottinghamshire 13
Derbyshire 50	Old Trafford Test 108
Drag 12	*Orcades (RMS)* 7
East Molesey 8	Oval Test 187
Edrich, W.J. 108	Oxford University 12
England 6	Pearce's XI 227
England selectors 16	*Playfair Cricket Annual* 6
Epitome of the Tests 228	Ring, D.T. 7
Essex 186	Scotland 227
Evans, T.G. 16	Second Test 52
Ferguson, W.H. 7	Simpson, R.T. 16
Festival matches 226	Somerset 224
Fifth Test 187	South 226
First Test 16	Statham, J.B. 16
Fourth Test 139	Surrey 9, 182
Gentlemen 224	Sussex 14
Gentlemen v Players 136, 226	Tallon, D. 7
Glamorgan 183	Tattersall, R. 16
Gloucestershire 106	Test trial 13
Graveney, T.W. 16	Third Test 108
Hampshire 14	Trent Bridge Test 16
Harvey, R.N. 6	Trueman, F.S. 108
Hassett, A.L. 6, 223	Wardle, J.H. 16
Headingley Test 139	Warwickshire 184
Hill, J.C. 7	Washbrook, C. 108
Hole, G.B. 6	Watson, W 52
Holland 137	Weather 227
Hutton, L. 6, 16, 223, 228	Worcestershire 8
Johnston, W.A. 7	Yorkshire 9, 51

MCC in Australia 1954-55

Hutton's last bow
ENGLAND KEEP THE ASHES !

Ball-by-ball
The story of the 1954-55 Test Series, England in Australia

Written and compiled by Barry Valentine

from the original MCC tour scorebook by George Duckworth

MCC in Australia 1954-55

CONTENTS

MAIN SOURCES 5
INTRODUCTON 7
   Damp preparations for the big venture 7
   # The touring team 7
   Seaside start: Western Australian Country XI, at Bunbury, October 11, 12 9
   Efficient opening: Western Australia at Perth, October 15,16,18,19 10
   Double victory: Combined XI at Perth, October 22, 23, 25 10
   # Denis Compton arrives: South Australia at Adelaide, Oct 29, 30 Nov 1, 2 10
   Rain arrives: Australian XI at Melbourne, November 5, 6, (7) (8) 11
   Cowdrey arrives: New South Wales, November 12, 13, 15 16 11
   Lindwall's secret: Queensland at Brisbane: Nov 19, 20, 22, 23 12

 # FIRST TEST AT BRISBANE 13
   FIRST DAY - Everything goes wrong 13
      Australia First Innings 13
   SECOND DAY – Australia consolidate 21
   THIRD DAY – England under the steam-roller 28
      England First Innings 30
   FOURTH DAY - England refuse to fold up 36
      England Second Innings 39
   FIFTH DAY - Rain mocks to deceive 45
      Queensland Country XI at Rockhampton, December 4 and 6 51
      Prime Minster's XI at Canberra, December 8 51
      Bailey opens: Victoria at Melbourne, December 10, 11, 13 and 14 51

 # SECOND TEST AT SYDNEY 52
   FIRST DAY – Can it get any worse? 52
      England First Innings 52
      Australia First Innings 59
   SECOND DAY – Once more unto the breach 60
   THIRD DAY – Young amateurs 67
      England Second Innings 67
   FOURTH DAY – Good day for Australia 75
      Australia Second Innings 80
   FIFTH DAY - Typhoon 83
   MCC v Northern New South Wales Country XI at Newcastle, December 27, 28 and 29. 87

 # THIRD TEST AT MELBOURNE 89
   FIRST DAY – Here we go again 89
      England First Innings 89
   SECOND DAY – Slow grind 98
      Australia First Innings 98
   THIRD DAY – Rising damp 104
      England Second Innings 106
   FOURTH DAY – May England win? 113
      Australia Second Innings 119
   FIFTH DAY – Typhoon strikes twice 121
   MCC v Combined XI at Hobart, January 8, 10 and 11 123
   MCC v Tasmania at Launceston, January 13, 14, 15 124
   MCC v South Australian Country XI at Mount Gambier, January 18 and 19 ... 124

    MCC v South Australia at Adelaide, January 21, 22 and 24 124
FOURTH TEST AT ADELAIDE **125**
  FIRST DAY – Australia miss the boat 125
    Australia First Innings... 125
  SECOND DAY – See-saw day 132
    England First Innings.. 137
  THIRD DAY – Australia Day grind... 140
  FOURTH DAY – Appleyard bites 149
    Australia Second Innings 154
  FIFTH DAY – Hutton's reward... 158
    England Second Innings 160
    MCC v Victorian Country XI at Yallourn, February 5 and 7 165
    MCC v Victoria at Melbourne, February 11, 12, 14 and 15. 165
    MCC v New South Wales at Sydney, February 18, 19, 21 and 22 165
FIFTH TEST AT SYDNEY **168**
  FOURTH DAY – Worth waiting for 168
    England First Innings.. 168
  FIFTH DAY – Drifting to a draw 174
    Australia First Innings... 180
  SIXTH DAY – Oops! 183
    Australia Second Innings 188
Farewell... **192**
  Epitome of the Tests 194
  MCC tour record 196
INDEX.. **197**

MAIN SOURCES

Books on the tour
Australian Test Journal by John Arlott (Phoenix 1955)
The Ashes Ablaze by Sidney Barnes (Kimber 1955)
The Picture Post *Book of the Tests 1954-55* by Denzil Batchelor (Hulton 1955)
The Urn Returns by A.E.R.Gilligan (Andre Deutsch, 1955)
Ashes Triumphant 1954-5 by Bruce Harris (Hutchinson 1955)
The Long Hop by Margaret Hughes (Stanley Paul 1955)
Cricket Typhoon by Keith Miller and R.S.Whitington (Macdonald 1955)
The Fight for the Ashes 1954-1955 by A.G.Moyes (Harrap 1955)
Peebles on the Ashes by Ian Peebles (Hodder & Stoughton 1955)
Australia '55 by Alan Ross (Michael Joseph 1955)
Victory in Australia by E.W.Swanton (Daily Telegraph 1955)
The Ashes Retained by E.M.Wellings (Evans Bros 1955)

Biographical
Wickets, Catches and the Odd Run by Trevor Bailey (Willow 1986)
Twin Ambitions by Alec Bedser (S. Paul 1986)
Anything but ... An Autobiography by Richie Benaud (Hodder & Stoughton 1998)
End of an Innings by Denis Compton (Oldbourne 1958)
Cricket and All That by Denis Compton and Bill Edrich (Pelham 1978)
Time for Reflection by Colin Cowdrey (Muller 1962)
MCC: the Autobiography of a Cricketer by Colin Cowdrey (Hodder & Stoughton 1976)
Fifteen Paces by Alan Davidson (Souvenir 1963)
Bill Edrich by Alan Hill (Deutsch 1994)
Round the Wicket by W.J.Edrich (Muller 1959)
Action in Cricket by Godfrey Evans (Hodder & Stoughton 1956)
The Gloves are Off by Godfrey Evans (Hodder & Stoughton 1960)
By Hook or by Cut by Les Favell (Investigator Press Adelaide, 1970)
Cricket through the Covers by Tom Graveney (Muller 1958)
Ray Lindwall Cricket Legend by John Ringwood (R Hale 1996)
Just My Story by Len Hutton (Hutchinson 1956)
Fifty Years in Cricket by Len Hutton/Alex Bannister (Stanley Paul 1984)
Len Hutton by Gerald Howat (Mandarin pbk 1990)
Cricket at the Crossroads by Ian Johnson (Cassell 1957)
A Game Enjoyed by Peter May and Michael Melford (Stanley Paul 1985)
Keith Miller the Golden Nuggett by R.S.Whitington (Rigby 1981)
Keith Miller a Cricketing Biography by Mihir Bose (Allen & Unwin 1979)
Parson's Pitch by David Sheppard (Hodder & Stoughton 1964)
Cricket Merry-go-round by Brian Statham (S.Paul 1956)
Flying Bails by Brian Statham (S.Paul 1961)
A Spell at the Top by Brian Statham (Souvenir 1969)
Fast Fury by Freddie Trueman (Stanley Paul 1961)
A Typhoon called Tyson by Frank Tyson (Heinemann 1961)
Happy Go Johnny by J.H.Wardle and A.A.Thomson (Hale 1957)

Australian Histories
First-class Cricket in Australia (Vol.2, 1945-46 to 1976-77) by Ray Webster (1997)
Test Cricket in Australia 18-2002 by Charles Davis (Davis 2002)

Other
The Rothmans Book of Test Matches (England v Australia 1946-1963) ed Ted Dexter (Barker 1964) [contains reviews of 1954-55 by Colin McDonald and Frank Tyson]
Close of Play by Neville Cardus (Collins 1956)
The Game is Not the Same ... by Alan McGilvray (David & Charles 1986)
The Cricketer's Bedside Book ed. Ron Roberts (Batsford 1966) [article by John Woodcock 'The Typhoon Strikes']
The Long Run by Alf Gover (Pelham 1991)
Cricket Decade by J.M.Kilburn (Heinemann 1959)
For the Love of the Game by David Lemmon (Pelham 1993)
Gentlemen & Players by Michael Marshall (Grafton 1987)

Periodicals
The Cricketer 1955
Wisden Cricketers' Almanack 1956
Playfair Cricket Annual 1954 and 1955 (tour review by W.E.Bowes)
The Times (London) [Cricket correspondent John Woodcock]

MCC in Australia 1954-55

INTRODUCTON

The euphoria of Kennington Oval in August 1953 was dampened in the following winter when Hutton's England side lost comfortably the first two Tests in the West Indies with some dismal batting. They won the Third and Fifth Tests to square the series. This was a great achievement for Len Hutton, the first professional to lead an MCC team abroad, but it did not disguise the disappointment of Lock and Trueman whose bowling made little impression. On the other hand, it was a very good tour for Hutton himself, Compton, May, Graveney, Bailey and Statham and moderately successful for Watson and Laker.

Damp preparations for the big venture

1954 was appallingly wet throughout. The visitors were the newest Test nation, Pakistan, who were allocated four Tests of five days.

In early May, the selectors appointed Hutton as captain for the First Test (In England the captain was usually appointed for one or two home Tests at a time.) The selectors were Norman Yardley, Leslie Ames and Walter Robins. To pick the team for Australia they would be joined by Gubby Allen and Charles Palmer.

In the First at Lord's play did not start until 3.45 on the fourth day! Pakistan made 87 (J.B.Statham 4-18, J.H.Wardle 4-33) and 123-1 (Hanif Mohammad 39, Waqar Hassan 53*) England 117-9 dec (R.T.Simpson 40, Fazal Mahmood 4-54, Khan Mohammad 5-61).

With less weather interference at Trent Bridge, England won in four days. Pakistan 157 (R.Appleyard 5-51) and 272 (Hanif Mohammed 51, Maqsood Ahmed 69) England 558-6 dec (R.T.Simpson 101, D.C.S.Compton 278 in 290 minutes, T.W.Graveney 84). Hutton was absent injured and England chose David S. Sheppard, a traditional amateur (Cranbourne, Cambridge Univ and Sussex), who had toured Australia with little success in 1950-51, captained Sussex with great success in 1953 and came within a whisker of being tried as Hutton's opening partner. Bailey had been vice-captain in West Indies and was also an amateur but he was now in the dog house because he had published a book in the spring which broke the rule about Test players not commenting on recent Test matches.

Sheppard again captained for the Third Test at Old Trafford where there was play only on the first and third days. England 359-8 dec (T.E.Bailey 42, D.C.S.Compton 93, T.W.Graveney 65, J.H.Wardle 54, Fazal Mahmood 4-107). Pakistan 90 (Wardle 4-19) and 25-4 (Bedser 3-9).

The touring team

There was some feeling in MCC circles that Sheppard should be made captain to tour Australia and he told the selectors that he would be available to tour if made captain, setting back his progress towards holy orders in the Church of England. Hutton first heard of rumours that Sheppard was favoured in newspapers. He wrote a letter to the MCC stating that he was available to tour Australia, as captain if asked, or under any other captain. Hutton himself told Sheppard that he thought Sheppard would be appointed and that Hutton would support him. However, in the end they reverted to Hutton, no doubt fearing a public outcry. One of the England Test selectors Walter Robins, told him "I fell we've been unfair to Len. He was in a very difficult position in the West Indies".

MCC announced that George Duckworth, pre-war Lancashire and England wicket-keeper, would be scorer and baggage master. For the first time, and at Hutton's strong request, an official MCC masseur, H.W.Dalton of Essex, would go with the team. The Lancashire CC Secretary who had played occasional games for Middlesex, Geoffrey Howard was appointed as tour manager.

On 27 July the team that Hutton would take to Australia was announced:
(with ages as at 1st November 1954)

Batsmen

Len HUTTON (Capt.) (Yorks), 38. England's established opening right-hand batsman and professional captain, who had missed the last two Tests because of back trouble

Reg T. SIMPSON (Notts) aged 34, amateur. Opening or middle-order bat, tall and elegant. Made the match-winning century in 1950-51

W.J.(Bill) EDRICH (Middlesex) aged 37, was a pugnacious and resolute right-hand batsman, specialist slip and now an occasional medium pace bowler. His golden years were from 1946 to 1950. He was wrongly dropped for the 1950-51 tour but was back in 1953. Became an amateur in 1947.

Peter B.H. MAY (vice capt.) (Surrey) aged 23. Amateur, powerful and solid right-hand bat. Now reaching his confident prime

Denis C.S. COMPTON (Middx) aged 35. Professional. Outstanding right-hand bat, slow left arm 'chinaman' bowler. Now back to something near his best.

Tom W. GRAVENEY (Gloucs) Professional. aged almost 26. Stylish right-hand bat.

M. Colin COWDREY (Kent) Young amateur (Tonbridge and Oxford Univ) aged almost 22. No Test experience, 12th man at the Oval Test 1954, naturally gifted right-handed stroker of the ball. Good close fielder. Occasional leg-spinner. Picked with an eye to the future.

All-rounder

Trevor E. BAILEY (Essex) Amateur. Aged 29 Infuriatingly adhesive middle-order bat and right fast medium bowler. Vice-captain in the West Indies. Much depended on him as the only all-rounder in the side

Pace bowlers

Alec V. BEDSER (Surrey) aged 36 Professional. outstanding right fast medium bowler. Rested for the tour of West Indies so he would be fresh for his third and last tour of Australia.

MCC in Australia 1954-55

J. Brian STATHAM (Lancs) Professional Aged almost 24. Fast right-hand bowler, unpretentious left-hand bat. Now established as England's fast bowler.

Frank H. TYSON (Northants). Aged 24, professional, a very fast right-hand bowler of a long run-up, qualified for Northants after trials for his home county Lancashire, a graduate of Durham University, useful low order right hand bat. A raw talent who needed to learn greater accuracy for Test achievement. Made his Test debut at the Oval 1954.

Peter J. LOADER (Surrey) professional, passing 25 in October, right-hand fastish bowler and low order right hand bat. Taking wickets for his county. Test debut at the Oval 1954.

Spinners

John H. WARDLE (Yorks) professional. Aged 31. Versatile slow left arm bowler who bowled only orthodox finger spin for Yorkshire but could also bowl 'chinamen', that is wrist spin off-breaks, and useful low order left hand bat. Preferred to Lock to the surprise of many.

Ron APPLEYARD (Yorks) aged 30, professional, right arm slow medium off-spinner/cutter. Took 200 wickets in his first full season 1951, then missed two whole seasons because of tuberculosis, a randomly fatal disease. Then came back in 1954 as if nothing had happened. Took seven wickets in England's victory at Lord's.

Jim E. MCCONNON (Glamorgan) aged 31, professional, a tall off-spinner and useful low order batsman, who made his debut only in 1950. He was injured and came home early from the Commonwealth tour of India in 1953-54. Played two Tests in 1954, taking 3-19 in his first innings.

Wicket-keepers

T. Godfrey EVANS (Kent) aged 32 Professional. Brilliant wicket-keeper and dashing low order bat.

Keith V. ANDREW (Northants) aged 24, a surprise choice as deputy to Evans, with only two seasons experience for the county, efficient and unobtrusive, and a stubborn right-hand batsman.

The vice-captaincy was announced with the team, and May had to read the papers to find out that he was the recipient of the post.

The general view was that it was a reasonable choice of batting squad, but many thought that Trueman would have got in ahead of Tyson and/or Loader and that Lock would be the first chosen spinner. Trueman and Lock had not been great successes in West Indies, and indeed Lock had been no-balled for throwing. Certainly both of these would have improved the close-in catching. In view of the dearth of all-rounders Allan Watkins of Glamorgan, also a brilliant close fielder, might have been considered.

Let's hear from our experts:

Arlott: Not as strong as side as it seemed at first. Trueman, Watkins and Watson are unlucky. Tyson is very fast, but wayward; and who will be good enough to hold catches off him? McConnon is picked ahead of Laker because he can flight the ball like Ian Johnson and is a good close fielder. There is a question whether Bedser's fitness will allow him to be at his best.

Swanton: it is a team very much as expected, with the best potential of any MCC side since the War. Stronger in bowling than batting. Lock and Trueman derive some sympathy. There is no leg-spinner and only one all-rounder in the side. The emphasis will be on pace bowling.

Wellings: It is a mistake to leave out Lock, who is now recovering his incidence and form after the shock of being no-balled for throwing in the West Indies. If the team had been chosen two weeks later he would have been picked. I would have picked Trueman and not Tyson. McConnon is very lucky to be chosen. Bailey would be the ideal vice-captain and he is being pettily punished for having published a book in 1954 describing recent Test matches. On the whole it is a well chosen team.

Barnes: The omission of Trueman is sensational and mysterious, and it is suspected that it was due to grounds other than cricketing ability.

Ross: Lock and Laker are our two best spinners

Harris: I cannot understand the exclusion of Trueman. Lock and Laker have taken a lot of wickets and would be much better than Wardle and McConnon

Miller and Whitington: Trueman, Laker and Lock were the best bowlers in the Ashes-wining test.

For the last Test was Hutton was again fit and the match was treated very much with the Australian tour in mind. Sheppard was obviously dropped. Bedser and Bailey were rested in order to blood Tyson and Loader. Rain was never far away and the whole second day was blanked out. Pakistan made 133 ((F.H.Tyson 4-35) England 130 (D.C.S.Compton 53, Fazal Mahmood 6-53, Mahmood Hussain 4-58). Pakistan made 164 (Wazir Mohammad 42*, J.H.Wardle 7-56). The last two Pakistan wickets had added 56 and 82 in the two innings. England, needing 168 to win with a day plus 2½ hours left, reached 109 before the third wicket fell and tried to get the runs on Monday evening. They were 125 for 6 at the close and next day were all out for 143 (P.B.H.May 53, Fazal Mahmood 6-46).

As cover for Compton, an 18th tourist was chosen:

J. Vic WILSON (Yorks) professional, aged 33, a farmer, left-handed batsman and specialist close fielder, who scored consistently since his 1946 debut.

Apart from Statham and Wardle, Wilson will be the only left-handed batsman in the side.

Wellings: Wilson's addition is a major surprise: he has never before been given a chance in any form of representative cricket If Compton proves fit enough to join the side, there will be 18 tourists, eight of them specialist batsmen. That is an unwieldy number for a tour of Australia.

Ross: would have much preferred Watson, the hero of Lord's 1953

Australia had no international cricket after the 1953 tour, except that the New Zealanders played three State sides on their way home from South Africa. Hassett and Tallon retired. In 1953-54 Keith Miller led New South Wales to a narrow victory in the Sheffield Shield. Morris, Benaud, Miller, Ken Mackay and McDonald all scored well. Ian Johnson the slow Victorian off-spinner, was the conspicuous bowling success. Other names to look out for were the openers Hallebone of Victoria and Briggs of NSW.

Sir Donald Bradman returns to the Australian selection Committee with another Australian captain Jack Ryder, and Dudley Seddon, a former NSW player.

The unusually large complement of 18 members (minus Compton) of the touring team, manager, masseur and baggage master/scorer were accompanied by a phalanx of 23 journalists and as always Alec Bedser's twin brother Eric. Interest in the series was enormous. If the post-First World War template were to be applied, England would retain the Ashes comfortably, like Chapman's side of 1928-29 which won 4-1.

The Australian Overseas Travel Service published information for anyone who wanted to watch the Test series in Australia. A return sea trip leaving London on 26 October and returning on 11 April would cost £307 first class, £182 tourist class. An air return journey leaving London on 20 November was first class £538, tourist £430. Hotel accommodation in Australia would be two Australian pounds per night.

The MCC side were seen off by the national dignitaries and numerous photographers at St. Pancras Station, where a railway worker chalked "Bring home the Ashes" on a brick wall, bound for the *Orsova* sailing from Tilbury docks on 15 September 1954. Many more went there to wave them off. There was a farewell lunch on board. Hutton went and spoke to young Cowdrey's parents and assured them that he would look after their son. The *Orsova,* having docked for half an hour at Gibraltar, docked in Naples and the cricketing party took a bus trip to Pompeii. Hutton and some others went to see the grave of Hedley Verity at Caserta and laid a wreath. En route to Port Said Hutton appointed his selection committee for the tour: himself, May, Edrich and Evans. Bailey was excluded, also Bedser who was designated 'senior professional'. Through the Suez Canal, British service families came out in small boats and Hutton got his team to sign photographs and throw them out to the boats. At the end of the canal, the Scots Guards pipes and drums played "Will ye no' come back again?"

The extra speed put on from Aden (costing Cunard over £1,000 in fuel) enabled the MCC to play five hours' cricket against Ceylon at Colombo. Before docking Hutton called Press Conference and, to much surprise, made a point of stating his opposition to the use of bouncers by fast bowlers. MCC made 178 for 8 dec (Cowdrey 66*) and Ceylon 101 for 4. Appleyard injured his ribs when colliding with a spectator as he ran off at the end of the match. The players and Press spent the evening at the Grand Oriental Hotel and got back to the ship for a midnight sailing.

The shores of Western Australia were reached on 7th October. At Freemantle the ship was invaded by Australian journalists and Hutton gave his first Press Conference, very successfully. He emphatically denied that he had ever told the selectors that he would pull out of Trueman were in the team; he would come no matter who else was selected; he would not discuss the secret deliberations of the selection committee, but did mention that Trueman's form in the West Indies was unimpressive. [In 1984 Hutton wrote that he in fact voted for Trueman]. He said again that 'bouncers' should be used sufficiently sparingly that the Umpires should not have to intervene. He disarmed the Australian Press by making out as if he had a rag-bag team "not much bowling, no real batsmen". "I think the chances are even, but of course Australia will be playing at home in conditions to which they are used."

Then they went up the Swan River towards Perth, for a few days of civic functions and net practices. On arrival at the hotel there was a cable saying that Colin Cowdrey's father was dead. Mr Cowdrey, aged 54 actually suffered a fatal heart attack listening to a radio report of the Ceylon match. Colin had been told on the ship that his father was ill. For some time after that the captain and manager took a special interest in keeping Cowdrey occupied

On the first full day ashore there was a bit of controversy when scorer and baggage man George Duckworth was reported as saying that Trueman's omission was a shock. Both Hutton and the manager Mr Howard had a word with Duckworth, reminding him of his contractual obligation not to give interviews. More serious was the news that MCC's primary bowler Alec Bedser had contracted a nasty attack of shingles on his bowling arm. He had a twinge of pain on his right shoulder on the last day at sea and was diagnosed by a doctor in Perth. He might be out of action for a month. On top of this Appleyard had his rib trouble diagnosed as a slipped cartilage with synovial fluid, a particular concern for someone with tuberculosis.

In the net practices, Hutton asked ageing leg-spinners, Ian Peebles and F.R.Brown to bowl in the nets.

Ahead lies a traditional itinerary, basically unchanged between 1932-33 and 1965-66: an anti-clockwise journey round the continental coast, First Test at Brisbane, Fourth Test at Adelaide, the other three Tests shared between Melbourne and Sydney.

In a troubled world the post-war patterns are being established. The formal occupation of Germany by the war Allies is ended. West Germany is admitted to NATO and signs an economic agreement with France, there is Communist insurgency in the French colony of Vietnam, Britain and Egypt agree on the evacuation of British troops from the Suez Canal.

Seaside start: Western Australian Country XI, at Bunbury, October 11, 12

The first match was at Bunbury, a thriving seaside port and resort 100 miles south of Perth. The Country XI contained mostly young farmers, many of whom came vast distances to play. Graveney passed 50 in an hour, striking 64444 off successive balls by a leg spinner. Edrich made a muddled start but reached his 100 in 195 minutes. On the second day (Tuesday) Australians were treated to their first sight of the 70 yard gap between the start of Tyson's run-up and the wicket-keeper, but Tyson's direction was wayward. Loader, McConnon and 'keeper Andrew looked good. In the follow on, Cowdrey's leg breaks got more turn than any body. A 17-year old lefthander, Barry Shepherd made a promising 14. Stephen's 54 runs in the match took 280 minutes.

MCC 344-5 dec (Hutton 59, Edrich 129, Graveney 58, Cowdrey 48*). WESTERN AUSTRALIAN COUNTRY XI 116 (Loader 4-35, McConnon 5-30) and 128-6 (E.Stephen 40, Cowdrey 4-35) *Drawn*

MCC in Australia 1954-55

Efficient opening: Western Australia at Perth, October 15,16,18,19

The W.A.C.A. ground at Perth is one of the best wickets in Australia, and with its recently erected scoreboard and roomy pavilion stands, it could well host a Test match. The MCC team almost picked itself: Bedser has shingles, Appleyard a rib strain, Andrew is injured and Compton is still in England. In beautiful weather and a fresh looking wicket Hutton put the State side into bat and Statham soon reduced them to 57 for 7, punctuated by a sudden 15 minute rain break. At that point the captain Carmody, who had retired when struck on the head from his first ball by Statham, returned and helped to lift the side to 103 all out. MCC's fielding was poor and three chances were dropped. Hutton dominated the MCC innings. 49 overnight, on the cooler Saturday he went on to 145 in 269 minutes when he retired with a leg strain. It was an unspectacular innings with three chances, until he reached his hundred. Wilson batted with determination and Cowdrey was very impressive. Western Australia were 32 for 3 at the close, but on the third day Carmody and Meuleman stayed nearly to tea-time. Carmody was dropped when 8, an easy catch to May at slip. When No.10 Price came in 21 were required to avoid an innings defeat. The innings survived until the final day. Meuleman's stubborn chanceless 109 lasted 385 minutes. MCC lost three wickets in wrapping it up by lunch time.

WESTERN AUSTRALIA 103 (Statham 6-23) and 255 (K.D.Meuleman 109, D.K.Carmody 75, Statham 3-68). MCC 321 (Hutton ret.145*, Wilson 38, Cowdrey 41, H.R.Gorringe 4-102) and 40-3. *MCC won by seven wickets.*

Keith Miller has been re-appointed captain of New South Wales. Those who favour Arthur Morris to move from vice-captaincy of the Test side to captain in succession to Hassett, would have hoped that Morris would displace Miller in the State position.

Double victory: Combined XI at Perth, October 22, 23, 25

With Hutton out of action, though watching and advising intently from the Pavilion, May captained the side against an XI consisting of the Western Australia team augmented by three Test players brought over specially from the East: Neil Harvey, Graham Hole and Ian Johnson. Meuleman had to drop out because of knee trouble. May put the Combined XI in and in 228 minutes they were all out for 86. Rutherford the opener, made 39 in 205 minutes, the only one to reach double figures. Harvey made 3, Hole 4, being two of Evans five victims. It was Bailey who made the breakthrough, and Tyson found the control which he lacked at Bunbury. MCC were 60 for 3 at the close and on Saturday May and Wilson took their partnership to 179 in 250 minutes, faultless but uninspiring. May achieved some domination later on and his 129 in 324 minutes contained 14 fours. The most successful bowler was Johnson, who on Friday had dismissed Simpson and Graveney in one over, and who was curiously under-bowled by Carmody. On Monday all ten Combined XI wickets fell and the match was over with one day and 17 minutes to spare.

COMBINED XI 86 (J.W.Rutherford 39, Statham 3-21) and 163 (G.B.Hole 33, D.K.Carmody 38, L.Pavy 36*, Wardle 4-34, Appleyard 3-36). MCC 311 (May 129, Wilson 72, Bailey 35, R.H.Price 3-73, I.W.Johnson 3-44). *MCC won by an innings and 62 runs.*

Denis Compton arrives: South Australia at Adelaide, Oct 29, 30 Nov 1, 2

On 26 October the MCC and its entourage flew to Adelaide, a six hour stretch at night. Previous touring teams had made that journey over three days by train. Denis Compton had just arrived on a flight from London. He was without his cricket gear, which was stolen from his car the day before his departure. Preparing for a short stop at Karachi the landing wheels refused to operate and after two hours circling while a strip was prepared, the plane landed safely on its belly. There was a very sober and ceremonial civic reception in the City Hall, where Hutton resuscitated the audience with a scintillating little speech. Those who were not playing flew on to see the Melbourne Cup (a horse race).

On the morning of the match Compton elected to play. Hutton won the toss. Edrich was caught and bowled off the first ball that he middled; Simpson skied a sweep. Compton hit a two off his first ball and, though not at his best, dominated the rest of the innings, with support from Hutton, Graveney and Cowdrey. Compton made 113 in 172 minutes with 10 fours. MCC's last five wickets fell for 35. South Australia were 5 for 0 at the first day close when bad light stopped play.

On Saturday Les Favell boosted his Test chances with an assured 84 in 158 minutes with two sixes. Hole was in poor form. The slow bowler Roxby and wicketkeeper Langley added 60 and at the close South Australia were equal to the MCC score with three wickets to fall. Tyson was impressive, off a very long run, fast and accurate. On Monday the home side squeezed only a small lead, with Wilson suffering a hard blow to the body from Tyson. Drennan took 3 for 13 in six overs but captain Ridings used Horsnell and Roxby after lunch and Hutton and Graveney added 65 in 75 minutes. McConnon stayed with Hutton until the latter was caught at slip for 98 in 251 minutes.

South Australia had the whole last day to score 174 to win on a slowly turning wicket. Harris and Hole went cheaply. At 51 for 2, Pinch ducked into a stump-high ball from Loader and retired hurt. Ridings was out just before lunch and Favell immediately afterwards, beaten by Tyson's pace. Pinch returned at the fall of the sixth wicket but lasted only three balls. Appleyard clinched victory, which was not quite as narrow as it looked, in a spell of 3 overs, 4 for 5.

At the same time as this match, the Australian domestic season opened. Because of fears that gate receipts would be so low as to make the normal programme uneconomic, as an experiment, the Sheffield Shield matches were drastically reduced. The major states (New South Wales, Victoria, South Australia, Queensland) will play only four Shield games, and the fledgling Western Australia two. Like the MCC state matches, games are limited to four days of five hours each. The Shield opened with Queensland at home to New South Wales in a dull draw, with centuries by Mackay and Burge for Queensland, and Benaud and Burke for the visitors.

Full scores:-

MCC in Australia 1954-55

MCC (won toss)

*L.Hutton c Roxby b Wilson	37	c Hole b Roxby	98
W.J.Edrich c and b Horsnell	0	c Langley b Drennan	2
R.T.Simpson c sub (J.C.Lill) b Wilson	26	b Drennan	16
D.C.S.Compton st Langley b Wilson	113	b Drennan	2
T.W.Graveney b Drennan	20	c Langley b Hole	34
M.C.Cowdrey st Langley b Roxby	20	c Hole b Wilson	7
J.E.McConnon st Langley b Roxby	4	lbw b Wilson	12
F.H.Tyson c Wilson b Roxby	8	not out	4
P.J.Loader c Ridings b Wilson	6	(10) c Pinch b Wilson	4
+K.V.Andrew c Favell b Wilson	2	(9) c Hole b Wilson	0
R.Appleyard not out	5	b Roxby	0
Extras (b 4, l-b 1)	5	(b 1, l-b 1)	2
Total (73.6 overs, 282 mins)	**246**	**(71.5 overs, 286 mins)**	**181**

WICKETS.- 1-4, 2-45, 3-92, 4-162, 5-211, 6-225, 7-227, 8-234, 9-236, 10-246.
BOWLING.-. Drennan 7-1-16-1; Hornsell 13-2-38-1; Roxby 23.6-4-82-3; Wilson 24-4-81-5; Hole 1-0-1-0; Dansie 5-0-23-0.

1-5, 2-29, 3-31, 4-96, 5-111, 6-173, 7-173, 8-173, 9-181, 10-181.
.Drennan 16-3-32-3; Horsnell 8-0-34-0; Roxby 16.5-3-59-2; Hole 10-3-14-1; Wilson 16-5-32-4; Dansie 5-1-8-0.

South Australia

L.E.Favell c Hutton b Tyson	84	b Tyson	47
D.Harris b Tyson	43	c and b Loader	0
G.B.Hole c Simpson b Loader	12	c McConnon b Appleyard	10
C.J.Pinch b McConnon	12	c Andrew b Appleyard	9
*P.L.Ridings c Andrew b Loader	19	c Graveney b McConnon	27
H.N.Dansie c Hutton b Tyson	11	lbw b Appleyard	18
+G.R..Langley not out	36	b McConnon	23
R.C.Roxby lbw b McConnon	28	not out	6
J.Drennan b Tyson	2	c Simpson b Appleyard	1
K.G.Horsnell b Tyson	0	b Appleyard	2
J.W.Wilson run out (Graveney/Andrew)	0	b Loader	2
Extras (b 3, l-b 3, n-b 1)	7	(b 5, l-b 1, n-b 1)	7
Total (61.1 overs, 317 mins)	**254**	**(39.6 overs, 217 mins)**	**152**

WICKETS.- 1-119 2-136 3-146 4-167 5-182 6-186 7-246 8-249 9-253 10-254
BOWLING.-.Tyson 19-3-62-5; Loader 17-0-73-2; Edrich 5-2-25-0; Appleyard 9-2-31-0; McConnon 11.1-1-56-2.

1-2 2-42 3-95 4-102 5-127 6-142 7-142 8-144 9-147 10-152
Tyson 12-3-37-1; Loader 8.6-2-25-2; Appleyard 11-1-46-5; McConnon 8-0-37-2.

Umpires: K.C.Buller and M.J.McInnes.
MCC WON BY 21 RUNS

Rain arrives: Australian XI at Melbourne, November 5, 6, (7) (8)

The tourists went south east on a sleeping train, 450 miles in 14 hours, to Melbourne, the most populous city and biggest cricket ground with a gaping gap beside the Members' Stand for new stands of the 1956 Olympics to be built, to play not Victoria but an Australian XI. May won the toss and batted and after Edrich scratched around for 90 minutes for 11. Simpson and May added 63. Simpson used his feet well to the spinners. In a feeble collapse against the spin of Johnson and Benaud, the last seven wickets fell for 52. From 12 for 0 at the close, the Australian XI scored 155 in 278 minutes on the second day, boring a crowd of 36,317. With no play on Monday, play was extended to a fifth day but to no avail as not another ball was bowled. Denis Compton, having forgotten to bring his ground pass, was refused entry through the turnstiles by a gatekeeper who recognised him. "Very well, I'll go home" he said and then jumped over the railings. Later several players in their MCC blazers and flannels, coming back from net practice, were also held up.
MCC 205 (Simpson 74, May 45, I.W.Johnson 6-66, R. Benaud 3-58). AUSTRALIAN XI 167-7 (R.E.Briggs 48, R. Benaud 47, Bailey 4-53). *Match drawn*

Cowdrey arrives: New South Wales, November 12, 13, 15 16

Another train journey to the state border, changing trains because Victoria and New South Wales have different track gauges. In New South Wales, where the public were now voting in a state referendum, by a narrow majority, to extend the licensing hours from a 6pm closure to 10pm, MCC now faced the biggest game of the tour so far. They unexpectedly rested Compton, Graveney and Bailey and gave Edrich another chance. The State captain Keith Miller put MCC in. After 75 minutes the score was 38 for 4, two caught by young Bobby Simpson at slip. The Cowdrey joined Hutton in a stand of 163 in even time, before the rest of the batting collapsed. Bedser's 'rabbit' Arthur Morris took 14 runs off Bedser's first over, and NSW closed at 19-0, though next day he had him caught in the covers for 26. Opener Willie Watson batted through the day for 138*, adding 161 in 140 minutes with Miller.

MCC in Australia 1954-55

Curiously at 4.45 the batsman de Courcy appeared to speak with Hutton and they agreed to come off the field for bad light, without involving the umpires. Mysteriously the umpires brought the players back on for another ten minutes play in no better light. On Monday NSW secured a lead of 130. Watson took his score to 155 in 380 minutes and in his second match for the State made himself a Test candidate. In the second innings Wilson and Cowdrey opened. Wilson was yorked by the tall fast bowler Crawford for nought. But Cowdrey went to 71 out of 138-3 at the close and on the final morning, after the end of another disappointing struggle by Edrich, Hutton joined Cowdrey. Cowdrey was out after lunch completing 103 in 280 minutes. Hutton was later caught off the leg spinner Treanor by Simpson diving full stretch to his right at slip. Tyson held on for an hour and NSW were left only 75 minutes to score 198. The match ended oddly for Cowdrey: having announced himself as a Test batsman with two centuries, he completely lost the confidence of his captain as a leg-spin bowler conceding 38 runs in three overs, including a six by Davidson onto the roof of the main Grandstand.

MCC 252 (Hutton 102, Cowdrey 110, P.A.Crawford 3-51, A.K.Davidson 3-41, J.C.Treanor 3-64) and 327 (Cowdrey 103, Edrich 37, Hutton 87, P.A.Crawford 4-86, J.C.Treanor 4-96). NEW SOUTH WALES 382 (W.J.Watson 155, K.R.Miller 86, A.K.Davidson 30, Bedser 4-117, Tyson 4-98) and 78-2 (J.W.Burke 34*). *Match Drawn.*

At the same time the Western Australians were earning a very creditable draw against South Australia at Adelaide.

Home team for First Test

On the 17 November Colonel Nasser took over a President of Egypt, and the Australian XII for the First Test was announced. It was:

Arthur Robert MORRIS (NSW), the vice-captain, a dominating left-hand batsman still in decline, who had been beaten to the captaincy of NSW by Miller.

Les(lie) E FAVELL (S Aus), a free-scoring right-handed opening batsman, yet to appear in a Test

R. Neil HARVEY (Victoria) the nimble, 5 ft 8 ins. left-hander, consistently devastating on good firm pitches.

Graeme B. HOLE (S. Aus), tall free-scoring front foot right hand batsman and excellent slip fielder.

Keith R. MILLER (NSW), one of the great all-rounders, powerful right hand batsman, on his day and in short spells a fast and fearsome right arm bowler. Captain of his State and the popular favourite to captain Australia in succession to Hassett

Ray(mond) R. LINDWALL (now playing for Queensland) renowned fast right-hand bowler and a positive contributor with the bat at No.9.

Ron G. ARCHER (Queensland), tall lanky lively fast medium bowler who could bat well at 9 or 10.

William (Bill) A. JOHNSTON (Victoria) the tall lively left arm swing bowler on the fast side of medium, who could cut down his pace to bowl spin. Still suffering from the effects of his leg injury in the 1953 tour. A confirmed left-hand No.11 bat.

Alan K. DAVIDSON (NSW) a similar type of bowler to Johnston, stockier and a little quicker, and a very useful left-hand bat.

Richie BENAUD (NSW) still a promising all-rounder, nippy leg-spinner and hard-hitting batsman.

Ian W. JOHNSON (Victoria), almost 34, a very slow off-break bowler with a slightly bent arm action that caused some comment, and useful No.9 batsman. He had not made the 1953 tour and had never been an automatic selection for the Test side.

Gilbert (Gil) R.A. LANGLEY (S Aus) highly efficient rather than brilliant wicket-keeper now unchallenged since Tallon's retirement.

In accordance with the Australian tradition, the captain was chosen the next day by the Board from the team provided by the Selectors. There were three candidates, Miller, who had beaten Morris to the captaincy of New South Wales, Morris and Johnson, successor to Hassett as captain of Victoria. Miller was clearly the popular choice. Johnson had not been selected to tour England in 1953. He was pleasant, diplomatic cricketer, very much part of the Australian establishment. For the first time for many years the Board had picked a captain who would not be regarded as an automatic member of the Test side and there was some suspicion that, contrary to the professed policy, he had been foisted into the team to be made captain. On the other hand, he was an experienced Test cricketer, who toured in 1948, and it would be hard to point to any other available spinner who should be ahead of him: Benaud? Johnston? Hill? It was his good figures for the Australian XI against MCC that probably secured his choice as captain. Arthur Morris was the vice-captain. It is believed that the Board delegates from South Australia and obviously Victoria voted for Johnson. The New South Wales voted for Miller and the Queensland for Morris

Lindwall's secret: Queensland at Brisbane: Nov 19, 20, 22, 23

Transfer from Sydney to Brisbane was by Australian National Airways. MCC were again put in to bat and again collapsed to 18 for 3. Simpson and Compton joined in a stand of 234. After taking 4 for 66 Lindwall was absent for the rest of the match with what was described with a gastric complaint and was in fact hepatitis. He kept it quiet and took on the diet and medicine prescribed, giving up beer, and hoped to be fit for the First Test. In the last over of the day, when the home side made 12 for 0, McConnon was felled by a body blow when fielding at short leg. Rain allowed only 140 minutes play on the second day when Queensland advanced to 97 for one. With Lindwall unable to bat they were held to a respectable total by a nine wicket stand between Flynn and wicket-keeper Grout. In their innings all but one batsman reached 20. Before the close Cowdrey had failed for the second time as an opening batsman. On the final day May and Compton made the game safe. Graveney has an attack of 'flu.

MCC 304 (Simpson 136, Compton 110, R.R.Lindwall 4-66) and 288 (Simpson 38, May 77, Compton 69, Bailey 51*). QUEENSLAND 288 (C.E.Harvey 49, Statham 3-74, Bailey 3-74) and 25-2 (Simpson 2-5). *Match Drawn*

There was even more rain at Melbourne where Les Favell of South Australia made a timely 56 and 160.

MCC in Australia 1954-55 – FIRST TEST

FIRST TEST AT BRISBANE

November 26, 27, 29, 30, Dec 1

On Wednesday 24th November the England team for the Test was announced:
Hutton, Simpson, Edrich, Compton, May, Cowdrey, Bailey, Evans, Tyson, Bedser, Statham. (12th man Wilson).

   Graveney is still indisposed. Simpson's century against Queensland gets him in to solve the problem of Hutton's opening partner. Edrich is in on his reputation. The sensation is that England commit themselves to playing four bowlers, all pace. Neither Wardle nor Appleyard have impressed so far. But not since the bodyline series has England omitted a specialist spinner from its team (and then suffered their only loss of that series). Trevor Bailey was not at all impressed when he was told the team by Evans and Edrich and ordered a double Scotch. It seems odd, therefore, that Compton was not given a decent spell of bowling his chinamen in the State match: perhaps May, who captained against Queensland, was not privy to Hutton's plans. Hutton is taking a big gamble, it is assumed that he is planning on putting Australia into bat first (a big mistake, thinks Moyes). Hutton watched every ball from a chair in front of the Pavilion and formed his view based on the lively nature of the wicket for the Queensland match. Four-pace attack needs a helpful pitch and atmosphere and it is too early to predict the conditions two days before the start, says Whitington. Gilligan agrees: 13 players should have been named and the final choice made on the morning of the match. The weather is pleasantly hot with the ever-present possibility of thunder. MCC practice on the wicket used for the state match. Now that the rules have been changed in Australia to allow the wicket to be covered at any time to prevent rain falling on it, there will be no fear of the sensational Brisbane 'sticky' on which batting becomes a pure lottery and where 20 wickets fell for 130 runs on one day in the Test of 1950-51, though a proper storm will probably percolate the strongest of covers.

   After vigorous exercise playing squash, on Thursday evening Evans took ill, having sunstroke, and he has to be replaced by Andrew. Evans will spend the first day of the Test in bed with a temperature of 102°F.

   The Woollongabba (or 'Gabba') is off Vulture Street in south east Brisbane

FIRST DAY - Everything goes wrong

Friday 26 November

   A warm breezy day, like a perfect summer's day in England, not humid. The temperature is under 80 degrees Fahrenheit. The Australians leave out Davidson.

   Out in the middle with Johnson, Hutton prods and feels the pitch, and walks its length twice, calls heads, correctly, prods and feels again several times. Walking back to the Pavilion he says "Ian, I think you can have the strike". He assumes the wicket to be damp and lively as was the pitch for the match against Queensland, and the constitution of the team commits him to bowling first. In this he may have made two errors: one, that the same careful preparation went in to the State game pitch as would go in for the Test pitch, and two, that the continuous dry sunshine since then has had no effect.

Umpires: C.Hoy and M.J.McInnes

Australia First Innings

Odd overs -] →   from Vulture St (Pavilion) End
Even overs - ← [from Railway (Stanley St) End

				Favell	Morris		
1	11.30	Bedser 1] →		- - 1 - - - -		 - 1	Favell hit high on pad by inswinger Favell pushes to mid-off Three onside fielders against Morris
2		Statham 1 ← [		- - - - - -		 - 1	 Favell plays and misses Favell plays and misses *Good over*
3		Bedser 2] →			- - - - - - 1		 *Morris thin edge dropped by Andrew* *Pitch playing fast but easy for batsmen*

13

MCC in Australia 1954-55 – FIRST TEST

#	Time	Bowler	B1	B2	Total	Notes
4		Statham 2 ← [	- - - 1 - - - -		- 2	
5		Bedser 3] → Off spell 3-1-2-0	- - 1 - - - -		- 3	Favell hits just outside Hutton's reach at fwd short leg. Tyson throws in quick but wide. Andrew gathers in mid pitch, throws to Bedser who if he took it cleanly, might just have run out Favell.
6		Statham 3 ← [Off spell 3-1-3-0	- - 2 - - - -		-5	*Statham, fast and accurate, has made good use of the new ball*
7		Tyson 1] →	- - - 3 (nb) - - 1 -		- 9	Morris drives for 3 off the mark after 30 mins
8		Bailey 1 ← [	- - - - - 1 4 -		- 14	Morris sweet drive past cover for 4
9	12.15	Tyson 2] →	1 - 4 - - - - -		- 19	Morris on drive for 4 *Morris ducks two bouncers. His cap falls off. He takes off his cap and gives it to the umpire* Drinks
10		Bailey 2 ← [Off spell 2-0-13-0	4 - - - - 4 -		- 27	Favell square cut for 4 Favell glides for 4
11		Tyson 3] → Off spell 3-0-15-0	- - 1 1 - 4 -		- 33	Morris cuts uppishly. Compton at third man collides with fence and hurts his hand

MCC in Australia 1954-55 – FIRST TEST

Over	Time	Bowler	Batsman 1	Batsman 2	Score	Notes
12		Bedser 4 ← [	- 1	- (1 nb) - - (4 byes) - - 6 (nb) -	- 45	*4 byes somewhere in this over* Morris pull for six disturbs two conversing ladies under parasols
13	12.35	Statham 4] →	- - 1	- - - - -	-46	*Compton leaves the field. Wilson substitutes*
14	 12.44	Bedser 5 ← [Off spell 2-0-11-0	- - - 4 - - -		- 50	All run 4. Tyson returns to Andrew who throws at bowler's stumps, just missing, with Morris well short. 50 up in 74 mins
15	 12.50 12.52	Statham 5] → 	 W Miller - 2	- - 1 - 	 1-51 - 53	Favell c Cowdrey, hooks too soon at bouncer, off gloves boot-high to short sq leg. 23 in 80 mins, 62 balls, 3 fours Miller almost c & b first ball
16		Tyson 4 ← [Spell 1-0-2-0	- 1	- - 1 - - -	- 55	
17	 1.00	Statham 6] → Spell 3-0-5-1	- - - 1	- - - - - -	- 56	England rush at change of ends to get in final over
		LUNCH	Miller 4 8 mins 10 balls	Morris 24 90 mins 67 balls	1-56 90 mins 139 balls	

Arlott: only Statham got past the bat this morning.

Swanton: the pitch has been dry, firm and evenly paced. Favell made an auspicious debut, generally playing with assurance.

Barnes: a refreshingly confident start by Favell. Has Morris's opening partner been found?

			Miller 4	Morris 24	1- 56	
18	1.40	Bedser 6 ← [	1	- - - - - -	- 57	

MCC in Australia 1954-55 – FIRST TEST

Over		Bowler	Runs		Total	Notes
19		Statham 7] →	- - - - 1	- -	- 58	
20		Bedser 7 ← [	2 - - - - 2 - (nb) 6 2		- 70	Miller a big high six to long on
21		Statham 8] → Off spell (incl. lunch) 5-0-8-1	- 1	1 - - - - -	- 72	
22		Bedser 8 ← [	1 -	- - - - - -	-73	
23		Tyson 5] →	- - (nb) 1 3 1 - 4 -		- 82	Morris perfectly timed 4 to sq leg
24		Bedser 9 ← [	- - 1	- 4 - - -	- 87	Three runs plus one overthrow
25		Tyson 6] → Off spell 2-0-19-0	4 - 2 - - 4 -		- 97	Miller superb cut for 4 Miller superb cut for 2 Miller superb cut for 4
26		Bedser 10 ← [	- 1	- - 1 - - - -	- 99	
27		Bailey 3] →	- - - - - -		- 99	

16

MCC in Australia 1954-55 – FIRST TEST

Over	Time	Bowler		Batsman		Score	Notes
28	2.30	Bedser 11 ← [		- (1 lb) - - - - -		-100	*100 up in 140 mins*
29		Bailey 4] →		- 2 1 4 - 3 -		- 110	
30		Bedser 12 ← [Off spell 7-1-25-0		- 1 1 1 - - -		- 113	*Miller stumping chance down leg-side, bounces off Andrew's pads*
31		Bailey 5] →		- - - - - 1 2		- 116	*Bailey bowls leg theory*
32	2.50	Edrich 1 ← [Off spell 1-0-6-0		1 1 - 4 - - -		- 122	*An over of long hops*
33	 2.58 3.00	Bailey 6] →		- - 1 - - - W Harvey -		 2-123 - 123	*News that Compton has fractured metacarpal bone* *Miller cutting again, plays on off gloves and edge, 49 in 86 mins, 88 balls, 4 fours, 1 six*
34		Statham 9 ← [		- - - - 1 - -		- 124	
35		Bailey 7] →		- - - 1 - - -		- 125	
36		Statham 10 ← [Off spell 1-0-5-0		- - (4 byes) - - - 1 -		- 130	*4 byes somewhere between overs 33.8 and 38.8*

MCC in Australia 1954-55 – FIRST TEST

Over	Time	Bowler	Batsman 1	Batsman 2	Score	Notes
37		Bailey 8] →		- 1		
	3.19	Off spell 6-1-21-1	2 - - - 3		- 136	Harvey off mark after 19 mins, off-drive for 2
38		Bedser 13 ← [	- - - - - 2 -		-138	
39	3.25	Statham 11] → Spell 1-0-4-0	- 1	2 1 - - - -		Morris 51 in 195 mins, 138 balls
	3.30				-142	
		TEA	Harvey 8 30 mins 24 balls	Morris 52 200 mins 143 balls	2-142 200 mins 317 balls	

SESSION 86-1 IN 110 MINS, 178 BALLS
Compton has fractured his hand and will only bat in an emergency

Over	Time	Bowler	Harvey 8	Morris 52	2- 142	Notes
40	3.50	Bedser 14 ← [	1	- - - 2 - -	- 145	
41		Tyson 7] →	- - 1 - 1 - -		- 147	
42		Bedser 15 ← [	- - - - - 1 -		- 148	Morris (55) hooks high to long leg, Bailey drops it
43		Tyson 8] →	- - - - - -	4	- 152	Morris snicks between wk and slip for 4
44		Bedser 16 ← [Off spell (incl. tea) 4-0-8-0	1 - - - 1	1	- 155	

18

MCC in Australia 1954-55 – FIRST TEST

Over		Bowler				Score	Notes
45		Tyson 9] → Off spell 3-0-12-0	4 - - - - 2 -			- 161	Harvey pulls and edges over wk's head for 4 to 3rd man
46		Statham 12 ← [		- - 1 - - -		- 162	Tyson leaves field with cramp. Graveney substitutes
47		Bailey 9] →		- - 4 1 - 1 -		- 168	Tyson leaves the field for a short time with cramp
48		Statham 13 ← [		- - - - - -		- 168	
49		Bailey 10] →		1 - 1 - - -		- 170	
50		Statham 14 ← [	2 - 1	2 - - -		- 175	
51		Bailey 11] → Off spell 3-0-13-0	- - - - 1 4 -			- 180	
52		Statham 15 ← [	- (1 b/ lb) -	- - 1 - -		-182	
53		Tyson 10] →		- - - - (1 b/lb) - - -		- 183	

MCC in Australia 1954-55 – FIRST TEST

54		Statham 16 ← [Off spell 5-1-12-0		- - - (1 b/lb) - 5 - - -	 - 189	4 overthrows
55		Tyson 11] →	2 - 4 - - 1	 1	 -197	
56		Bedser 17 ← [		- - - - - - -	 - 197	
57		Tyson 12] → Spell 3-1-13-0	1 - - 1 - 2 1		 - 202	
58		Bedser 18 ← [Spell 2-1-6-0	- 1 - - -	- 4 1 -	 -208	New ball now available
	5.30	CLOSE	Harvy 41 130 mins 103 balls	Morris 82 300 mins 216 balls	2-208 300 mins 469 balls	Attendance: 16,500

SESSION 66-0 IN 100 MINS, 152 BALLS

The first day of the series could hardly have gone worse for England and for Hutton. He put Australia in and took two wickets in the day, the fielding was patchy, the bowling innocuous, and England may have lost one of their premier batsmen. Compton has a metacarpal fracture of the fourth finger of the left hand

Swanton: Miller played the best innings of the day. Morris started well but after he lapsed in concentration. Harvey came in at an ideal time, when the bowling was flagging, but he never quite found his touch.

Arlott: Wilson drew the admiration of the crowd for his perfectly accurate long throw-ins into Andrews' gloves. If England do not break through tomorrow, they will spend five days struggling for a draw.

Cardus: Morris has freed himself from the dominance of Bedser's bowling

Peebles: The gamble has failed and it is now a question of trying to save the game.

Gilligan: Most of the Press this morning thought Hutton was right to bowl first, and the gamble was lost because of dropped catches.

Wellings: Bailey, a specialist close fielder, was at long leg because of his injured hand, where he dropped Morris

Times correspondent: Statham was fast and accurate, Tyson hurled everything into his task, Bedser bowled with his usual heroic intent, Bailey kept the batsmen quiet after a loose start.

Moyes: The English attack was never hostile and they bowled too short. Simpson, Cowdrey and substitute Wilson stood out in the field.

Hughes: Hutton fairly thought that the pitch would be as fiery as in the State game and rightly wanted to have a go at the Australian batsmen who were not yet in the runs. Bedser is half as good a bowler without Evans at the stumps. If Morris had been caught for 0, he might have run through the side

Harris: Groundsman Jack McAndrew told me that he would have advised the winner of the toss to bat. Hutton made a simple mistake, as anyone could.

Hutton says that he put Australia in because he expected a lively wicket and because no Australian batsman was as yet in form. The fielding today was the worst in his memory. [In 1984 he writes that he should have abandoned his plan to bowl first when it was clear that Evans would not play]

MCC in Australia 1954-55 – FIRST TEST

SECOND DAY – Australia consolidate

Saturday 27 November

			Harvy 41	Morris 82	2-208	
59	11.30	Statham 17] →		- - 4 - - 1 - -	- 213	Morris powerful 4 through covers
60		Bedser 19 ← [		2 - - 1 - - -	- 216	*Spectators complain of commentary being heard from portable radio in the stand. Police intervene* New ball – Morris edges just past May's fingertips at 2nd slip Harvey plays and misses
61		Statham 18] →		- - 1 - 2 - -	- 219	
62		Bedser 20 ← [		2 - - - - - -	- 221	
63	11.53	Statham 19] → Off spell 3-0-19-0	4 - - - - 3	4	- 232	Harvey 50 in 153 mins, 120 balls
64	12.00	Bedser 21 ← [	- - - 1	- - 4 -	- 237	Morris 101 in 330 mins, 242 balls
65		Bailey 12] →	4 1	- - 1 2 - -	- 245	Harvey cuts square for 4
66		Bedser 22 ← [Off spell 4-0-14-0		- - - - - - 4	- 249	

MCC in Australia 1954-55 – FIRST TEST

Over	Time	Bowler			Notes
67		Bailey 13] →	- - - 4 - - -	- 253	*Bailey tries leg theory* *Harvey on 58 dropped by Bedser at leg slip, ball bouncing out as he fell*
68		Edrich 2 ← [	- - 4 - - - 3	- 260	
69		Bailey 14] → Off spell 3-0-19-0	- - - - 6 1 -	- 267	Morris 6 flicked to long leg. Even Bailey applauds.
70	12.15	Edrich 3 ← [Off spell 2-0-22-0	4 4 - 1 4 - 1	- 282	
71		Tyson 13] →	- - 1 2 - 1 -	- 286	
72		Statham 20 ← [	- - 1 - - - -	- 287	
73		Tyson 14] →	4 - - 1 1 1 -	- 294	Harvey almost ct down leg-side by Andrew who gets end of gloves to it.
74		Statham 21 ← [Off spell 2-0-2-0	- 1 - - - - -	- 295	
75		Tyson 15] → Spell 3-0-13-0	- - 1 - - 1 -	- 297	

MCC in Australia 1954-55 – FIRST TEST

Over	Time	Bowler	Batsman 1	Batsman 2	Score	Notes
76		Bedser 23 ← [Spell 1-0-2-0		- 1 - - - -	1	
	1.00				- 299	
		LUNCH	Harvey 76 220 mins 161 balls	Morris 138 390 mins 302 balls	2- 299 390 mins 613 balls	

SESSION 91-0 IN 90 MINS, 144 BALLS
Bailey's short-lived attempt at leg theory is deprecated by Lindsay Hassett.

Over	Time	Bowler	Harvey 76	Morris 138	2- 299	Notes
77	1.40	Tyson 16] →	- 2 - - - -		- 301	
78		Bailey 15 ← [	 1 1	4 1 - 1 -	- 309	
79		Tyson 17] →	- 1 - 1 - -		- 311	Tyson is bowling off half his usual run, at Hutton's request
80		Bailey 16 ← [	 - 1 3	3 - 3 -	- 321	
81	2.00	Tyson 18] →	1 - - 1 - -	- 1 - 1	- 325	200 partnership in 240 mins
82	2.09 2.10	Bailey 17 ← [	 - 1	- W Hole 1 - -	3- 325 - 327	Morris c Cowdrey, edging drive waist high to the only slip, 153 in 419 mins, 321 balls, 8 fours 2 sixes. Morris has become the third highest Australian Test run-scorer (after Bradman and C.Hill)
83		Tyson 19] → Off spell (incl.lunch) 7-0-29-0	2 - - 2 - - 4		- 335	Harvey edges for 4

MCC in Australia 1954-55 – FIRST TEST

84		Bailey 18 ← [		- - 1 - 1 - -	- 337	
85	2.20	Bedser 24] →	4 - 2 - 1	- -	- 344	Harvey pushes firmly to sq leg, 101 in 265 mins, 200 balls. His first 100 v England in Australia. *Harvey hard c & b chance*
86		Bailey 19 ← [	1 1	- 1 - - 1 -	- 348	
87		Bedser 25] →		- - - 1 - - -	- 349	
88		Bailey 20 ← [Off spell 6-1-31-1	4 -	- - - - 1	- 354	
89		Bedser 26] →	1	3 - 4 - - 1	- 363	
90		Statham 22 ← [	1 - - 4	- 3 1	- 372	Only slip close up for Harvey
91		Bedser 27] →		- - - - - - 1	- 373	
92		Statham 23 ← [	2 -	- - 1 -	- 376	

24

MCC in Australia 1954-55 – FIRST TEST

Over	Time	Bowler	Batsman 1	Batsman 2	Total	Notes
93		Bedser 28] → Off spell 5-0-21-0		2 - - - 1 - -	- 379	
94		Statham 24 ← [	- 2 - 1	- 1 - - - 1	- 384	
95		Tyson 20] →	- 4 - 4	4 2 1	- 399	
96		Statham 25 ← [Off spell 4-0-24-0	- - 1 - - 1	- - 1 - 4 1	- 406	
97	3.30	Tyson 21] →	- 4 1	- 1 - -	- 412	
		TEA	Harvy 135 330 mins 241 balls	Hole 39 80 mins 69 balls	3- 412 500 mins 781 balls	

SESSION 113-1 IN 110 MINS, 168 BALLS

Over	Time	Bowler	Batsman 1	Batsman 2	Total	Notes
			Harvy 135	Hole 39	3- 412	
98	3.50	Bedser 29 ← [	(1 b/lb) - - - - - 1	1	- 415	Unexplained change of ends ?
99		Tyson 22] →	- - - 2 - 4		- 421	New ball Tyson uses long run Harvey off-drive for 4
100		Bedser 30 ← [	- - -	- 4 2 1 - - -	- 428	101 stand in 95 mins

MCC in Australia 1954-55 – FIRST TEST

101		Tyson 23] →	- - - - 2 -	- (1 b/lb)	- 431	
102		Bedser 31 ← [(1 b/lb) -	2 1 2 - - -		- 437	Hole 50 in 105 mins, 79 balls
103		Tyson 24] → Off spell (incl. tea) 5-0-40-0	- 4 1 3 (1 b/lb) - 1	1 1	- 448	
104	 4.30 4.32	Bedser 32 ← [4 (1 bye/lb) -		 2 1-W Benaud -	 4- 456 - 456	*Harvey difficult chance to Statham at mid-off* Hole run out (Tyson/Andrew) perfect throw from deep sq leg, 57 in 120 mins, 87 balls, 4 fours
105		Statham 26] →	- 4 1	2 - - - -	- 463	
106	4.40 4.42	Bedser 33 ← [	W Archer - - - - -		5- 463 - 463	Harvey c Bailey diving low to left at bkwd sq leg, hooking 162 in 380 mins, 282 balls, 1 five 17 fours *First maiden of the day*
107	4.47 4.49	Statham 27] →	 W Lindwall - (1 b/lb) - - -	1	6- 464 - 465	Archer c Bedser, prodding to gully, 0 in 5 mins, 8 balls, 0 fours
108		Bedser 34 ← [Off spell 6-1-22-1	- - 1 - - - -		- 466	
109		Statham 28] →	- - - 1 - - 1		- 468	

26

MCC in Australia 1954-55 – FIRST TEST

110		Bailey 21 ← [	- - - 4 - 4	1	- 477	
111		Statham 29] →	1 1	- 1 1 - 4	- 485	
112		Bailey 22 ← [	- 4 - - 4 - 1		- 494	Lindwall dropped at leg-slip by Cowdrey
113		Statham 30] → Spell 5-0-20-1	- - - 1 - - - 1		- 496	
114	5.30	Bailey 23 ← [Spell 3-0-25-0	1 4 -	- - 1 1	- 503	
		CLOSE	Lindwl 27 41 mins 38 balls	Benaud 14 58 mins 31 balls	6- 503 600 mins 917 balls	Attendance: 30,329

Session 91-3 in 100 mins, 136 balls

Australia have not passed 500 against England since the First Test of 1948. England's four pace bowlers and Edrich have averaged under 92 balls per hour, in the unrelenting sunshine.

Morris was dropped 4 times, and Harvey 3.

Swanton: England's bowlers have not concentrated on a consistency of direction, and with a split 5-4 field all day, runs have been there to be had in all directions.

Arlott: Australia are virtually impregnable.

Moyes: The slow over rate was due to bowlers like Tyson fielding in the deep, and having to walk in for each over, and time spent on meticulous field placing. To relieve the monotony of the attack, Cowdrey should have been given a few overs. Neither Appleyard nor Wardle has impressed on the tour, but at least a spinner could have pinned down one end economically.

Fingleton: Australia have had enough luck in two days to last all the series.

Hassett has criticised England's resort to leg theory tactics, through Bailey, on the early stages of Saturday morning, an ugly spectacle, he said, when aggressive bowling was needed.

Alf Gover, the Surrey fast bowler of the 1930s and owner of a world-famous coaching school in London, is reporting the tour for the *Sunday Mirror*. He has coached Tyson and this Saturday evening he mentioned to Len Hutton that Tyson stutters in the middle of his long run up and he might gain more fluency without loss of pace if he started his run at that point.

MCC in Australia 1954-55 – FIRST TEST

THIRD DAY – England under the steam-roller

Monday 29 November
Johnson decides to bat on

			Lindwl 27	Benaud 14	6- 503	
115	11.30	Tyson 25] →		- - 1 - - 1	 - 505	Only one slip Two slips for Lindwall *Tyson beats bat 4 times in this over*
116		Statham 31 ← [	- - - 1 4 2	 1 	 - 513	Five fielders on leg side Yorker jammed and edged over wk's head for 4
117		Tyson 26] →		2 - 2 1 - 4 1 -	 - 523	 Lindwall drive. 4 all run
118		Statham 32 ← [	- - 1 -	 2 - 1 	 - 527	
119		Tyson 27] →	- 1 1	1 - (1 b/lb) 2 -	 - 533	 Tyson almost runs out Beno from 7 yds
120		Statham 33 ← [	1 - 4 - -	6 1 	 - 545	Benaud 6 over long on Lindwall 4 punched through covers
121	12.07 12.09	Tyson 28] →		W Langley 4 - - - - 1	7- 545 - 550	Benaud c May, hit across line skied to cover, 34 in 93 mins, 51 balls, 1 six 1 four 4 past cover
122	 12.20	Statham 34 ← [Off spell 4-0-29-0		1 - - - - - 4	 - 555	 4 cut past cover, Ldwl 52 in 91 m, 74 b

MCC in Australia 1954-55 – FIRST TEST

Over	Time	Bowler		Batsman	Score	Notes
123		Tyson 29] → Off spell 5-0-30-1		- - - - 2 2 4	- 563	
124		Bailey 24 ← [		- - - 2 - - 4	- 569	Lindwall 2 over mid on. Statham gets right hand to it.
125		Bedser 35] →		1 - 1 - - 1 -	- 572	
126	12.38 12.40	Bailey 25 ← [		W JohnSon 1 - 1 4 -	8- 572 - 579	Langley bld off stump, 16 in 29 mins, 21 balls, 2 fours
127		Bedser 36] →		- - - - 2 1 -	- 582	
128		Bailey 26 ← [Spell 6-0-18-1		- 4 - 1 (nb) - - -	- 587	JohnSon 4 over mid off JohnSon 'caught'
129		Bedser 37] → Spell 3-0-20-0		6 - 2 - 4 2 -	- 601	JohnSon steepling pull for 6 JohnSon dropped by Simpson JohnSon dropped by Cowdrey in gully, thought he was out and had to be called back
	1.00	LUNCH	Lindwl 64 131 mins 95 balls 11 fours	JonSn 24 20 mins 23 balls 2 fours 1 six	8- 601 690 mins 1038 balls	

Session 98-2 in 90 mins, 123 balls
During the lunch interval Johnson declares.

Australia First Innings

L.E.Favell	c Cowdrey b Statham	23	80 mins, 62 balls, 3 fours	1- 51
A.R. Morris	c Cowdrey b Bailey	153	419 mins, 321 balls, 8 fours 2 sixes	3- 325
K.R. Miller	b Bailey	49	86 mins, 88 balls, 4 fours, 1 six	2- 123
R.N.Harvey	c Bailey b Bedser	162	380 mins, 282 balls, 1 five 17 fours	5- 463
G.B. Hole	run out (Tyson/Andrew)	57	120 mins, 87 balls, 4 fours	4- 456
R. Benaud	c May b Tyson	34	93 mins, 51 balls, 1 six 1 four	7- 545
R.G. Archer	c Bedser b Statham	0	5 mins, 8 balls, 0 fours	6- 464
R.R. Lindwall	not out	64	131 mins, 95 balls, 11 fours	

MCC in Australia 1954-55 – FIRST TEST

G.R.A. Langley	b Langley		16	29 mins, 21 balls, 2 fours	8- 572
I.W.Johnson	not out		24	20 mins, 23 balls, 2 fours 1 six	
Extras	(b 11, lb 7, nb 1)		<u>19</u>		
TOTAL	(8 wkts dec)		601	690 mins, 129 overs, 1038 balls	

BOWLING

Bedser	37	4	131	1	(1 nb)
Statham	34	2	123	2	
Tyson	29	1	160	1	
Bailey	26	1	140	3	
Edrich	3	0	28	0	

Arlott: Four more catches dropped today, making a total of 12 catches, a stumping and a run out missed

Wellings: It was the third day before Tyson took a wicket, but he persisted keenly as a bowler and fielder throughout. Statham was the best bowler on the first day. The four-pace attack was let down by the fielders. It is unfair to criticise Hutton for putting his bowlers in the deep field: it is no more restful to field close in.

Cardus: Statham and Tyson bowled tenaciously and were not downcast, but with a tendency to short-pitched balls on the leg stump.

Peebles: England must now dig in and hope for bad weather.

England First Innings

Odd overs   ] →   from Vulture St End
Even overs ←]   from Railway End

				Hutton	Simpson		
1	1.40		Lindwall 1] →	4 - - - - -			Hutton steers 4 sweetly past gully *Umbrella field of 7, plus short mid-on and short mid-off*
	1.44			W Edrich		1-4	Hutton c Langley, half-cock, trying to leave late outswinger, 4 in 4 mins, 7 balls. Sympathetic applause.
	1.46			4		- 8	Edrich cuts full toss for 4 past gully
2			Miller 1 ← [		- 2 -		*Umbrella field* Simpson 2 to third man
	1.50				W May	2-10	Simpson bld, pushing forward, no feet, to fast late inswinger, 2 in 10 mins, 5 balls
	1.52				1 - -	-11	May snicks off his pads, quick single Edrich plays and misses Edrich plays and misses
3			Lindwall 2] →		- - - -		
	1.57				W Cowdrey	3-11	May bld, leg-side ball, shaping to on, via boot, 1 in 5 mins, 7 balls
	1.59				- -	-11	
4			Miller 2 ← [	1	- - - - 1 -	- 13	
5			Lindwall 3] →		- - - - - - -	- 13	
6			Miller 3 ← [Off spell 3-1-5-1		- - - - - (1 lb) - -	- 14	

MCC in Australia 1954-55 – FIRST TEST

7		Lindwall 4] →	- - - - 1		- - - 15	
8		Archer 1 ← [	- - 4 4 - - -		- 23	Edrich hooks 4 to square leg Edrich hooks 4 to square leg
9		Lindwall 5] →	- - - 1 - 1 -		-25	Long PA announcement about parked cars
10	2.28 2.30	Archer 2 ← [	W Bailey - - - - - -		4 -25 -25	Edrich c Langley, playing late, chasing off-side ball, thin edge, 15 in 42 mins, 28 balls, 3 fours
11		Lindwall 6] → Off spell 6-3-11-2	- - - - - - -		-25	
12		Archer 3 ← [	- - 1 - - - 4		-30	
13		Miller 4] →	- - - - - - -		- 30	
14		Archer 4 ← [Off spell 4-1-14-1	1 - - - - - -		- 31	
15		Miller 5] →	- - - - - - -		-31	

MCC in Australia 1954-55 – FIRST TEST

Over	Time	Bowler					Notes
16	3.05	JohnSon 1 ← [		- - 1 - - - -		- 32	*First spin bowling of the match.*
17		Miller 6] → Off spell 3-3-0-0	(4 lb)	- - - - - - -		- 36	4 leg byes somewhere between overs 16.1 and 18.8.
18		JohnSon 2 ← [		- - 1 4 - - -	1	-42	Cowdrey goes down pitch to drive straight high and safe for 4, just short of six
19		Benaud 1] →		- - - - - - -		- 42	
20		JohnSon 3 ← [	(1 lb)	- - - - - - -		- 43	
21		Benaud 2] →		- - - - - - -		- 43	
22		JohnSon 4 ← [		- 1 - - 4 - - -		-48	Cowdrey goes down pitch to drive over mid-off for 4 Johnson puts fielder at long-off
23		Benaud 3] →		- - - - - - -		- 48	
24	 3.25	JohnSon 5 ← [Off spell 5-1-16-0		- - - - - - 4 -		-52	Cwdry cuts through slips for 4. 52 up 105 mins in 85 balls

MCC in Australia 1954-55 – FIRST TEST

Over	Time	Bowler	Bailey	Cowdry	Total	Notes
25		Benaud 4] → Off spell 4-4-0-0	- - - - - - -			
	3.30				-52	
		TEA	Bailey 4 60 mins 67 balls	Cowdry 20 91 mins 86 balls	4-52 110 mins 200 balls	

Swanton: only the manner and time of defeat seem now in question.

Over	Time	Bowler	Bailey	Cowdry	Total	Notes
			Bailey 4	Cowdry 20	-52	
26	3.50	JohnsTon 1 ← [		- - 4 - - - -	-56	*JohnsTon bowling over the wicket* Cowdrey 4 full toss punched though covers
27		Benaud 5] →	- - - - - -		- 56	Benaud's fifth maiden in a row to Bailey
28		JohnsTon 2 ← [		- - 4 - - -	-60	Cowdrey 4 through covers
29		Benaud 6] →	- - 4 - - -		- 64	Bailey cuts for 4, doubling his score
30		JohnsTon 3 ← [	- 1	1 4 - - -	-70	Cowdrey 4 through covers
31	4.05	Benaud 7] →	4 4 - - 4 - -		- 82	Bailey pulls long hop to sq leg for 4 Bailey pulls long hop to mid wkt for 4, for 53 partnership in 75 mins Bailey 4 to long leg
32		JohnsTon 4 ← [		- - 1 - - - 5	-88	4 overthrows

MCC in Australia 1954-55 – FIRST TEST

Over	Time	Bowler	Runs	Batsman	Score	Notes
33		Benaud 8] → Off spell (incl.tea) 4-1-20-0	4 - - - - - -		- 92	
34		JohnsTon 5 ← [		- - - 1 1 - -	-94	*JohnsTon adopts leg-side attack with five close fielders*
35		Lindwall 7] →	- - - - - - -		- 94	
36		JohnsTon 6 ← [		- - - - - - -	-94	
37		Lindwall 8] →	- - - 1 - - -		- 95	
38		JohnsTon 7 ← [		- - - - - - -	-95	
39		Lindwall 9] →	- - 2 1 - - -	1	-99	
40		JohnsTon 8 ← [Off spell 8-3-22-0		- - - - - - -	-99	
41	4.50	Lindwall 10] →		- - 1 - - - -	-100	100 up in 170 mins

MCC in Australia 1954-55 – FIRST TEST

42		JohnSon 6 ← [		- - - - - - -	- 100	
43		Lindwall 11] → Off spell 5-1-7-0	1	- - - - - -	- 101	
44		JohnSon 7 ← [	- - 1	 - - - -	-102	
45		Miller 7] →	- - - - - -		- 102	*Miller bowling medium pace off-breaks*
46		JohnSon 8 ← [		- - - - - 1 -	- 103	
47		Miller 8] → Off spell 2-1-1-0	1 - - - - - -		- 104	
48		JohnSon 9 ← [Off spell 4-2-2-0	- - - - - - -		-104	
49		JohnsTon 9] →	- - 1	 - - -	- 105	
50		Benaud 9 ← [Spell 1-0-1-0	- - - (1 b/lb) - - 1 -		-107	

35

MCC in Australia 1954-55 – FIRST TEST

51	5.29	JohnsTon 10] →		W Tyson - - - - -	5- 107	Cowdrey c Hole simple catch to 1st slip, 40 in 190 mins, 183 balls, 7 fours. Cowdrey hesitates and is given out– ball hit toe? The scorers had to check how he was out
	5.30	Spell 2-1-1-1				
	5.33			-	-107	
		CLOSE	Bailey 38 163 mins 171 balls	Tyson 0 3 mins 7 balls	5-107 213 mins 408 balls	Attendance: 16,142

Session 55-1 in 103 mins, 208 balls
The only defiant session of the match for England so far.
Swanton: Cowdrey was surprised to be given out: perhaps the ball hit his toe or the ground and then, unknown to him, nicked the bat.
Arlott: Cowdrey may have made his mark as a new Test cricketer, showing his technique (though perhaps to slavish in his tendency to play forward) and temperament. England are being steam-rollered and a determined effort in the second innings will be too late.
Peebles: Cowdrey showed his class and his maturity

FOURTH DAY - England refuse to fold up

Tuesday 30 November
Compton will bat "only in an emergency". An ambiguous phrase, for in one sense there is no emergency unless the rest of the batting holds out for a very long time. He has a metacarpal fracture of the fourth finger of the left hand: his hand in is plaster and he cannot move his fingers.

			Bailey 38	Tyson 0	5-107	Only 4,000 crowd at start
52	11.30	JohnSon 10 ← [	- - 2 1 -	1	- 111	
53		JohnsTon 11] →	- 1 - 1	- - 3 3 -	- 119	Tyson 3 through covers Tyson 3 through covers
54		JohnSon 11 ← [	4 - - - - 1		- 124	
55		JohnsTon 12] →	- - (2 byes) - - - -		- 126	2 byes somewhere between overs 52.1 and 58.1
56		JohnSon 12 ← [		- - - - - - -	- 126	

MCC in Australia 1954-55 – FIRST TEST

#	Time	Bowler	B1	B2	Score	Notes
57	11.47	JohnsTon 13] →	4 2 - - - -		- 130	Bailey 52 in 180 mins, 198 balls
58	11.52	JohnSon 13 ← [		- W Bedser - - - - -	6-132 -132	Tyson bld, hypnotised by full length ball, 7 in 23 mins, 23 balls
59		JohnsTon 14] → Off spell 4-1-18-0	- 4 - - - - -		-136	
60	12.00 12.02	JohnSon 14 ← [		- 1 4 W Andrew - - -	7-141 -141	One short? Bedser 4 to midwkt Bedser bld, 5 in 8 mins, 10 balls, 1 four
61		Lindwall 12] →	1 - - - 1 -	2 1 - - - -	-146	*England have achieved a minor triumph in forcing Lindwall to come back on.*
62		JohnSon 15 ← [	- 6 - - 1 -	- - - - - 1	-154	Bailey 6 drive over long on, wins £A100 prize offered in today's local newspaper by Mr.Coles Smith, local businessman. Johnson congratulates him
63	12.15 12.17	Lindwall 13] →		- - - 2 W Statham - -	8-156 -156	Andrew bld, faster ball, 6 in 13 mins, 15 balls
64		JohnSon 16 ← [Off spell 7-2-23-2	- - - - 1 -		-157	
65		Lindwall 14] → Off spell 3-0-9-1	- - - - 2 -		-159	

MCC in Australia 1954-55 – FIRST TEST

Over	Time	Bowler		Batsman 1	Batsman 2	Score	Notes
66		Benaud 10 ← [			- - - 1 - 1	-161	
67		Miller 9] →			- - - 1 - - -	-162	
68		Benaud 11 ← [		- - 4 - - -		-166	Bailey hits over mid on, one bounce over boundary
69		Miller 10] →			- - - 4 - 4 -	- 174	Statham snicks through legs for 4 Statham powerful straight drive for 4
70		Benaud 12 ← [Off spell 3-0-7-0		- - - 1	- - -	-175	
71		Miller 11] → Off spell 3-0-13-0		- - - - 4 -		- 179	
72		JohnSon 17 ← [			2 - - - - -		
	12.54				W Compton	9-181	Statham bld, wild swing at full length ball, 11 in 37 mins, 33 balls, 2 fours
73	12.56	JohnsTon 15] →		- - - - -			Compton, to great cheers, comes out because Bailey is still in. He wears an elastic crepe bandage, having removed the plaster
	1.00				1 -	-182	JohnsTon bowls well wide of stumps
		LUNCH		Bailey 82 253 mins 272 balls	Compton 0 4 mins 1 ball	9-182 303 mins 584 balls	

SESSION 75-4 IN 90 MINS, 176 BALLS

Compton decided to bat, and the batsmen were so informed, if the ninth wicket to fall was not Bailey.

Arlott: Clearly Compton decided to bat as a support for Bailey. The only ball he received was well wide.

MCC in Australia 1954-55 – FIRST TEST

			Bailey 82	Compton 0	9-182	
74	1.40	JohnSon 18 ← [	- 1 - - - - -		-183	
75		JohnsTon 16] →	- - 4 - - - 1		-188	Bailey pull-drive for 4 Bailey gives hard c & b chance Bailey dropped by Favell at gully
76		JohnSon 19 ← [Spell (incl.lunch) 3-0-5-1	- - - 2 - - -		-190	Unexplained change of ends *Four short legs for Compton* Compton almost ct by Benaud diving in *from silly point* Compton cut for 2 to third man
77	1.51	JohnsTon 17] → Spell (incl. lunch) 2.1-0-5-1	W		10 –190	Bailey bld, swinging across full length ball, 88 in 264 mins, 283 balls, 11 fours, 1 five 1 six
				Comptn 2 15 mins 15 balls	10-190 314 mins 609 balls	

Session to date: 8-1 in 11 mins, 25 balls

Arlott: Bailey has introduced resistance. Australia are winning but no longer look superhuman.

Swanton: Bailey's judgement and concentration overcame his poor form.

Hughes: Every shot by Compton was vociferously cheered as if he were a home player.

England First innings

* L. Hutton	c Langley b Lindwall		4	4 mins, 7 balls	1-4
R.T. Simpson	b Miller		2	10 mins, 5 balls	2-10
W.J. Edrich	c Langley b Archer		15	42 mins, 28 balls, 3 fours	4-25
P.B.H. May	b Lindwall		1	5 mins, 7 balls	3-11
M.C. Cowdrey	c Hole b Johnston		40	190 mins, 183 balls, 7 fours	5-107
T.E. Bailey	b Johnston		88	264 mins, 283 balls, 11 fours, 1 five 1 six	10-190
F.H. Tyson	b Johnson		7	23 mins, 23 balls	6-132
A.V. Bedser	b Johnson		5	8 mins, 10 balls, 1 four	7-141
+ K.V. Andrew	b Lindwall		6	13 mins, 15 balls	8-156
J.B. Statham	b Johnson		11	37 mins, 33 balls, 2 fours	9-181
D.C.S. Compton	not out		2	15 mins, 15 balls	
Extras	(b 3, l-b 6)		9		
TOTAL	(for 10 wkts – all out)		190	314 mins, 76.1 overs, 609 balls	

BOWLING

Lindwall	14	4	27	3
Miller	11	5	19	1
Archer	4	1	14	1
Johnson	19	5	46	3
Benaud	12	5	28	0
Johnston	16.1	5	47	2

England Second Innings

Odd overs   ] →   from Vulture St End
Even overs   ← [from Railway End

Follow on 411 behind

			Hutton	Simpson		
1	2.03	Lindwall 1] →	4 - - - - - -	-4		Again Hutton hits first ball of innings for 4, flicked through short legs *3 slips, 2 gullies, 2 short legs, mid on, mid off* lbw appeal Hutton almost cocks up catch to JohnsTon

MCC in Australia 1954-55 – FIRST TEST

2		Miller 1 ← [	- 2 - - 1 - -	-7	*Same field as Lindwall* Simpson 2 to third man
3		Lindwall 2] →	- - - 2 - 2 - -	- 11	Simpson hit on foot by inswinging yorker, almost going onto stumps
4		Miller 2 ← [Off spell 2-0-4-0	- - - - 1 - -	-12	
5		Lindwall 3] →	- - - 4 2 - -	- 18	Hutton 4 to long leg Hutton 2 past gully yorker played safely
6		Archer 1 ← [	- - - - - - -	-18	*Good over*
7		Lindwall 4] →	- - - - - - -	-18	
8		Archer 2 ← [	- 1 - - - - -	-19	
9	 2.43 2.45	Lindwall 5] → Off Spell 5-1-17-0	1 2 - - (W) Edrich - - -	 1-22 - 22	Simpson 1 past JohnSon at cover Hutton 2 to long leg Hutton edges between Hole and Archer at slip. Archer checks it. Favell at 3rd slip runs behind and throws down wkt. Simpson, realising urgency too late, run out 9 in 40 mins, 27 balls
10		Archer 3 ← [	- - - - - - -	-22	

40

MCC in Australia 1954-55 – FIRST TEST

11		Miller 3] →		- - - - - - -	- 22	*Edrich dropped waist high by Archer at 2nd slip. Next ball bounces over his head.*
12		Archer 4 ← [	- - - (1 lb) - - - -		- 23	
13	3.03 3.05	Miller 4] →	- - - - - W May -		2-23 -23	Hutton lbw, playing too early at low slower ball, 13 in 60 mins, 61 balls, 2 fours
14		Archer 5 ← [		1 - - - - - -	-24	
15		Miller 5] → Off spell 3-2-1-1	- - - - - - 1		-25	
16		Archer 6 ← [		- - - - - 4 -	-29	Edrich late cut for 4
17		Lindwall 6] →	- - - - - - -		- 29	
18		Archer 7 ← [Off spell 7-3-10-0		- - - - 4 - -	-33	
19	3.30	Lindwall 7] → Spell 2-1-11-0	3 - - 4 - 4		- 44	*Still 7 men in umbrella field* Edrich off-drive for 4

MCC in Australia 1954-55 – FIRST TEST

	3.30	TEA	May 3 25 mins 17 balls	Edrich 18 45 mins 47 balls	2-44 87 mins 152 balls	

Session (both innings) 52-3 in 98 mins, 177 balls
Arlott: The openers seemed to have passed the test just when Simpson got run out.

			May 3	Edrich 18	2-44	
20	3.50	Archer 8 ← [	- - 2 - 1 - - -		-47	
21		Miller 6] →	4 - 2 - - 4 - -		- 57	
22		Archer 9 ← [Off spell 2-0-4-0	- - - - - 1 -		-58	
23		Miller 7] → Off spell 2-0-12-0	- - - - 2 - -		-60	
24		JohnsTon 1 ← [	- - - - - - -		-60	
25		JohnSon 1] →	- - 4 - - - -		-64	
26		JohnsTon 2 ← [	- - - - - - -		-64	
27		JohnSon 2] →	- - - - - - 1		- 65	*Edrich dropped at slip by Hole*

MCC in Australia 1954-55 – FIRST TEST

28		JohnsTon 3 ← [		- - - 4 - 2 -	-71	
29		JohnSon 3] →	- 4 - - - -		-75	May straight drive for 4. His first run for half an hour.
30		JohnsTon 4 ← [		- - - - 6 (nb) - -	-81	Edrich punches six straight
31		JohnSon 4] →	- 1 - - - - -		-82	
32		JohnsTon 5 ← [		- - - - - -	-82	
33		JohnSon 5] →		- - - - - 1	-83	
34		JohnsTon 6 ← [		- - - 2 - 4 -	-89	
35		JohnSon 6] →	- - - - 1	- -	-90	
36		JohnsTon 7 ← [	- - - - - - -		-90	*May gives high c & b chance*

MCC in Australia 1954-55 – FIRST TEST

Over	Time	Bowler		Balls	Total	Comments
37		JohnSon 7] →		- - - - - -	- 90	
38		JohnsTon 8 ← [		- - - - - -	-90	
39		JohnSon 8] → Off spell 8-1-14-0		- - - - 2 -	-92	
40		JohnsTon 9 ← [Off spell 9-5-23-0	- 1	4 - - - -	-97	Edrich off-drive for 4, 51 in 140 balls
41	5.10	Archer 10] →	- 1	- 4 - -	-102	Edrich late cut for 4
42		Benaud 1 ← [	4 3 - 1	4 1 - 1	-116	May pulls long hop for 4
43		Archer 11] →		- - - 4 - -	- 120	Edrich late cut for 4
44		Benaud 2 ← [	- 2 - - - -		-122	
45		Archer 12] → Spell 3-1-9-0		- - - - - -	- 122	

MCC in Australia 1954-55 – FIRST TEST

			May 39	Edrich 68	2-130	
46		Benaud 3 ← [Spell 3-0-24-0	- 1 - - - 4 -	3	-130	
	5.30	CLOSE	May 39 125 mins 109 balls	Edrich 68 145 mins 172 balls	2-130 187 mins 369 balls	Attendance: 9,237

Session 86-0 in 100 mins, 217 balls

Bailey received his £100 this evening in his room, and throws a small party.

Swanton: More backbone and purpose from the England batting today, though with 10 hours left there can only be one result unless the present heavy atmosphere turns to rain. Edrich, after slip chances at 0 and 24, found form remarkably. May looks very good.

Arlott: The batsmen are still to timid. Edrich could not decide whether to play or leave, but acquired new confidence after his chances. At last England survived a session without losing a wicket

Peebles: There is much talk of a depression in Central Australia which may bring rain to Brisbane

FIFTH DAY - Rain mocks to deceive

Wednesday 1 December

Weather has turned cloudy, mild with a hint of rain, but more than that is needed for England. All English players including Compton have a practice.

			May 39	Edrich 68	2-130	
47	11.30	Lindwall 8] →		1 - - - - - -	- 131	
48		JohnsTon 10 ← [		4 - 1 4 - -	-140	long hop late cut for 4 full toss hit straight for 4
49		Lindwall 9] →		- 2 - - - - -	-142	*Lindwall bowling a lesser speed*
50		JohnsTon 11 ← [	1 - - - 4 - - -		-147	May late cuts for 4
51	11.50 11.52	Lindwall 10] →	- - W Cowdrey - - -		3-147 - 147	May lbw playing round an inswinger that kept low, 44 in 145 mins, 126 balls, 6 fours. Looks sadly at stumps as he leaves.

MCC in Australia 1954-55 – FIRST TEST

52		JohnsTon 12 ← [		- 1 - - - - -	- 148	
53		Lindwall 11] → Off spell 4-1-5-1		- 2 - - - (2 byes) - -	- 152	Edrich 2 past short legs. 150 up 2 byes somewhere between overs 53.3 and 54.8
54		JohnsTon 13 ← [	- 4 - - - - -		-156	Cowdrey cover drive for 4
55		Miller 8] →		- - - - 2 -	- 158	*Miller bowling leg theory*
56		JohnsTon 14 ← [	2 - - - - - -		-160	
57		Miller 9] → Spell 2-0-5-0		3 - - - - - -	-163	
58	12.18 12.20 12.25	JohnsTon 15 ← [Off spell 6-1-21-1		- W Bailey - - - - -	4-163 -163	Edrich bld, hooking ball too far up, 88 in 193 mins, 212 balls, 13 fours 1 six Drizzle starts Cowdrey has rain blowing into his face, suggests going off. Johnson says it is a matter for the umpires Bailey appeals. Rain stops play
		LUNCH	Cowdrey 6 33 mins 33 balls	Bailey 0 5 mins 6 balls	4-163 242 mins 465 balls	

Session 33-2 in 55 mins, 96 balls

Drizzle turns into heavy rain for 20 minutes. Pitch is covered. Covers start to be removed at 12.45, but it takes too long for a pre-lunch resumption

Wellings: It is a sad commentary on the spirit of the game that JohnSon insisted on playing on in the rain until the umpires were consulted.

Whitington: JohnSon was merely using the sensible tactic of playing on whilst the wicket was exposed to the wet, until the umpires were asked to decide.

MCC in Australia 1954-55 – FIRST TEST

			Cowdrey 6	Bailey 0	4-163	Sun shining
59	1.40	JohnSon 9] →	- (4 b) - - - -		 - 167	Seven close fielders 4 byes somewhere in this over
60		JohnsTon 16 ← [		- - - 1 - - -	 - 168	Eight close fielders
61		JohnSon 10] →	- - - - - -	1	 - 169	*JohnSon bowls round the wicket* *Cowdrey and Bailey are sticking out the front pad, knowing that umpires are reluctant to give lbws to batsmen playing forward*
62		JohnsTon 17 ← [		- - - - - 4	 - 173	Bailey drives to leg for 4
63		JohnSon 11] →	- - - - - -		- 173	
64		JohnsTon 18 ← [		- - - - - -	- 173	
65		JohnSon 12] →	- - - - - -		- 173	
66		JohnsTon 19 ← [		- - - - 4 - -	- 177	
67		JohnSon 13] → Off spell 5-4-1-0	- - - - - -		- 177	

MCC in Australia 1954-55 – FIRST TEST

68		JohnsTon 20 ←[		- - - - - -	-177	
69	2.15 2.17	Benaud 4]→	4 - - - - W Tyson -		5-181 - 181	Cowdrey's first run since lunch, 4 edged Cowdrey bld, no stroke to googly, off gloves or under-edge, 10 in 68 mins, 83 balls, 2 fours
70		JohnsTon 21 ←[Off spell 6-2-15-0	- - - - 2 - 4 -		-187	Bailey drives for 2 Bailey drives for 4
71		Benaud 5]→	- - - - - - - -		-187	
72		JohnSon 14 ←[Off spell 1-0-8-0	- 4 - - 1 -	3	-195	
73		Benaud 6]→ Off spell 3-1-9-1	1 - - 4 - - - -		- 200	Bailey cuts late for four. 200 up in 290 mins
74		Miller 10 ←[	- 1 - - - - - -		-201	
75		Lindwall 12]→	- - - - - - 3 -		- 204	New ball Tyson driving, inside edge to fine leg for 3
76		Miller 11 ←[	- - 1 1 - -	- (1 b or lb)	-207	

48

MCC in Australia 1954-55 – FIRST TEST

Over	Time	Bowler	B1	B2	Score	Notes
77		Lindwall 13] →	- 2 - 3	- - -	-212	Tyson straight drives for 3
78		Miller 12 ← [Off spell 3-0-8-0	- 2 - 2 - - 1		-217	
79		Lindwall 14] →	- - - 1	- - -	-218	
80		Archer 13 ← [	- - 1	- - - - -	-219	
81	3.10	Lindwall 15] →	1 - - - - -	W Bedser	6 -220	Bailey has not scored for half an hour Bailey dropped by Langley down leg side Bailey c Langley, edged outswing to wk diving wide, 23 in 95 mins, 91 balls, 4 fours
82	3.12	Archer 14 ← [	- - 1	- - -	-221	
83		Lindwall 16] →	- - 2 - - 2		-225	
84		Archer 15 ← [Off spell 3-0-5-0	- 1	1 - - - 1 -	- 228	
85	3.30	Lindwall 17] → Off spell 6-0-17-1		- - 3 - - - -	-231	

MCC in Australia 1954-55 – FIRST TEST

			Tyson 31	Bedser 5	6-231	
		TEA	73 mins	18 mins	352 mins	
			69 balls	12 balls	681 balls	

SESSION 68-2 IN 110 MINS, 216 BALLS

			Tyson 31	Bedser 5	6-231	
	3.50					
86	3.51	JohnSon 15		W	7-231	Bedser c Archer, long hop hit high, ct by
		] →		Andrew		mid on running to deep mid wkt, 5 in 19
	3.53		1			mins, 13 balls (batsmen crossed)
				1		
				-		
				-		
				2		
				-	- 235	
87		Benaud 7		-		
		← [		-		
				-		
				4		
				-		
				-		
				-	- 239	
88		JohnSon 16		-		
		] →		-		
				-		
			2			
			(1 b/lb) -	-		
				-		
	4.00			W	8 - 242	Andrew bld, 5 in 7 mins, 12 balls, 1 four
				Compton		
89	4.02	Benaud 8	1	-		
		← [		-		
	4.04			W	9-243	Compton c Langley, pushing forward, 0 in
				Statham		2 mins, 3 balls
	4.06			-		
				-		
				4		
				1	-248	
90		JohnSon 17		-		
		] →		4		
				-		
		Spell 4-0-15-2		-		
				2		
				2		
				1	-257	
91	4.12	Benaud 9		W	-257	Statham c Harvey, running to long on, one
		← [				hand above head, 14 in 6 mins, 13 balls,
		Spell 2.1-0-10-2				2 fours
			Tyson 37		10- 257	Attendance: 4,800
			85 mins		374 mins	Attendance for 5 days: £77,008
			81 balls		722 balls	Match receipts: £A 22,604

SESSION 26-4 IN 22 MINS, 41 BALLS

The Australians walked off the field to minimal acclaim. Ian Johnson is not popular in Queensland.
Peebles: Tyson looks an orthodox straight hitter with a good defence. Moyes: Tyson played well and naturally.
One link in the England tail may have disappeared.
Barnes: Apart from fresh overs by Lindwall and Miller, the Australian bowling in this Test was limp.

England Second innings

* L. Hutton	lbw b Miller	13	60 mins, 61 balls, 2 fours	2-23
R.T. Simpson	run out (Favell)	9	40 mins, 27 balls	1-22
W.J. Edrich	b JohnsTon	88	193 mins, 212 balls, 13 fours 1 six	4-163
P.B.H. May	lbw b Lindwall	44	145 mins, 126 balls, 6 fours	3-147
M.C. Cowdrey	b Benaud	10	68 mins, 83 balls, 2 fours	5-181
T.E. Bailey	c Langley b Lindwall	23	95 mins, 91 balls, 4 fours	6-220
F.H. Tyson	not out	37	85 mins, 81 balls, 1 four	
A.V. Bedser	c Archer b Johnson	5	19 mins, 13 balls	7-231
+ K.V. Andrew	b JohnSon	5	7 mins, 12 balls, 1 four	8-242

MCC in Australia 1954-55 – FIRST TEST

D.C.S.Compton	c Langley b Benaud			0	2 mins, 3 balls		9-243
J.B. Statham	c Harvey b Benaud			16	6 mins, 13 balls, 2 fours		10-257
Extras	(b 7, lb 2)			9			
TOTAL	(10 wkts – all out)			257	374 mins, 90.1 overs, 722 balls		

BOWLING

Lindwall	17	3	50	2
Miller	12	2	30	1
Archer	15	4	28	0
JohnsTon	21	8	59	1
JohnSon	17	5	38	2
Benaud	8.1	1	43	2

Australia won by an innings and 154 runs

At the end of the Test, Tyson had a few words with Lindwall and asked him about the proper way to bowl a bumper. Lindwall said "Next time I'll show you."

Choosing a man of the match is difficult in this Test: obviously it must be an Australian, Harvey and Morris made large scores but had a lot of luck and were not at their best. Lindwall hit late runs and made the first innings breakthrough. I am inclined to award it to Ian Johnson, who captained well, scored runs and took wickets.

Swanton: Australia will be much harder to beat now, but the series is not yet half lost.

Compton is going to Sydney for treatment.

Arlott: Few consolations for England. Australia are keen and confident. Edrich has re-established himself. Cowdrey looks Test class. Tyson improves as a batsman and fielder. Andrew kept confidently and superbly standing up to Bedser but does not match Evans' vitality. We lacked the ability in specialist fielding positions.

Moyes: Compton might have led a fightback and inspired aggression. Hutton was too defensive a batsman and captain to give a lead, for the Australian attack was nothing special after the new-ball period.

Next day Hutton had all his team except the injured Compton and McConnon out on the field for a practice.

Queensland Country XI at Rockhampton, December 4 and 6

A disheartened side flew north to the costal town of Rockhampton, a few miles within the Tropics. On the Rodeo ground, used because it housed more spectators than the cricket ground, MCC entertained the crowd well with 317 in 245 minutes. MCC decided to overlook the fact that contrary to tour regulations the wicket was watered over the weekend. Having followed on the Country XI were six down with four minutes to go. Hutton asked the home captain to agree to an extra fifteen minutes and he reluctantly agreed. Under the tour conditions such an alteration of the hours requires consent of the Australian Board of Control. Appleyard then finished off the innings

MCC 317 (Hutton 40, Edrich 74, May 69, Wilson 61, D.Watt 5-56). QUEENSLAND COUNTRY XI 95 (Loader 3-22, Graveney 2-8) and 210 (W.Brown 78, R.Sippel 45, Appleyard 7-51). MCC WON BY AN INNINGS AND 12 RUNS

MCC now flew from Rockhampton to Sydney, then to Canberra

Prime Minster's XI at Canberra, December 8

This was a light-hearted affair, in which Lindsay Hassett renewed his acquaintance with the old enemy and the gate money plus bonuses for sixes raised over £700 for Legacy, a war veterans charity.

MCC 278-7dec (May 101, Graveney 56) Prime Minister's XI 247 (R. Benaud 117, S.J.E.Loxton 47, Wardle 4-73, Hutton 3-15). MCC WON BY 31 RUNS.

Bailey opens: Victoria at Melbourne, December 10, 11, 13 and 14

Hutton's continual attempts to find an opening partner seemed to be met with success when he and Bailey opened with a slow but solid 97. The only brightness came from Graveney and Cowdrey between lunch and tea. In the full five hours MCC made only 253 for 8. When Victoria went in just before lunch on Saturday, Tyson bowled off a much shorter run, which he had been trying net practice, and hit McDonald on the fingers and on the arm in his first over. Ten minutes after lunch, heavy rain stopped play. After two inspections and much activity by the umpires and groundstaff, play was abandoned without further cricket action. Many of the 18,000 crowd had come in at lunchtime and they expressed their dissatisfaction loudly. On Monday Tyson took 3 for 15 in 4.2 overs before Hutton took him off. Victoria flourished against the indifferent bowling of Wardle and McConnon. In all Tyson took six wickets, for five of which sheer pace was enough. On the final day Hutton delayed his declaration to enable May to reach his excellent century in 198 minutes. In the final stages there was nothing to play for except that in six overs Tyson split McDonald's thumb against his bat handle and forced him to retire hurt.

MCC 312 (Hutton 41, Bailey 60, Graveney 48, Cowdrey 79) and 236-5 dec (May 105*, Cowdrey 54). Victoria 277 (R.N.Harvey 59, J.L.Chambers 42, Tyson 6-68) and 88-3 (Ray Harvey 38*). MATCH DRAWN.

MCC in Australia 1954-55 – SECOND TEST

SECOND TEST AT SYDNEY

December 17, 18, 20, 21, 22

For the Second Test, there were a few mainly enforced changes.

For Australia, Johnson (pulled leg muscle) and Miller (fluid on knee) are unfit. Davidson, 12th man at Brisbane comes in to the XI. The balance of the side is shifted towards the batting by the selection of Burke. Young Watson of NSW is named as 12th man. Obviously Morris is named as captain - would he have been preferred to Miller?

James W. BURKE (NSW) aged 24, a solid right-hand batsman, and occasional off-spinner with a very suspect action, who scored a century on his Test debut in 1950-51 against England.

According to Whitington, Hutton was thinking of dropping Tyson for the Test. At the Windsor Hotel lounge, before leaving for the ground on the second day of the Victoria match, he happened to engage in conversation with some Australian Press men. One of them showed Len the story he had filed for his Sydney newspaper, saying that Tyson was the one bowler that Australia feared. That day Tyson took 6 for 68.

England bring in Graveney to replace the injured Compton. Evans replaces Andrew now that he is fit again. Simpson is inevitably dropped, replaced in the XII by the two spinners Appleyard and Wardle. Therefore they commit themselves to six batsmen, including Bailey who seems likely to open the batting, and five bowlers: probably Bedser (if he feels fit enough), Tyson, Statham, Bailey and one of the spinners. Peebles thinks that Bedser is competing for two places with Appleyard and Wardle. If Bedser is not at his best form, he should be held back for the Melbourne Test. So also Ross who says it will be a nasty decision. Gilligan thinks that Bedser may have to be dropped because the four-pace strategy should not be continued, and Wardle is a better batsman and fielder and can be used as a stock bowler.

FIRST DAY – Can it get any worse?

Friday 17 December

Violent storm overnight. Cloud still heavy. Stiff breeze across wicket from mid off at City End. Hutton himself says that it was his hope even before the tour started that Tyson and Statham would be his main strike bowlers. His conclusion from the Brisbane defeat is that England need five bowlers. Bedser bowled heroically and unluckily at Brisbane but below fitness and form and the strain was causing him to bowl no-balls.. The prospect of dropping his friend Alec made him sleep badly for three nights before the Test.

Some say that Hutton, understandably, could not bring himself to speak to Bedser directly, and the first news of it came when the team sheet was posted in the dressing-room, but Hutton says that he discussed the possibility privately with Bedser before the decision was taken by the selection committee. Cowdrey thinks that Hutton did not cross out Bedser's name until he was walking out to toss with Arthur Morris. Bedser's omission is cruel, and perhaps unfair: he should bowl at Sydney in these conditions at least as well as he did at Brisbane, and the two spinners who replace him do not exactly pick themselves, though says Swanton, it is less surprising to those who have watched the MCC tour unfold. Wellings was adamant that Bedser should play, he may be below top form but is still fit enough and certainly to be preferred to either of the spinners. Ross says that there are few who think it wise to drop Bedser; the atmosphere is heavy and the wicket green, ideal for him. Kilburn: though past his peak, conditions are never likely to be better for Bedser. Moyes: Australia would never have left Bedser out. Bowes: It seems the wrong moment to drop Bedser: the pitch would not suit him better if he had ordered it. Woodcock: it is a momentous step, not justified by the form of Appleyard and Wardle. Hughes: "Perhaps it was because Morris was so delighted with his Christmas present of Bedser's absence that he felt he had to make a counter-present to Hutton of first use of the pitch". Cardus: Bedser should not have been discarded on the evidence of Brisbane, but courage and lack of sentiment make it right to have Tyson and Statham with the new ball.

Tyson is retained on the strength of his performance against Victoria, to his own surprise. Bedser makes no complaint about his omission. In retrospect he should have not have come back so soon after his shingles. Though Sydney's wicket is at its liveliest on the first day, Hutton would hardly risk putting Australia in again. Ironically, it is Morris who wins the toss and puts England in.

Sydney Cricket Ground is in the Paddington suburb, the most distinguished of Australian venues, similar in atmosphere to Lord's.

Umpires: M.J.McInnes and R.J.J.Wright

England First Innings

Odd overs →\ from Hill End
Even overs ←\ from City (Pavilion) End
All fielders except Morris wear sweaters

			Hutton	Bailey		
1	11.30	Lindwall 1 →\	2			Hutton 2 past Morris at silly mid on
			-			Field: 4 slips, gully, 2 leg slips, 1 silly mid on,
			-			
			-			
			-			
			-			
			4		- 6	Hutton glides full toss past gully for 4

52

MCC in Australia 1954-55 – SECOND TEST

2		Archer 1 ←\		- - - - - -		- 6	Field for Bailey: 3 slips, 2 gullies, 2 sht legs, silly mid on, silly mid off
3		Lindwall 2 →\		- - 4 - 1		- 11	*Appeal for caught behind* Hutton 4 through covers
4		Archer 2 ←\		- - 1 - - - -		- 12	
5		Lindwall 3 →\ Off spell 3-0-13-0		- - - - 2 - - -		- 14	
6		Archer 3 ←\ Off spell 3-2-1-0		- - - - - - -		-14	
7	12.00	Davidson 1 →\ Off spell 1-1-0-0		- - - - - - -		- 14	
8	 12.07 12.09	Lindwall 4 ←\		- - - - W May - - 1	 1-14 - 15		Bailey tempted by fast leg side ball; crowd appeal *Lindwall bowling into the wind* Bailey b Lindwall, beaten by fast yorker, 0 in 37 mins, 28 balls
9		Archer 4 →\		- - - 1 - - -		- 16	
10		Lindwall 5 ←\		- - - - - - 3 -		- 19	

MCC in Australia 1954-55 – SECOND TEST

11	12.21 12.23	Archer 5 →\		- - W Graveney - - -	2- 19 - 19	May c Johnston, stabbed rising ball to short sq leg, 5 in 12 mins, 18 balls, 0 fours
12		Lindwall 6 ←\		- - - - - - 4	- 23	
13		Archer 6 →\		- - - - - - -	- 23	
14		Lindwall 7 ←\ Off spell 4-1-8-1		- - - - - - -	- 23	
15		Archer 7 →\ Off spell 4-2-3-1	1	- - (1 lb) - - - 1	- 26	
16		Davidson 2 ←\		- - - (2 lb) - - 1 -	- 29	2 leg-byes somewhere in this over
17		JohnsTon 1 →\		- - - - 3 - -	- 32	
18		Davidson 3 ←\ Off spell 2-0-2-0		1 - - - - -	- 33	

MCC in Australia 1954-55 – SECOND TEST

Over	Time	Bowler	Hutton	Graveney	Total	Notes
19		JohnsTon 2 →\		- - - - 1 - -		
	1.00				- 34	
		LUNCH	Hutton 19 90 mins 70 balls	Gravny 7 37 mins 36 balls	2-34 90 mins 152 balls	

Arlott: surely one of the slowest openings in Test cricket.

Over	Time	Bowler	Hutton 19	Gravny 7	2-34	20,000 crowd in coats
20	1.40	Lindwall 8 ←\		- .. - 2 1 - 1	- 38	
21		JohnsTon 3 →\	- - 1 - - - -		- 39	
22		Lindwall 9 ←\		- - - - - -	- 39	
23		JohnsTon 4 →\		- 1 - 1 4 - -	- 45	*Graveney crashes cover boundary.*
24		Lindwall 10 ←\	- - 1 - - - 1		- 47	
25		JohnsTon 5 →\		1 - - - - 1 -	- 49	
26		Lindwall 11 ←\ Off spell 4-1-	3	- - - - - - -	- 52	Hutton glances for 3. 52 up in 2 hours

MCC in Australia 1954-55 – SECOND TEST

Over	Time	Bowler	Batsman 1	Batsman 2	Score	Notes
27		JohnsTon 6 →\	- - - - - - 1		- 53	
28		Davidson 4 ←\	- 1 1	- - 1 - 2	- 58	*This may have been a seven-ball over*
29	2.22 2.24	JohnsTon 7 →\	W Cowdrey - - - - -	-	3-58 - 58	Hutton c Davidson, diving to left like a cat, firm leg glance, 30 in 132 mins, 109 balls, 3 fours. Hutton flabbergasted
30		Davidson 5 ←\	1 - - 2 - - 2		- 63	
31	2.31 2.33	JohnsTon 8 →\		- W Edrich 2 - - - -	4- 63 - 65	Graveney c Favell, diving to right at 3rd slip, both hands, casually cutting wide ball, 21 in 88 mins, 74 balls, 1 four. Edrich two edged to square leg
32		Davidson 6 ←\ Off spell 3-0-16-0	- 3 - - - 2 -	1	- 71	
33		JohnsTon 9 →\		- - - - 3 - -	- 74	
34		Archer 8 ←\		- - - - 4 (nb) - -	- 78	
35		JohnsTon 10 →\	- - - 2 4 -		- 84	

MCC in Australia 1954-55 – SECOND TEST

36	2.54 2.56	Archer 9 ←\		W Tyson - - - - -	5-84 - 84	Edrich c Benaud at gully, ball popped, 10 in 21 mins, 23 balls, 1 four
37		JohnsTon 11 →\ Off spell (ncl. Lunch) 11-1-26-2	- - - - 1	- -	- 85	
38		Archer 10 ←\	- - - - - -		- 85	
39	3.10 3.12	Lindwall 12 →\		- - W Evans - 3 -	6-85 - 88	Tyson bld, driving over and round, 0 in 14 mins, 13 balls
40	3.15 3.17	Archer 11 ←\		W Wardle - - - - -	7- 88 - 88	Evans c Langley, wk, sparring at short ball, inside edge, 3 in 3 mins, 3 balls
41		Lindwall 13 →\	- - - - - -		- 88	
42		Archer 12 ←\ Off spell 5-3-8-2	- - 4 - - - -		- 92	
43	3.30	Lindwall 14 →\ Spell 3-1-5-1	2 - - - - -		- 94	
		TEA	Cowdry 18 66 mins 62 balls	Wardle 4 13 mins 15 balls	7-94 200 mins 345 balls	

SESSION 60-5 IN 110 MINS, 193 BALLS

Swanton: Davidson's catch was of the type that can win a Test match. Cowdrey is showing how to bat confidently on this wicket.

Peebles: what is lacking in Graveney for top-class cricket?

MCC in Australia 1954-55 – SECOND TEST

				Cowdry 18	Wardle 4	7-94	
44	3.50		Davidson 7 ←\		- - - - - - -	 - 94	
45			Lindwall 15 →\	- - - - 2 - - 3		 - 99	*Cowdrey dropped by Benaud at slip* Cowdrey straight drive 3
46	4.00 4.02		Davidson 8 ←\	W Appleyard - 2 1 (1 lb) -	 - - 1	8-99 - 104	Cowdrey c Langley, wk, flash outside off-stump, 23 in 76 mins, 71 balls, 1 four
47			Lindwall 16 →\	- 1 - 3	 - 1 1	 - 110	
48			Davidson 9 ←\		- - - - - - -	 - 110	
49			Lindwall 17 →\ Off spell (incl. tea) 6-1-17-1	- - - - 1	 - -	 - 111	
50	 4.22 4.24		Davidson 10 ←\	- - W Statham 1 2 -	 - (1 lb)	9-111 - 115	Appleyard c Hole, 1st slip, low to right hand, 8 in 20 mins, 17 balls, 0 fours Wardle 7 in 42 balls
51			JohnsTon 12 →\	 2	4 2 2 4 4 - 1	 - 134	Wardle 4 cover-drive on the hop *Wardle two swipes over in-field, Benaud gets is hands to one* Wardle 4 cut over 2nd slip Wardle 4 cut over 3rd slip Smiling JohnsTon puts in a fly slip Wardle 1 swipe over in-field
52			Davidson 11 ←\	- - - - 1 -	- - - 1 -	 - 136	

MCC in Australia 1954-55 – SECOND TEST

53		JohnsTon 13 →\		- - - 2 1 4 2		- 145	Wardle off-drives for 4 Wardle dropped by Beno at midwkt
54		Davidson 12 ←\ Spell 6-2-16-2		- 1 1 - 3 1 1		- 152	*Rain falling*
55	4.47	JohnsTon 14 →\ Spell 2.3-0-30-1			- 2 W	10-154	Wardle c Burke, long on, 35 in 70 mins, 63 balls, 5 fours
			Statham 14 23 mins 17 balls 0 fours			10-154 257 mins 436 balls	Wardle scored his last 28 in 21 balls

SESSION TO DATE 60-3 IN 57 MINS, 91 BALLS

Arlott: The familiar tragedies of 1946 to 1951 are being played out again. Lindwall bowled magnificently and got wickets for other bowlers.

Swanton: ironic that England were girding themselves for a burst of fast bowling against Australia in the evening, and Statham and Wardle in trying to get out managed to make 43 runs.

Woodcock: Hutton seems to have ordered Wardle to hit out or get out

Peebles: Lindwall was the backbone. He pitched the ball up whereas Archer bowled an economically short length.

Fingleton: Sweating under the covers and humid conditions made the pitch grassier than usual and gave extra pace. Wardle's innings restored some much-needed respect.

Moyes: Wardle's buccaneering innings might not have endured if Langley had stood up to the stumps. Statham says that Wardle's innings was thanks to the wicket-keeper standing back while Wardle was making excursions down the wicket

Gilligan: The batting was worse than poor, Archer was outstanding in an excellent attack.

England First innings

* L. Hutton	c Davidson b Johnston	30	132 mins, 109 balls, 3 fours	3-58
T.E. Bailey	b Lindwall	0	37 mins, 28 balls	1-14
P.B.H. May	c Johnston b Archer	5	12 mins, 18 balls, 0 fours	2- 19
T.W. Graveney	c Favell b Johnston	21	88 mins, 74 balls, 1 four	4- 63
M.C. Cowdrey	c Langley b Davidson	23	76 mins, 71 balls, 1 four	8-99
W.J. Edrich	c Benaud b Archer	10	21 mins, 23 balls, 1 four	5-84
F.H. Tyson	b Lindwall	0	14 mins, 13 balls	6-85
+ T.G. Evans	c Langley b Archer	3	3 mins, 3 balls	7- 88
J.H. Wardle	c Burke b Johnston	35	70 mins, 63 balls, 5 fours	10-154
R. Appleyard	c Hole b Davidson	8	20 mins, 17 balls, 0 fours	9-111
J.B. Statham	not out	14	23 mins, 17 balls, 0 fours	
Extras	(lb 5)	5		
TOTAL	(10 wkts – all out)	154	257 mins, 54.3 overs, 436 balls	

BOWLING

Lindwall	17	3	47	2
Archer	12	7	12	3
Davidson	12	3	34	2
Johnston	13.3	1	56	3

Australia First Innings

Odd overs →\ from Hill End
Even overs ←\ from City (Pavilion) End

The pitch was being rolled until a short downpour required the covers to be put on. Start delayed by resumption of the rolling of the pitch. Poor light.

MCC in Australia 1954-55 – SECOND TEST

				Favell	Morris		
1	5.13	Statham 1 →\		- - - - - 4 -		- 4	Favell 4 to square leg
2		Bailey 1 ←\			- - - - 2 (nb) 4 - -	-10	Morris cover drives for 4
3		Statham 2 →\ Spell 2-0-6-0		- - - 2 - - -		- 12	
4		Bailey 2 ←\ Spell 1.6-0-12-1			- - 2 - 4 W	1 -18	Morris c Hutton, leg slip, riser, off glove, 12 in 18 mins, 15 balls, 2 fours
	5.31			Favell 6 18 mins 16 balls		1-18 18 mins 31 balls	Attendance: 23,312

SESSION (BOTH SIDES) 78-4 IN 75 MINS, 122 BALLS
Moyes and Wellings think that at the time of contact Morris's glove was off his bat.
Peebles: A very good day for entertainment but not for standard of cricket.

SECOND DAY – Once more unto the breach
Saturday 18 December

				Favell 6	Burke	1-18	
4 ctd	11.30	Bailey 2 Ctd			- -	- 18	
5		Statham 3 →\		2 2 - - - - -		- 22	Favell cuts twice for 2s *Field : 2 slips 2 gullies, 3 leg slips*
6		Bailey 3 ←\ Off spell (today) 1.2-0-6-0			3 2 - - 1 -	-28	
7		Statham 4 →\		4 - 3 - - 2 3 -		-40	

60

MCC in Australia 1954-55 – SECOND TEST

Over	Time	Bowler	Batsman	Balls	Score	Notes
8		Tyson 1 ←\		2 - 2 - 1 (nb) - - -	- 45	*Tyson struggling for rhythm on shorter 15 yard run-up*
9	11.56	Statham 5 →\ Off spell 3-0-24-0		2 - (4 byes) - - 1 2 3	- 57	*51 in 44 mins*
10		Tyson 2 ←\ Off spell 2-0-12-0	1	- - 2 4 (nb) - - (1 nb) - -	- 65	
11	12.10 12.12	Bailey 4 →\	W Harvey	- - - - - -	2-65 - 65	*Bailey on at other end to get cross-wind to help outswing.* *Favell c Graveney, low at 2nd slip, driving full length ball, 26 in 58 mins, 45 balls, 2 fours*
12		Statham 6 ←\		- - 3 - - 1 1	- 70	*Statham changes ends to use the cross-wind for his inswing*
13		Bailey 5 →\		- 1 - 1 - - (1 b/lb)	- 73	
14		Statham 7 ←\		- - - - - 2 1	- 76	
15		Bailey 6 →\	- 1	1 - - 2 - -	- 80	*Burke dropped by Graveney at 2nd slip, striking his left boot*

MCC in Australia 1954-55 – SECOND TEST

Over	Time	Bowler	Batsman L	Batsman R	Score	Notes
16		Statham 8 ←\	- - - 1 - -	1	- 82	
17		Bailey 7 →\	- - 2 - - -		- 84	
18		Statham 9 ←\ Off spell 4-0-12-0	- - 1 - - 1 -		-86	
19		Bailey 8 →\ Off spell 5-1-9-1	- - - - 1 -		- 87	
20	1.00	Tyson 3 ←\	- - - 1 - - -		- 88	
		LUNCH	Harvey 5 48 mins 29 balls	Burke 39 90 mins 75 balls	2- 88 108 mins 164 balls	

SESSION 70-1 IN 90 MINS, 133 BALLS

Arlott: Not a good morning for England. There is potent batting to come and Hutton may not be able to risk his spinners. Favell and Burke batted enterprisingly and England should have tempted them to flash more at well pitched-up balls

Over	Time	Bowler	Harvey 5	Burke 39	2- 88	Notes
21	1.40	Bailey 9 →\	- 2 1 - - -	1	- 92	
22		Tyson 4 ←\	- 3 - - (1 nb) - - -	2	- 98	
23	1.55 1.57	Bailey 10 →\	- 1 - - -	1 W Hole - 1	3- 100 - 101	Burke c Graveney, no feet movement, edges half-volley to 2nd slip, ct shoulder high, 44 in 105 mins, 85 balls, 1 four

MCC in Australia 1954-55 – SECOND TEST

Over	Time	Bowler	Benaud	Other	Score	Notes
24		Tyson 5 ←\	3 - -			
	2.04		W Benaud		4- 104	Harvey c Cowdrey, round arm delivery, rising ball fended gently to gully, 12 in 72 mins, 45 balls, 0 fours
	2.06		- -		- 104	*Benaud twice beaten for pace*
25		Bailey 11 →\	- - 1			
			3			Benaud straight drive for 3
			- 4		- 112	Hole drives 4 imperiously though covers
26		Tyson 6 ←\	- 4 - (1 nb) - 1 - - 1 -		- 119	Benaud edges high over Edrich in slips Benaud dropped by Graveney at bkwd square leg
27		Bailey 12 →\	- - 1 - - -		- 120	*Hole beaten on forward stroke*
28		Tyson 7 ←\	1 - 1 - - -			
	2.28		W Archer		5- 122	Hole bld, fast straight ball, 12 in 31 mins, 23 balls, 1 four
29	2.30	Bailey 13 →\	- - - - - -		- 122	
30		Tyson 8 ←\	- - - - 1 -		- 123	
31		Bailey 14 →\ Off spell (incl. lunch) 11-2-25-2	- - - - - -		- 123	
32		Tyson 9 ←\ Off spell (incl. lunch) 7-0-24-2	- 2 1 - - 2 -		- 128	*Tyson now tiring*

MCC in Australia 1954-55 – SECOND TEST

33		Appleyard 1 →\	- - - - 4 -		- 132	*Applyrd's first bowl of the series. A very good over. A wktkpr stands up at the stumps for first time in match* Benaud near catch to Edrich bkwd sht leg. Lock would have caught it. Benaud 4 over mid on
34		Statham 10 ←\	2 1	- - 1 - 4 -	- 140	
35		Appleyard 2 →\	- - 1	- - -	- 141	
36	3.10 3.12	Statham 11 ←\	W Davidson	- - - - - -	6- 141 - 141	Appeal for ct behind off bouncer Benaud lbw, playing back, 20 in 64 mins, 51 balls, 2 fours
37		Appleyard 3 →\		1 - - - - -	- 142	
38		Statham 12 ←\		1 - - 1 - - 1	- 145	
39		Appleyard 4 →\ Off spell 4-0-17-0		- - 4 - 6 1 -	- 156	Archer off drives for 4 Archer 6 pulled over wide mid on. Australia take 1st inns lead
40	3.30	Statham 13 ←\ Off spell 4-1-12-1		- - - - (1 b/lb) - 1	- 158	
		TEA	Davdsn 2 18 mins 17 balls	Archer 22 60 mins 45 balls	6-158 218 mins 326 balls	

SESSION 70-4 IN 110 MINS, 162 BALLS

MCC in Australia 1954-55 – SECOND TEST

#	Time	Bowler	Davdsn 2	Archer 22	6-158	Notes
41	3.50	Bailey 15 →\	- - 4 - - - -		- 162	
42		Tyson 10 ←\	1 (1 b/lb) - -	1 1 - 1	- 167	
43		Bailey 16 →\	1	- - - 4 1 -	- 173	
44		Tyson 11 ←\ Off spell 2-0-9-0	- - - - 1	4	- 178	
45		Bailey 17 →\ Off spell 3-0-12-0	- - - - 1	- 1	- 180	
46		Statham 14 ←\	- - - 3	- - 1 -	- 184	
47		Appleyard 5 →\	- - 1 -	- - 1	- 186	
48	4.32 4.34	Statham 15 ←\	- 4 2 W Lindwall - -	1	7-193 - 193	Davdsn square cuts: 50 stand Davdsn edges chance to May at 2nd slip Davidson bld, hitting across ball on leg stump, 20 in 60 mins, 54 balls, 2 fours
49		Appleyard 6 →\		- - - - -	- 193	

MCC in Australia 1954-55 – SECOND TEST

Over	Time	Bowler	Batsman 1	Batsman 2	Score	Notes
50		Statham 16 ←\	- - - - - 1		- 194	
51		Appleyard 7 →\ Off spell 4-1-15-0	4 1 - - 4 - 4 -		- 207	Lindwall edges for 4 Archer 4 snicked though empty slip area. becomes top-scorer. 203 up in 4½ hrs Archer 4 to mid wkt
52		Statham 17 ←\	2 1 - - 2 - 1		- 213	New ball *Archer plays and misses twice*
53	4.58 5.00	Tyson 12 →\	-	W Langley - - - - -	8-213 - 213	Archer plays and misses Archer c Hutton, well ct at 3rd slip, 49 in 128 mins, 91 balls, 6 fours, 1 six *4 slips and no short leg for Tyson*
54		Statham 18 ←\ Off spell 6-0-29-1	3 - 1 - 2 4 - 1		- 224	
55	5.11 5.13	Tyson 13 →\ Spell 2-2-0-2	- - - - - -	W JohnsTon - - - - -	9- 224 - 224	Lindwall c Evans, wk, skied innocuous head-high bouncer, 19 in 37 mins, 23 balls, 2 fours. Tyson's bouncer to Lindwall – a big mistake. *Obvious delays in fielding side to prevent having to bat again tonight. Tyson bowls wide of leg stump to prevent bowling Johnston. The over lasts 9 mins*
56	 5.22	Bailey 18 ←\ Spell 0.4-0-4-1		- - 4 W	- 228	Langley bld, 5 in 22 mins, 12 balls, 1 four
			Johnston 0 8 mins 6 balls		10- 228 310 mins 450 balls	Att: 44,897

SESSION 70-4 IN 92 MINS, 124 BALLS

Arlott: Australia's lead may be enough but at least Australia have been engaged in an equal challenge.
Swanton: Australia bowled out for 228 without Bedser, or would his presence have done it more cheaply? Moyes thinks yes.
Peebles: Tyson's shorter run has brought greater control with no loss of pace. Bailey led the way in the morning.
Woodcock: A thrilling and heartening day
Ross: Led by Bailey, England have counter-attacked and must continue to do so.
England have bowled about the same number of overs in almost an hour longer than did Australia, and Australia have scored 74 more runs.

Australia First innings

* A.R. Morris	c Hutton b Bailey	12	18 mins, 15 balls, 2 fours	1-18
L.E. Favell	c Graveney b Bailey	26	58 mins, 45 balls, 2 fours	2-65
J.W. Burke	c Graveney b Bailey	44	105 mins, 85 balls, 1 four	3-100
R.N. Harvey	c Cowdrey b Tyson	12	72 mins, 45 balls, 0 fours	4- 104
G.B. Hole	b Tyson	12	31 mins, 23 balls, 1 four	5-122
R. Benaud	lbw b Statham	20	64 mins, 51 balls, 2 fours	6-141

MCC in Australia 1954-55 – SECOND TEST

R.G. Archer	c Hutton b Tyson	49	128 mins, 91 balls, 6 fours, 1 six	8-213
A.K. Davidson	b Statham	20	60 mins, 54 balls, 2 fours	7-193
R.R. Lindwall	c Evans b Tyson	19	37 mins, 23 balls, 2 fours	9-224
+G.R. Langley	b Bailey	5	22 mins, 12 balls, 1 four	10-228
W.A. Johnston	not out	0	8 mins, 6 balls	
Extras	(b 5, lb 2, nb 2)	9		
TOTAL	(10 wkts – all out)	228	310 mins, 55.4 overs, 450 balls	

BOWLING

Statham	18	1	83	2
Bailey	17.4	3	59	4
Tyson	13	2	45	4
Appleyard	7	1	32	0

Wardle, England's top-scorer, has not bowled a ball.
On Sunday the wicket is exposed to bake in the sun.

THIRD DAY – Young amateurs

Monday 20 December

England Second Innings

Odd overs →\ from Hill End
Even overs ←\ from City End
The pitch looks easier – less green – and the air is less humid.

			Hutton	Bailey		
1	11.30	Lindwall 1 →\	- 1 - - - 4	- 1 -	- 6	Yorker Hutton pushes wide of mid on for 1 Bailey quick single to sq leg Hutton 4 struck to 3rd man
2		Archer 1 ←\		- - - - - -	- 6	*An over of half-volleys patted back.*
3		Lindwall 2 →\	1	4 - 1 - -	- 12	Bailey 4 off full toss to long leg
4		Archer 2 ←\		- - - - - -	- 12	*Archer, generally full length, slips in attempted bouncer; Bailey ducks and is hit on back; lbw appeal*
5		Lindwall 3 →\	- - - - - -		- 12	
6		Archer 3 ←\		- - - - - -	- 12	

MCC in Australia 1954-55 – SECOND TEST

Over	Time	Bowler	Batsman 1	Batsman 2	Score	Notes
7		Lindwall 4 →\	- - - - 1	- -	- 13	Hutton pushes to mid-off for 1. First run for 15 mins Bailey almost tempted to edge outswinger
8	12.06 12.08	Archer 4 ←\	- - - 4 1	- W May 3	 1- 18 - 21	Hutton uppish 4 to square leg Bailey c Langley wk, ball moved away late off seam, 6 in 36 mins, 33 balls, 1 four. Bailey 'walks' May flicks 3 to square leg
9		Lindwall 5 →\		- - 4 - - - -	 - 25	May plays and misses May hits inswinger to long leg for 4 May checks stroke to dig out fast ball
10		Archer 5 ←\	3	- - - - 4 -	 - 32	May 4 to square leg
11	12.20	Lindwall 6 →\	- - - - - - -		- 32	
12	12.30	Archer 6 ←\ Off spell 6-4-15-1	- - - - - - -		- 32	Drinks
13		Lindwall 7 →\ Off spell 7-2-26-0	- 4 - - 4 1 -		 -41	Hutton wild slash outside off-stump Hutton 4 to point boundary Hutton 4 to long leg in the air near Dvdsn short single Lindwall goes off for boot repairs
14		JohnsTon 1 ←\	- 1	- - 4 - 3 -	 - 49	May straight drive for 4 May pushes to on for 3
15		Davidson 1 →\		- 1 - - 3 - 1 -	 - 54	50 up in 73 mins

MCC in Australia 1954-55 – SECOND TEST

Over	Time	Bowler			Score	Notes
16	12.47	JohnsTon 2 ←\	- W Graveney -	- 1	2- 55	Hutton, c Benaud, head-high at gully, driving with no feet movement, 28 in 77 mins, 54 balls, 4 fours
	12.50		W Cowdrey -		3- 55	Graveney plays and misses first ball Graveney c Langley, straight-driving leg-cutter, casual shot, 0 in 2 mins, 3 balls
	12.52				- 55	
17		Davidson 2 →\ Off spell 2-1-5-0		- - - - - -	- 55	
18		JohnsTon 3 ←\	- 3 - - - -			
	1.00		-	-	- 58	
		LUNCH	Cowdrey 3 8 mins 4 balls	May 21 52 mins 50 balls	3- 58 90 mins 144 balls	

Arlott: Edrich should open the batting rather than Bailey. It looks as if the match balance has finally tilted to Australia.

Moyes: May has started with more assurance than usual

Over	Time	Bowler			Score	Notes
			Cowdrey 3	May 21	3- 58	
19	1.40	Lindwall 8 →\	- - - - - -		- 58	*May has said to Cowdrey on walking out, "if I am to play the innings of my life, I would like to do it this afternoon".*
20		JohnsTon 4 ←\		- 1 - 2 - -	- 61	
21		Lindwall 9 →\		- - - - - -	- 61	
22		JohnsTon 5 ←\	- - - - - -		- 61	
23		Lindwall 10 →\		- 1 - - - -	- 62	4 runs in 25 mins

MCC in Australia 1954-55 – SECOND TEST

24		JohnsTon 6 ←\		- 4 1		May 4 to square leg
			- 1	- 3 -	- 71	May 4 to square leg
25		Lindwall 11 →\	- 1	1 - 2 - - -	- 75	
26		JohnsTon 7 ←\	- - - - 3 -		- 78	
27		Lindwall 12 →\ Off spell 5-2-6-0	- - 1 1 - - -		- 79	
28		JohnsTon 8 ←\	- 1 - - - - -		- 80	
29		Davidson 3 →\	- 3 - - - 4 -		- 87	
30		JohnsTon 9 ←\ Off spell 9-1-29-2	- - - 1 - -		- 88	
31		Davidson 4 →\	- 4 - - - - -		- 92	Cowdrey 4 swept through leg trap
32		Archer 7 ←\		- - - - 4 - -	- 96	May hooks for 4

70

MCC in Australia 1954-55 – SECOND TEST

Over		Bowler	Balls	Balls	Score	Notes
33		Davidson 5 →\	- 4 1	- - - -	- 101	Cowdrey straight drive for 4. 100 up in 155 mins
34		Archer 8 ←\	- - - - - -		- 101	
35		Davidson 6 →\	- 1 - 4 1 -	-	- 107	Cowdrey off-drive for 4. 51 stand in 79 mins
36		Archer 9 ←\ Off spell 3-1-8-0	- - - - 4 -		- 111	
37		Davidson 7 →\ Off spell 5-0-28-0	4 1 - 1 - - -		- 117	
38		Benaud 1 ←\	1 - - - - 1 -		- 119	
39		Archer 10 →\	- - - - 4 - -		- 123	May hooks 4, 53 in 140 mins, 129 balls
40		Benaud 2 ←\	1 - - - - - 1		- 125	
41		Archer 11 →\	- 1 - - - - -		- 126	

MCC in Australia 1954-55 – SECOND TEST

Over	Time	Bowler	Cowdrey	May	Total	Notes
42		Benaud 3 ←\		2 - - - - - -	- 128	
43		Archer 12 →\	- - - - - - -		- 128	
44		Benaud 4 ←\		- - - 1 - - -	- 129	
45	3.30	Archer 13 →\ Off spell 4-2-5-0	- - - - - - -		- 129	
		TEA	Cowdry 37 118 mins 109 balls	May 58 162 mins 161 balls	3- 129 200 mins 360 balls	

Session 71-0 in 110 mins, 216 balls

Arlott: The score belies the fact that this has been a momentous session for England, two batsmen holding out for the whole period from a near-indefensible position.

Cardus: What a great pleasure to see the revival of the spirit of amateur batsmanship in the persons of May and Cowdrey. They brought back graciousness, driving beautifully between cover and mid-on

Over	Time	Bowler	Cowdrey	May	Total	Notes
			Cowdry 37	May 58	3- 129	
46	3.50	Benaud 5 ←\	2 - - - - - -		- 131	
47		Lindwall 13 →\		- - - - - - 1	- 132	Lindwall discards umbrella field; 5 men in front
48		Benaud 6 ←\		- - - - - 1 2	- 136	
			1			
49		Lindwall 14 →\	1	- - - - - - -	- 137	Cowdrey nearly lbw

72

MCC in Australia 1954-55 – SECOND TEST

Over	Time	Bowler			Total	Notes
50		Benaud 7 ←\	3 - - - - -	-	- 140	
51		Lindwall 15 →\	- - - - - 4 (1 lb)	-	- 145	
52		Benaud 8 ←\	- - - - - -		- 145	
53		Lindwall 16 →\	-	- - - - 1	- 146	
54	4.20	Benaud 9 ←\	-	4 - - - - -	- 150	
55	4.25	Lindwall 17 →\	4 - - - - -	-	- 154	Cowdrey 52 in 153 mins, 146 balls
56		Benaud 10 ←\	-	- - - - - -	- 154	
57	4.35	Lindwall 18 →\	- - - 1 - -	- (1 lb)	- 156	100 partnership in 163 mins
58		Benaud 11 ←\	-	- - 3 - - -	- 159	

MCC in Australia 1954-55 – SECOND TEST

Over	Time	Bowler		Batsman	Runs	Score	Notes
59		Lindwall 19 →\ Off spell 7-0-17-0			- - 2 - - - 3 -	- 164	
60		Benaud 12 ←\			- - - - - - - -	- 164	
61		JohnsTon 10 →\			- - - - - -	- 164	JohnsTon bowls in slow style
62		Benaud 13 ←\			2 - - - - - - -	- 166	
63		JohnsTon 11 →\		(nb) 1	- - - - - - 3	- 170	
64	5.05 5.07	Benaud 14 ←\		 W Edrich	- - 1 - - 1	 4- 171 - 172	Cowdrey c Archer, down pitch lofted drive to deep mid-off 54 in 193 mins, 184 balls, 4 fours. Batsmen crossed
65		JohnsTon 12 →\			3 - - - - - 4	- 179	Edrich 4 hook
66		Benaud 15 ←\			- - - - 3 - -	- 182	
67		JohnsTon 13 →\		4 (4 nb) -	- - 3 - - -	 - 193	May 3 wide of mid-on Edrich off-drive for 4 Lbw appeal Edrich swings and misses no ball, unsighting Langley. *

MCC in Australia 1954-55 – SECOND TEST

Over	Time	Bowler	Batsman 1	Runs	Batsman 2	Total	Notes
68		Benaud 16 ←\		- 1 - - 4 - -		- 198	Edrich punches short ball to square leg for 4
69		JohnsTon 14 →\ Spell 5-1-23-0		4 - 1 - - - -		- 203	May 4 wide of mid-off
70	5.30	Benaud 17 ←\ Off spell (incl. tea) 17-3-36-1		- 1 - - - - -		- 204	
		CLOSE	Edrich 12 23 mins 32 balls	May 98 262 mins balls		4- 204 300 mins 562 balls	Attendance: 31,679

* (67th over) Wrongly called runs to Edrich but corrected overnight
Session 75-1 in 100 mins, 202 balls
England lead by 130.
Arlott: England now have half a chance.
Swanton: The wicket is now plumb so England need a lot more runs. May supplied the grace, Cowdrey the calm
  certainty of judgement and common sense. Australia's out-cricket kept to a high standard all day. Lindwall
  bowled for nearly three hours, and was the linchpin of the bowling though he took no wicket.
Fingleton: nothing finer on the tour has been seen than May's straight and on-driving
May had dinner at the Union Club as a guest of Ian Peebles, who allowed him only one glass of wine and sent him
off to an early bed.

FOURTH DAY – Good day for Australia

Tuesday 21 December
Stormy night

Over	Time	Bowler	Edrich 12	May 98	4- 204	Notes
			Edrich 12	May 98	4- 204	
71	11.30	Lindwall 20 →\ Off spell 1-0-5-0		- 2 - - 1 - 2	- 209	May turns for 2 past short leg, 100 in 263 mins, 258 balls Light drizzle
	11.36	RAIN				
72	11.53	Davidson 8 ←\		1 - - - - - -	- 210	
73		JohnsTon 15 →\		- - 1 - - - -	- 211	*Morris delays new ball because of wet outfield*

75

MCC in Australia 1954-55 – SECOND TEST

Over	Time	Bowler	Batsman 1	Batsman 2	Score	Notes
74		Davidson 9 ←\		- - - (1 lb) - - - -	- 212	
75		JohnsTon 16 →\		- - (1 lb) - - 1 - -	- 214	
76		Davidson 10 ←\	- 2 - - 1 - - -		- 217	
77		JohnsTon 17 →\ Off spell 3-0-6-0	- 4 - - - - -		- 221	Edrich 4 through covers. 50 partnership
78		Davidson 11 ←\ Off spell 4-1-5-0		- - - - 1 - -	-222	Edrich almost c & b
79	12.23 12.25	Lindwall 21 →\		- - - W Tyson - - -	5- 222 - 222	New ball taken at last May bld off-stump, fast break-back full length, 104 in 298 mins, 286 balls, 10 fours
80		Archer 14 ←\	- - 1 - 1 1	- - 1 -	- 225	
81		Lindwall 22 →\	- - - - - -		- 225	
82		Archer 15 ←\		- - - - - - -	-225	

MCC in Australia 1954-55 – SECOND TEST

Over	Time	Bowler		Batsman	Score	Notes
83		Lindwall 23 →\	- - - 1 - -			
	12.45			- ret Evans	- 226	Tyson retired hurt, hit on back of head by bouncer, 1 in 20 mins, 17 balls
84	12.47	Archer 16 ←\	- - - 3 - 1	1	- 231	Tyson taken to hospital for X-ray Evans dropped by Hole at slip
85		Lindwall 24 →\ Spell 4-3-1-1	- - - - - -		- 231	
86	1.00	Archer 17 ←\ Spell 3.6-1-9-1	- - - W	1	6 -232	Edrich bld, wide ball, pulling out of stroke, played on inside edge, 29 in 96 mins, 108 balls, 4 fours
		LUNCH		Evans 2 13 mins 3 balls	6- 232 373 mins 688 balls	

SESSION 28-2 IN 73 MINS, 126 BALLS

Whether Tyson will bat again is not known. Peebles thinks not. Ross, Harris and Gilligan fear that he may not bat or bowl in the match.
Moyes: England should have pushed the score along before Lindwall returned with the new ball.
Ross: May must throw off his habit of being a second innings batsman.

Over	Time	Bowler		Wardle	Evans 2	6- 232	Notes
86 ctd	1.40	Archer 17 Ctd	- -			- 232	
87		Lindwall 25 →\	- - - 1 - 1 1			- 236	
88	1.50 1.52	Archer 18 ←\	- 3 - - -	W Tyson 1	7-239 - 240	Evans c Lindwall, off-side flash, ct at 2nd slip, 4 in 23 mins, 10 balls, 0 fours
89		Lindwall 26 →\	- - - - 3	- 1 1	- 245	Wardle hooks for 3

MCC in Australia 1954-55 – SECOND TEST

Over	Time	Bowler		Runs	Score	Notes
90		Archer 19 ←\		4 - - - - - -	- 249	Tyson straight drive for 4
91	2.05 2.07	Lindwall 27 →\	W Appleyard	- - - - - - -	8- 249 - 249	Wardle lbw, off-cutter, 8 in 25 mins, 19 balls, 0 fours
92		Archer 20 ←\		- - 1 - - -	- 250	
93	2.15 2.17	Lindwall 28 →\	W Statham	- - - 4 - -	9- 250 - 254	Tyson bld. slow yorker, 9 in 43 mins, 37 balls, 1 four Statham drives straight for 4
94		Archer 21 ←\		- - - - - -	- 254	
95		Lindwall 29 →\		- - - (2 lb) - - - -	- 256	
96		Archer 22 ←\ Off spell 9-2-25-2	1	- - 2 - 4 -	- 263	
97		Lindwall 30 →\		- - - 1 - -	- 264	
98		Davidson 12 ←\		- - 2 3 - 4	- 273	

MCC in Australia 1954-55 – SECOND TEST

99		Lindwall 31 →\ Off spell 11-6-15-3	- - - - - - -		- 273	
100		Davidson 13 ←\ Off spell 2-0-14-0	- - 1 - - - 4		- 278	Appleyard cuts for 4
101		JohnsTon 18 →\	- - - - 2 4 - -		- 284	
102		Benaud 18 ←\	- - - - - 1 4 -		- 289	
103		JohnsTon 19 →\	- - 2 - - - 1		- 292	
104		Benaud 19 ←\ Spell 2-0-6-0	- - - - - - 1		- 293	
105	3.10	JohnsTon 20 →\ Spell 2.3.-0-12-1	- 3	W	10- 296	Statham c Langley wk, edged push, 25 in 53 mins, 39 balls, 5 fours
			Applyd 19 63 mins 64 balls 1 four		10-296 463 mins 837 balls	

SESSION 64-4 IN 90 MINS, 149 BALLS

Swanton: Until the last wicket partnership the Englishman was filled with gloom. The innings ended with Langley's fifth catch of the match and no bye conceded. Only Evans at his best can surpass him.

Ross: Langley's virtues hide behind his rubicund and undemonstrative exterior.

Arlott: Langley ended the innings: he is undemonstrably as good as any wicket-keeper.

Peebles: Appleyard reaped the reward of his persistent practice in the nets

Australian innings will commence and tea will be taken late. They need 223 to win on a pitch that is getting easier. England must make the most of the new ball.

England Second innings

* L. Hutton	c Benaud b Johnston	28	77 mins, 54 balls, 4 fours	2-55
T.E. Bailey	c Langley b Archer	6	36 mins, 33 balls, 1 four	1-18
P.B.H. May	b Lindwall	104	298 mins, 286 balls, 10 fours	5-222
T.W. Graveney	c Langley b Johnston	0	2 mins, 3 balls	3-55
M.C. Cowdrey	c Archer b Benaud	54	193 mins, 184 balls, 4 fours	4-171
W.J. Edrich	b Archer	29	96 mins, 108 balls, 4 fours	6-232
F.H. Tyson	b Lindwall	9	43 mins, 37 balls, 1 four	9-250
+ T.G. Evans	c Lindwall b Archer	4	23 mins, 10 balls, 0 fours	7-239

MCC in Australia 1954-55 – SECOND TEST

J.H. Wardle	lbw b Lindwall	8	25 mins, 19 balls, 0 fours	8-249
R. Appleyard	not out	19	63 mins, 64 balls, 1 four	
J.B. Statham	c Langley b Johnston	25	53 mins, 39 balls, 5 fours	10-296
Extras	(lb 6, nb 4)	10		
TOTAL	(10 wkts – all out)	296	463 mins, 104.3 overs, 837 balls	

Tyson retired hurt 1 in 20 mins, 17 balls at 226-5, returned at 7-239

BOWLING

Lindwall	31	10	69	3
Archer	21	9	53	3
Johnston	19.3	2	70	3
Davidson	13	2	52	0
Benaud	19	3	42	1

Australia Second Innings

Odd overs ← \ from City (Pavilion) End
Even overs → \ from Hill End
Australia need 223 to win, which most think is well within their powers

			Favell	Morris		
1	3.20	Statham 1 ← \ bowling into wind	- - 2 - - 4 -	 - 6		Favell nearly plays on Lbw appeal Favell cuts hard through Edrich's finger tips at 1st slip, 2 runs Favell almost bowled Favell flicks inswinger to long leg for 4
2		Tyson 1 → \ has large bump on his head	- - - - - 2	1 -		
3		Statham 2 ← \	3 - - (4 lb) - - 4 -			4 leg byes somewhere in first 5 overs
4		Tyson 2 → \	- 2 4 - - - -	 -		Morris 4 off full toss to long leg, ball retrieved by a small black spaniel before May could get there. A boy retrieves the ball. *Morris plays and misses twice*
5	3.45	Statham 3 ← \	1 - - - - W	 1- 27		*Morris hooks at good-length ball, lbw appeal, also plays and misses four times* Morris lbw hooking, ball kept low, 10 in 25 mins, 16 balls, 1 four
		TEA	Favell 13 25 mins 23 balls	1- 27 25 mins 39 balls		

			Favell 13	Burke	1- 27	
5 ctd	4.03	Statham 3 ctd		-	- 27	
6		Tyson 3 → \	3 - - 3 - -	 - (1 nb) 		
	4.10 4.12		W Harvey -	 - -	2- 34 - 34	Favell c Edrich at 1st slip, both hands head high to right, 16 in 32 mins, 27 balls, 2 fours Harvey plays and misses first two balls

MCC in Australia 1954-55 – SECOND TEST

7		Statham 4 ← \		- - - - - - -	- 34	*Statham twice hits Burke hard on right thigh*
8		Tyson 4 → \ Off spell (incl. tea) 4-0-18-1	- - - - - 3	- -	- 37	
9		Statham 5 ← \		- - - - - - -	- 37	
10		Bailey 1 → \		- - - (1 lb) - 2 -	- 40	
11		Statham 6 ← \ Off spell 6-3-14-1		- - - - - - -	- 40	
12		Bailey 2 → \ Off spell 2-0-3-0	- - - - 1	- -	- 41	
13		Appleyard 1 ← \		- - - - - - -	- 41	
14		Wardle 1 → \		- - - - - - -	- 41	
15		Appleyard 2 ← \	2 - - - - - -		- 43	

MCC in Australia 1954-55 – SECOND TEST

Over	Time	Bowler			Score	Notes
16		Wardle 2 → \		- - - - - - -	- 43	
17		Appleyard 3 ← \ Off Spell 3-1-6-0	1	- - - - 3 - -	- 47	
18		Tyson 5 → \		- (1 nb) - - - - 4 1 -	- 53	*Burke hit on chest and badly winded*
19		Statham 7 ← \ Off spell 1-0-2-0	1	- - 1 - - - -	- 55	
20		Tyson 6 → \ Off spell 2-0-11-0	- - - 2 2 2		- 61	
21		Wardle 3 ← \	2	- - - - - 1	- 64	
22		Statham 8 → \ Spell 1-1-0-0		- - - - - - -	- 64	*Crowd start to drift away*
23	5.30	Wardle 4 ← \ Spell 2-0-11-0	- 4 4 - - - - -		- 72	Harvey 4 through extra cover Harvey 4 to long leg
		CLOSE	Harvey 26 78 mins 65 balls	Burke 13 87 mins 78 balls	2- 72 112 mins 186 balls	Attendance: 20,909

SESSION 45-1 IN 87 MINS, 147 BALLS
Arlott: Australia are still the likely winners. When the next new ball is due the match will be nearly over.
Swanton: The not out pair have added only 38 in the last 80 minutes

MCC in Australia 1954-55 – SECOND TEST

FIFTH DAY - Typhoon

Wednesday 22 December

			Harvey 26	Burke 13	2- 72	
24	11.30	Tyson 7 →\		- - 1 - 3 - (1 nb) - - -	 - 77	*Weather cool with a refreshing breeze from the south*
25		Statham 9 ←\	- - - - - -		 - 77	*Pitch seems lifeless*
26	 11.45 11.47 11.51 11.53	Tyson 8 →\		- - W Hole - - W Benaud -	 3- 77 4 – 77 4- 77	Burke, bld, yorker, 14 in 102 mins, 88 balls, 1 four Hole bld yorker, 0 in 4 mins, 4 balls
27		Statham 10 ←\ Off spell 2-1-3-0	- - - - 2 1		 - 80	
28		Tyson 9 →\	- - - - - 1		 - 81	
29		Bailey 3 ←\	- - - - 4 -		 - 85	Lbw appeal
30		Tyson 10 →\ Off spell 4-1-8-2	 1	- - - 1 - 1	 - 88	
31		Bailey 4 ←\		- - - 2 - - -	 - 90	

MCC in Australia 1954-55 – SECOND TEST

#	Time	Bowler	Bat1	Bat2	Score	Notes
32		Statham 11 →\	- 3 - - - -		- 93	
33		Bailey 5 ←\ Off spell 3-0-10-0	- 3 - - -	1	- 97	
34	12.34	Statham 12 →\	- - - (1 lb) -	- - 1 - (1 lb)	- 100	100 up in 176 mins
35		Appleyard 4 ←\		- - - - - 1	- 101	Benaud almost bowled through the gate *Benaud makes an injudicious swipe, stopped by Statham with his foot*
36		Statham 13 →\ Off spell 3-0-9-0	-	- - - - 2 3	- 106	
37	12.44 12.46	Appleyard 5 ←\	1	W Archer - - - 1	5- 106 - 108	Benaud c Tyson behind sq leg. High hit, Tyson gets out of position and makes a desperate lunge. Batsmen crossed, 12 in 51 mins, 47 balls, 0 fours Harvey takes a risky single, giving Archer the strike
38		Tyson 11 →\	1 - 4 - - 2 - -		- 115	Harvey 50 in 115 mins
39	1.00	Appleyard 6 ←\	-	- - - 2 1 -	- 118	
		LUNCH	Harvey 51 160 mins 120 balls	Archer 5 14 mins 13 balls	5- 118 202 mins 315 balls	

SESSION 46-3 IN 90 MINS, 129 BALLS
Arlott: For the first time in the match, probability favours England

			Harvey 51	Archer 5	5- 118	

MCC in Australia 1954-55 – SECOND TEST

Over	Time	Bowler		Batsman	Wicket	Score	Notes
40	1.40	Tyson 12 →\		- - 1 - - 2 - 1		 - 122	Harvey 2 off hip to long leg
41		Statham 14 ←\		- - - - - - -		 - 122	
42	1.53 1.55	Tyson 13 →\		- - W Davidson 2 - 2 1 -	6- 122 - 127		Lbw appeal Archer bld 6, cutting breakback, played on? 6 in 27 mins, 19 balls, 0 fours. Davidson 2 to off Davidson 2 to off
43	2.00 2.02	Statham 15 ←\		- W Lindwall - 4 - 2 2 -	7-127 - 135		Davidson c Evans, wk, edged off shoulder of bat, diving in front of 2nd slip, ball drops out of left hand and re-caught in right, 5 in 5 mins, 6 balls, 0 fours Lindwall 4 through covers
44	 2.11 2.13	Tyson 14 →\	- - 1 	 - W Langley - -	 8-136 - 136		Tyson ignores advice from the Hill to bowl a bumper at Lindwall Fast breakback, just kept out Lindwall bld, yorked, 8 in 9 mins, 8 balls, 1 four
45		Statham 16 ←\	- - - 4 1	 - - -	 - 141		
46		Tyson 15 →\	- - - - - 3	 - -	 - 144		
47	 2.29 2.31	Statham 17 ←\	- 1 	 W JohnsTon - - -	 9- 145 - 145		Langley bld off stump, inswinger, 0 in 13 mins, 8 balls, stump broken Johnston almost bowled Appeal for lbw Harvey refuses single

MCC in Australia 1954-55 – SECOND TEST

48		Tyson 16 →\	4 - - 2 4 - 1		- 156	Harvey sweeps over Bailey at long leg for 4
49		Statham 18 ←\	- 2 - - - - -		- 158	Statham bowls slow and wide of leg
50		Tyson 17 →\		4 1 2 - 2 - 1	- 168	Jnstn glances full toss one-handed for 4 Johnston sneaks a single *Harvey could have been run out in this over but for a bad throw*
51		Statham 19 ←\ Off spell 6-1-17-2	- - - - 1 - -		- 169	*Statham, after six overs in to the wind, is flagging in his run-up*
52		Tyson 18 →\	- - - 1 - - 2		- 172	
53		Bailey 6 ←\ Spell 1-0-8-0	- 4 - - - 4 -		- 180	Defensive field Harvey straight drive over bowler's head for 4 Harvey pull-drive for 4 Hutton asks Tyson to bowl one more over
54	3.11	Tyson 19 →\ Spell (incl. lunch) 8.4-0-48-3		- - 4 W	10- 184	Jstn glances full toss one-handed for 4 Johnston c Evans, swings at leg side ball, 11 in 40 mins, 17 balls, 2 fours
		Best innings I ever saw Harvey play, says Evans	Harvey 92 251 mins 191 balls 9 fours		10- 184 293 mins 431 balls	Johnston shakes hands with Tyson and Statham, and the crowd cheers them off. Attendance: 14,575. Attendance for 5 days: 135,354, Receipts: £A 23,334

SESSION 66-5 IN 91 MINS, 116 BALLS

First visitor to the England dressing room is Mr Menzies.

Hutton tells the Press that Statham and Tyson did a wonderful job on a good pitch. He had seen Statham in the West Indies but Tyson "far exceeded the expectations I had of him when we left England." He said he would have been tempted to put Australia in if he had won the toss, if there were no critics to worry about. Did he miss Bedser? "We always miss Alec" was his coy reply.

Tyson and Statham were at the end of their tether. Statham went straight back to the hotel and slept for two hours.

Arlott: 90 minutes of insufferable suspense. England showed a hard edge. Hutton decided to keep Tyson on all afternoon till he was near his limit, because he would stiffen up if rested. The victory is all the sweeter because it was achieved by the new young players, Tyson, Statham, May and Cowdrey. Harvey was in total command.

Swanton: The batting in this match has been of very moderate standard. Harvey was tremendous when Johnston came taking the necessary risks without making any mistake. In farming the strike he was helped by England's slow fielders. It was perhaps his finest innings yet for his country. Tyson has made his reputation with as fine display of stamina and speed as I have ever seen from an English fast bowler. The causes of England's success are four players – May, Cowdrey, Statham and Tyson – under 25.

Cardus: Another defeat here would have broken the team spirit so much that the series would have been lost.

MCC in Australia 1954-55 – SECOND TEST

Fingleton: Against bowling fit to rank with Larwood for sheer pace, Australia's batting was pathetic

Moyes: Harvey played selflessly for the side and did not worry about a century. Statham, bowling into the wind, was inferior to Tyson only in figures.

Wellings: The last wicket fell just in time for Tyson and Statham were exhausted. The omission of Bedser nearly cost England the match.

Ross: Bedser's omission was justified; though Wardle hardly bowled the balance of the attack was improved and both spinners scored vital runs. Morris used the umbrella field, 5 slips 2 leg slips, for the pace attack whereas Hutton usually had a third man and long leg, and often only one slip. By doing so England saved over 40 runs and no real chance was missed.

Australia Second innings

L.E. Favell	c Edrich b Tyson	16	32 mins, 27 balls, 2 fours	2-34
* A.R. Morris	lbw b Statham	10	25 mins, 16 balls, 1 four	1-27
J.W. Burke	b Tyson	14	102 mins, 88 balls, 1 four	3-77
R.N. Harvey	not out	92	251 mins, 191 balls, 9 fours	
G.B. Hole	b Tyson	0	4 mins, 4 balls	4-77
R. Benaud	c Tyson b Appleyard	12	51 mins, 47 balls, 0 fours	5-106
R.G. Archer	b Tyson	6	27 mins, 19 balls, 0 fours	6-122
A.K. Davidson	c Evans b Statham	5	5 mins, 6 balls, 0 fours	7-127
R.R. Lindwall	b Tyson	8	9 mins, 8 balls, 1 four	8-136
+ G.R. Langley	b Statham	0	13 mins, 8 balls	9-145
W.A. Johnston	c Evans b Tyson	11	40 mins, 17 balls, 2 fours	10-184
Extras	(lb 7, nb 3)	10		
TOTAL	(10 wkts – all out)	184	293 mins, 53.4 overs, 431 balls	

BOWLING

Statham	19	6	45	3
Tyson	18.4	1	83	6
Bailey	6	0	21	0
Appleyard	6	1	12	1
Wardle	4	2	11	0

England won by 38 runs

May deserves mention for his century which turned the game around, but there can only be one man of this match: Frank Tyson.

After the stunning victory at Sydney, the MCC celebrated a much more cheerful Christmas at the Oceanic Hotel in Coogee Bay. Cowdrey had his 22nd birthday on Christmas 'Eve. Recorded Christmas messages from their families back home were played.

The margin was 38 runs. England last wicket contributed 43 and 46 in each innings.

Swanton thinks that England cannot hope to win the series on the strength of this narrow victory and indeed, seem likely to lose unless the administrative arrangements are changed. Mr. Howard the manager has taken part in team selection but has otherwise steered clear of cricketing matters. Hutton has not been able the bear the burden of organising proper practices for the players. For example, during the Brisbane Test, net practice before each day's play was not provided by the home authority and MCC accepted the refusal. Compulsory fielding practices have not been organised.

MCC v Northern New South Wales Country XI at Newcastle, December 27, 28 and 29.

Newcastle is the second city of New South Wales, 60 miles north up the coast from Sydney. The opposition were a mixture of players from New South Wales country sides. Even though it would not rank as first-class, the match was allocated an unnecessary three days, Monday to Wednesday. The Country side collapsed after a good start and by the end of the first day, MCC were 116 for 4. On Tuesday they added 322 in only 207 minutes, with May driving towards his fourth century in consecutive matches. It was a bumper day for the spectators (only 5,000 compared with 7,000 on the first day), for the home side raced to 143 for 2 in the remaining 110 minutes. On the final day Bedser took two quick wickets, then taken off for Wardle, and Appleyard ran through the rest. It was a good match for Compton, who seemed unaffected by his hand injury, Bedser who seemed to have recovered his normal energy, and for MCC who received £800 as share of the gate money

NORTHERN NSW 211 (R.Harvey 41, R.MacDonald 63, Wardle 6-36) and 246 (R.Harvey 36, R.Wotton 52, Bedser 3-49, Appleyard 5-59). MCC 438 (McConnon 43, Compton 60, May 157, Evans 69, J.Bull 5-80, W.Wellham 4-107) and 20-1. MCC WON BY NINE WICKETS.

In the Sheffield Shield, the four main states were playing, Victoria at home to New South Wales, South Australia to Queensland (the latter commencing on Christmas Day). And two absorbing matches they were, Victoria winning by 36 runs with 55 minutes left, Queensland by 34 runs with 74 minutes left. Catching the selectors' eyes were Colin McDonald of Victoria with 94 and 54, Jack Hill (leg-spinner of the 1953 tour) with seven wickets for them, for NSW leg-spinner Jim Treanor and tall lanky fast bowler Pat Crawford each with seven wickets. With Johnson resting his knee for the Test, young spinner W.A.Dick was a late call-up and took 5 for 31. The Adelaide game was marked by tedious

MCC in Australia 1954-55 – SECOND TEST

Queensland batting (Ken Mackay, a left-handed caricature of Trevor Bailey, making 55 in 195 minutes). For the home team Graeme Hole made a glorious 140 in 204 minutes. Ron Archer (Queensland) had a good match with 66 and 44, 3-67 and 3-47. Drennan of South Australia took nine wickets in the match. Test wicket-keeper Gil Langley got hit on the eye by the ball that bowled Archer and was unfit for the rest of the match, good news for the contender for his place, Len Maddocks, who batted well for Victoria.

THIRD TEST AT MELBOURNE

December 31, January 1, 3, 4, 5

England's only change from the Sydney Test is Compton in for Graveney. Bedser is retained in the XII. For Australia Johnson and Miller are now fit and returned. His doctor has told Miller to bowl only in short spells. Out go Davidson and, despite his runs in the Second Test, Burke. Langley then withdrew due to his eye injury and Maddocks, a useful batsman, replaces him. Archer and Hole retain their places after their good state performances.

Leonard (Len) V. MADDOCKS (Victoria), aged 28, a small, wiry, wicket-keeper, not quite as good as Langley, but a very useful right-hand batsman.

Northerly winds, bringing heat from the desert, are forecast

For some reason, a Shield game was taking place during the Test, New South Wales beating Queensland in a low scoring game.

FIRST DAY – Here we go again

Friday 31 December

It has been a hot sticky night. Hutton is doubtful with back ache and a bad cold. He has to be persuaded out of bed and accompanied to the ground by Evans and Edrich who tell him that the side's morale depends on him playing. At 11.30 he is announced as playing. The Bedser problem has been praying on his mind. Evans, Edrich and Compton all suggested that Bedser should be left out. Bedser is invited by Hutton to inspect the pitch with Denis Compton. Hutton says that during the pitch inspection he got the impression that Alec was not 100 per cent confident about his fitness. Bedser has had his greatest successes at the MCG. Wardle, a bowler who was entrusted with only four overs in the Second Test, stays in. On the other hand Bedser's inclusion would require reversion to the four-pace attack. Hutton resolves that Bedser must drop out. But this time, much to his subsequent regret, Hutton bottles out of telling Bedser directly.

Bedser was under the firm impression that his place was secure and is unhappy about the way in which he found out otherwise.

Australia leave out Burke. At breakfast Miller tells Sir Donald Bradman that he is worried about bowling as his knee is still painful. Bradman tells him to have a go and stop if it hurts.

'MCG' is a monumental stadium, the biggest in Australia at Yarra Park Yolimont, South Melbourne. In the 1950s it could accommodate nearly 90,000 but now it can only take about 65,000 because of demolition work in preparation for the 1956 Olympics. After dissatisfaction with the pitch for the MCC match, the Club has brought in a new curator, Jack House of the Albert Cricket Ground.

Umpires: C. Hoy and M.J.McInnes

England First Innings

Odd overs] →) from Pavilion End
Even overs] ←) from Southern Stand End

Apart from his hepatitis, still a secret, Lindwall has a leg strain.
Hutton wins the toss and gratefully bats.

			Hutton	Edrich		40,000 at start in sweltering sunshine
1	12.00	Lindwall 1] →)	(4 byes) - - 3			Inswinger down leg side. Hutton loses his footing
				4 -		Hutton cover-drive for 3
				- -		Edrich glance to long leg for 4
					- 11	
2		Miller 1] ←)	- - - (1 bye) -	-		Crowd cheer Miller
				- -		*Miller gets some lift in this over and wraps Edrich on upper arm*
					- 12	
3		Lindwall 2] →)	- - - - 2 -			Miller tells the captain that his knee feels alright for full-pace bowling
					- 14	

MCC in Australia 1954-55 – THIRD TEST

4	12.17 12.19	Miller 2] ←)		- - W May - - - -	1-14 - 14	Edrich c Lindwall, leg-glance ct in midriff at leg slip, 4 in 17 mins, 11 balls, 1 four May nearly bowled
5	 12.26	Lindwall 3] →)	4 3	- - - - - W Cowdrey	 2 - 21	Hutton turns to leg for 3 May c Benaud, gully, lifter off bat handle, 0 in 7 mins, 6 balls
6	12.28	Miller 3] ←)		- - - - - -	 - 21	*May, on his birthday, has walked back head down and missed the pavilion gate by ten yards*
7		Lindwall 4] →)		- 4 4 - - -	 - 29	Cowdrey edged past 3rd slip Cowdrey glances to fine leg for 4
8	12.37 12.39	Miller 4] ←)		W Compton - - 3 - 2 - -	3- 29 - 34	Hutton c Hole low at 1st slip, late out-swinger, 12 in 37 mins, 32 balls, 1 four Compton 3 past extra cover. First runs off Miller Cowdrey 2 past gully
9		Lindwall 5] →)	1	- - - (4 byes) - 2 -	 - 41	4 byes somewhere between overs 8.2 and 10.4
10	 12.50 12.52	Miller 5] ←)		- - - - W Bailey - -	 4- 41 - 41	Compton c Harvey, off right thumb to 2nd gully, 4 in 11 mins, 9 balls, 0 fours. Compton winces in pain
11		Lindwall 6] →) Off spell 6-0-34-1		- - - 3 4 - -	 - 48	Bailey turns off his legs for 4

MCC in Australia 1954-55 – THIRD TEST

12		Miller 6] ←)		- - - - - -	- 48	
13		Archer 1] →)	- - - - - -		- 48	
14		Miller 7] ←)		- - - - - -	- 48	
15		Archer 2] →)	- - - - - -		- 48	
16		Miller 8] ←)		- - - - - -	- 48	*Five successive maidens*
17		Archer 3] →) Off spell 3-2-6-0	1 3 - 2 - -		- 54	Bailey steals single to mid-off. Archers throw misses stumps with Bailey yards short Cowdrey 3 through short legs. 52 up in 75 mins
18		Miller 9] ←) Off spell 9-8-5-3		- - - - - -	- 54	
19		Benaud 1] →) Off spell 1-0-5-0	- - 1	- - 4 -	- 59	
	1.30	LUNCH	Bailey 8 38 mins 31 balls	Cowdry 22 62 mins 63 balls	4- 59 90 mins 152 balls	

Compton visits hospital for an X-ray. His thumb was bruised by the ball that dismissed him.
Arlott: the pitch is true and hard. Miller has risen magnificently to the occasion.
Swanton: Miller bowled devastatingly on a traditionally lively Melbourne wicket.

MCC in Australia 1954-55 – THIRD TEST

				Bailey 8	Cowdry 22	4- 59	
20	2.10	Archer 4] ←)		- - - - - -		- 59	
21		Lindwall 7] →)			- 1 -	- 60	
22		Archer 5] ←)		- - - - -	1	- 61	*The wicket has now settled down.*
23		Lindwall 8] →)			- 4 - 4 - -	- 69	Cowdrey off-drive for 4 Cowdrey pushes off legs to fine leg, all-run 4
24		Archer 6] ←)		- - 1 - - -	1	- 71	
25		Lindwall 9] →) Off spell 3-0-12-0		2	- - 1 - - -	- 74	
26		Archer 7] ←)			- - - - 4 1 -	- 79	Cowdrey cuts square for 4
27		Benaud 2] →)		- - - -	- - - 3	- 82	
28		Archer 8] ←) Off spell 6-1-11-0		- - - - -	3	- 85	

MCC in Australia 1954-55 – THIRD TEST

29		Benaud 3] →)		4 - - 1 4 - - -	- 94	Cowdrey chops past slip for 4 Cowdrey 50 in 95 balls Bailey sweeps for 4, stand 53
30		JohnsTon 1] ←)		2 - - - - - -	- 96	
31		Benaud 4] →)	- - - 2 - - 1		- 99	
32		JohnsTon 2] ←)	- - - - - - -		- 99	*JohnsTon has five fielders in front of square on off-side*
33		Benaud 5] →)	- - - - - - 4		- 103	Cowdrey drives for 4 past mid-on
34		JohnsTon 3] ←)	- 2 3 - - - -		- 108	Bailey late cut Bailey late cut
35		Benaud 6] →)	- - - - - 2 -		- 110	Bailey late cut
36		JohnsTon 4] ←)	- - - - - - -		- 110	
37		Benaud 7] →) Off spell 6-0-25-0	- - - 4 - - -		- 114	

MCC in Australia 1954-55 – THIRD TEST

#	Time	Bowler	Fielder	Runs	Score	Notes
38		JohnsTon 5] ←)		- - - - - - -	- 114	
39		JohnSon 1] →)		- - 1 - - - -	- 115	
40	3.30 3.32	JohnsTon 6] ←)	W Evans	- - - - -	5- 115	Bailey c Maddocks, wk, hooking long-hop, edged onto pad, 30 in 118 mins, 118 balls, 3 fours
41		JohnSon 2] →)		- - - - - - -	- 115	
42		JohnsTon 7] ←)		- - - - - - 1	- 116	
43		JohnSon 3] →)		- - - - - - -	- 116	
44		JohnsTon 8] ←)		- - - - - - -	- 116	
45		JohnSon 4] →)		- 1 - - 4 - -	- 121	Cowdrey moves off 56 after 40 mins, lofting over Archer at mid on, almost caught, through outstretched finger tips
46		JohnsTon 9] ←)		- - - - - - -	- 121	

MCC in Australia 1954-55 – THIRD TEST

Over	Time	Bowler	Evans	Cowdrey	Score	Notes
47		JohnSon 5] →) Off spell 5-2-10-0		- - - 4 - - - -	 - 125	Cowdrey drive for 4 to mid wkt
48	 4.00	JohnsTon 10] ←) Spell 10-6-13-1	- 1	- 4 - - - -	 - 130	Cowdrey pulls 4 to long leg
		TEA	Evans 3 28 mins 35 balls	Cowdry 68 172 mins 173 balls	5- 130 200 mins 384 balls	

SESSION 71-1 IN 110 MINS, 232 BALLS

Over	Time	Bowler	Evans	Cowdrey	Score	Notes
			Evans 3	Cowdry 68	5- 130	
49	4.20	Lindwall 10] →)	1 -	- - - - 1	 - 132	
50		JohnsTon 11] ←)		- - 4 - - - 4 1	 - 141	Cowdrey 4 past extra cover Cowdrey turns to leg for 4
51		Lindwall 11] →)	 1 - - 1 -	- -	 - 143	
52		JohnsTon 12] ←) Off spell 2-0-13-0	- - - - 3 - 1		 - 147	
53		Lindwall 12] →)	- - 1 - 3	- - - 4	 - 155	Cowdrey hit on heart by bouncer Cowdrey drives to off for 4
54		Miller 10] ←)	- - - - - 4 -		 - 159	Evans strikes over mid on or 4. Miller shakes his hand

MCC in Australia 1954-55 – THIRD TEST

55		Lindwall 13] →) Off spell 4-0-13-0		- - - 1 - - -	- 160	
56		Miller 11] ←) Off spell 2-0-9-0	4	- - - - - 1	- 165	
57		JohnSon 6] →)		- - - - 2 -	- 167	
58	5.04 5.06	Archer 9] ←)	1 W Wardle	- - 1 - - -	6- 169 - 169	Evans lbw, no real stroke, 20 in 72 mins, 63 balls, 2 fours
59		JohnSon 7] →)		- - - - - 3	- 172	Cowdrey late cut for 3
60		Archer 10] ←)		- - - 4 3 - -	- 179	Cowdrey straight drive for 4 Cowdrey 3 wide of mid on for his 100 off 236 balls
61		JohnSon 8] →)		- - - - - - 2	- 181	
62	5..21 5.23	Archer 11] ←)	- - W Tyson -	- - - - -	7- 181 - 181	Wardle bld, too far across, behind legs, 0 in 15 mins, 9 balls
63	5.27 5.29	JohnSon 9] →)	W Statham	- - - - - -	8- 181 - 181	Cowdrey bld, too far across, no stroke to big off-break, behind legs, 102 in 239 mins, 247 balls, 15 fours

MCC in Australia 1954-55 – THIRD TEST

64		Archer 12] ←)	- - - - - 3	-	- 184	
65		JohnSon 10] →) Off spell 6-1-10-1	- - - - - 1	-	- 185	
66		Archer 13] ←)	- 1 - - - -	-	- 186	
67		JohnSon 11] →)	- - - 1 - -	1	- 188	*Australia will not have to bat tonight.*
68	5.52 5.55	Archer 14] ←) Spell 5.6-1-16-4		- 2 W Appleyard - 1 W	9- 190 10- 191	Statham bld, 3 in 23 mins, 17 balls Tyson bld, 6 in 32 mins, 28 balls, 0 fours
				Applyd 1 2 mins 2 balls	10- 191 295 mins 542 balls	Attendance 63,814

SESSION 61-5 IN 95 MINS, 158 BALLS

Compton suffered an injury to his right thumb when he was out, but it is not fractured and he will probably bat again.

Arlott: 191 is a poor score but it gives Tyson something to bowl at. Miller's high action was well suited to the hard wicket.

Swanton: Cowdrey's greatest strength is his utter calmness of nerve. Apart from Maddocks' nervous start, the fielding was immaculate, especially Favell's throwing.

England First innings

* L. Hutton	c Hole b Miller	12	37 mins, 32 balls, 1 four	3-29
W.J. Edrich	c Lindwall b Miller	4	17 mins, 11 balls, 1 four	1-14
P.B.H. May	c Benaud b Lindwall	0	7 mins, 6 balls	2-21
M.C. Cowdrey	b Johnson	102	239 mins, 247 balls, 15 fours	8-181
D.C.S. Compton	c Harvey b Miller	4	11 mins, 9 balls, 0 fours	4-41
T.E. Bailey	c Maddocks b Johnston	30	118 mins, 118 balls, 3 fours	5-115
+ T.G. Evans	lbw b Archer	20	72 mins, 63 balls, 2 fours	6-169
J.H. Wardle	b Archer	0	15 mins, 9 balls	7-181
F.H. Tyson	b Archer	6	32 mins, 28 balls, 0 fours	10-191
J.B. Statham	b Archer	3	23 mins, 17 balls	9-190
R. Appleyard	not out	1	2 mins, 2 balls	
Extras	(b 9)	9		
TOTAL	(10 wkts – all out)	191	295 mins, 67.6 overs, 542 balls	

BOWLING

Lindwall	13	0	59	1
Miller	11	8	14	3
Archer	13.6	4	33	4
Benaud	7	0	30	0
Johnston	12	6	26	1
Johnson	11	3	20	1

MCC in Australia 1954-55 – THIRD TEST

SECOND DAY – Slow grind
Australia First Innings

Odd overs] →) from Pavilion End
Even overs] ←) from Southern Stand End

Looking at the rock-hard wicket this morning, Hutton and the groundsman agree that it is so hard it will hardly last two more days.
Wilson substitutes for Compton.

			Favell	Morris		
1	12.00	Tyson 1] →)	- - - - - - 3		- 3	*Lbw appeal* Favell 3 through Bailey's legs at gully
2		Statham 1] ←)	4 1 - 3 - 1 -		- 12	Favell top-edge past 2nd slip. 3rd slip added Favell hit on hand Morris hooks to long leg
3	 12.17	Tyson 2] →)	3 - - - - - W Miller		1- 15	 Morris lbw, playing back to half volley, 3 in 17 mins, 10 balls
4	12.19	Statham 2] ←) Off spell 2-0-16-0	4 - (2 b) - - 1 - 2 -		- 24	Favell drives straight for 4 2 byes somewhere in over 4 or 5
5		Tyson 3] →) Off spell 3-0-14-1	- 4 - (1 nb) - - - 4		- 33	Favell square cuts for 4
6		Bailey 1] ←)		- 4 1 - - - -	- 38	Miller glorious 4 through square cover
7	12.40 12.42	Statham 3] →)		W Harvey - - 4 - 1	2- 38 - 43	Miller, c Evans (wk) push outside off, dive in front of 1st slip to scoop it up, 7 in 21 mins, 7 balls, 1 four Harvey thumps 4 past cover

MCC in Australia 1954-55 – THIRD TEST

Over	Time	Bowler	Batsman 1	Batsman 2	Total	Notes
8		Bailey 2] ←)		- .. - - - - -	- 43	
9	12.53 12.55	Statham 4] →)	- W Hole - - 1 4	3- 43 - 48	Favell lbw, playing back to creeper, 25 in 53 mins, 35 balls, 4 fours Harvey cuts past 3rd man for 4
10		Bailey 3] ←)	1 - - 1 - -	- 50	
11		Statham 5] →) Off spell 3-0-16-2	- - - - - - 4	- 54	
12		Bailey 4] ←) Off spell 4-1-9-0	- 1 - 1 - -	- 56	
13	1.15	Tyson 4] →)	- - 1 1 - - -	- 58	
14		Appleyard 1] ←) Off spell 1-0-7-0	- 4 - 2 1 - -	- 65	Hole cuts wide of slip for 4 Hole cuts for 2
15	1.27 1.29 1.32	Tyson 5] →)	- - - - W Benaud - -	4- 65 - 65	Hole bld, yorked off stump by full toss, 11 in 32 mins, 24 balls, 1 four
		LUNCH	Benaud 0 3 mins 3 balls	Harvey 16 50 mins 42 balls	4- 65 92 mins 121 balls	Only 15 overs bowled in 92 minutes

Arlott: English bowlers trudged slowly back in the heat, and could not get the lift that Miller did. Statham with 2 for 14 in his second spell, looked the best bowler. The best fielding came from substitute Wilson.

MCC in Australia 1954-55 – THIRD TEST

				Benaud 0	Harvey 16	4- 65	
16	2.10	Statham 6] ←)			- - - 1 - - -	- 66	
17		Tyson 6] →)			- - - - (1 lb) - - 1 3	- 71	
18		Statham 7] ←) Off spell 2-0-3-0		1 - - - - - - 1	- 73	*Benaud is barracked by the crowd for his studied defence, but he is having to cope with very variable bounce from Tyson and Statham*
19		Tyson 7] →)			- - - 1 1 - 2	- 77	
20		Bailey 5] ←)			1 - - 3 - - -	- 81	
21		Tyson 8] →) Off spell (incl. lunch) 5-1-15-1		- - - (1 nb) - 1	- - 4	- 87	Benaud 'caught' by Hutton at short leg Harvey drive for 4
22		Bailey 6] ←) Off spell 2-0-8-0		1	1 - - 2 1 - -	- 91	
23		Statham 8] →)			1 - - - - - -	- 92	Drinks interval
24	3.00 3.02	Appleyard 2] ←)			- - W Archer 4 - - 1	5- 92 - 97	*Appleyard bowls over the wicket* Harvey bld, beaten in air and by spin, 31 in 100 mins, 71 balls, 4 fours Archer edges btwn wk and slip for 4

MCC in Australia 1954-55 – THIRD TEST

#	Time	Bowler		Batsman	Score	Notes
25		Statham 9] →)		2 2 2 1 - - - -	- 104	Archer 2 edged through slips. 101 up
26		Appleyard 3] ←)		- - - (1 lb) - 3 - - -	- 108	*Archer misses and edges several times*
27		Statham 10] →)		- - - 1 - - -	- 109	*Statham slips in delivery and turns full cartwheel. Hutton inspects his boots and borrows a penknife from Ump. McInnes to scrape away soil.*
28	3.25 3.27	Appleyard 4] ←)		1 4 1 W Maddocks (4 b) - 2 - -	6- 115 - 121	Archer drives straight first bounce for 4. Hutton takes man out of leg trap. Benaud c sub (Wilson), dollies off-break straight to bkwd sht leg, 15 in 78 mins, 54 balls, 0 fours. After a warm welcome Maddocks is beaten first ball. *Archer should have been run out by Wardle from mid on*
29		Statham 11] →) Off spell 4-0-10-0		- - 1 - - - -	- 122	
30		Appleyard 5] ←)		- - - - - - -	- 122	
31		Tyson 9] →)		- - - 1 1 - (1 b) -	- 125	
32		Appleyard 6] ←)		- - - (1 lb) - - 1 - -	- 127	
33		Tyson 10] →)		1 - - - - - -	- 128	

MCC in Australia 1954-55 – THIRD TEST

34		Appleyard 7] ←) Off spell 6-2-17-2		- - - - - - -	- 128	
35	 4.00	Tyson 11] →) Off spell 3-0-7-0	- - 2 2 - -		- 132	
		TEA	Madoks 7 33 mins 36 balls	Archer 21 58 mins 45 balls	6- 132 202 mins 282 balls	

SESSION 67-2 IN 110 MINS, 161 BALLS

Appleyard's ball to bowl Harvey was a beauty: bowling over the wicket, he beat his forward defensive in the air, pitched leg and hit the top of off stump.

Arlott: Harvey and Benaud were tied down despite aggressive intentions. Hutton has not enough runs to play with to risk spin at both ends.

Swanton: Benaud is full of talent and an excellent fielder but he still cannot score the runs

	4.20		Madoks 7	Archer 21	6- 132	
36		Wardle 1] ←)		- - 1 - - -	- 133	Wardle bowls over the wicket.
37		Tyson 12] →)		- 1 - - - -	- 134	
38	4.32 4.34	Wardle 2] ←)	 1	- W Lindwall 1 - 4 - -	7- 134 - 140	*Wardle bowling round the wicket* Archer bld by quick shooter, 23 in 70 mins, 53 balls, 2 fours Lindwall all run 4 cover drive. Tyson hurts back in chasing it.
39		Tyson 13] →) Off spell 2-1-1-0	- - - - - - -		- 140	
40		Wardle 3] ←) Off spell 0-14-1		- 2 - 2 3 - -	- 147	

MCC in Australia 1954-55 – THIRD TEST

41		Statham 12] →)	2 1	- 1 - - W JohnSon -	8- 151 - 151	Lindwall bld, near yorker, 13 in 20 mins, 15 balls, 1 four
	4.54 4.56					
42		Tyson 14] ←)	4 - - - - 3	- -	- 158	
43		Statham 13] →)	- - - 1	 - - -	- 159	Hutton, not anxious to bat this evening, slows game up. England ground fielding poor in last hour
44		Tyson 15] ←) Off spell 2-0-11-0	1 2 -	- - -]	- 163	
45		Statham 14] →) Off spell 3-0-6-1	 - -	- - 1 - -	- 164	
46		Wardle 4] ←)	 1	- - - - - 1	- 166	
47		Appleyard 8] →)	- -	- - - - - -	- 166	
48		Wardle 5] ←)	 2	- - - - - 1	- 169	
49		Appleyard 9] →) Off spell 2-1-11-0	 2 4 - 3	- 1 1	- 180	Cheers for Maddocks who becomes top-scorer of the day

103

50	Wardle 6] ←) Off spell 3-0-6-0	- - - - - -	1	- 181	
51	Tyson 16] →)	- 1 - - - -		- 182	
52	Bailey 7] ←)	- - - - 1 - -		- 183	
53	Tyson 17] →) Off spell 2-0-3-0	- - - - - - 2		- 185	
54	Bailey 8] ←) Spell 2-0-4-0	- - - - 1 1 -	1	- 188	
6.00	CLOSE	Madoks 36 133 mins 114 balls	JonSn 12 64 mins 51 balls	8- 188 302 mins 434 balls	Attendance: 65,515

SESSION 56-2 IN 100 MINS, 152 BALLS

Only 54 overs bowled in 5 hours. The crowd were very impatient with England's slowness. One explanation given is that Hutton could not give instructions to his players over the noise of the crowd

Arlott: the last 65 minutes were England's worst performance of the day. Tyson and Statham both attacked the stumps but both lost their sparkle. But England still have the psychological advantage and if Australia do not squeeze a substantial lead, the advantage should be with England.

Swanton: No catches were dropped but slowness in the field must have lost England about 30 runs. The over-rate was far too slow and one sympathised with the crowd's annoyance at the interminable conferences and slow change-overs.

Moyes: Putting bowlers in the deep field does not help the over-rate.

Ross: Appleyard should have been kept going after tea.

Hughes: The players say that the cracks on the pitch are half an inch thick, and most people think the game will be over on Monday

THIRD DAY – Rising damp

Monday 3 January

Unbearable heatwave on Sunday. Dust from the desert makes the sky look cloudy. The wicket, which was pale yellow before, is now darker grey, with black on the old creases: as if it has been watered. All the players of both sides look at it closely. Their spikes sink into the turf. Hutton says: "Let's win the game first and complain if we have to afterwards". Pitch appears moist when play starts despite having been left uncovered during Sunday's 105°F. Last night it was 94°. A 50 mile-an-hour northerly breeze wafted the heat of the desert into the city. People slept on the beaches.

			Madoks 36	JonSn 12	8- 188	Crowd 60,000. Not so hot.

MCC in Australia 1954-55 – THIRD TEST

Over	Time	Bowler	Batsman 1	Batsman 2	Score	Notes
55	12.00	Tyson 18] →)	2 - 1 - 1	1	- - 193	Maddocks 2 to long leg quick single on leg side – scores even
56		Appleyard 10] ←) Off spell 2-0-3-0	1 - - - - 1	-	- 195	
57		Tyson 19] →)	- - - 1 - 1	1	- 198	
58		Appleyard 11] ←)	1 - - - - -		- 199	
59		Tyson 20] →)	1 - - 2 - 3	- -	- 205	
60	 12.29 12.31	Statham 15] ←)	- - - W JohnsTon 1	 - 2	9- 205 - 208	Maddocks c Evans wk, 47 in 162 mins, 140 balls, 2 fours
61		Tyson 21] →) Off spell 4-0-17-0	- 2 - 1 - -	-	- 211	
62		Statham 16] ←)	4 - 3	 1 - - -	- 219	JohnsTon 4 skied over cover Misfield by Wardle at 3rd man *JohnsTon takes wild swings and Statham pretends to follow the path of the ball into the crowd*
63		Bailey 9] →) Spell 1-0-12-0		4 - 4 4 - - -	- 231	*JohnsTon three drives for 4* Bailey moves to leg-side field. Crowd slow handclap

MCC in Australia 1954-55 – THIRD TEST

64	12.53	Statham 17] ←) Spell 2.3-0-11-2	- - W		10 - 231	JohnsTon bld off-stump, 11 in 22 mins, 15 balls, 1 four
		LUNCH		JonSn 33 117 mins 85 balls 3 fours	10- 231 355 mins 509 balls	

SESSION 43-2 IN 53 MINS, 75 BALLS

Arlott: The batsmen took advantage of leisurely outfielding.

Swanton: Crowds greeted JohnsTon as a kind of licensed humorist.

Peebles: Statham bowled with impeccable technique, apart from the fact that three times he slipped and fell in his delivery stride, with no injury. Perhaps his boot studs need repair.

Miller and Whitington: Tyson is below his Sydney pace.

Australia First innings

L.E. Favell	lbw b Statham	25	53 mins, 35 balls, 4 fours	3-43
A.R. Morris	lbw b Tyson	3	17 mins, 10 balls	1-15
K.R. Miller	c Evans b Statham	7	21 mins, 7 balls, 1 four	2-38
R.N. Harvey	b Appleyard	31	100 mins, 71 balls, 4 fours	5-92
G.B. Hole	b Tyson	11	32 mins, 24 balls, 1 four	4-65
R. Benaud	c sub (Wilson) b Appleyard	15	78 mins, 54 balls, 0 fours	6-115
R.G. Archer	b Wardle	23	70 mins, 53 balls, 2 fours	7-134
+ L.V. Maddocks	c Evans b Statham	47	162 mins, 140 balls, 2 fours	9-205
R.R. Lindwall	b Statham	13	20 mins, 15 balls, 1 four	8-151
* I.W. Johnson	not out	33	117 mins, 85 balls, 3 fours	
W.A. Johnston	b Statham	11	22 mins, 15 balls, 1 four	10-231
Extras	(b 7, lb 3, nb 2)	12		
TOTAL	(10 wkts – all out)	231	355 mins, 63.3 overs, 509 balls	

BOWLING

Tyson	21	2	68	2
Statham	16.3	0	60	5
Bailey	9	1	33	0
Appleyard	11	3	38	2
Wardle	6	0	20	1

England Second Innings

Odd overs] →) from Pavilion End
Even overs] ←) from Southern Stand End

			Hutton	Edrich		
1	1.06	Lindwall 1] →)	- - 1 (1 wide) . -	1 - 3		
2		Miller 1] ←)		- - - - - - -3		Edrich beaten twice in this over
3		Lindwall 2] →)	- 1 - - - -	- - - - - 4		
4		Miller 2] ←)	- - - 1 - -	- 5		

MCC in Australia 1954-55 – THIRD TEST

			Hutton	Edrich		
5		Lindwall 3] →)	- - 1 -	 - - - - -	 - 6	
	1.30	LUNCH	Hutton 4 24 mins 17 balls	Edrich 1 24 mins 23 balls	0- 6 24 mins 41 balls *	* incl. one wide

Session (both sides) 49-2 in 77 mins, 116 balls

			Hutton 4	Edrich 1	0- 6	
6	2.10	Miller 3] ←) Off spell (incl. lunch) 3-1-7-0	- - 1 - 2 -	 - 3 	 - 12	
7		Lindwall 4] →) Off spell 4-0-5-0	 - - - 1 - -	- - (1 lb) - - - -	 - 14	
8		Archer 1] ←)	4 - - - - 1	 -	 - 19	
9		JohnsTon 1] →)	- - - - 1	 2 -	 - 22	*JohnsTon bowling spin*
10		Archer 2] ←)	- - - 1 - - -	 4 - -	 - 27	
11		JohnsTon 2] →)	- - - - 4 - -	 -	 - 31	
12		Archer 3] ←)	 	- - - 2 - - (1 lb) -	 - 34	

MCC in Australia 1954-55 – THIRD TEST

13		JohnsTon 3] →)	- - 1 - - 1 -	- 36	
14		Archer 4] ←)	- 2 - 1 - - -	- 39	
15	2.51 2.53	JohnsTon 4] →)	- - - - 1 W May -	1- 40 - 40	Edrich bld, playing forward, beaten by leg break, 13 in 65 mins, 52 balls, 1 four
16		Archer 5] ←)	- - - - - -	- 40	
17		JohnsTon 5] →)	- - - - 1 -	- 41	
18		Archer 6] ←)	- - - 3 - 4 -	- 48	May 3 racing past Harvey in covers Hutton 4 edged between wk and slip
19		JohnsTon 6] →)	3 - - - - - -	- 51	
20		Archer 7] ←) Off spell 7-1-23-0	- - - - - 1 -	- 52	
21		JohnsTon 7] →) Off spell 7-0-18-1	2 - - 2 - - -	- 56	

MCC in Australia 1954-55 – THIRD TEST

22		Miller 4] ←)	2 - 1 - - 1 - -		- 60	
23		JohnSon 1] →)		- - - - - - 1	- 61	
24		Miller 5] ←)	1 - - - - 1		- 63	
25		JohnSon 2] →)	- - 1	- - - 4 -	- 68	May straight drive for 4
26		Miller 6] ←)	1	4 - - - - 1	- 74	May straight drives for 4. Miller applauds.
27		JohnSon 3] →)	1 - - - - -		- 75	
28		Miller 7] ←)		- - - - (1 lb) - - 1	- 77	
29		JohnSon 4] →)	- - - - - - -		- 77	
30		Miller 8] ←)		- - - - - -	- 77	

MCC in Australia 1954-55 – THIRD TEST

Over	Time	Bowler	Batsman 1	Batsman 2	Score	Notes
31		JohnSon 5] →) Off spell 5-2-7-1	- - - - - - -		- 77	*Hutton is barracked and holds out his bat towards the crowd*
32		Miller 9] ←) Off spell 6-1-20-0	1 - 2 1 - - 2	1	- 84	Cheers for run by Hutton. He doffs his cap.
33	4.00	Benaud 1] →) Off spell 1-0-4-0	- - - 3 1 - -		- 88	
		TEA	Hutton 39 134 mins 135 balls	May 32 67 mins 77 balls	1- 88 134 mins 265 balls *	* incl. one wide

SESSION 82-1 IN 110 MINS, 223 BALLS
Arlott: England are painstaking yet precarious. Hutton has batted wearily and the crowd resent it.
A story appears in Sydney that the Melbourne pitch has been watered at the weekend.

Over	Time	Bowler	Hutton 39	May 32	1- 88	Notes
34	4.20	Archer 8] ←)	1 - - 1 - - -	- 1 - - - -	- 91	
35		Lindwall 5] →)	- 1 - 4 - - -		- 96	
36	4.32 4.34	Archer 9] ←)	- W Cowdrey - - - -		2- 96 - 96	Hutton lbw, break-back ball kept low, 42 in 146 mins, 141 balls, 3 fours Cowdrey pads up. Big appeal from crowd.
37		Lindwall 6] →)		4 - - - - 1 1	- 102	May off drive for 4 *Lindwall gives a courteous warning to Cowdrey for backing up out of crease too soon*
38		Archer 10] ←)	- 1 - - 1 -		- 104	

MCC in Australia 1954-55 – THIRD TEST

Over	Time	Bowler	Batsman L	Batsman R	Score	Notes
39		Lindwall 7] →)		- - - - - -	- 104	
40		Archer 11] ←)	- - - 2 - -		- 106	
41		Lindwall 8] →) Off spell 4-1-17-0		2 - 2 2 - - -	- 112	
42		Archer 12] ←)	- - - - - -		- 112	
43		Benaud 2] →)		- - 4 1 - -	- 117	May moves out and hits through mid on, 53 off 120 balls
44		Archer 13] ←) Off spell 6-2-14-1	- - - 4 3 - -		- 124	
45		Benaud 3] →)		1 - - - - - 1	- 126	
46		JohnsTon 8] ←)	2 - - - - - -		- 128	*Unexplained change of ends*
47	5.25 5.27	Benaud 4] →)		- - - - - W Compton -	3- 128 - 128	Cowdrey bld, back-stroke, rolls slowly on to stumps as May shouts to him, 7 in 51 mins, 55 balls, 0 fours.

MCC in Australia 1954-55 – THIRD TEST

Over	Time	Bowler	Batsman 1	Batsman 2	Score	Notes
48		JohnsTon 9] ←)	- 2 - - -	- 3	- 133	*Compton has bruised thumb*
49		Benaud 5] →)	- 1 -	4 - - 1 - -	- 139	
50		JohnsTon 10] ←) Off spell 3-0-11-0	- 1	- 3 - - -	- 143	
51		Benaud 6] →)		1 - - - - -	- 144	
52		Lindwall 9] ←)	1	- - 1 - - -	- 146	
53		Benaud 7] →)	- - - - - -		- 146	
54		Lindwall 10] ←)	- - - - - -	1	- 147	
55		Benaud 8] →) Off spell 7-2-21-1	4 -	- - - - 3	- 154	Compton 4 to long leg
56	6.00	Lindwall 11] ←) Spell 3-0-8-0	1 -	- 3 1 -	- 159	
		CLOSE	Comptn 10 33 mins 49 balls	May 83 167 mins 151 balls	3- 159 234 mins 449 balls *	Attendance: 63,040 * incl. one wide

MCC in Australia 1954-55 – THIRD TEST

SESSION 71-2 IN 100 MINS, 184 BALLS
England lead by 119.

Arlott: an unspectacular, indecisive and graceless day. Compton was spiritless. Only a few drives by May lightened the mood.

Swanton: the widening cracks appearing on the pitch on Saturday seem to have been replaced by binding moisture. This suggests that there may have been some thundery rain on Sunday.

Newspapers allege that the pitch has been watered during the weekend. Percy Beames will say so in tomorrow's Melbourne *Age*. [It is rumoured that he actually saw a hose being used when he happened to call in on Sunday evening, but according to Richie Benaud, Beames was told by a 'phone call from the curator whom Jack Howse replaced, Bill Vanthoff, that the ground was watered.] Jack Howse tells the Press that it was not watered. The cover was taken off from 7am to 6.15pm on Sunday but the wicket was never left unattended; that Sunday night was very humid and caused seating under the covers so that the turf was quite damp when the covers were removed at 7am on Monday. The official denial is treated with scepticism. The obvious explanation is that the new groundsman saw to his horror that he had produced a wicket that would last hardly three days and did what was necessary to avoid that, regardless of which side would be advantaged.

Cardus: If there is any truth in the rumour, then the match should at once declared void.

FOURTH DAY – May England win?

Tuesday 4 January

The groundsman denies that pitch has been illegally watered or that it was ever unattended when left open during Sunday. After an inquiry the Melbourne CC and Victoria CA issue a joint statement denying that any part of the wicket has been watered since Friday. MCC players were not consulted during the enquiry. An expert from Melbourne University says that a tarpaulin cover on a very hot day can draw up moisture from the soil.

Whitington claims without equivocation that the pitch was watered on Sunday well before dusk, openly, but unknown to Club or State officials.

But for the appearance of moisture, however it came, the match would have been over in four days, and probably not to England's advantage. For that reason the matter is closed.

Compton is wearing a shield on his right thumb and a shield on the back of his left hand.

			Comptn 10	May 83	3- 159	
57	12.00	JohnsTon 11] →)		- - - 1 - -	- 160	*Compton has sore thumb*
58		Lindwall 12] ←)		- - - - - -	- 160	
59		JohnsTon 12] →)	- - - - 1	-	- 161	*Both batsmen out of touch.*
60		Lindwall 13] ←) Off spell 2-1-7-0	- 1	- 4 2 - -	- 168	May 4 past mid on
61		JohnsTon 13] →)	- - - 2 - -		- 170	

MCC in Australia 1954-55 – THIRD TEST

Over	Time	Bowler	Batsman 1	Batsman 2	Wicket	Score	Notes
62		Miller 10] ←)		- 1 - - - -		- 171	
63		JohnsTon 14] →)		- - - - - -		- 171	
64		Miller 11] ←) Off spell 2-0-3-0	2 - - - - -			- 173	Today May 8 in 32 mins
65	12.32 12.34	JohnsTon 15] →)		- W Bailey - 4 - -	4- 173	- 177	May beaten. Stumping attempted. May bld pushing tentatively, ball flicks pad, 91 in 199 mins, 183 balls, 8 fours. Bailey leg glances 4
66		Archer 14] ←)	- - - 1 - -	1		- 179	
67		JohnsTon 16] →)		- - - - - -		- 179	
68		Archer 15] ←)	1 - - - - -			- 180	
69		JohnsTon 17] →)		- - - - 4 1		- 185	Compton square drive for 4
70	12.56 12.58	Archer 16] ←)		- W Evans - 2 1 - -	5- 185 - 188		Compton c Maddocks, wk, off leg glance, 23 in 89 mins, 101 balls, 2 fours *Evans dropped by Lindwall at short leg*

MCC in Australia 1954-55 – THIRD TEST

Over	Time	Bowler	Batsman 1	Batsman 2	Score	Notes
71		JohnsTon 18] →)	- - 2 - 1 - -		- 191	
72		Archer 17] ←) Off spell 4-0-7-1	- - - - 1 -		- 192	
73		JohnsTon 19] →) Off spell 9-2-24-1	4 - - 4 - -		- 200	Evans sweeps to leg for 4 Evans steers past gully for 4
74		Miller 12] ←)		- - - - - -	- 200	
75	1.15	Lindwall 14] →)	1 - - - 1 2 -		- 204	New ball
76		Miller 13] ←)		- - - - - - -	- 204	
77	1.30	Lindwall 15] →)	- 3 - - - 1 -	1	- 209	
		LUNCH	Evans 22 32 mins 31 balls	Bailey 7 56 mins 53 balls	5- 209 324 mins 617 balls*	* incl. one wide

SESSION 50-2 IN 90 MINS, 168 BALLS

Arlott: It was not a good idea to take the new ball as the ball is coming slowly off the pitch. The game is poised. England lead by 119. Much depends on Bailey.

Hughes: JohnSon should have persisted with JohnsTon rather than take the new ball immediately.

Over	Time	Bowler	Evans 22	Bailey 7	5- 209	
78	2.10	Miller 14] ←)		- - - (1 bye) - - - -	- 210	

MCC in Australia 1954-55 – THIRD TEST

Over	Time	Bowler	Extras	Runs	Score	Comments
79		Lindwall 16] →)	- - (1 lb) - - - -		- 211	
80	2.19 2.21	Miller 15] ←)	- W Wardle 1 - - -		6- 211 - 212	Evans c Maddocks, wk, edges outswinger, 22 in 41 mins, 41 balls, 2 fours
81		Lindwall 17] →)	- - 2 (1 b/lb) - -	1	- 216	
82		Miller 16] ←)	3 - - - - -		- 219	
83		Lindwall 18] →) Off spell 5-1-15-0	- - - 2 - 1 -		- 222	Ran one short?
84		Miller 17] ←)	1 - - - - - -		- 223	
85		JohnsTon 20] →) Off spell 1-0-16-0	- - 4 4 4 - - 4		- 239	Wardle sweeps with the spin for 4 Wardle punches short ball thro covers 4 Wardle hits to mid wkt for 4 Wardle hits to leg for 4
86		Miller 18] ←) Off spell (incl. lunch) 7-4-5-1	- - - - - - -		- 239	*Crowd barrack Bailey*
87		JohnSon 6] →)	4 - 2 - 4 4 -		- 253	Wardle late cuts sweetly for 4 Wardle sweeps sweetly for 4 Wardle sweeps sweetly for 4

MCC in Australia 1954-55 – THIRD TEST

88		Archer 18] ←)		- 1 - - - 1 -	- 255	
89	3.02 3.04	JohnSon 7] →)		- - 2 - - W Tyson -	7- 257 - 257	Wardle bld, shorter flighted ball, violent sweep, 38 in 41 mins, 45 balls, 7 fours
90		Archer 19] ←)		- - - - 1 - -	- 258	
91		JohnSon 8] →) Off spell 3-0-18-1		2 - - - - - -	- 260	
92		Archer 20] ←)		- - - - - - -	- 260	
93		JohnsTon 21] →)		- - - 4 - - -	- 264	
94		Archer 21] ←)		- - - - - - -	- 264	
95	3.29	JohnsTon 22] →)		- - 1 - 4 - -	- 269	Tyson off mark with straight drive to screen
96		Archer 22] ←)		- - - - 1 2 -	- 272	

MCC in Australia 1954-55 – THIRD TEST

97		JohnsTon 23] →)		-		
	3.37		W Statham	- - 1	8- 273	Tyson c Harvey, skied to covers, knocks up and spins round, second attempt, 6 in 33 mins, 27 balls, 1 four
	3.39			- -	- 273	
98		Archer 23] ←)		- - - - - - -	- 273	
99	3.47	JohnsTon 24] →)	W Appleyard	- - - -	9- 273	Statham c Favell, deep extra cover, 0 in 8 mins, 6 balls
	3.49			2 -	- 275	Appleyard edges for 2
100		Archer 24] ←) Spell 7-4-6-0		- - - - - -	- 275	
101		JohnsTon 25] →)		- 4 -		Appleyard cuts edgily for 4
	3.57	Spell 4.5-0-16-3	W	-	10- 279	Appleyard bld, shooter, 6 in 8 mins, 10 balls, 1 four
				Bailey 24 163 mins 144 balls 2 fours	10-279 431 mins 806 balls*	* incl. one wide

SESSION 70-5 IN 107 MINS, 189 BALLS

Arlott: England are in with a chance. JohnsTon was Australia's best bowler. Wardle's batting was no comedy act, he kept the ball on the ground and found the gaps. It is easy to criticise Bailey for not hitting hard when the tail-enders were in but it is hard for him to change the mental attitude which has brought him such success.

Swanton: The latter part of Bailey's innings was not worthy of his reputation.

Moyes: Bailey should have tried to hit harder when the tail were in, but never minimise his nuisance value

Ross: Bailey limits himself to three strokes, forward defensive, and very occasionally a late cut and a swing to leg, but he is in form, unruffled and devoted to the team

England Second innings

* L. Hutton	lbw b Archer	42	146 mins, 141 balls, 3 fours	2-96
W.J. Edrich	b Johnston	13	65 mins, 52 balls, 1 four	1-40
P.B.H. May	b Johnston	91	199 mins, 183 balls, 8 fours.	4-173
M.C. Cowdrey	b Benaud	7	51 mins, 55 balls, 0 fours	3-128
D.C.S. Compton	c Maddocks b Archer	23	89 mins, 101 balls, 2 fours	5-185
T.E. Bailey	not out	24	163 mins, 144 balls, 2 fours	
+ T.G. Evans	c Maddocks b Miller	22	41 mins, 41 balls, 2 fours	6-211
J.H. Wardle	b Johnson	38	41 mins, 45 balls, 7 fours	7-257
F.H. Tyson	c Harvey b Johnston	6	33 mins, 27 balls, 1 four	8-273
J.B. Statham	c Favell b Johnston	0	8 mins, 6 balls	9-273
R. Appleyard	b Johnston	6	8 mins, 10 balls, 1 four	10-279
Extras	(b 2, lb 4, w 1)	7		
TOTAL	(10 wkts – all out)	279	431 mins, 100.5 overs, 806 balls (incl.1 wide)	

BOWLING

Lindwall	18	3	52	0
Miller	18	6	35	1
Archer	24	7	50	2
Johnston	24.5	2	85	5
Johnson	8	2	25	1
Benaud	8	2	25	1

MCC in Australia 1954-55 – THIRD TEST

Australia Second Innings

Odd overs] →) from Pavilion End
Even overs] ←) from Southern Stand End

Australia need 240 to win.

#	Time	Bowler		Favell	Morris		Notes
1	4.17	Tyson 1] →)		1 - - - -	1 - 2		
2		Statham 1] ←)		1 - - 2 - 1 -	 - 6		
3		Tyson 2] →)		- - - 2 - - -	 - 8		*Tyson bowling too short*
4		Statham 2] ←)		- - - 1 - 2 - 1	 - 12		Nine-ball over ?
5		Tyson 3] →)		- - - - - - 1	 - 13		
6		Bailey 1] ←)		- - 4 - 1 - - 1	 - 19		*Morris almost c & b, tricky left-handed catch*
7		Tyson 4] →)			- (4 lb) - - W Benaud - - (4 lb) - -	1- 23 - 27	4 leg-byes somewhere between overs 6.1 and 7.3 Morris c Cowdrey, ct in right hand, diving forward at silly mid on, 4 in 36 mins, 14 balls, 0 fours 4 leg byes between Evans and Edrich
	4.53	Off spell 4-1-5-1					
	4.55						
8		Bailey 2] ←)		- 2 - 1 - - - -	 - 30		

MCC in Australia 1954-55 – THIRD TEST

Over	Time	Bowler	Batsman 1	Batsman 2	Score	Notes
9		Statham 3] →)	- - - 1 3	4 1 -	- 39	
10		Bailey 3] ←) Off spell 3-0-14-0	- - 4 - 1	- -	- 44	
11		Statham 4] →)	- - 1	- - -	- 45	
12		Appleyard 1] ←)	1 4 - - - - 2		- 51	Benaud 4 to long on, one bounce
13		Statham 5] →) Off spell 5-0-19-0	- 1	- - - (4 lb) - - -	- 57	
14	5.33 5.35	Appleyard 2] ←)	W <u>Harvey</u> 2 4 - - - -		2- 57 - 63	Favell bld, hitting over late in-dipper, 30 in 76 mins, 61 balls, 2 fours Harvey 2 to square leg Harvey hooks 4 over leg slip
15		Tyson 5] →)		- - - 1 (1 lb) - 3 -	- 68	
16		Appleyard 3] ←)	4 - - - - - -		- 72	Benaud 4. First signalled as six, then policeman on sightscreen boundary told the deep fielder Cowdrey
17		Tyson 6] →) Off spell 2-0-6-0	- - - - - - 2		- 74	

MCC in Australia 1954-55 – THIRD TEST

18		Appleyard 4] ←) Off spell 4-1-17-1	- - - - - - -		- 74	*Play interrupted by drunk man running on pitch.*
19	 6.03	Wardle 1] →) Spell 1-0-1-0	- - - - - 1	-	- 75	
		CLOSE	Harvey 9 28 mins 24 balls	Benaud 19 68 mins 53 balls	2- 75 106 mins 152 balls	Attendance: 57,418

Arlott: Australia are on the way to victory, unless the wicket deteriorates.

Peebles, Ross and Swanton note that at Sydney at the same stage Australia were 71-2 with Morris and Favell out needing another 151, here they are 75-2 with Morris and Favell out needing another 165. The wicket is not helping the fast bowlers.

Swanton: An intriguing decision to send in Benaud at No.3 perhaps because he is on edge waiting to bat.

Hughes: Most people are inclined to expect Australia to win.

Wellings: "England appear to have the better chance and I fancy they will win provided this self-irrigating pitch does not unearth another mysterious and secret reservoir"

Mr. Vernon Ransford, the Melbourne CC Secretary, announced that after an inquiry, the Club were satisfied that no watering of the pitch or any part of the ground has occurred. None of the MCC party were consulted or invited to give their views during the inquiry.

FIFTH DAY – Typhoon strikes twice

Wednesday 5 January
Packed crowd anticipates an exciting day.

			Harvey 9	Benaud 19	2- 75	
20	12.00 12.04 12.06	Tyson 7] ←)	2 - - - - W Miller -		 3- 77 - 77	Harvey 2 to square leg Cowdrey is moved up to fine leg *Tyson is on a longer run, bowling up the slope* Harvey c Evans, wk, diving, very fine glance, 11 in 32 mins, 31 balls, 1 four Miller beaten by pace
21		Statham 6] →)		- 2 - 1 - - 1 -	 - 81	 Statham bowls three shooters in succession Miller drives edged down long leg
22		Tyson 8] ←)	- - 1 - - - -		 - 82	*The wicket has come to life again, and both bowlers regularly hit the cracks*
23		Statham 7] →)		- - 4 - - - -	 - 86	*Four successive shooters* Miller 4 'Harrow glide'

MCC in Australia 1954-55 – THIRD TEST

Over	Time	Bowler	Batsman 1	Batsman 2	Score	Notes
24	12.23	Tyson 9] ←)		W <u>Hole</u> - - 1	4- 86	Benaud bld, under-edge hooking, 22 in 91 mins, 63 balls, 3 fours Hole late cut for 1
	12.28 12.30		W <u>Archer</u> 1	- 1	5- 87 - 89	Miller c Edrich, 1st slip, via drop by Hutton 2nd slip, lifting ball, 6 in 22 mins, 17 balls, 1 four Archer pushes square to off for 1 Hole cuts for 1
25		Statham 8] →)	- - - - - - -		- 89	
26		Tyson 10] ←)	- 1	- - 2 - -	- 92	
27		Statham 9] →)	2 (1 lb) - 1	- - - 1		*Three successive yorkers to Hole*
	12.47			W <u>Maddocks</u>	6 - 97	Hole c Evans wk, edged drive, 5 in 17 mins, 24 balls, 0 fours
28	12.49	Tyson 11] ←)	- - - 1			
	12.53			W <u>Lindwall</u> - W <u>JohnSon</u> -	7- 98 8- 98 - 98	Maddocks bld, yorker, plays on, 0 in 4 mins, 1 ball Lindwall lbw, ball kept low, 0 in 1 min, 2 balls
	12.55 12.56 12.58					
29		Statham 10] →)	- - - 3	- 2 -	- 103	*After consulting May, Hutton decides to let Tyson and Statham continue* Archer drives to extra cover for 3
30		Tyson 12] ←)	- 4 - 1	- - -	- 108	Archer square cut for 4
31		Statham 11] →)	- 1 - -	- 1		
	1.13 1.15	Spell 6-1-19-2		W <u>JohnsTon</u> -	9- 110 - 110	Archer bld, full toss yorked via pads, 15 in 43 mins, 22 balls, 1 four
32	1.19	Tyson 13] ←) Spell 6.3-0-16-6	W	- 1	10- 111	JohnsTon c Evans wk, swatting at yorker, dive in front of 1st slip, 0 in 4 mins, 3 balls

MCC in Australia 1954-55 – THIRD TEST

				JohnSon 4 21 mins 13 balls	10- 111 185 mins 251 balls	Attendance: 50,483 Match attendance, 5 days: 300, 270. Receipts £A 47,933

SESSION 36-8 IN 79 MINS, 99 BALLS

Hutton: "Both men bowled wonderfully well. I switched Tyson to the end that Miller used, hoping he would get some lift, and it was gratifying that he got Miller himself with a ball that kicked. Evans too was magnificent. The team rose to the occasion."

Johnson: "Both men bowled extremely well – I emphasise both."

Tyson thinks that he was lucky to get the wickets of Harvey, Benaud, Maddocks, Miller and Lindwall, and that he bowled better in the Sydney Test.

Arlott: "As exciting and moving a day as I have ever seen"

Swanton: Tyson today did not do much more than bowl fast and straight. His progress on the tour, especially since he took a third off his run, has been phenomenal. If Australia had batted as they should, Bedser's absence might have been crucial.

Cardus: Logic suggested that on the crumbling but slow wicket and an old ball, Hutton should have started with his spinners, but psychologically, Hutton made the right choice to start with Tyson and Statham

Miller and Whitington: Despite his increasing weight, Evans is still able to dive mercurially for any chance that comes his way

Gilligan: The batsmen showed no fight; they nudged and glanced and failed to get behind the line of the ball.

Hughes: Some sixth sense told me that the match was decided when Harvey was out at 77-3. Tyson thought so as well.

Ross: Favell and Harvey are the only Australian batsmen who have the temperament and technique to deal with fast pitched up bowling. Once again England's four stars were under 25.

Australia Second innings

A.R. Morris	c Cowdrey b Tyson	4	36 mins, 14 balls, 0 fours	1-23
L.E. Favell	b Appleyard	30	76 mins, 61 balls, 2 fours	2-57
R. Benaud	b Tyson	22	91 mins, 63 balls, 3 fours	4-86
R.N. Harvey	c Evans b Tyson	11	32 mins, 31 balls, 1 four	3-77
K.R. Miller	c Edrich b Tyson	6	22 mins, 17 balls, 1 four	5-87
G.B. Hole	c Evans b Statham	5	17 mins, 24 balls, 0 fours	6-97
R.G. Archer	b Statham	15	43 mins, 22 balls, 1 four	9-110
+L.V. Maddocks	b Tyson	0	4 mins, 1 ball	7-98
R.R. Lindwall	lbw b Tyson	0	1 min, 2 balls	8-98
*I.W. Johnson	not out	4	21 mins, 13 balls	
W.A. Johnston	c Evans b Tyson	0	4 mins, 3 balls	10-111
Extras	(b 1, lb 13)	14		
TOTAL	(10 wkts – all out)	111	185 mins, 31.3 overs, 251 balls	

BOWLING

Tyson	12.3	1	27	7
Statham	11	1	38	2
Bailey	3	0	14	0
Appleyard	4	1	17	1
Wardle	1	0	1	0

England win by 128 runs

May and Cowdrey made crucial contributions to this Test which so closely matched the Sydney Test. Tyson probably should be made man of the match, but since he got it at Sydney, I am awarding the honour to Brian Statham for the way in which his support for Tyson kept the Australian batsmen under constant pressure.

At the end of the match two civil engineers, Aitcheson and Trollope, of Melbourne University write an unsolicited letter to the Victorian CA that extreme heat followed by a cooler temperature on Monday morning, combined with unventilated covers to bring up moisture and trap it in the surface soil, causing the dry crust and closing of the cracks. Still no one believes this explanation. [Years later Hutton was told that indeed the pitch had been watered.]

MCC v Combined XI at Hobart, January 8, 10 and 11

MCC now flew to the temperate climate of Tasmania, though now parched after a long drought, to play first a Combined XI in the capital Hobart on the southern coast, the islanders re-inforced by Neil Harvey, Favell, Davidson and Benaud from the 'mainland'. Bedser got Favell out fourth ball after two lbw appeals. Bedser continued to trouble everyone with his movement in the air. Harvey was dropped twice and outshone by home captain Rodwell, an Army clerk. On Monday MCC struggled hard and slowly to achieve a first innings lead. Wilson and Graveney failed again. Davidson was the best bowler and also took a magnificent catch to send back McConnon. On the final day Harvey and Benaud scored freely on a dead pitch. A drive by Harvey broke McConnon's finger and it was soon decided to send him home. (It was Harvey's brother Clarence who had injured McConnon in the Queensland match in November.) A tea-time declaration set MCC 164 in 95 minutes. They disappointed the large crowd by taking batting practice. Wilson made 33 in the last half hour. The match attendance is 20,783, a Tasmanian record.

COMBINED XI 221 (R.N.Harvey 82, E.E.Rodwell 70, Bedser 3-56, Loader 4-81, Bailey 3-29) and 184-6 dec (R.N.Harvey 47, R. Benaud 68*). MCC 99-2 (Graveney 37*). MATCH DRAWN.

MCC in Australia 1954-55 – THIRD TEST

MCC v Tasmania at Launceston, January 13, 14, 15

The MCC batsmen came alive at Launceston ground perched on a hill on the north side of the island, making 377 for 5 on the first day, led by the elegant Graveney (twice dropped). On Monday Tasmania fell to Loader who took 3 for 4 in a spell of 3 overs. Tyson, at reduced pace, forced Rodwell to retire for a time when he hit him on the knee. At the request of the Tasmanian authorities Hutton did not enforce the follow on, and promoted Tyson and Appleyard in the batting order. On the final day Compton and Cowdrey bowled generously to prolong the entertainment then Wardle came back on and MCC won with 14 minutes to spare.

MCC 427-7 dec (Hutton 61, Graveney 134, Compton 50, Wilson 62*, Wardle 63, N.V.Diprose 4-107) and 133-6 dec (T.J.Cowley 4-53). TASMANIA 117 (Loader 6-22) and 200 (B.J.Hyland 49, J.M.Maddox 62*, Wardle 4-37). MCC WON BY 243 RUNS.

On a grassy Sydney pitch New South Wales beat Victoria in two days. Bobby Simpson scored a decisive 104 in 159 minutes.

MCC fly out of Launceston on Sunday morning, lunch in Melbourne, drive out to Essendon to catch a 4.30 plane to Mount Gambier, the City of the Blue Lake

MCC v South Australian Country XI at Mount Gambier, January 18 and 19

Mount Gambier is a little city of limestone houses near a Tourquoise Blue Lake in the craters of an old volcano, on the south-eastern tip of the State, 10 miles from the sea and ten miles from the Victoria border. On a lovely wicket, MCC scored 328 in 248 minutes, despite Gross, a left arm medium pace bowler dismissing Bailey, Evans and Tyson in two overs. On the second day 19 Country XI wickets fell. In the follow on, Statham hit the stumps six times in 26 balls without a run off him.

MCC 328 (Simpson 68, May 62, Graveney 44, Compton 53, G.Gross 3-31). SOUTH AUSTRALIAN COUNTRY XI 106 (K.Hanna 34, Appleyard 6-26) and 45 (Statham 6-3-3-6, Bedser 3-11). MCC WON BY AN INNINGS AND 177 RUNS.

A big crowd and the Girls of the Blue Lake Scottish Band see the MCC players off on the 8.45pm train to Adelaide, where Hutton who skipped Mount Gambier, is waiting for them at the Pier Hotel in Adelaide's seaside suburb, Glenelg, their home for the next fortnight.

MCC v South Australia at Adelaide, January 21, 22 and 24

MCC achieved an easy victory in the return match against South Australia. Langley, having been left out of the Test side, was loudly cheered when he came in at 80 for 5. He was last out for 53. Yet another English opening combination was tried, Edrich and Graveney. Both were out before the close at 52 for 2. Then Compton rolled back the years in the stark sunshine (Adelaide started 1955 with a stifling heatwave) in stands of 92 with Cowdrey and 234 with May. MCC scored 367 in the 5½ hour day. On Monday South Australia were bowled out in 190 minutes and the match ended soon after tea. Bedser was taken off after 11 overs 3 for 20, and not brought back

SOUTH AUSTRALIA 185 (P.L.Ridings 40, G.R.A Langley 53) and 123 (P.L.Ridings 40*, D.F.Trowse 32, Bedser 3-20, Loader 4-32). MCC 451 (Cowdrey 64, Compton 182, May 114, D.M.Gregg 4-117). MCC WON BY AN INNINGS AND 143 RUNS.

Queensland drew with Victoria at Brisbane where torrential rain wiped out the second day. Lindwall pulled a muscle driving at his first ball and did not bowl again. This makes New South Wales the champions for 1954-55, though with so few matches the result is somewhat devalued.

FOURTH TEST AT ADELAIDE

28, 29, 31 January, 1, 2 February

Australia elected not to restore the now fit Langley to appear on his home ground and preferred the better batting of Maddocks. They dropped Hole and Morris no less, for Burke and McDonald. The changes, and the retention of Johnson as captain, come in for vigorous home criticism. Johnson was not fit at Melbourne and will have to pass a medical test. Ex-Test players Bill O'Reilly and Jack Fingleton make noises in their newspaper columns, about the dropping of Morris and retention of Johnson.

Colin C. McDonald (Victoria) aged 26, a pugnacious right-hander, a regular state player only since 1951 who toured England in 1953.

When Lindwall reported unfit, Davidson was brought in and Morris was added to the XII.

England have nominated the same XI as at Melbourne. Edrich can consider himself lucky, Graveney not. Graveney has made a big effort to get himself fit and in form and is very disappointed.

Wednesday: Swanton: "An old English cricketer, old enough to know better, is bowling in the nets to a young England batsman who has dispensed with the formality of a shirt – and the thermometer is rising implacably from its breakfast-time score of 92."

Thursday: Miller hurts his right hand when batting in the nets, causing a blister which is slow to harden.

FIRST DAY – Australia miss the boat

Friday 28 January

On the morning of the match the home selectors decided to play Morris in preference to the originally selected Favell. It has not rained in Adelaide for 22 days. A short distance away, the Australian open tennis championships are taking place.

Adelaide Oval is situate in parkland with St Peter's Cathedral peering through the trees to the right of its famously huge scoreboard, one of the prettiest Test grounds in the world

Umpires: M.J.McInnes and R.J.J.Wright

Australia First Innings

Odd overs △ →/ from Cathedral End
Even overs △ ←/ from River (Pavilion) End

			McDonald	Morris		
1	12.00	Tyson 1 △ →/	2 - 1 - - 1 - -		- 4	McDon 2 to Statham at deep sq leg McDon 1 to fine leg Field: 3 slips (Edrich Bailey May), gully (Cowdrey), 2 leg slips (Compton Hutton), cover, mid on, deep sq leg
2		Statham 1 △ ←/		- 2 - - 2 - -	- 8	Field similar, but only one short leg
3		Tyson 2 △ →/	- 4 - 4 - - - -		- 16	McDonald 4 through gully McDonald 4 through covers
4		Statham 2 △ ←/ Off spell 2-0-5-0	- - - - -	- - 1 - -	- 17	
5		Tyson 3 △ →/ Off spell 3-0-15-0		- 2 - - - - 1	- 20	

MCC in Australia 1954-55 – FOURTH TEST

6		Appleyard 1 △ ← /		- - - - - -	- 20	
7		Bailey 1 △ → /	- - - - - -		- 20	
8		Appleyard 2 △ ← /		1 - - - - 2	- 23	
9		Bailey 2 △ → / Off spell 2-2-0-0	- - - - - -		- 23	
10		Appleyard 3 △ ← / Off spell 3-2-3-0	- - - - - -		- 23	
11		Statham 3 △ → /		2 - - 2 - -	- 27	Morris swings straight to Hutton at leg-slip, who drops it
12		Tyson 4 △ ← /	(nb) 4 2 - - - (1 nb) - - -		- 34	*Tyson off target*
13		Statham 4 △ → / Off spell 2-0-11-0	- 1 4 - 1	- 1 	- 41	Morris hooks for 4
14		Tyson 5 △ ← / Off spell 2-0-8-0	- 1	- 1 - - -	- 43	

126

MCC in Australia 1954-55 – FOURTH TEST

Over	Time	Bowler	McDon	Morris	Score	Notes
15		Wardle 1 △ → /		- - 1 - - 1 -	- 45	
16		Appleyard 4 △ ← /		- - - (3 lb) - - -	- 48	
17		Wardle 2 △ → / Off spell 2-1-2-0		- - - - - -	- 48	
18	1.30	Appleyard 5 △ ← / Off spell 2-1-3-0	- - - - 3 -	- -	- 51	
		LUNCH	McDon 25 90 mins 71 balls	Morris 22 90 mins 75 balls	0- 51 90 mins 146 balls	

Arlott: a cautious start on a quiet pitch.
Swanton: Runs came only from pushes and glides.

Over	Time	Bowler	McDon 25	Morris 22	0- 51	Notes
19	2.10	Statham 5 △ → /	- - - - 4 - -		- 55	McDon cover-drives for 4. Highest opening stand of the series to date
20		Tyson 6 △ ← /		- - 2 - 1 - -	- 58	
21		Statham 6 △ → /		- - - - - - -	- 58	*Morris edges into slips* *Morris hooks and swats ball to prevent it from dropping from his gloves onto bails*
22	2.30 2.32	Tyson 7 △ ← /	1	- W Burke - - - -	1- 59 - 59	Morris c Evans wk, playing back, off glove attempting to leave, 25 on 110 mins, 90 balls, 1 four

MCC in Australia 1954-55 – FOURTH TEST

23		Statham 7 △ → /	- - 1	- - - - -	- 60	
24		Tyson 8 △ ← / Off spell 3-0-8-1	3	- - - - 1	- 64	
25		Statham 8 △ → /		- - - - - - -	- 64	
26		Appleyard 6 △ ← /	- - - - 3 - -		- 67	
27		Statham 9 △ → / Off spell 5-2-8-0	2 - - 1	- - -	- 70	
28		Appleyard 7 △ ← /	- - - - 3 - -	- 1	- 74	
29		Wardle 3 △ → /		- - - - - - -	- 74	
30		Appleyard 8 △ ← /	- - - - - - -		- 74	
31		Wardle 4 △ → / Off spell 2-1-9-0	1 4 -	- 1 3 - -	- 83	McD pulls high agst spin. Cmptn at wide mid on drops it off balance, distracted by screams from Ladies enclosure? McDon pulls 4 to square leg

MCC in Australia 1954-55 – FOURTH TEST

Over	Time	Bowler	Batsman 1	Batsman 2	Score	Notes
32	3.20	Appleyard 9 △ ← /	W Harvey - - (2 lb) - -	- - 3	2- 86 - 88	McDonald c May, flicking to fwd sht leg, 48 in 160 mins, 117 balls, 5 fours
33		Statham 10 △ → /		- - - - - - -	- 88	
34		Appleyard 10 △ ← / Off spell 5-1-19-1	4 1 - - - -	4 	- 97	Harvey drives thro extra cover for 4, Tyson chasing. Burke 4 through two short legs
35		Statham 11 △ → /	2 - 2 1 - -	1	- 103	101 up in 175 mins
36		Tyson 9 △ ← /		- - - 1 -	- 104	*Burke rapped on knuckles*
37		Statham 12 △ → / Off spell 3-1-15-0	1 - 4 2	- 1 - 1	- 113	Harvey drives for all run 4
38	3.53 3.55 4.00	Tyson 10 △ ← /	1	1 W Miller - - 4 -	3- 115 - 119	Burke c May, drive to fwd sht leg, 18 in 81 mins, 74 balls, 1 four *Miller pulls injured hand away in defensive stroke* Miller edges past Edrich at slip for 4
		TEA	Harvey 18 40 mins 20 balls	Miller 4 5 mins 5 balls	3- 119 200 mins 306 balls	

SESSION 68-3 IN 110 MINS, 160 BALLS

Over	Time	Bowler	Batsman 1	Batsman 2	Score	Notes
			Harvey 18	Miller 4	3- 119	
39	4.20	Wardle 5 △ → /	- - - 3 - -	1	- 123	

129

MCC in Australia 1954-55 – FOURTH TEST

Over	Time	Bowler		Runs	Score	Notes
40		Tyson 11 △ ← /		- - - - - - -	- 123	
41		Wardle 6 △ → / Off spell 2-0-8-0		- - - - 4 - -	- 127	
42		Tyson 12 △ ← /		- - - - 1 - -	- 128	
43	4.44 4.46	Bailey 3 △ → /	W Benaud	- 1 - - - - -	4- 129 - 129	Harvey c Edrich, 1st slip, driving, 25 in 64 mins, 42 balls, 3 fours
44		Tyson 13 △ ← / Off spell (incl. tea) 5-2-8-0		- - - - - - -	- 129	
45		Bailey 4 △ → /	1	- - - - - 1	- 131	
46		Statham 13 △ ← /		- - - - - - -	- 131	
47		Bailey 5 △ → /		- - - - - - -	- 131	
48		Statham 14 △ ← / Off spell 2-1-2-0		- - - 2 - -	- 133	Miller cuts for 2 – ironic applause

MCC in Australia 1954-55 – FOURTH TEST

#		Bowler			Score	Comments
49		Bailey 6 △ → /	4 - (1 nb) – - - - - -		- 138	19 in hour after tea
50		Appleyard 11 △ ← /	- - - - - 4	- 1 	- 143	*Many of the crowd are leaving for home*
51		Bailey 7 △ → / Off spell 5-1-16-1		4 - 4 - - 1 -	- 152	Miller straight drive for all run 4 Miller square cuts for 4
52		Appleyard 12 △ ← / Off spell 2-0-6-0		- - - - 1 -	- 153	
53		Wardle 7 △ → /		- 1 - - - -	- 154	
54		Tyson 14 △ ← /		- - - 1 - -	- 155	
55		Wardle 8 △ → /		- - - - - 1	-156	
56		Tyson 15 △ ← /	2 1	- 1 - - -	- 160	
57		Wardle 9 △ → / Spell 3-1-2-0		- - - - - -	- 160	

MCC in Australia 1954-55 – FOURTH TEST

58		Tyson 16 △ ← / Spell 3-0-6-0		- - - 1 - - -		
	6.00				- 161	
		CLOSE	Benaud 12 74 mins 51 balls	Miller 26 105 mins 93 balls	4- 161 300 mins 467 balls	Attendance: 29,136

SESSION 42-1 IN 100 MINS, 161 BALLS

Swanton: England fielded much better today. The bowling was accurate and purposeful. The pitch was placid and easy for batting.

Moyes: Considering that they are 2-1 down, Australia's batting, especially Burke, was too slow. They failed to capitalise on their best start of the series.

Barnes: A shocking display of stubbornly timid batting.

SECOND DAY – See-saw day

Saturday 29 January
Weather cooler and windy.

			Benaud 12	Miller 26	4- 161	
59	12.00	Statham 15 △ → /	1	- 1 2 - 1 -	- 166	
60		Tyson 17 △ ← /		- - - - - -	- 166	*Lbw appeal against Miller*
61		Statham 16 △ → / Off spell 2-0-9-0	1 1	- - 1 - 1	- 170	*Benaud glances very difficult leg-side chance to Evans*
62		Tyson 18 △ ← / Off spell 2-1-3-0		- - - - - 3	- 173	
63		Wardle 10 △ → /		- - 1 - - - -	- 174	
64		Appleyard 13 △ ← /		- 1 - - -		*Benaud almost stumped, difficult chance*
	12.30 12.32		W Maddocks -		5 -175	Benaud c May, pushing gently to fwd sht leg, 15 in 104 mins, 66 balls, 2 fours Maddocks sportingly cheered by crowd

MCC in Australia 1954-55 – FOURTH TEST

Over	Time	Bowler		Runs	Batsman	Score	Notes
65		Wardle 11 △ → /		4 - 1 - - - -		- 180	Miller 4 high to sightscreen
66		Appleyard 14 △ ← /		- - - 1 - - -		- 181	*Maddocks dropped by May at fwd sht leg*
67		Wardle 12 △ → /		- 1 - - - - -		- 182	
68	12.46	Appleyard 15 △ ← /		- - - - - - W	Archer	6- 182	Miller c Bailey, drive too soon to mid wkt, 44 in 151 mins, 142 balls, 4 fours
69	12.48	Wardle 13 △ → /	(3 b) -	- - - - - 6		- 191	Archer six into members stand at square leg. Ball hits elderly woman.
70	12.56	Appleyard 16 △ ← /		- - 1 1 - -		- 193	Maddocks first run after 23 mins Archer almost run out, Bailey hits stumps from mid on
71		Wardle 14 △ → /		- - - - - - -		- 193	
72		Appleyard 17 △ ← /		- - - - - - -		- 193	
73		Wardle 15 △ → /		1 - - - - 1 -		- 195	

MCC in Australia 1954-55 – FOURTH TEST

Over	Time	Bowler	Batsman 1	Batsman 2	Wkt	Score	Notes
74		Appleyard 18 △ ← /		- - - - - 1		- 196	
75		Wardle 16 △ → / Off spell 7-2-15-0		- - - - - -		- 196	
76	1.15	Appleyard 19 △ ← / Off spell 7-2-11-2		- - 4 - - 2 - -		- 202	Archer sweeps thro leg trap for 4. 200 up in 375 mins
77		Statham 17 △ → / Off spell 1-0-8-0	3	4 - 1 - -		- 210	Archer 4 square to off
78	1.25 1.27 1.30	Tyson 19 △ ← /		2 - W Davidson 2 1 4 2 -	7- 212	- 221	New ball taken Archer c May, low at 3rd slip off back stroke, 21 in 37 mins, 27 balls, 2 fours 1 six Madoks edges past Evans for 4
		LUNCH	Madoks 12 58 mins 67 balls	Davdsn 3 3 mins 2 balls		7- 221 390 mins 627 balls	

SESSION 60-3 IN 90 MINS, 160 BALLS
Arlott: Australia's position is below standard for this pitch.

Over	Time	Bowler	Madoks 12	Davdsn 3	Wkt	7- 221	Notes
79	2.10	Bailey 8 △ → /		- 2 - - - - -		- 223	*Statham has injured toe-nail. Visiting English eminence, Gubby Allen, a Test fast bowler of the 1930s, suggests that he cut a hole in the toe cap, and masseur Harold Dalton does it.*
80		Tyson 20 △ ← /	2 - - - - - 1			- 226	
81	 2.24 2.26	Bailey 9 △ → /	- 2 - - 1	 W JohnSon 2 -	8- 229	- 231	Davidson c Evans wk, off-driving, 5 in 17 mins, 11 balls, 0 fours

MCC in Australia 1954-55 – FOURTH TEST

82		Tyson 21 △ ← /	- - - (1 lb) - - - -		- 232	
83		Bailey 10 △ → / Off spell 3-0-9-1	1	- 1 - - - -	- 234	
84		Tyson 22 △ ← /		1 - - - - 1	- 236	
85		Appleyard 20 △ → / Off spell 1-1-0-0	- - - - - - -		- 236	
86		Tyson 23 △ ← / Off spell 5-1-19-1		- - 2 - - - 1	- 239	
87		Wardle 17 △ → /	1	- - 4 4 - 1	- 249	JohnSon 4 to long on JohnSon 4 to square leg Field drops back
88		Appleyard 21 △ ← /	- - - 1 1	1 -	- 252	
89		Wardle 18 △ → /	- 3 - - - -	1	- 256	
90		Appleyard 22 △ ← /	1 3	- 1 - 1	- 262	Madoks drives over bowler's head

MCC in Australia 1954-55 – FOURTH TEST

Over	Time	Bowler	Batsman 1	Batsman 2	Score	Notes
91		Wardle 19 △ → / Off spell 3-0-23-0	- 4 - 4 - 1 - -		- 271	Madoks sweeps 4 to square leg Madoks 4 to sightscreen *Three expensive overs by Wardle*
92		Appleyard 23 △ ← / Off spell 3-0-16-0	4 - 1 1 1 - -		- 278	
93	3.25	Statham 18 △ → /	- - - 1 - - 4		- 283	*Madoks hits to mid wkt and runs, sent back. Applyd lobs return high over Evans' head and Madoks gets back* 50 stand in 59 mins Madoks cover drive for 4
94	3.30	Tyson 24 △ ← /	2 1 1 1 1 - - 4		- 293	 Madoks 50 in 138 mins Maddocks hooks bouncer to fine leg for 4
95	3.40	Statham 19 △ → / Off spell 2-0-12-0	- 1 - - - 4 2 -		- 300	 Maddocks magnificent cover drive for 4 Maddocks leg glance for 2 - 300 up in 480 mins
96		Tyson 25 △ ← /	- - (1 lb) 1 1 - - -		- 303	
97		Bailey 11 △ → /	- - 4 1 - 1 1 4		- 314	
98		Tyson 26 △ ← /	- 4 - - 1 - -		- 319	
99	4.00	Bailey 12 △ → /	1 - 1 - - W		9- 321	JohnSon c Statham at mid off, 41 in 94 mins, 62 balls, 5 fours. Batsmen crossed
		TEA	Madoks 67 168 mins 163 balls		9- 321 500 mins 794 balls	

136

MCC in Australia 1954-55 – FOURTH TEST

SESSION 100-2 IN 110 MINS, 167 BALLS

Arlott: slack fielding has allowed what may prove to be the decisive stand

Swanton: Hutton lost his grip of the situation by giving three costly overs to Wardle. Maddocks saw himself through a painful start; he was inspired by Johnson.

Miller and Whitington: The first nine wickets have fallen to catches, indicating a pitch with bounce. Appleyard has got some lift by his slightly slower back-spinning ball, where the first and second fingers whip under the ball at delivery.

Gilligan: Statham bowled as well as Appleyard for no reward

			Madoks 67	JohnsTon	9- 321	
99	4.20	Bailey 12 ctd Spell 2-0-14-1	1		- 322	
100	4.21	Tyson 27 ◇ ← / Spell (incl. tea) 3.1-0-18-0	(r o) 1		10- 323	Maddocks run out, going for second to long leg to keep bowling, beaten by Wardle's throw, 69 in 169 mins, 165 balls, 7 fours
				JonsTn 0 1 min 0 balls	10- 323 501 mins 796 balls	Standing ovation for Maddocks

Australia First innings

C.C. McDonald	c May b Appleyard	48	160 mins, 117 balls, 5 fours	2-86
A.R. Morris	c Evans b Tyson	25	110 mins, 90 balls, 1 four	1-59
J.W. Burke	c May b Tyson	18	81 mins, 74 balls, 1 four	3-115
R.N. Harvey	c Edrich b Bailey	25	64 mins, 42 balls, 3 fours	4-129
K.R. Miller	c Bailey b Appleyard	44	151 mins, 142 balls, 4 fours	6-182
R. Benaud	c May b Appleyard	15	104 mins, 66 balls, 2 fours	5-175
+ L.V. Maddocks	run out (Wardle)	69	169 mins, 165 balls, 7 fours	10-323
R.G. Archer	c May b Tyson	21	37 mins, 27 balls, 2 fours 1 six	7-212
A.K. Davidson	c Evans b Bailey	5	17 mins, 11 balls, 0 fours	8-229
* I.W. Johnson	c Statham b Bailey	41	94 mins, 62 balls, 5 fours	9-321
W.A. Johnston	not out	0	1 min, 0 balls	
Extras	(b 3, lb 7, nb 2)	12		
TOTAL	(10 wkts – all out)	323	501 mins, 99.1 overs, 796 balls	

BOWLING

Tyson	26.1	4	85	3	nb 1
Statham	19	4	70	0	
Appleyard	23	7	58	3	
Bailey	12	3	39	3	nb 1
Wardle	19	5	59	0	

England First Innings

Odd overs ◇ ← / from River End
Even overs ◇ → / from Cathedral End

			Hutton	Edrich		
1	4.32	Miller 1 ◇ ← /	(1 b/lb) - 1 - - 4 - 3		- 9	Hutton 4 drive through covers, all run Hutton cuts for 3
2		Archer 1 ◇ → /	2 1 1	- (1 b/lb) - 2 - -	- 16	
3		Miller 2 ◇ ← /	- 1 - 1 - - -	1	- 19	

137

MCC in Australia 1954-55 – FOURTH TEST

4		Archer 2 △ → / Off spell 2-0-8-0	1 - - - - -	1	- 21	
5		Miller 3 △ ← / Off spell 3-1-11-0	- - - - - - -		- 21	
6		JohnSon 1 △ → /	- - - 1 - - -		- 22	
7		Davidson 1 △ ← /	- 1 - - - - -	1	- 24	*Hutton complains that Davidson is running onto wicket on follow through*
8		JohnSon 2 △ → /	- - - - - - -		- 24	
9		Davidson 2 △ ← /	1 - - - - - -		- 25	
10		JohnSon 3 △ → /	- - - - - - -		- 25	
11		Davidson 3 △ ← /	- - - - - 1	1	- 27	
12		JohnSon 4 △ → /	- - - - - - -		- 27	

MCC in Australia 1954-55 – FOURTH TEST

13		Davidson 4 △ ← /		- 1 - - -	- 29	
14		JohnSon 5 △ → /		- - - 1 - -	- 30	
15		Davidson 5 △ ← / Off spell 5-0-11-0	- - - - 3	- 1	- 34	
16		JohnSon 6 △ → /		- - - - - - -	- 34	
17		JohnsTon 1 △ ← /		- - - 1 - -	- 35	
18		JohnSon 7 △ → /		- - - - - -	- 35	
19		JohnsTon 2 △ ← /	1 - 2 - 1	-	- 39	
20		JohnSon 8 △ → /	- 1	- - - -	- 40	First run off JohnSon since his first over
21		JohnsTon 3 △ ← / Off spell 3-0-12-0	3	4 - - - -	- 47	Edrich hooks for 4

MCC in Australia 1954-55 – FOURTH TEST

			Hutton 34	Edrich 21	0-57	
22		JohnSon 9 △ → / Off spell 9-6-3-0	- - - - - -		- 47	
23	 6.00	Benaud 1 △ ← / Off spell 1-0-10-0	- - 1 - 3 2 - 4		- - - - - - - 57	Edrich edges over slips for 2 Edrich hooks for 4
		CLOSE	Hutton 34 88 mins 98 balls	Edrich 21 88 mins 86 balls	0- 57 88 mins 184 balls	Attendance: 43,983

This is already England's best opening stand of the series.

Moyes: Hutton's complaint against Davidson is unconvincing. The left-handed bowler is swinging his feet clear of the pitch as well as he can.

Woodcock: JohnSon bowled ball after ball of full flight and late dip and nearly broke through.

THIRD DAY – Australia Day grind

Monday 31 January

Australia Day ceremony. The band plays "Song of Australia" and Ian Johnson hoists the national flag with the two teams lined up.

			Hutton 34	Edrich 21	0- 57	
24	12.00 12.04 12.06	JohnSon 10 △ → /	- - - 3 - 	 - W May -	 1- 60 - 60	Hutton 3 off full toss, misfield by McDonald at mid on Edrich bld through gate, 21 in 92 mins, 88 balls, 2 fours
25		Benaud 2 △ ← /	- - - - - -		 - 60	
26		JohnSon 11 △ → /	 1	- - 1 - -	 - 62	Benaud in very close at short leg
27	 12.15	Benaud 3 △ ← /	- - - 1 	 - - W Cowdrey	 2 - 63	May pulls bat away from vicious spinner May c Archer, brilliantly to his right at slip, 1 in 9 mins, 10 balls
28	12.17	JohnSon 12 △ → /	- - - - - -		 - 63	JohnSon brings in a second short leg

MCC in Australia 1954-55 – FOURTH TEST

Over		Bowler		Ball	Score	Notes
29		Benaud 4 △ ← /		- - - 1 - 2 -	- 66	
30		JohnSon 13 △ → /		- - - - - - -	- 66	
31		Benaud 5 △ ← /	- - - - 1	2 1	- 70	
32		JohnSon 14 △ → /		- - - - - - -	- 70	*Cowdrey pads up and ball canons off back of leg close to stumps*
33		Benaud 6 △ ← /	- 1	- - - 3 -	- 74	Cowdrey off drives for 3
34		JohnSon 15 △ → /		- 4 - - - - -	- 78	Cowdrey drives past point for 4
35		Benaud 7 △ ← /	- - - - - -		- 78	
36		JohnSon 16 △ → /		- - 1 - - -	- 79	JohnSon bowls round the wicket
37		Benaud 8 △ ← /		- - - - - - 4	- 83	Cowdrey drives past point for 4

141

MCC in Australia 1954-55 – FOURTH TEST

Over	Time	Bowler		Batsman 1	Batsman 2	Score	Notes
38		JohnSon 17 △ → /		- - - - 1 1	1	- 86	
39		Benaud 9 △ ← /		- - 1 - - -	3	- 90	
40	1.00	JohnSon 18 △ → / Off spell 9-4-13-1		- - - - - -		- 90	
41	1.02	Benaud 10 △ ← / Off spell 9-2-28-1		- - 4 - 1 -	3	- 98	Hutton 4 to fine leg all run, 50 in 150 mins, 170 balls
42		JohnsTon 4 △ → /		- - - - - -		- 98	
43		JohnSon 19 △ ← /		- 1 - - - -		- 99	
44		JohnsTon 5 △ → /		- 1 - - 4 -		- 104	100 up in 162 mins Cowdrey hooks for 4
45		JohnSon 20 △ ← / Off spell 2-1-1-0		- - - - - -		- 104	
46		JohnsTon 6 △ → / Off spell 3-1-7-0		- - 2 - - -		- 106	Cowdrey turns to leg

MCC in Australia 1954-55 – FOURTH TEST

#	Time	Bowler	Hutton	Cowdrey	Total	Comments
47		Davidson 6 △ ← / Off spell 1-0-1-0	- - - - 1	-	- - 107	*Loud lbw appeal against Hutton*
48	1.30	Burke 1 △ → / Off spell 1-0-4-0	- - 4 - -	-	- - 111	Hutton 4 off back foot past cover's left
		LUNCH	Hutton 58 / 178 mins / 201 balls	Cowdry 29 / 73 mins / 85 balls	2-111 / 178 mins / 384 balls	

Arlott: England have had difficulty with the ball pitching in the rough from the bowlers' follow through.
Swanton: the spinners are only getting turn well wide of the off-stump.

Tom Graveney and Johnny Wardle, in their flannels and MCC blazers, took a walk out during the lunch interval for a quick look at the Australian Tennis championships, but their arrangement for getting in fell foul of the officious tennis stewards. Then the gateman at the Cricket ground wouldn't let them in again. Wardle was stopped as he jumped the turnstile and the MCC manager was called to sort things out.

#	Time	Bowler	Hutton 58	Cowdry 29	2-111	Comments
49	2.10	JohnSon 21 △ ← /	- - - 1 - - -		- 112	Hutton props out ball just short of Benaud at short leg
50		JohnsTon 7 △ → /		- - - - - - -	- 112	
51		JohnSon 22 △ ← /	- 2 - - - -		- 114	Hutton 2 via painful blow to Benaud's back at short leg. Applause as Benaud resumes his silly leg position. Almost scoops up catch off defensive stroke.
52		JohnsTon 8 △ → /		- - - - - -	- 114	
53		JohnSon 23 △ ← /		- - - - - -	- 114	
54		JohnsTon 9 △ → /		- - - - - 3 -	- 117	

143

MCC in Australia 1954-55 – FOURTH TEST

55		JohnSon 24 △ ← /	1	- - - 1 - -	- 119	
56		JohnsTon 10 △ → /	- - 2 - - -		- 121	Hutton 2, his first off-drive today
57		JohnSon 25 △ ← /	-	- - - - - -	- 121	
58		JohnsTon 11 △ → /	- - - 4 - 1	-	- 126	Hutton drives through extra cover for 4
59		JohnSon 26 △ ← /	- 1	- - - - -	- 127	
60		JohnsTon 12 △ → / Off spell 6-3-10-0	- - - - - -		- 127	
61		JohnSon 27 △ ← / Off spell 6-2-10-0		- - - - 4 - -	- 131	Last over of Johnson's long spell. He has had several lbw appeals turned down when batsmen were on the front foot Cowdrey on drives for 4 JohnSon 27-13-27-1
62	3.00	Benaud 11 △ → /	- 1	- 1 - - -	- 133	
63		Miller 4 △ ← /		- - - 4 - - -	- 137	Miller one over of off-breaks

MCC in Australia 1954-55 – FOURTH TEST

64		Benaud 12 △ → /	- 4 - - 2 -		 - 143	Hutton 4 through covers Hutton leg glances for 2
65		Miller 5 △ ← / Off spell 2-1-4-0		- - - - - -	 - 143	Miller one over at full pace
66		Benaud 13 △ → /	- - - 2 - -		 - 145	
67		Davidson 7 △ ← /		1 - - - - -	 - 146	
68		Benaud 14 △ → /		- - 4 - - -	 - 150	Cowdrey flicks to leg for 4
69		Davidson 8 △ ← /		- - - - - -	 - 150	
70	3.25	Benaud 15 △ → /		- - - - 4 - -	 - 154	Cowdrey 4 hooks to fine leg, 52 in 150 mins, 176 balls
71		Davidson 9 △ ← / Off spell 3-1-3-0	- - 1	- 1 - -	 - 156	
72		Benaud 16 △ → / Off spell 6-0-22-0		- - - - 4 - -	 - 160	Cowdrey square drives for 4

MCC in Australia 1954-55 – FOURTH TEST

Over	Time	Bowler	Batsman 1	Batsman 2	Score	Notes
73	3.42 3.44	JohnsTon 13 △ ← /	1 - - W Compton - 3	1 - -	3- 162 - 165	*Hutton almost gives catch to Davidson at short leg* Hutton c Davidson, at short leg, fierce hook, stuck in hands, 80 in 270 mins, 294 balls, 5 fours Compton late cuts for 3
74		JohnSon 28 △ → /	- - - - - -		- 165	
75		JohnsTon 14 △ ← /	- - - 3 -		- 168	
76		JohnSon 29 △ → /	- - - - - - -		- 168	
77		JohnsTon 15 △ ← /	- - (1 lb) - - - -		- 169	
78	4.00	JohnSon 30 △ → / Off spell 3-3-0-0 JohnSon's figures so far: 30-16-27-1	- - - - - -		- 169	
		TEA	Comptn 3 16 mins 23 balls	Cowdry 61 183 mins 209 balls	3- 169 288 mins 624 balls	

Session 58-1 in 110 mins, 240 balls
Arlott: Hutton and Cowdrey have batted with skill and judgement.

Over	Time	Bowler	Batsman 1	Batsman 2	Score	Notes
			Comptn 3	Cowdry 61	3- 169	
79	4.20	JohnsTon 16 △ ← /	- - - - - -		- 169	
80		Benaud 17 △ → /	- - - - 1 -		- 170	*Some barracking. Both batsmen are out of touch. Cowdrey reacts (on his own admission) by trying to play some chancy shots*

MCC in Australia 1954-55 – FOURTH TEST

81		JohnsTon 17 △ ← /	4 - - - - 1	-	- 175	Follow on avoided
82		Benaud 18 △ → /	- - " 3 - - -	-	- 178	
83		JohnsTon 18 △ ← /	- - - - - -		- 178	*Continuous slow handclapping*
84		Benaud 19 △ → /	- - 3 - - -		- 181	*12th man Wilson comes out with 'new bat' and a banana to give instructions to Cowdrey to keep his head down "After seeing a couple of wild shots from you just now, skipper thought you might be hungry".*
85		JohnsTon 19 △ ← /	(1 nb) - 1	- 1 - - -	- 184	
86		Benaud 20 △ → /	- - - - - -		- 184	
87		JohnsTon 20 △ ← / Off spell (incl. tea) 8-3-16-1		- - - - 1 -	- 185	*Cowdrey is drained by the nervous tension*
88		Benaud 21 △ → /		- - - - - -	- 185	
89		Davidson 10 △ ← /	- - - 1 - -	1	- 187	

MCC in Australia 1954-55 – FOURTH TEST

90		Benaud 22 △ → /		- - - - - - 1 -	- - 188	
91		Davidson 11 △ ← /		- - - - - - - -	- 188	
92		Benaud 23 △ → /	4 - - 1	- - - -	- 193	
93		Davidson 12 △ ← /	1 - - 3 - 1	- -	- 198	
94		Benaud 24 △ → / Off spell 8-2-16-1	- - - - - 3 -	-	- 201	201 up in 350 mins
95		Davidson 13 △ ← / Off spell 4-1-11-0	- - - - - - 4		- 205	*New ball not taken*
96		JohnSon 31 △ → /		- - 4 - - - 1 -	- 209	
97	5.36	JohnsTon 21 △ ← /		- - - 2 - - 4 -	- 215	Compton off-drives for 4, 53 stand in 92 mins
98		JohnSon 32 △ → /		- - - - - - - -	- 215	

MCC in Australia 1954-55 – FOURTH TEST

99		JohnsTon 22 △ ← /	- - - - - - -		- 215	
100		JohnSon 33 △ → /		- - - 1 - - -	- 216	
101		JohnsTon 23 △ ← / Off spell 3-1-9-0	- - - - 3	- (3 nb) - - - -	- 222	
102		JohnSon 34 △ → /	- - - - - 1		- 223	
103		Burke 2 △ ← / Off spell 1-0-3-0	1 1	1 - - - -	- 226	
104		JohnSon 35 △ → / Off spell 5-1-10-0	- - - 4 - -	- - - - - -	- 230	
	6.00	CLOSE	Comptn 44 116 mins 139 balls	Cowdry 77 283 mins 303 balls	3- 230 388 mins 834 balls	Attendance: 39,876

SESSION 61-0 IN 100 MINS, 210 BALLS
England 93 runs behind. An exhausted Cowdrey falls asleep on the massage table.
Swanton: Play got very slow after tea because runs were coming only from one end. A large crowd of 40,000 saw a day devoid of colour and excitement.

FOURTH DAY – Appleyard bites

Tuesday 1 February
Heavy rain during the night. Cowdrey and even Compton have a net practice.

			Comptn 44	Cowdry 77	3- 230	Field full of seagulls
105	12.00	Davidson 14 △ ← /		- - - - - 1	- 231	

149

MCC in Australia 1954-55 – FOURTH TEST

Over	Time	Bowler	Batsman 1	Batsman 2	Score	Notes
106	12.08 12.10	Miller 6 △ → /	W Bailey - - -	- - 1	4- 232 - 232	New ball after 3 balls Compton lbw, back to late inswinger 44 in 124 mins, 140 balls, 5 fours. Only Miller appealed.
107	12.13 12.15	Davidson 15 △ ← /	2 -	W Evans - - 4 3	5- 232 - 241	Cowdrey c Maddocks, cutting, half forward, kicker, 79 in 296 mins, 315 balls, 9 fours Evans 4 square to off Evans 3 edged to 3rd man Bailey drives for 2
108		Miller 7 △ → /	- 1 -	- 1 4 - 1 -	- 248	Evans 4 to long leg Evans dropped by Burke at 3rd slip
109		Davidson 16 △ ← /	2 -	- 2 - 5 - -	- 257	Evans 5 straight all run chased by Morris from short mid off Bailey 2 to third man
110		Miller 8 △ → / Off spell 3-0-18-1	- 1 1	4 1 - 2 1	- 267	Evans 4 to square leg Evans hooks over short leg field
111		Davidson 17 △ ← / Off spell 4-0-24-1	- - 1	- - 4 - -	- 272	Evans 4 through covers
112		Benaud 25 △ → /	- - 4 1	- - 4 - -	- 281	Bailey square cuts for 4 Quick single. Harvey nearly beats Evans Evans hooks square for 4
113		Miller 9 △ ← /	- - - - - -		- 281	Drinks interval
114	12.51 12.53	Benaud 26 △ → / Off spell 2-0-17-1	1 1	1 - W Wardle - - - 6	6- 283 - 289	50 partnership Evans c Maddocks wk, off back foot faint edge, 37 in 36 mins, 28 balls, 5 fours 1 five Wardle high six to wide long on towards Cathedral

150

MCC in Australia 1954-55 – FOURTH TEST

#		Bowler			Score	Notes
115		Miller 10 △ ← / - - - - - - -			- 289	
116		Davidson 18 △ → /	1	- - - 1 - - -	- 291	
117		Miller 11 △ ← / Off spell 3-2-1-0	1	- - - - - - -	- 292	
118		Davidson 19 △ → /	- - 3	- - - -	- 295	
119		Benaud 27 △ ← /	- - - - 2 - -		- 297	Unexplained change of ends
120		Davidson 20 △ → / Off spell 3-1-5-0	- - - - - - -		- 297	
121		Benaud 28 △ ← /		- - - 1 - - -	- 298	
122		Archer 3 △ → / Off spell 1-0-4-0	- - - 2 - 1	1	- 302	

MCC in Australia 1954-55 – FOURTH TEST

123		Benaud 29 △ ← /	- - - - - 1			
	1.30	LUNCH	Bailey 25 80 mins 82 balls	- Wardle 9 37 mins 29 balls	- 303 6- 303 478 mins 986 balls	

Session 73-3 in 90 mins, 152 balls

			Bailey 25	Wardle 9	6- 303	
124	2.10	Davidson 21 △ → /	- - - - - -		- 303	
125		Benaud 30 △ ← /		- - - - 3 - -	- 306	
126		Davidson 22 △ → /		- - - - - - -	- 306	
127		Benaud 31 △ ← /	2 - 1	- - - 3	- 312	
128		Davidson 23 △ → /		- - - - - - -	- 312	
129		Benaud 32 △ ← / Off spell (incl. lunch) 6-1-13-0	- - - - - - -		- 312	
130		Davidson 24 △ → /		- - - - - - -	- 312	

MCC in Australia 1954-55 – FOURTH TEST

131		JohnSon 36 △ ← / Off spell 1-0-9-1 2.40 2.42	- - 1 4 4 - W Tyson -		7- 321 - 321	JohnSon has arm strain Wardle 4 through covers Wardle 4 straight Wardle c & b, hard catch, 23 in 67 mins, 68 balls, 2 fours 1 six
132		Davidson 25 △ → / Off spell 5-5-0-0	- - - - - - -		- 321	Davidson five successive maidens
133		Benaud 33 △ ← /	- - - - 1 -		- 322	
134		JohnsTon 24 △ → /	- - - - - - -		- 322	Tyson almost caught at slip
135		Benaud 34 △ ← /	1 - - - - - -		- 323	323 in 523 mins. Scores level
136		JohnsTon 25 △ → /	- - - - - - -		- 323	
137		Benaud 35 △ ← / 3.04 3.06	- - - - W Appleyard -		8- 323 - 323	*Tyson has hardly middled the ball* Tyson c Burke running in from deep mid wkt, 1 in 22 mins, 29 balls. Batsmen crossed.
138		JohnsTon 26 △ → /	- - - 1 4 1 -		- 329	Applyd push to short leg. England ahead
139		Benaud 36 △ ← /	- - 2 1 - - 4		- 336	

MCC in Australia 1954-55 – FOURTH TEST

140	3.15 3.17	JohnsTon 27 △ → / Spell 4-3-6-1	- - - W Statham - - - -		9- 336 - 336	Bailey c Davidson, drive to wide slip, 38 in 145 mins, 136 balls, 2 fours
141	3.24	Benaud 37 △ ← / Spell 4.6-1-14-2	4 1 - - - W		 10- 341	Applyd straight drive for 4 Applyd straight drive for 1 Statham c Madoks wk, slash at flighted leg break, 0 in 7 mins, 8 balls
			Applyd 10 18 mins 12 balls 2 fours	10- 341 552 mins 1128 balls		

SESSION 38-4 in 74 mins, 142 balls

Arlott: Johnston was under-used.

Moyes: Johnson relied on his spin attack, though he himself was unfit to bowl, and his spinners could not deliver the goods

England First innings

* L. Hutton	c Davidson b JohnsTon	80	270 mins, 294 balls, 5 fours	3-162
W.J. Edrich	b JohnSon	21	92 mins, 88 balls, 2 fours	1-60
P.B.H. May	c Archer b Benaud	1	9 mins, 10 balls	2-63
M.C. Cowdrey	c Maddocks b Davidson	79	296 mins, 315 balls, 9 fours	5-232
D.C.S. Compton	lbw b Miller	44	124 mins, 140 balls, 5 fours	4-232
T.E. Bailey	c Davidson b Benaud	38	145 mins, 136 balls, 2 fours	9-336
+ T.G. Evans	c Maddocks b Benaud	37	36 mins, 28 balls, 5 fours 1 five	6-283
J.H. Wardle	c & b JohnSon	23	67 mins, 68 balls, 2 fours 1 six	7-321
F.H. Tyson	c Burke b Benaud	1	22 mins, 29 balls	8-323
R. Appleyard	not out	10	18 mins, 12 balls, 2 fours	
J.B. Statham	c Maddocks b Benaud	0	7 mins, 8 balls	10-341
Extras	(b 1, lb 2, nb 4)	7		
TOTAL	(10 wkts – all out)	341	552 mins, 140.6 overs, 1128 balls	

BOWLING

Miller	11	4	34	1	
Archer	3	0	12	0	
JohnSon	36	17	46	2	
Davidson	25	8	55	1	
JohnsTon	27	11	60	2	(nb 4)
Benaud	36.6	6	120	4	
Burke	2	0	7	0	

Australia Second Innings

Odd overs △ ← / from River End
Even overs △ → / from Cathedral End
England lead of 18. Twelve hours left for play.

			McDonald	Morris		
1	3.35	Tyson 1 △ ← /	- - - 4 - - -	 - 4		
2		Statham 1 △ → /	2 - - 2 1 - -	 - 9		

154

MCC in Australia 1954-55 – FOURTH TEST

Over	Time	Bowler	Batsman 1	Batsman 2	Score	Notes
3		Tyson 2 △ ← /		- - 1 (nb) 1 - 1 -	1 1 - 14	
4		Statham 2 △ → / Off spell 2-0-13-0		- 3 - - 1 - 4	- 22	Australia lead by 4 runs
5		Tyson 3 △ ← / Spell 3-0-11-0		- - 1 - - - 1	- 24	
6	4.06 4.14	Appleyard 1 △ → /		- - - - - W	1-24	Two short legs and one slip Morris cuts hard, ball bounces and hits Cowdrey gully on nose. Carried off. Five mins stoppage. Wilson substitutes Morris c & b, playing too soon, 16 in 39 mins, 27 balls, 1 four
		TEA	McDon 8 39 mins 20 balls		1-24 39 mins 47 balls	

Arlott: Appleyard is at his best on the slow turning wicket; he pushes the ball through with some spin. Swanton: he runs the ball out of his first and second fingers.

Harris: The Adelaide infield is very rough.

Over	Time	Bowler	McDon 8	Burke	1-24	
6 ctd	4.35	Appleyard 1 Ctd		- -	- 24	
7		Tyson 4 △ ← /	1	- 3 (nb) - - - - -	- 28	
8		Appleyard 2 △ → /		- - - - - - -	- 28	
9		Tyson 5 △ ← / Off spell 5-0-22-3	2 2 - 1 - 1	- - - - - 1	- 35	

155

MCC in Australia 1954-55 – FOURTH TEST

Over	Time	Bowler	Runs	Batsman	Score	Notes
10		Appleyard 3 △ → /	- - - - - - 3		- 38	
11		Statham 3 △ ← /	- 1	- - 1 - -	- 40	
12	5.02 5.04	Appleyard 4 △ → /		W Harvey - - - - - -	2- 40 - 40	Burke bld, off break between bat and pad, 5 in 27 mins, 19 balls, 0 fours
13		Statham 4 △ ← /	1 2 1 -	- 1 1	- 46	
14		Appleyard 5 △ → /		- 1 - - 2 - -	- 49	
15		Statham 5 △ ← / Off spell 3-0-13-0	- - 1	- 1 - 2 1	- 54	
16	5.25 5.27	Appleyard 6 △ → /		- - W Miller 1 - - -	3- 54 - 55	Harvey bld, missing a hook shot, 7 in 21 mins, 21 balls, 0 fours Miller quick single to mid on
17		Tyson 6 △ ← / Off spell 1-1-0-0		- - - - - - -	- 55	*Miller misses several cut shots*
18		Appleyard 7 △ → /	- - - 1 3		- 59	Miller drives for 3

MCC in Australia 1954-55 – FOURTH TEST

19		Wardle 1 △ ← /		- - - - - - -	- 59	
20		Appleyard 8 △ → /	- - - - - -		- 59	
21		Wardle 2 △ ← /		2 - - - - -	- 61	
22		Appleyard 9 △ → /	- - 1 - - 1		- 63	
23		Wardle 3 △ ← /		- 1 - 1 - - -	- 65	
24		Appleyard 10 △ → / Spell 10-5-13-3	- - - - - - -		- 65	
25	6.00	Wardle 4 △ ← / Off spell 4-1-8-0		- - - - - 4 -	- 69	
		CLOSE	McDon 29 124 mins 92 balls	Miller 12 33 mins 43 balls	3- 69 124 mins 202 balls	Attendance 26,298

SESSION 45-2 IN 85 MINS, 155 BALLS

Australia lead by 51 runs. Miller and McDonald are fighting to stay in the match. Cowdrey will be able to bat tomorrow.

Peebles: Appleyard has bowled very well, helped by some injudicious shots

MCC in Australia 1954-55 – FOURTH TEST

FIFTH DAY – Hutton's reward

Wednesday 2 February

Hutton adjudges the wicket to be in good condition; Appleyard may not repeat his success of last evening, so he starts with his main fast bowlers.

			McDon 29	Miller 12	3- 69	
26	12.00	Statham 6 △ → /	- -			
	12.02		W Maddocks (1 bye) -		4- 69	McDonald bld, off pads?, hitting across full toss, shaping to leg, 29 in 126 mins, 95 balls, 1 four
	12.04		- - -		- 70	
27		Tyson 7 △ ← /	2 - (2 byes) - - - -		- 74	Maddocks leg glances for 2
28		Statham 7 △ → /		- 2		Miller leg glances for 2
	12.14			W Benaud	5- 76	Miller bld, lunging forward, ball kept low, flicked leg bail, 14 in 47 mins, 50 balls, 1 four
	12.16			- 1 - -	- 77	
29	12.21	Tyson 8 △ ← /		- W Archer	6- 77	Benaud lbw, half volley, head in air, late on shot, 1 in 5 mins, 4 balls
	12.23			- 1 - - -	- 78	Archer batting with torn muscle.
30		Statham 8 △ → /	- - -	1		
	12.32		W Davidson		7- 79	Maddocks lbw, covering up, 2 in 28 mins, 20 balls
	12.34		1		- 80	
31		Tyson 9 △ ← /	1	1 - - 1		
	12.40			W JohnsTon	8- 83	Archer c Evans wk, top edge cutting, 3 in 17 mins, 7 balls
	12.42			-	- 83	
32		Statham 9 △ → /	- - 2 - - 1		- 86	

MCC in Australia 1954-55 – FOURTH TEST

33		Tyson 10 △ ← /	- 2 - - 1 - -	- (1 bye)	- 90	
34		Statham 10 △ → /	- 1 - - - -	- (1 lb)	- 92	
35		Tyson 11 △ ← /	- 1 - 2 - -	1	- 96	
36		Statham 11 △ → /	- - - - 1 - -		- 97	
37		Tyson 12 △ ← /	- 2 1 - -	1 W JohnSon	9- 101	JohnsTon c Appleyard, cross-batted drive skied to mid-off, 3 in 35 mins, 19 balls
	1.17					
38	1.19	Statham 12 △ → / Off spell 7-1-12-3	1 - - - 1 -	- - - - -	- 103	JohnSon has damaged right elbow, injected with local anaesthetic
39		Tyson 13 △ ← / Spell 7-1-17-3	- - - - - -		- 103	
	1.30					
		LUNCH	Davdsn 17 56 mins 38 balls	JohnSon 1 11 mins 14 balls	9- 103 214 mins 314 balls	

The Australian batting this morning has been so out of character that it has been a disappointment.
Moyes: everyone thought that Appleyard would be the match-winner, but Hutton had a hunch that Statham would make the ball hurry through low.

			Davdsn 17	JohnSon 1	9- 103	
40	2.10	Appleyard 11 △ → /	- - - - - -		- 103	

MCC in Australia 1954-55 – FOURTH TEST

41		Tyson 14 △ ← /		- - - 1 - - -	- 104	
42		Appleyard 12 △ → / Off spell 2-2-0-0		- - - - - - -	- 104	
43		Tyson 15 △ ← / Off spell (incl. lunch) 9-1-25-3	1 - - - 4 1	1	- 111	
44	2.30	Wardle 5 △ → / Spell 0.2-0-0-1	- W		10- 111	Dvdsn hooks at long hop and misses Davidson lbw, sweeping, 23 in 76 mins, 56 balls, 4 fours
				JohnSon 3 31 mins 30 balls	10- 111 234 mins 348 balls	

Session so far: 8-1 in 20 mins, 34 balls

As in the Melbourne Test, Australia collapse for the dreaded 'Nelson' 111, which is supposed to be unlucky for the English.

Moyes: "Thou are weighed in the balance, and found wanting".

Australia Second innings

C.C. McDonald	b Statham	29	126 mins, 95 balls, 1 four	4-69
A.R. Morris	c & b Appleyard	16	39 mins, 27 balls, 1 four	1-24
J.W. Burke	b Appleyard	5	27 mins, 19 balls, 0 fours	2-40
R.N. Harvey	b Appleyard	7	21 mins, 21 balls, 0 fours	3-54
K.R. Miller	b Statham	14	47 mins, 50 balls, 1 four	5-76
+ L.V. Maddocks	lbw b Statham	2	28 mins, 20 balls	7-79
R. Benaud	lbw b Tyson	1	5 mins, 4 balls	6-77
R.G. Archer	c Evans b Tyson	3	17 mins, 7 balls	8-83
A.K. Davidson	lbw b Wardle	23	76 mins, 56 balls, 4 fours	10-111
W.A. Johnston	c Appleyard b Tyson	3	35 mins, 19 balls	9-101
* I.W. Johnson	not out	3	31 mins, 30 balls	
Extras	(b 4, lb 1)	5		
TOTAL	(10 wkts – all out)	111	234 mins, 43.2 overs, 348 balls	

BOWLING

Tyson	15	2	47	3
Statham	12	1	38	3
Appleyard	12	7	13	3
Wardle	4.2	1	8	1

England Second Innings

Odd overs △ ← / from River End
Even overs △ → / from Cathedral End

England need 94 to win, with three hours to do it if they want to win to-day. Despite his injury JohnSon comes out with his team. Hutton at first asks Compton to open the innings then changes his mind and padded up himself. Cowdrey has a broken nose: May asks Hutton who he wants to bat in Cowdrey's place; Hutton says "no one".

				Hutton	Edrich		
1	2.41	Miller 1 △ ← /		- - - 3			
	2.43				W	1- 3	Hutton pushes 3 wide of JohnSon at mid off Edrich bld, inswinger through the gate, 0 in 2 mins, 2 balls
	2.45				May - (1 lb) 2	- 6	

160

MCC in Australia 1954-55 – FOURTH TEST

2		Davidson 1 △ → /		- - 2 - - - 1	- 9	May 2 to deep cover
3	2.52 2.54	Miller 2 △ ← /	W Cowdrey	1 - - - - -	2- 10 - 10	Hutton c Davidson, out swinger, low to his left at 2nd slip, 5 in 11 mins, 6 balls, 0 fours Cowdrey comes in with blackened face
4		Davidson 2 △ → / Off spell 2-0-7-0		- 2 2 - - - -	- 14	
5	3.03 3.05	Miller 3 △ ← /	- 4 - W Compton 1	- - -	3- 18 - 19	Cowdrey square cuts for 4 Miller strikes Cowdrey on thigh Cowdrey c Archer, outswinger, 1st slip, 4 in 9 mins, 10 balls, 1 four *In the dressing-room, Hutton puts his head in his hands and stops watching.*
6		Archer 1 △ → /	- - - - - 1		- 20	
7		Miller 4 △ ← /	- - - - - -		- 20	
8		Archer 2 △ → /		- - - - - - 2	- 22	
9		Miller 5 △ ← /	- - - 1 - 1 1	- - 1 	- 25	*RAAF jets fly over the ground* May spoons catch to mid off area. Miller tries to get over to it.
10		Archer 3 △ → / Off spell 3-0-10-0	1	- - - 2 - - 4	- 32	May pulls for 4

161

MCC in Australia 1954-55 – FOURTH TEST

11		Miller 6 △ ← /	- - 2 - - - -		- 34	
12		Benaud 1 △ → /	- - - - - - -		- 34	
13		Miller 7 △ ← / Off spell 7-1-20-3	- - - 1	- - 3	- 38	
14		Benaud 2 △ → /	- - - 1 - 1	1	- 41	
15		JohnsTon 1 △ ← /		4 - - - - - -	- 45	May edges for 4
16		Benaud 3 △ → /	- - 1	- - - -	- 46	
17		JohnsTon 2 △ ← /	(3 lb) - - - -			
	3.56 3.58 4.00			W Bailey -	4- 49 - 49	May c Miller, extra cover, diving to left, hard flat drive, 26 in 71 mins, 75 balls, 1 four
		TEA	Comptn 10 55 mins 42 balls	Bailey 0 2 mins 1 ball	4- 49 79 mins 136 balls	

SESSION 47-5 IN 99 MINS, 170 BALLS

Compton was doubtful whether Miller had held onto the catch off May as he rolled over. He shouted for May to come back, but May did not hear over the din of the crowd and appeared satisfied that he was out. Miller would never claim a catch if he was doubtful about it. In fact Miller did drop the ball but Miller, and May, were of the opinion that he held it long enough to constitute a catch.

Miller has put the game back in the melting pot.

At some point, either the fall of the third wicket or during the tea interval, Hutton's nerve snapped for a moment. "We're done in" he said. Compton then grabbed his bat and said "I'll show who's done who".

MCC in Australia 1954-55 – FOURTH TEST

			Comptn 10	Bailey 0	4-49	
18	4.20	Benaud 4 △ → /	4 - - - - - -		- 53	Compton 4 square of cover, 53 up in 80 mins
19		JohnsTon 3 △ ← /		- - - - 4 - -	- 57	Bailey hooks long hop 4 over leg field
20		Benaud 5 △ → /	- - - - - - -		- 57	
21		JohnsTon 4 △ ← / Off spell (incl. tea) 4-2-8-1		- - - - - - -	- 57	
22	4.40	Benaud 6 △ → / Off spell (incl.tea) 6-2-10-0	- - (2 byes) - - - - 1	1	- 61	
23		Miller 8 △ ← /		- - - - - - -	- 61	Miller attacks Bailey with five close fielders.
24		JohnsTon 5 △ → /	- - 3 - - - -	- - - - 4 - -	- 68	Compton glances for 3 Bailey hooks one bounce into crowd
25	4.50	Miller 9 △ ← /	- - - 2 - - 2		- 72	Compton 2 past Harvey at cover Compton glances, superb throw by Burke
26		JohnsTon 6 △ → /	-	- - - - - 1 -	- 73	Bailey quick single to Miller at fine leg

MCC in Australia 1954-55 – FOURTH TEST

27		Miller 10 △←/ Off spell 3-1-14-0		2 - 3 - 2 - - 3	- 83	Bailey steers 2 through gully Bailey straight drive for 3
28		JohnsTon 7 △→/		- - - - - 3 -	- 86	*Benaud at gully is hit on body as ball bounces unevenly.* Compton late cut for 3
29		Archer 4 △←/ Off spell 1-0-4-0		- 2 1 - - - -	- 89	
30	5.15 5.17	JohnsTon 8 △→/ Spell 4-0-12-1		- - 1 - W Evans - (1 bye) - -	5- 90 - 91	Bailey lbw, slower ball, driving, 15 in 57 mins, 49 balls, 2 fours Evans swings hard and misses
31	 5.20	Miller 11 △←/ Spell 0.4-0-6-0		- 2 - 4		Chancy second run to 3rd man, Compton reluctant Evans 4 to mid wkt
			Comptn 34 115 mins 97 balls 1 four	Evans 6 3 mins 5 balls 1 four	5- 97 139 mins 244 balls	Attendance: 23,206. Attendance for 5 days: 162,499, receipts £A 28,703

SESSION 42-1 IN 60 MINS, 108 BALLS

Compton loses £5 offered by someone else for hitting the winning runs. If he told him, Evans would have let Compton do it and halve the proceeds

England Second innings

* L. Hutton	c Davidson b Miller	5	11 mins, 6 balls, 0 fours	2-10
W.J. Edrich	b Miller	0	2 mins, 2 balls	1-3
P.B.H. May	c Miller b Johnston	26	71 mins, 75 balls, 1 four	4-49
M.C. Cowdrey	c Archer b Miller	4	9 mins, 10 balls, 1 four	3-18
D.C.S. Compton	not out	34	115 mins, 97 balls, 1 four	
T.E. Bailey	lbw b Johnston	15	57 mins, 49 balls, 2 fours	5-90
+ T.G. Evans	not out	6	3 mins, 5 balls, 1 four	
Extras	(b 3, lb 4)	7		
TOTAL	(5 wkts)	97	139 mins, 30.4 overs, 244 balls	

BOWLING

Miller	10.4	2	40	3
Davidson	2	0	7	0
Archer	4	0	13	0
Benaud	6	2	10	0
Johnston	8	2	20	2

England win by five wickets

Arlott: Compton and Bailey's determination have seen England through. If Lindwall were playing, the result might have been different. JohnSon was so injured that he could hardly pick up the ball or throw more than 15 yards. He should have been off the field: Favell, a fine fieldsman, could have substituted for him; and Miller, as captain on the field, might have inspired a miracle.

Swanton: Nine weeks after the humiliating defeat at Brisbane England have won the series and retained the Ashes.

Moyes: On a slowish good wicket, England were superior in every department except fielding. Hutton followed a policy of attrition in batting and made Cowdrey do the same.

Ross's view of this match comes entirely second-hand, from his bed in Calvary Hospital, after an operation for appendicitis. He managed to toddle to a seat in the ground to watch England score 97 runs on the final afternoon

MCC in Australia 1954-55 – FOURTH TEST

Man of the match is hard to decide in this Test. The contenders are Hutton, Cowdrey, Compton, Bailey, Tyson and Appleyard. After some cogitation, I give it to Appleyard.

Hutton devoted nearly an hour to the questions of the Press in the dining room of the George Giffen Pavilion. He again attributed victory to the four young men of the side, May, Cowdrey, Statham and Tyson, and to Evans' wicket-keeping, said how happy he was to see the old stalwarts Compton and Evans in at the end and paid tribute to Keith Miller's bowling. He told the BBC early morning radio audience that his team were tired but happy. He praised the bowling of Statham and Tyson and of Miller "who gave us a lot to worry about". He denied that he deliberately slowed down the over-rate, thanked the crowds for their patience and said that his young fast bowlers needed a lot of help with field placings. [Does that include Statham and Bailey who made their Test debuts in 1951 and 1949 respectively?] Congratulatory telegrams were sent from Pudsey Leeds, and from MCC assistant secretary S.C.Griffith. Frank's mother Mrs.Violet Tyson has been staying with friends in Blackpool to avoid publicity.

The MCC hotel in Glenelg was an entertaining place to be this evening. At least sixty bottles of champagne were sacrificed to the jollity. Hutton did his best to join the celebrations though he is mentally and physically exhausted and, after he was asked why he was "born so beautiful" or "born at all" he renders *On Ilkly Moor bah t'at,* and then, with Bill Edrich "Susie, Susie, sitting in the shoe-shine shop". At 10.30am (GMT) Cowdrey made a three–minute call costing £1 per minute to Penelope Chiesman at her Chislehurst home to wish her a happy 22nd birthday. Evans climbed up a marble pillar in the hotel foyer, winning a bet of £100, then losing it on a toss of coin for double or quits. Edrich disappeared with an old RAF comrade and was not seen again until hauled out of his bed to the plane to Melbourne two days later. The morning after the Test Statham went for a walk and found Hutton sitting alone on a bench on Glenelg beach. The two sat and smoked in silence.

Thursday 3 February

The Australian touring team to go to West Indies is announced. Johnson remains captain and there are no new faces except Peter Burge of Queensland (whose father is the manager).

A delayed morning flight took the happy Englishmen to Melbourne, for lunch at the Windsor Hotel, then a fleet of hired cars took them to the garden town of Yallourn, built beside an open-cut coal mine owned by the Electricity Commission. There they had to contend with oppressive heat, brown coal dust and a plague of flies.

MCC v Victorian Country XI at Yallourn, February 5 and 7

In continuing heat, MCC found more opposition from the local flies than the local cricketers. One of them (a fly that is) made Loader ill when he swallowed it. The MCC manager Geoffrey Howard played and scored 0 not out having run out Wardle.

VICTORIAN COUNTRY XI 182 (W.Young 56, Loader 4-29, Wardle 5-46) and 99 (Wardle 7-45). MCC 307-8 dec (Hutton 75, Simpson 59, Graveney 50, Edrich 36). MCC WON BY AN INNINGS AND 26 RUNS.

MCC v Victoria at Melbourne, February 11, 12, 14 and 15.

Rain ruined this match, with play under dark-clouded skies only on Saturday. It was perfect wicket, but Victoria were reduced to 39 for 6. The captain Sam Loxton was joined by bespectacled Dick in a stand of 53. (Ian Johnson rested himself as a precaution though he played for his club). There was time for Edrich to fail again. He was lbw to Bill Johnston in what turned out to be the latter's last first class match in Australia. Trevor Bailey found that he had broken a finger when fielding. This is the last cricket match at MCG until 1957. After the 1955 Football season, the pitch is to be dug up for the Olympics.

VICTORIA 113 (S.J.E.Loxton 27, W.A.Dick 41, Statham 3-23, Bailey 3-22, Appleyard 3-14). MCC 90-1 (Simpson 33*, May 33*). MATCH DRAWN

In Perth, the last Sheffield Shield match of the season, Western Australia v South Australia, rain prevented any play on the last two days. New South Wales are champions for the fifth time since the War.

MCC v New South Wales at Sydney, February 18, 19, 21 and 22

MCC came back to Sydney to complete the tour of Australia with a State match and the Fifth Test. Morris and Watson missed this game because of their vaccinations for touring the West Indies, and in came two youngsters, Peter Philpott a leg-spinner and Brian Booth, a tall thin shy Hurlstone Agricultural High School teacher. Miller won the toss and Bedser from the Hill end dismissed Briggs with a lifter and had Burke caught at short leg in his first over. In Bedser's third over Benaud swung hard to the onside and Wardle ran from behind square along the fence to take a diving left-hand catch at absolutely full stretch. Miller and Simpson edged drives to first slip and the Shield Champions were 26 for 5 on a blameless pitch. Philpott, short and stocky, joined the lanky nervous Booth and eased him into form. Philpott scored 46 out of their 83 partnership in 128 minutes, falling to an Evans leg-side stumping. Thereafter only Crawford gave Booth any support. NSW were all out for 172 in 291 minutes.

MCC came out to bat in dour light. Wilson was bowled first ball, and May was caught behind. Loader came in and after facing one ball appealed successfully against the light. On Saturday morning, dull

MCC in Australia 1954-55 – FOURTH TEST

again, Miller's masterly captaincy reduced MCC to 35 for 5. Graveney and then Evans helped Hutton to stage a recovery. At 130 Hutton late cut a leg-spinner off the middle of his bat and Simpson moved and dived to his right to catch him one-handed. Simpson set new and unsurpassed standards for slip fielding. Wardle hit hard for 15 minutes till he hit straight to cover. Tyson was called for a run by Evans but lost the race with Briggs. The first innings scores were tied.

Bowling with the wind, Tyson made Briggs play on for a pair, but Graveney dropped Simpson at slip. And NSW were 18 for 1 at the close. Simpson, so timid in the first innings, dominated the scene on Monday in a stand of 159 with Burke. Burke scored only 15 in the 110 minutes before lunch. Tyson was not bowling. In the afternoon light drizzle was falling with Simpson on 98. At this point, according to a later MCC Press statement, Hutton said to the umpires "What about it?"; the umpires replied "it's up to you". Hutton lead his team off. The batsmen, who had not been consulted, stayed put. By now the rain had stopped and the Umpires ordered the MCC team to resume the game, which they did at once. Simpson then played a silly shot and was stumped. The crowd who had already booed when the English went off were irate. The umpires version of events was that Umpire Wigzell had said some time earlier "It's up to *the players*", and that when Hutton went off, they assumed that the batsmen had agreed with Hutton about the rain - noticing that the batsmen did not go off they then found out that they had not been consulted and ordered the game to re-start. According to the tour playing conditions, going off for bad weather was to be agreed between the fielding captain and the batsmen, and the umpires would decide only if the two sides disagreed.

Benaud made 57 in 46 minutes, Miller 71 in 57 minutes against the attack missing Tyson and Loader. Miller declared setting MCC 315 to win. Graveney and Simpson survived to the close at 26 for 0. On the final day from 68 for 3 May and Hutton took MCC past lunch to 145 though May had great difficulty in reading Benaud's leg-breaks and 'bosies'. Lambert was hit on the nose in keeping to Benaud's first over after lunch and Simpson took over the gloves. Miller, who had bowled little up to now because of the effects of his West Indies inoculations, came on and at once bowled May playing across the line – 145-4. Cowdrey came in wearing a sweater because he had 'flu. At 189 Hutton was caught at second attempt by Simpson behind the stumps. Evans stayed with Cowdrey till tea when 95 were needed in 110 minutes. Miller was now feeling too weak to bowl and Crawford was handicapped by a bruised heel. Miller gave the bowling to an astonished Booth, who soon had Cowdrey caught down the leg side by the deputy wicket-keeper. Wardle was caught at deep mid-off by the airborne Philpott, Evans, Tyson and Loader were caught in the slips. With an hour to spare MCC lost the gallant battle and much praise was heaped on Miller's bold, imaginative, intelligent and lucky captaincy.

New South Wales

R.E.Briggs c Evans b Bedser	0	b Tyson	0
J.W.Burke c Cowdrey b Bedser	0	c Graveney b Wardle	62
R.B.Simpson c Graveney b Tyson	6	st Evans b Wardle	98
R. Benaud c Wardle b Bedser	1	(5) st Evans b Wardle	57
* K.R.Miller c Graveney b Loader	11	(6) c May b Bedser	71
P.I.Philpott st Evans b Bedser	46	(8) b Wardle	11
B.C.Booth not out	74	c Evans b Bedser	0
A.K.Davidson c Graveney b Bedser	9	(4) c Cowdrey b Wardle	0
P.A.Crawford c Evans b Wilson	19	not out	0
+ O.Lambert c Cowdrey b Wardle	1		
J.C.Treanor c Graveney b Wilson	0		
Extras (b 1, lb 3, nb 1)	5	(lb 10, w 2, nb 3)	15
TOTAL (all out, 291 mins, 57.1 overs)	172	- (8 wkts dec, 327 mins, 70.2 overs)	314

WICKETS. – 1-0, 2-3, 3-3, 4-16, 5-26, 6-109, 7-127, 8-167, 9-168, 10-172.
1-2, 2-161, 3-161, 4-196, 5-260, 6-263, 7-314, 8-314.

BOWLING. – Bedser 20-3-57-5; Tyson 16-4-27-1; Loader 12-2-56-1; Wardle 8-2-26-1; Wilson 1.1-0-1-2.
Bedser 22.2-4-87-2; Tyson 9-2-24-1; Loader 10-2-28-0; Wardle 25-0-118-5; Wilson 4-0-42-0.

MCC

R.T.Simpson c Briggs b Davidson	6	c Davidson b Benaud	24
J.V.Wilson b Miller	0	(4) b Davidson	4
P.B.H.May c Lambert b Crawford	3	b Miller	42
P.J.Loader b Davidson	0	(11) c Benaud b Treanor	8
T.W.Graveney c Lambert b Davidson	35	(2) lbw b Benaud	28
M.C.Cowdrey c Lambert b Davidson	12	c Simpson (wk) b Booth	33
* L.Hutton c Simpson b Treanor	48	(5) c Simpson (wk) b Burke	59
+ T.G.Evans b Crawford	40	(7) c Miller b Davidson	39
J.H.Wardle c Crawford b Treanor	16	(8) c Philpott b Treanor	12
F.H.Tyson run out (Briggs)	3	(9) c Benaud b Treanor	0
A.V.Bedser not out	2	(10) not out	0
Extras (b 1, lb 1, nb 5)	7	- (b 13, lb 3, w 1, nb 3)	20
TOTAL (all out, 243 mins, 52 overs)	172	- (all out, 297 mins, 71.7 overs	269

MCC in Australia 1954-55 – FOURTH TEST

WICKETS. -- 1-1, 2-4, 3-10, 4-13, 5-35, 6-94, 7-130, 8-153, 9-157, 10-172.
BOWLING. - Crawford 15-3-47-2; Miller 10-0-31-1; Davidson 12-3-25-4; Treanor 11-4-44-2; Benaud 3-0-10-0; Philpott 1-0-8-0.

WICKETS. – 1-36, 2-63, 3-68, 4-145, 5-189, 6-222, 7-250, 8-261, 9-261, 10-269.
Crawford 8-0-37-0; Miller 5-0-15-1; Davidson 13-1-43-2; Benaud 21-7-62-2; Philpott 6-2-22-0; Treanor 13.7-7-54-3; Burke 3-1-6-1; Booth 2-1-10-1.

NEW SOUTH WALES WON BY 45 RUNS

FIFTH TEST AT SYDNEY

(25, (26), (28) Feb, 1, 2, 3 March

For the Fifth and non-decisive Test, Australia dropped Morris, Burke and Johnston, and in come Watson, Burge and Lindwall. The two newcomers have been selected for the tour of West Indies.

William J. WATSON (NSW) aged 24, a right-handed opener who scored 155 against MCC at the start of the season.

Peter J.P. BURGE (Queensland), aged 23, tall but stocky strong-armed right hand middle order batsman who showed promise in his appearances for his State.

England foresaw serious selection problems, Tyson not fully fit, Bailey having a broken finger and Cowdrey suffering $100°$ with influenza in a nursing home. All were included in the XIII announced which was the XI at Adelaide plus Graveney and Bedser.

During the NSW match, a Sydney newspaper published photographs of Tyson showing his back foot well over the line in the act of delivery, allegedly proof that he was consistently no-balling. The fact is that many fast bowlers, Lindwall among them, 'drag' their back foot over the line having grounded behind the line. Umpires pass these deliveries as fair for the simple reason that it is impossible to have in view both the bowler's back foot and his arm at the moment when the ball is released

Two days before the scheduled start the rain came and stayed in Sydney, causing major flooding to large areas in the Hunter Valley and some loss of life. Les Favell's flight from Adelaide was diverted to Canberra because of the fog and rain in Sydney, and from there he shared a taxi arriving in Sydney at 10.30pm on the 'eve of the Test. He needn't have bothered. On Friday the first day, play was abandoned before it was due to start. Saturday was worse. Sunday was sunny and the groundsmen got to work. Monday saw more rain.

FOURTH DAY – Worth waiting for

Tuesday 1 March

On Tuesday morning there was no actual rain but little optimism. The wicket was of course completely protected and white and dry. The outfield is lush with areas where the water was still just under the surface. The captains inspected at 11.30 and again at 12.15 when they decided to start after lunch if no rain came.

England have left out Edrich, unsurprisingly, and a disappointed Bedser. Surely some consideration should have been given to Bedser who is now fully fit and bowled well in the State match, for whom the wicket would be suitable, and who might be allowed to play one last Test match in Australia. Admittedly it was difficult to see who should be left out: it would have to be Wardle. Hutton chooses Graveney as his third, and least likely, opening partner of the Test series. Graveney finds out ten minutes before the start that he is playing and that he is opening. Cowdrey is now fit to play.

Australia leave out Archer who is top of their bowling averages

Australia win toss.

Umpires: M.J.McInnes and R.J.J.Wright

England First Innings

Odd overs \\→ from City (Pavilion) End
Even overs \\← from Hill End

			Hutton	Graveney		
1	2.00	Lindwall 1 \\→	-			
			4			Hutton 4 to fine leg
			2			Hutton 2 to fine leg
	2.03		W		1- 6	Hutton c Burge, bkwd short leg, juggling catch, 6 in 3 mins, 4 balls, 1 four.
			May			Burge's first touch of the ball in Test cricket
	2.05		-			
			-			
			-		1- 6	
2		Miller 1 \\←		2		Graveney 2 to the on
				4		Graveney straight drive for 4
				-		
				-		
				-		
				-		
				-	- 12	
3		Lindwall 2 \\→	-			
			-			
			-			
			-			
			-			
			-			
			-	- 12		

MCC in Australia 1954-55 – FIFTH TEST

4		Miller 2 \ ←		- 2 4 3 - 1 -	- 22	Graveney 2 to square leg Graveney straight drive for 4 Graveney pulls for 3 to fine leg May off mark, 1 to cover
5		Lindwall 3 \ →	1	- 1 - 1 - 1	- 26	
6		Miller 3 \ ←	1	- - - - -	- 27	
7		Lindwall 4 \ →		- - 2 - - 1	- 30	
8	2.40	Miller 4 \ ←		2 1 - - 4 -	- 37	May straight drive for 4
9		Lindwall 5 \ → Off spell 5-2-13-1		- - - - - - -	- 37	
10		Miller 5 \ ←	- - 4 1	- - - -	- 42	
11		Davidson 1 \ →	- - - - 1	- 1	- 44	
12		Miller 6 \ ← Off spell 6-0-34-0	- 1	1 - 3 - -	- 49	

MCC in Australia 1954-55 – FIFTH TEST

13		Davidson 2 \ →		- - 2 - - - -	- 51	51 up in 54 mins
14	3.00	JohnSon 1 \ ←	1	- - - - - - 4	- 56	50 stand in 55 mins
15		Davidson 3 \ →		- - 1 - - 4 -	- 61	
16		JohnSon 2 \ ←		- - - - 2 -	- 63	May mis-hits over mid on; Favell slow to go back for catch
17		Davidson 4 \ → Off spell 4-0-17-0		2 - - 2 4 - -	- 71	
18	3.15	JohnSon 3 \ ←	1	- - - 4 4 - -	- 80	Gravny pulls to midwkt for 4, 51 in 75 mins, 76 balls
19		Benaud 1 \ →		- - - 1 - - -	- 81	
20		JohnSon 4 \ ←		- - 2 - - - -	- 83	
21		Benaud 2 \ →	3	- - 3 - - -	- 89	

MCC in Australia 1954-55 – FIFTH TEST

Over	Time	Bowler	Batsman 1	Batsman 2	Score	Notes
22		JohnSon 5 \ ←	4 2 - - -			May drive high over mid on
		Off Spell 5-0-24-0				
	3.30		-		- 95	
		TEA	May 31 85 mins 83 balls	Gravny 58 90 mins 89 balls	1- 95 90 mins 176 balls	

Arlott: Putting England in was a mistake

Over	Time	Bowler	Batsman 1	Batsman 2	Score	Notes
			May 31	Gravny 58	1- 95	
23	3.50	Benaud 3 \ →		- - - 2 - - -	- 97	
24	3.56 4.00	Davidson 5 \ ←	- 1 4 4 - - 1	3	- 110	101 in 96 mins May straight drive for 4 May cover drive for 4, 103 stand in 95 mins
25		Benaud 4 \ →	- 2 - - - -		- 112	
26		Davidson 6 \ ←	- - 1	- - 1 1 (nb) - - -	- 115	
27		Benaud 5 \ →		2 - 2 - 1 - -	- 120	
28		Davidson 7 \ ←	- - -	- - 1 - - -	- 121	
29		Benaud 6 \ →	- - 1	- - 1 - - -	- 123	*Graveney is going through a difficult patch*

171

MCC in Australia 1954-55 – FIFTH TEST

30		Davidson 8 \ ←	-			
			-			
			-			
		Off	-			
		Spell 4-0-22-0	4			
			-			
	4.21		1		- 128	May 50 in 116 mins, 122 balls
31		Benaud 7 \ →	-			
			-			
			-			
			-			
			-			
			-			
			-		- 128	
32		Miller 7 \ ←	-	1		
			4			
			-			
			-			
			-			
			-			
			-		- 133	
33		Benaud 8 \ →	-			
			-			
			-			
			-			
			-			
			-			
			-		- 133	
34		Miller 8 \ ←	-			
			-			
			-			
			4			
			-			
			-			
			-		- 137	
35		Benaud 9 \ →	-			*Graveney fights his way back into his stride*
			-			
			2			
			-			
			-			
			4			
			-		- 143	
36		Miller 9 \ ←	-			
			1			
				1		
			-			
			-			
			-			
			-		- 145	
37		Benaud 10 \ →	-			Graveney c & b chance, past Benaud
			-			Graveney two stinging drives straight to
			-			Miller and JohnSon
		Off	-			
		spell (inc. tea)	4			Graveney cuts square off front foot for 4
		10-2-29-0	-			
			1			
			-		- 150	
38		Miller 10 \ ←	-			
			-			
			4			Graveney on drive 4
		Off	-			
	4.49	Spell 4-0-27-0	4			Gravny cover drive past Harvey, 150 stand
			4			Graveney straight drive 4
			-			Miller bowls deliberate long hop
	4.51		4		- 166	Grny sweeps full toss, 101, 151m, 148b

MCC in Australia 1954-55 – FIFTH TEST

Over	Time	Bowler	Batsman 1	Batsman 2	Score	Notes
39		Lindwall 6 \ →	- 2 1 - 3 - -	- 1	- 173	*All the Australians came up to congratulate Graveney at the end of he over*
40		JohnSon 6 \ ←	- - - - - - 3		- 176	
41		Lindwall 7 \ →	- - 3 - - -	3	- 182	
42	5.06 5.08 5.09 5.11	JohnSon 7 \ ←		- 2 4 W Cowdrey W Compton - -	2- 188 3- 188 - 188	Graveney lofted drive for 2 Graveney sweeps to leg for 4 Graveney c & b, hard drive to stomach, 111 in 166 mins, 157 balls, 14 fours Cowdrey c Maddocks wk, pushing out, 0 in 1 min, 1 ball
43		Lindwall 8 \ →	- - - - - -		- 188	
44		JohnSon 8 \ ←	- - - - - -		- 188	
45		Lindwall 9 \ → Off spell 4-1-21-0	- - 2 - 2 2 2		- 196	
46		JohnSon 9 \ ← Off spell 5-2-9-3	- - - - - - -		- 196	*Light now poor*
47	5.29	Benaud 11 \ → Spell 0.2-0-0-0	- W		4- 196	May c Davidson, pushing forward, 1st slip, 79 in 184 mins, 190 balls, 8 fours
		CLOSE		Comptn 0 18 mins 19 balls	4- 196 189 mins 371 balls	Attendance: 7,402

SESSION 101-2 IN 99 MINS, 195 BALLS

MCC in Australia 1954-55 – FIFTH TEST

Arlott: Graveney has played the most brilliant innings of the series, using his high back lift on the slow-paced pitch. Miller bowled deliberately to let him get his hundred.
Moyes: Graveney gave a masterly display of terrific driving, despite the damp outfield.
Fingleton: The opening position may suit Graveney; he just has to curb himself to be a terrific England player.
The MCC manager has declined a request from NSW treasurer Frank Cush to add two days onto the Test.

FIFTH DAY – Drifting to a draw

Wednesday 2 March

				Bailey	Comptn 0	3- 196	
47 ctd	11.30	Benaud 11 ctd \ → Off spell today 0.6-0-0-0		- - - - -		- 196	
48		Miller 11 \ ←		- 1 - - 4 -		- 201	Compton off mark, 1 to fine leg, after 22 mins Bailey hooks slower ball for 4
49		Lindwall 10 \ →		- - - 1 2 -		- 204	New ball
50		Miller 12 \ ←		- 1 - - - -		- 205	
51		Lindwall 11 \ →		- - - - 1 1		- 207	
52		Miller 13 \ ← Off spell 3-0-9-0		- 3 - - - -		- 210	
53		Lindwall 12 \ →		- - - - - -		- 210	
54		JohnSon 10 \ ←		3 - - 2	1 1	- 217	

174

MCC in Australia 1954-55 – FIFTH TEST

55		Lindwall 13 \→ Off spell 4-1-13-0	- 1	1 - - 4 - 2	- 225	
56		JohnSon 11 \←	- - 4 - - - -		- 229	
57		Davidson 9 \→		- - - - - - -	- 229	Compton almost bld playing no stroke
58		JohnSon 12 \←	- - - - - - -		- 229	
59		Davidson 10 \→		1 - - - 2 - -	- 232	
60		JohnSon 13 \←		- 4 - - - - -	- 236	
61		Davidson 11 \→	- - - - - - -		- 236	
62		JohnSon 14 \←		- - - - - - -	- 236	40 runs in first hour
63		Davidson 12 \→	- 1	- - - - - -	- 237	

MCC in Australia 1954-55 – FIFTH TEST

64		JohnSon 15 \ ← Off spell 4-1-15-0	- - - - - - -		- 237	
65		Davidson 13 \ → Off Spell 5-2-8-0	1	- 3 - - - -	- 241	
66		Benaud 12 \ ←	3 - - - - - -		- 244	
67		Miller 14 \ →	- - - - - - -		- 244	
68		Benaud 13 \ ← Off spell 2-0-5-0	- - - - 1	- - 1 - - -	- 246	50 stand in 87 mins
69		Miller 15 \ → Off Spell 2-1-1-0	1	- - - - -	- 247	
	1.00					
		LUNCH	Bailey 29 90 mins 98 balls	Comptn 22 108 mins 103 balls	4- 247 279 mins 553 balls	

SESSION 51 IN 90 MINS, 182 BALLS

Arlott: Compton and Bailey have made England completely safe but have also removed the small chance of victory.

Moyes: Compton should have taken the initiative this morning. England batted as if they were desperately fighting for a draw.

Miller and Whitington: the fielding was appalling.

Hughes: This dead bat morning was totally pointless. We expected England to give some entertainment to the crowd with the match safe. As it transpired, more runs would have allowed Hutton to declare at lunch and given time for England to win the series 4-1.

Bowes: Bailey and Compton did the right thing. Test cricket is not an exhibition match.

			Bailey 29	Comptn 22	4- 247	
70	1.40	Benaud 14 \ ←	- - - - - -		- 247	

MCC in Australia 1954-55 – FIFTH TEST

71		Lindwall 14 \ →		- 1 - - -	- 248	*Compton dropped by JohnSon at mid on, dolly catch*
72		Benaud 15 \ ←		- - - 1		*Compton should be stumped by Maddocks*
			2	- -	- 251	*Bailey dropped at slip by Davidson*
73		Lindwall 15 \ →		- - - 2 - - (1 lb)	- 254	*Crowd on the Hill are impatient for some action*
74		Benaud 16 \ ←	1	- 3 4 - - 3	- 265	*Compton edged through slips*
75		Lindwall 16 \ → Off Spell 3-0-4-0		- 1 - - - -	- 266	
76		Benaud 17 \ ←	1	1 - 2 1 -	- 271	
77	2.12	Davidson 14 \ →	1	3 - 4 - 2 -	- 281	*Compton 2 to third man, 50 in 140 mins, 133 balls*
78		Benaud 18 \ ←	1	- - 3 - - -	-285	
79		Davidson 15 \ →		- - - - - - -	- 285	

MCC in Australia 1954-55 – FIFTH TEST

Over	Time	Bowler	Batsman 1	Batsman 2	Score	Notes
80		Benaud 19 \ ←	1	- - - 1 - 2	- 289	
81		Davidson 16 \ →	3	- - - 3 -	- 295	
82	2.28	Benaud 20 \ ← Off spell 7-1-45-0	1	4 4 - - 4 4 1	- 313	100 stand in 137 mins Compton square cut for 4. 300 in 327m Compton off drive for 4 Compton sweeps for 4 Compton sweeps for 4
83		Davidson 17 \ →		2 - 3 - - - -	- 318	Compton dropped by Miller in slips
84		JohnSon 16 \ ←	1	- - 1 - - -	- 320	
85		Davidson 18 \ → Off spell 5-1-22-0		- - - - - - 1	- 321	74 in hour after lunch
86		JohnSon 17 \ ←	2 1	- - 1 - -	- 325	
87		Lindwall 17 \ →		- - - - - -	- 325	
88		JohnSon 18 \ ←	1	- - - - - -	- 326	

178

MCC in Australia 1954-55 – FIFTH TEST

Over	Time	Bowler	Batsman 1	Batsman 2	Score	Notes
89		Lindwall 18 \→	- 1	- - 3 - -	- 330	
90	3.02 3.04 3.05	JohnSon 19 \←	1 1	W Evans 1 - - 1	5- 330 - 334	Compton c & b, 84 in 190 mins, 196 balls, 8 fours. Special applause for Compton's last innings in Australia. Bailey 50 in 175 mins, 170 balls
91		Lindwall 19 \→	4 - 1 4	- 2 1 -	- 346	
92		JohnSon 20 \← Off spell 5-0-20-1	2 2 2 1	- 1 - 1	- 355	
93	3.18 3.20	Lindwall 20 \→	1	- 2 1 - W Wardle 1	6- 359 - 360	Evans c McDonald deliberately skied to mid on. 10 in 14 mins, 14 balls, 0 fours. Lindwall 99th wkt. Batsmen crossed
94		Davidson 19 \← Spell 1-0-3-0	- (1 b/lb) - 1 1	- (1 lb) 1 - (1 lb)	- 366	
95	3.28	Lindwall 21 \→ Spell 4.6-1-26-2	1 W	2 - 1 1	7- 371	Wardle 2, dropped by Dvdsn at long off. Bailey bld, moves clear to leg side, no stroke, 72 in 198 mins, 190 balls, 3 fours
	TEA			Wardle 5 8 mins 7 balls 0 fours	7- 371 387 mins 759 balls	

SESSION 124-3 IN 108 MINS, 206 BALLS

Bailey gave his wicket to Lindwall deliberately, prompted by Evans' suggestion. Lindwall's wife Peggy, his brother, two sisters and his 2½ year old son are all there.

Arlott: Bailey's gesture was so pleasant that one doubted whether one was watching an England Australia Test Match.

Moyes: It is a pity that Lindwall could not have achieved his 100 English wickets by normal means.

Barnes: This was not a gesture of sportsmanship, it subjugated Test cricket to a farcical celebration of statistical records.

Gilligan: The deliberate sacrifice of his wicket cheapens Lindwall's magnificent record.

Batchelor: Lindwall should have taken 100 wickets, not taken 98 and then been presented with two by Evans and Bailey

Peebles: One cannot begrudge Lindwall the gift of one wicket after such a career.

MCC in Australia 1954-55 – FIFTH TEST

England First innings

* L. Hutton	c Burge b Lindwall	6	3 mins, 4 balls, 1 four	1-6
T.W. Graveney	c & b Johnson	111	166 mins, 157 balls, 14 four	2-188
P.B.H. May	c Davidson b Benaud	79	184 mins, 190 balls, 8 fours	4-196
M.C. Cowdrey	c Maddocks b Johnson	0	1 min, 1 ball	3-188
D.C.S. Compton	c & b Johnson	84	190 mins, 196 balls, 8 fours	5-330
T.E. Bailey	b Lindwall	72	198 mins, 190 balls, 3 fours	7-371
+ T.G. Evans	c McDonald b Lindwall	10	14 mins 14 balls, 0 fours	6-359
J.H. Wardle	not out	5	8 mins, 7 balls, 0 fours	
Extras	(b 1, lb 3)	4		
TOTAL	(7 wkts dec)	371	387 mins, 94.6 overs, 759 balls	

F.H.Tyson, R. Appleyard and J.B. Statham did not bat

BOWLING

Lindwall	20.6	5	77	3
Miller	15	1	71	0
Davidson	19	3	72	0
JohnSon	20	5	68	3
Benaud	20	4	79	1

Australia First Innings

The target is 222 to avoid the follow on
Odd overs   → \   from Hill End
Even overs   ← \   from Pavilion End

			Watson	McDonald	
1	3.49	Tyson 1 → \	1 - - 6 - - -	- 7	Probably 2 + 4 overthrows
2		Statham 1 ← \	(4 byes) - 3 - - - 3 -	- 17	ball breaks from outside off and just misses leg stump
3		Tyson 2 → \ Off spell 2-0-15-0	1 4 - - 2 - 1	- 25	
4		Statham 2 ← \	- - - - - - -	- 25	*Watson hit on groin*
5		Appleyard 1 → \ Off spell 1-0-4-0	- - - - - - 4	- 29	
6		Statham 3 ← \	- - - - - 1 -	- 30	

MCC in Australia 1954-55 – FIFTH TEST

7		Wardle 1 →\	- - - - - -			- 30	
8		Statham 4 ←\ 4-1-16-0	- - - 1 - 3	4 1		- 39	
9		Wardle 2 →\	- - - - - 4 -			- 43	
10		Tyson 3 ←\	- - - 2 1 - - 2			- 48	
11		Wardle 3 →\	- - - - - - -			- 48	
12		Tyson 4 ←\	- - - - - 2 -			- 50	50 up in 57mins
13	4.52 4.54	Wardle 4 →\	- - 2 - W Favell - 1			1- 52 - 53	Watson bld, chinaman, 18 in 63 mins, 57 balls, 1 four
14	4.56 4.58	Tyson 5 ←\ Off spell 3-0-13-1	W Harvey - 3 - 3 - -			2- 53 - 59	Favell bld, playing back to half volley, fine inside edge, 1 in 2 mins, 3 balls
15		Wardle 5 →\	- - 1 - 1 - - 2			- 63	

MCC in Australia 1954-55 – FIFTH TEST

Over	Time	Bowler	Batsman 1	Batsman 2	Total	Notes
16		Appleyard 2 ←\	3 - - - 1 - -	- - - - - - -	- 67	
17		Wardle 6 →\		- - - (2 byes) - - - -	- 69	2 byes somewhere between overs 16.1 and 22.8
18		Appleyard 3 ←\	- 1 - - - - -		- 70	
19		Wardle 7 →\		- - - - - - -	- 70	
20		Appleyard 4 ←\	4 - - - 4 - -		- 78	
21		Wardle 8 →\ Spell 15-4-15-1		- - - - - 4 -	- 82	
22	5.30	Appleyard 5 ←\ Spell 4-1-13-1		- - - - - - -	- 82	
		CLOSE	Harvy 12 32 mins 27 balls	McDon 45 101 mins 89 balls	2- 82 101 mins 176 balls	Attendance: 13,357

Arlott: Australia have declined after a good start, against slow-turning spin. If an extra day were added, England would have an outside chance of winning.

Moyes: The Australians could not read Wardle's spin and he beat the bat frequently.

MCC in Australia 1954-55 – FIFTH TEST

SIXTH DAY – Oops!

Thursday 3 March
A small smattering of a crowd.

			Harvy 12	McDon 45	2- 82	
23	11.30	Wardle 9 →\	- - 1 -	- - - 1	 - 84	
24	11.39 11.41	Tyson 6 ←\	 W Miller - - -	- - 1	3- 85 - 85	Harvey c & b, too high on the blade, 13 in 41 mins, 32 balls, 1 four
25		Wardle 10 →\	-	- - - 2 - -	- 87	
26		Tyson 7 ←\	3 - - - -	1	- 91	Maddocks 50 off 105 balls
27		Wardle 11 →\		- - - - - 3	- 94	
28		Tyson 8 ←\ Off spell 3-1-5-1		- - - - - (1 bye) - - -	- 95	
29		Wardle 12 →\	- - 2	- - - 1	- 98	
30		Statham 5 ←\	4 -	- - - - 1	- 103	

MCC in Australia 1954-55 – FIFTH TEST

Over	Time	Bowler		Runs		Score	Notes
31		Wardle 13 →\ Off spell 5-0-23-0		3 - 1 - 2 2 1 4		- 116	
32		Statham 6 ←\		- - - 1 2 - -		- 119	
33		Appleyard 6 →\		- 3 - - - - -		- 122	
34		Statham 7 ←\ Off spell 3-0-9-0		- - - - - 1 -		- 123	
35	12.35 12.37	Appleyard 7 →\	(W) Burge	2 1 3 - - - -		4- 129 - 129	Miller run out, McDon called single to Cwdry at mid wkt, Miller too slow to beat wide throw to Evans, 19 in 54 mins, 34 balls, 2 fours
36		Wardle 14 ←\		- 1 - 4 - 2 2		- 138	
37	12.44 12.46	Appleyard 8 →\	W Benaud	- - W - 3 - 2		5- 138 - 143	McDonald c May at deepish sq leg, hooking against spin, 72 in 175 mins, 157 balls, 5 fours 1 six
38	12.50 12.52	Wardle 15 ←\	W Maddocks	- - - - 4 W -		6- 147 - 147	Benaud bld btwn bat and pad by spinning chinaman, 7 in 4 mins, 9 balls, 1 four
39		Appleyard 9 →\		- - - - - - -		- 147	

MCC in Australia 1954-55 – FIFTH TEST

40		Wardle 16 ←\ Spell 3-1-13-1		- - - - - - -	- 147	
41	 1.00	Appleyard 10 →\ Off spell 5-1-18-0	- - - - - - 4		- 151	
		LUNCH	Burge 14 23 mins 27 balls	Madoks 0 8 mins 9 balls	6- 151 191 mins 328 balls	

SESSION 69-4 IN 90 MIN 152 BALLS
Woodcock: McDonald scratched and snicked his way to 72.

			Burge 14	Madoks 0	6- 151	
42	1.40	Tyson 9 ←\ Off spell 1-0-5-0	- 2 - 1 1	- 1 	- 156	
43	 1.50 1.52	Wardle 17 →\	 - W Davidson - - 1	- (1 lb) 1 	7- 157 - 159	Burge c Appleyard, long hop swung to short mid wkt, 17 in 33 mins, 34 balls, 2 fours. Batsmen crossed
44		Appleyard 11 ←\	- (2 byes) - - 1 - - 2		- 164	
45		Wardle 18 →\	- - - - - -		- 164	
46		Appleyard 12 ←\	- - - - - -	- 1 	- 165	
47		Wardle 19 →\		- - - - 4 -	- 169	

MCC in Australia 1954-55 – FIFTH TEST

48		Appleyard 13 ← \	3 - 3 - - - -		- 175	
49		Wardle 20 → \	- 4 1 - 1 4 - -		- 185	
50		Appleyard 14 ← \	- 1 - - - - 1		- 187	
51		Wardle 21 → \	- 2 - - - - -		- 189	
52		Appleyard 15 ← \	- - 4 - - 2 - -		- 195	
53		Wardle 22 → \	- 2 - - - - - -		- 197	
54		Appleyard 16 ← \ Off spell 6-0-19-0	- - 1 - - - -		- 198	Unexplained change of ends
55	2.38 2.40	Wardle 23 → \ Off spell 10-2-39-3	- 4 - W JohnSon 2 - - -		8- 202 - 204	Maddocks c Appleyard, low at short mid wkt, 32 in 66 mins, 65 balls, 4 fours 18 needed to avoid follow on
56		Tyson 10 ← \	- - 4 - - - -		- 208	New ball

186

MCC in Australia 1954-55 – FIFTH TEST

Over	Time	Bowler	Batsman	Runs	Score	Notes
57		Statham 8 →\ Off spell 1-0-4-0		4 - - - - - - (1 bye)	- 213	
58		Tyson 11 ←\ Off spell 2-0-8-0		- - - - 2 1 1	- 217	
59	3.02 3.04	Wardle 24 →\	W Lindwall 1	- - - -	9 – 217 - 218	Davidson c Evans wk, googly, Dvdsn looks surprised, 18 in 70 mins, 61 balls, 1 fours.
60		Statham 9 ←\ Off spell 1-0-2-0		- - 1 - - 1 -	- 220	Four runs needed to avoid follow on
61	3.12	Wardle 25 →\ Spell 1.4-0-2-1		- 1 - - (W)	10- 221	Two needed to avoid follow on Graveney makes great stop at slip JohnSon run out. Ldwl stroke to Cmptn at sq cover, Jsn sent bank, slips, throw to Wardle. 11 in 32 mins, 25 balls, 1 four
	TEA			Lindwl 2 8 mins 7 balls	10- 221 283 mins 484 balls	

SESSION 70-6 IN 92 MINS, 156 BALLS

JohnSon's average is halved by the run out from 116 to 58.

Australia First innings

W. Watson	b Wardle	18	63 mins, 57 balls, 1 four	1-52
C.C. McDonald	c May b Appleyard	72	175 mins, 157 balls, 5 fours 1 six	5-138
L.E. Favell	b Tyson	1	2 mins, 3 balls	2-53
R.N. Harvey	c & b Tyson	13	41 mins, 32 balls, 1 four	3-85
K.R. Miller	run out (Cowdrey/Evans)	19	54 mins, 34 balls, 2 fours	4-129
P.J. Burge	c Appleyard b Wardle	17	33 mins, 34 balls, 2 fours	7-157
R. Benaud	b Wardle	7	4 mins, 9 balls, 1 four	6-147
+ L.V. Maddocks	c Appleyard b Wardle	32	66 mins, 65 balls, 4 fours	8-202
A.K. Davidson	c Evans b Wardle	18	70 mins, 61 balls, 1 fours	9-217
* I.W. Johnson	run out (Compton /Wardle)	11	32 mins, 25 balls, 1 four	10-221
R.R. Lindwall	not out	2	8 mins, 7 balls	
Extras	(b 10, lb 1)	11		
TOTAL	(10 wkts – all out)	221	283 mins, 60.4 overs, 484 balls	

BOWLING

Tyson	11	1	46	2
Statham	9	1	31	0
Appleyard	16	2	54	1
Wardle	24.4	6	79	5

MCC in Australia 1954-55 – FIFTH TEST

Australia Second Innings

Australia follow on against England for the first time since 1938

Odd overs → \ from Hill End
Even overs ← \ from Pavilion End

			Watson	McDonald		
1	3.33	Statham 1 → \	- 1 - - - - -	 - 1		
2		Tyson 1 ← \	- - - - - - -	 - 1		Tyson shortens his run to save time
3		Statham 2 → \	2 - - - 3 - -	 - 6		
4		Tyson 2 ← \ Off spell 2-1-6-0	- - - 2 - - 4	 - 12		
5		Statham 3 → \	- 2 - - - -			
	3.59		W Favell		1 - 14	Watson c Graveney, 1st slip, 3 in 26 mins, 20 balls
6	4.01	Wardle 1 ← \	- 4 - - - - -	 - 18		
7		Statham 4 → \	- - - - - 1 -	 - 19		
8		Wardle 2 ← \	4 - - 4 - -			Favell sweeps for 4 Favell sweeps for 4
	4.12		W Harvey		2 - 27	Favell c Graveney, slip, 9 in 11 mins, 15 balls, 2 fours

MCC in Australia 1954-55 – FIFTH TEST

#	Time	Bowler	Batsman	Runs	Total	Notes
9	4.14	Statham 5 → \ Off spell 5-0-11-0		1 - - - 1 - -	- 29	
10	4.21 4.23	Wardle 3 ← \	W Miller	- - - 1 - 1	3- 29 - 31	Harvey c & b, driving, twice in one day, 1 in 7 mins, 9 balls 67 mins play left
11		Tyson 3 → \		- - - - - - -	- 31	
12		Wardle 4 ← \		1	- 1 2 - - -	- 35	
13		Tyson 4 → \		1	1 - - - 1 - -	- 38	
14		Wardle 5 ← \		1	- 1 - - 3 -	- 43	
15		Tyson 5 → \ Off spell 3-1-14-0		1 2 4	- 1 - 1 3 -	- 54	
16		Wardle 6 ← \		2	- - 1 - - -	- 57	
17		Graveney 1 → \		1	- - - - - -	- 58	

MCC in Australia 1954-55 – FIFTH TEST

18		Wardle 7 ← \	4	4 - 1 - - -	- 67	
19	4.54 4.56	Graveney 2 → \	1	- - W Burge 3 - - -	4- 67 - 71	McDonald c Evans wk, cutting leg break, 37 in 81 mins, 75 balls, 3 fours 34 mins play left
20		Wardle 8 ← \	- 1 4 2 - - -		- 78	*Hutton refuses a drinks interval*
21		Graveney 3 → \	4 4 - 1 - - -		- 87	
22	5.05 5.07	Wardle 9 ← \		W Benaud - - - - - 1	5- 87 - 88	Miller bld, aiming a vast sweep, 28 in 42 mins, 37 mins, 4 fours 23 mins play left
23		Graveney 4 → \	- - 4 4 - - -		- 96	
24		Wardle 10 ← \		- - - 1 - -	- 97	
25		Graveney 5 → \	1	- 1 - - 1 -	- 100	
26		Wardle 11 ← \		- - - - - -	- 100	

190

MCC in Australia 1954-55 – FIFTH TEST

27		Graveney 6 →\ Off spell 6-0-34-1	- - 4 - 4 - 1		- -109	
28		Wardle 12 ←\ Spell 21-1-53-3	1 - 1 - - 1 4		- 116	
29	5.29	Hutton 1 →\ Spell 0.6-0-2-1	- 1 - - 1 W		6- 118	Benaud almost bowled Benaud bld, 'bailer' 22 in 22 mins, 35 balls, 4 fours
		CLOSE		Burge 18 33 mins 39 balls 2 fours	6- 118 116 mins 230 balls	Attendance: 8,905 Attendance for match (3 days): 29,844, receipts £A 4,284

Australia Second innings

W. Watson	c Graveney b Statham	3	26 mins, 20 balls	1-14
C.C. McDonald	c Evans b Graveney	37	81 mins, 75 balls, 3 fours	4-67
L.E. Favell	c Graveney b Wardle	9	11 mins, 15 balls, 2 fours	2-27
R.N. Harvey	c & b Wardle	1	7 mins, 9 balls	3-29
K.R. Miller	b Wardle	28	42 mins, 37 mins, 4 fours	5-87
P.J. Burge	not out	18	33 mins, 39 balls, 2 fours	
R. Benaud	b Hutton	22	22 mins, 35 balls, 4 fours	6-118
Extras		0		
TOTAL	(6 wkts)	118	116 mins, 28.6 overs, 230 balls	

+ L.V.Maddocks, A.K.Davidson, *I.W.Johnson and R.R.Lindwall did not bat

BOWLING

Statham	5	0	11	1
Tyson	5	2	20	0
Wardle	12	1	51	3
Graveney	6	0	34	1
Hutton	0.6	0	2	1

Match drawn

Only two men are in the frame for man of the match: Graveney and Wardle. Because he provided the only spectacular stroke-play in this series of grey batting, Graveney gets it.

Swanton: Badly as Australian batted there was never enough time for defeat.

Arlott: Thanks to some capable but not great bowling by Wardle on a slow spinning pitch, and to poor batting, England almost won a game which should have been an anti-climactic boring draw.

Peebles: This match signifies little and there was never any chance of a result

Moyes: England fielders ran to their places, Tyson cut his run to nine yards. Hutton should have used Appleyard in the second innings.

Barnes: Wardle spun the ball and he kept an excellent length.

Arlott: England were slightly the better of two indifferent teams and won because of the determined spirit. Hutton made superb tactical use of his only two strike weapons, Tyson and Statham, and kept them always fresh and ready.

Wellings: Wardle concentrated on wrist spin, chinamen and googlies, and although his length and direction were variable, the batsmen were puzzled by him

Fingleton: Wardle's googly, or 'bosie' was apparent from a long way off but the batsmen tied themselves in all sorts of knots.

FAREWELL

At 6pm, the MCC players were presented with cigarette cases by the NSW Cricket Association. At 10pm, they left for the airport and soon after midnight, having been seen off by Ian Johnson and Keith Miller, they were in the air on the way to New Zealand. There was one week between the ending of the Test series and the departure of the *Orsova* for those who were going home to England. Denis Compton went to Melbourne then flew off to South Africa to join his wife. (Interesting to note, the wives of Len Hutton, Godfrey Evans and Trevor Bailey came out to Australia in the later stages of the tour.) In New Zealand they easily beat Canterbury, Wellington and New Zealand in both Test matches. In the Auckland Test, the home side were bowled out for 26, the lowest innings total in Test history.

On this tour there was a very noticeable step in the eventual decline in over rates which have been the major problem with Test cricket in the last 30 years. Much of the blame has been attributed to Hutton for this and the figures certainly bear this out. Emphasis on fast bowlers, deliberation in field placings, consultations with bowlers between and during overs, bowlers fielding in the deep and having a long walk to and from their bowling marks. Some like Wellings suggest that Hutton learnt these tricks from watching Bradman in 1946-47

In his 1984 book Hutton denied that he deliberately slowed down the rate. He learnt from Bradman and other opposing captains the value of talking to the young fast bowlers and helping them with their field placings. In Australia the noise of the crowd was such that he could not talk to his players from a distance. An incident during an innings by Neil Harvey on the first day of the Adelaide Test has been used as evidence against him. Hutton says that he did tell Tyson to slow down the tempo, because Harvey had the effect of subconsciously inducing bowlers to quicken up the over rates when he was in aggressive mood. He said to Tyson "Ease up Frank, take your time. You're doing exactly what he wants you to do".

Alan McGilvray, the Australian radio commentator, says that when he suggested at the start of the tour that Australia should win the series, Hutton said "We will win" Why? "Because we'll give them less balls to hit than they give us".

In an article called "Blame the Yawns on Hutton", in Pollard's *Six and Out* (Angus & Robertson 1965), Arthur Morris claims that time wasting was started by Hutton in 1953 and developed on the 1954-55 tour, and Trevor Bailey was his willing accomplice. He describes Hutton as an unimaginative captain - make as few decisions as possible, wait and see, never take a risk.

I must say that the statistics compiled for this Book below do present a powerful case for the accusation of slowing down the over-rates. England provided 22 balls per hour less than Australia did about 14 overs fewer in a five-hour day. In the first-class matches outside the Tests MCC bowled about 102 balls per hour; in the Tests England bowled 91 balls per hour.

And yet, not only by his results is Hutton's reputation secured. The journalists who watched, and the players who served under him all give him the highest praise, although there are three instances of surprisingly unprofessional behaviour chronicled in this Book; his indecision when Australia were making hay in the run chase in the Headingley Test of 1953, his unwillingness to get out of bed on the morning of the Third Test at Melbourne, and his despair at Adelaide when Miller threatened to stop England getting 94 to win. But his handling of his attack in the second innings of the Second, Third and Fourth Tests, when England were so close to the precipice, was masterly.

Hutton was fêted on his eventual return to England: no longer were voices raised against him. He was appointed captain for all five Tests at home against South Africa in 1955, but fibrositis in his back prevented him from playing in any of them. May got the job by default. If Hutton had kept going, as he might have done if fit, until the end of the 1956 series, Cowdrey might have been his successor.

Miller and Whitington, writing at the end of the 1954-55 series prophetically compared the battle-worn Hutton and the tall young, handsome dapper May to Britain's aged Prime Minister Sir Winston Churchill and his Deputy Sir Anthony Eden. By the time that May captained England, Churchill had, in April, at last stood down for Eden.

May, Cowdrey, Statham and above all Tyson were the young players who carried off the victory for England, and all went on to great careers for England, except, oddly, Tyson. The Typhoon, as he quickly became known, suffered injury and in competition with Trueman he could not reach similar heights again. But his name will forever be synonymous with 1954-55 as Botham's is with 1981. Bailey was wholly in tune with Hutton's philosophy and tactics and played his role to perfection, being the most decisive contributor in the two series covered by this Book. Compton came through disastrous luck to finish the tour in comparative triumph; of course he had to be there again in the middle when the series was won at Adelaide, but he struggled for fluency against the best bowling as he had never done in his golden years. Evans was at his best behind and in front of the stumps and stood unchallenged for several years to come. Appleyard was the surprise success of the tour, a very English type cutter of the ball who took vital wickets on the dry wickets of Australia. Graveney had a disappointing tour until his classic innings at Sydney when the pressure was off. Wardle did more with the bat than with the ball until he got some turn on the dampish wicket at Sydney. The rest of the touring party achieved little of note, Bedser for reasons much discussed, and it is strange that the most successful English side to tour Australia since the war should actually be not that illustrious. Consider those left at home: Trueman, Lock, Laker, Watson, Sheppard.

For Johnson it had been a difficult season, because he lost the series and because he never had the support of the general public in Australia. And yet it is difficult to see how he could have done any better, as captain and player. He scored vital runs consistently, took several wickets and was able to tie down the England batsman for long time. If most of his victims were tailenders, that is a valuable contribution: witness the Second Test where with Johnson absent, England's last wicket partnerships in each innings made the different. His captaincy in the field was positive and intelligent and basically he was let down by his batsman. But he led Australia to defeat in England in 1956 and goes down in history as one of Australia's least esteemed leaders. Cardus thought that Australia were handicapped in this series by having second rate all-rounders: mediocrity on one department and mediocrity in another add up to a sum no higher than mediocrity. Although Lindwall and Miller could not be at top flight for as long as in their younger days, and the younger bowlers, Benaud and Davidson disappointed, Australia were not let down by their bowling and fielding. It was their batting which failed. Batsmen with high backlifts like Hole, Miller, Morris were not best suited to the speed of Tyson and Statham. Harvey could not capture his best form against England. Ultimately it was timidity and lack of application in five out of six innings in the three middle Tests which settled the series.

This was (I think) the first Ashes series in history in which the playing regulations required the wicket to be covered at all times to protect it from rain. There was virtually no interference from the weather, not even from bad light, until the Fifth Test when the series was decided. Yet in few other battles between England and Australia have been so dominated by the bowlers. No single batsman on either side rose above struggle.

One odd feature of this series is the total absence of any controversy concerning the umpires. The number of disputed decisions could be counted on the fingers of one hand and none of them created much fuss. Whereas in England most umpires were paid and former county cricketers, in Australia they were neither. Only three umpires were used in the series: Colin McCoy, whose test debut was the Test in his native Brisbane, Mel McInnes from Adelaide, and Ronald Wright.

There was one major potential controversy, the watering of the Melbourne wicket during the Third Test, which might not have been forgotten today if events had turned out differently. Watering was done for the reputation of the groundsman and not to favour Australia, but if, say, Australia's last two wickets had added another 100 runs on the easier pitch on the Monday morning, and the wicket were beginning to deteriorate again when England batted, and Australia had then won, there is a possibility that that the MCC management would have demanded that the match be abandoned or declared void. As it was, England won and no murmur of protest came from the English. Little more was heard about it. Indeed the English magazine, *The Cricketer*, does not even mention it in its reports on the tour, except obliquely by Fingleton.

MCC in Australia 1954-55

Epitome of the Tests
(8-ball overs)

In the following Test statistics, for the purposes of balls received by an individual, no-balls are included (since the batsman can score off them) but not wides. For the purposes of balls received by the team, no-balls and wides are included (since they accrue runs to the innings total). Aggregates of overs bowled exclude no-balls and wides.

ENGLAND

TEST	Wkts	Runs	Mins	Balls	Overs	Wides
1st	10	190	314	609	76.1	0
	10	257	374	722	90.1	0
2nd	10	154	257	436	54.3	0
	10	296	463	837	104.3	0
3rd	10	191	295	542	67.6	0
	10	279	431	806	100.5	1
4th	10	341	552	1128	140.6	0
	5	97	139	244	30.4	0
5th	7	371	387	759	94.6	0
Totals	**82**	**2176**	**3212**	**6083**	**759.3**	**1**

England scored 26.54 runs per wkt, 40.65 runs per hour, 35.77 runs per 100 balls, 2.87 runs per over.
Australia bowled 113.63 balls per hour, 14.18 overs per hour, 39.2 mins per wkt, 74.18 balls per wkt, 9.26 overs per wkt.

AUSTRALIA

TEST	Wkts	Runs	Mins	Balls	Overs	Wides
1st	8	601	690	1038	129.0	0
2nd	10	228	310	450	55.4	0
	10	184	293	431	53.4	0
3rd	10	231	355	509	63.3	0
	10	111	185	251	31.3	0
4th	10	323	501	796	99.1	0
	10	111	234	348	43.2	0
5th	10	221	283	484	60.4	0
	6	118	116	230	28.6	0
Totals	**84**	**2128**	**2967**	**4537**	**564.3**	**0**

Australia scored 25.33 runs per wkt, 43.03 runs per hour, 46.90 runs per 100 balls, 3.77 runs per over.
England bowled 91.75 balls per hour, 11.41 overs per hour, 35.3 mins per wkt, 54.01 balls per wkt, 6.72 overs per wkt.

TEST AVERAGES

ENGLAND –batting and fielding

	M	I	NO	Runs	HS	Avge	100s -50s	Runs per hour	Runs per 100 balls	Ct
T.W. Graveney	2	3	0	132	111	44.00	1-0	30.9	56.4	4
P.B.H. May	5	9	0	351	104	39.00	1-2	22.6	38.9	6
D.C.S. Compton	4	7	2	191	84	38.20	-1	21.0	34.0	0
T.E. Bailey	5	9	1	296	88	37.00	-2	15.9	27.7	2
M.C. Cowdrey	5	9	0	319	102	35.44	1-2	17.0	27.8	4
L. Hutton	5	9	0	220	80	24.44	-1	17.8	31.1	2
W.J. Edrich	4	8	0	180	88	22.50	-1	20.5	34.4	3
R. Appleyard	4	5	3	44	19*	22.00	0	23.8	41.9	4
J.H. Wardle	4	6	1	109	38	21.80	0	28.9	51.7	1
T.G. Evans	4	7	1	102	37	17.00	0	31.9	62.2	13
J.B. Statham	5	7	1	67	25	11.16	0	25.6	50.4	1
F.H. Tyson	5	7	1	66	37*	11.00	0	15.7	27.5	2
R.T. Simpson	1	2	0	11	9	5.50	0	13.2	34.4	0
K.V. Andrew	1	2	0	11	6	5.50	0	33.0	40.7	0
A.V. Bedser	1	2	0	10	5	5.00	0	22.2	43.5	1

. J.V. Wilson held one catch as substitute. There were no stumpings in the series
Wicket-keepers: Andrew conceded 11 byes for no dismissals. Evans conceded 30 byes for 13 dismissals

ENGLAND bowling

	Overs	Mdns	Runs	Wkts	Avge	10wM-5wI	Balls per wkt	Runs per 100 balls
L. Hutton	0.6	-	2	1	2.00	0	6.0	33.3
R. Appleyard	79	22	224	11	20.36	0	57.4	35.4
F.H. Tyson	151	16	583	28	20.82	1-2	43.1	48.3

MCC in Australia 1954-55

J.H.Wardle	70.6	15	229	10	22.90	1-2	56.6	40.4
J.B.Statham	143.3	16	499	18	27.72	-1	63.7	43.5
T.E.Bailey	73.4	8	306	10	30.60	0	58.8	52.0
T.W.Graveney	6	0	34	1	34.00	0	48.0	70.8
A.V.Bedser	37	4	131	1	131.00	0	296.0	44.2
W.J.Edrich	3	0	28	0	-	0	-	116.7

AUSTRALIA – batting and fielding

	M	I	NO	Runs	HS	Avge	100s-50s	Runs per hour	Runs per 100 balls	Ct
I.W. Johnson	4	6	4	116	41	58.00	0	22.1	48.7	1
C.C. McDonald	2	4	0	186	72	46.50	-1	20.6	41.9	0
R.N. Harvey	5	9	1	354	162	44.25	1-1	21.9	49.0	3
P.J. Burge	1	2	1	35	18*	35.00	0	31.8	47.9	0
A.R. Morris	4	7	0	223	153	31.85	1-0	20.1	45.2	0
L.V. Maddocks	3	5	0	150	69	30.00	-1	21.0	38.4	6
R.R. Lindwall	4	6	2	106	64*	26.50	-1	30.9	70.7	0
K.R. Miller	4	7	0	167	49	23.85	0	23.7	44.5	1
J.W. Burke	2	4	0	81	44	20.25	0	15.4	30.4	2
L.E. Favell	4	7	0	130	30	18.57	0	25.0	52.4	2
G.B. Hole	3	5	0	85	57	17.00	-1	25.0	51.8	3
R.G. Archer	4	7	0	117	49	16.71	0	21.5	51.5	4
R. Benaud	5	9	0	148	34	16.44	0	17.3	38.9	3
A.K. Davidson	3	5	0	71	23	14.20	0	18.7	37.8	4
W. Watson	1	2	0	21	18	10.50	0	14.2	27.3	0
G.R.A. Langley	2	3	0	21	16	7.00	0	19.7	51.2	9
W.A. Johnston	4	6	2	25	11	6.25	0	13.6	41.7	1

There were no stumpings in the series.

Wicket-keeping
Langley conceded 10 byes for 9 dismissals. Maddocks conceded 14 byes for 6 dismissals.

AUSTRALIA bowling

	Overs	Mdns	Runs	Wkts	Avge	10wM-5wI	Balls per wkt	Runs per 100 balls
R.G.Archer	97.6	32	215	13	16.53	0	60.2	27.5
I.W.Johnson	111	37	243	12	20.25	0	74.0	27.4
W.A.Johnston	141.4	37	423	19	22.26	-1	59.6	37.4
K.R. Miller	88.4	28	243	10	24.30	0	70.8	34.3
R.R.Lindwall	130.6	28	381	14	27.21	0	74.7	36.4
R.Benaud	116.7	23	377	10	37.70	0	93.5	40.3
A.K. Davidson	71	16	220	3	73.33	0	189.3	38.7
J.W.Burke	2	0	7	0	-	0	-	43.7

Men of the Match
(selected by B.Valentine)
First Test: Ian Johnson
Second Test: Frank Tyson
Third Test: Brian Statham
Fourth Test: Bob Appleyard
Fifth Test: Tom Graveney

MCC in Australia 1954-55

MCC tour record

Played 17, won 8, lost 2, drew 7

	MCC/England						Home team			
Result	Runs	W	Mins	Balls	w/nb	Opponent	Runs	W	Mins	Balls	w/nb
W	321	9	360	660	6	West Aus.	103	10	184	282	2
	40	3	48	101	1		255	10	441	763	3
W	311	10	414	846	5	Comb.XI	86	10	228	342	1
	0	0	0	0	0		163	10	310	518	0
W	246	10	282	590	0	South Aus.	254	10	317	489	1
	181	10	286	573	0		152	10	217	318	1
d	205	10	288	542	2	Aust XI	167	7	305	545	1
d	252	10	304	618	3	NSW	382	10	437	709	5
	327	10	409	885	6		78	2	75	128	3
d	304	10	308	578	1	Queensld	288	9	443	788	1
	288	9	282	640	0		25	2	34	60	0
L	190	10	314	609	0	First Test	601	8	690	1032	1
	257	10	374	721	0		0	0	0	0	0
d	312	10	375	718	2	Victoria	277	10	336	557	2
	236	5	221	424	3		88	3	113	208	0
W	154	10	257	435	0	2nd Test	228	10	310	444	2
	296	10	463	835	4		184	10	293	428	3
W	191	10	295	542	0	Third Test	231	10	355	507	2
	279	10	431	805	1		111	10	185	251	0
d	242	10	358	653	5	Comb.XI	221	10	253	442	0
	99	2	95	192	0		184	6	210	384	1
W	427	7	388	752	2	Tasmania	117	10	207	344	0
	133	6	149	296	0		200	10	206	393	0
W	451	10	427	867	0	South Aus.	185	10	264	493	3
	0	0	0	0	0		123	10	190	360	9
W	341	10	542	1126	4	Fourth Test	323	10	501	793	2
	97	5	139	244	0		111	10	234	346	0
d	113	10	199	313	0	Victoria	90	1	104	200	1
L	172	10	243	416	5	NSW	172	10	291	457	1
	269	10	297	575	4		314	8	327	562	5
d	371	7	387	758	0	Fifth Test	221	10	283	484	0
	0	0	0	0	0		118	6	116	230	0
	7105	253	8935	17314	54		6052	262	8459	13857	50

MCC/England scored
28.08 runs per wkt
47.71 runs per hour
41.04 runs per 100 balls
(40.72 adjusted to exclude w/nb from runs)
(40.91 adjusted to add w/nb to balls)
Opponents bowled
116.27 balls per hour (excl w/nb)
68.43 balls per wkt (excl w/nb)

Opponents scored
23.10 runs per wkt
42.93 runs per hour
43.67 runs per 100 balls
(43.31 adjusted to exclude w/nb from runs)
(43.83 adjusted to add w/nb to balls)
MCC/England bowled
98.29 balls per hour (excl w/nb)
52.89 balls per wkt (excl w/nb)

History had repeated itself. Just as 1953 mirrored 1926, so 1954-55 revisited 1928-29 when England under Percy Chapman won 4-1. In that season, Australia got better and more competitive with each Test and their victory came in the Final Test. In 1954-55, Australia got worse and worse and by the end looked as if they were trying to lose.

Well what happened next? Ian Johnson took them straight to the West Indies and their younger players began to come good, winning an incredibly high scoring series. This ensured that he retained the captaincy ahead of Miller. The 1956 tour of England broke the sequence, instead of winning 2-1, as in 1930, Australia lost by the same margin, being Lakered rather than Typhooned. In 1958-59 Peter May led his world-dominant England side to Australia, with a team that looked on paper better than Hutton's. But now England's luck ran out.

England have had glorious moments against Australia since then, but Australia's total supremacy since 1989 is unprecedented. Will it end in 2005?

INDEX

1954 7	Loader, P.J. 8
Adelaide Test 125	Maddocks, L.V. 89
Andrew, K.V. 8	May, P.B.H. 7
Appleyard, R. 8	MCC tour record 196
Archer, R.G. 12	McConnon, J.E. 8
Australian XI 11	McDonald, C.C. 125
Bailey, T.E. 7	Melbourne Test 89
Bedser, A.V. 7	Miller, K.R. 12
Benaud, R. 12	Morris, A.R. 12
Bibliography 5	Mount Gambier 124
Brisbane Test 13	New South Wales 11, 165
Bunbury 9	New Zealand 192
Burge, P.J. 168	Newcastle 87
Burke, J.W. 52	*Orsova* 9
Canberra 51	Over rates 192
Ceylon 9	Pakistan 7
Combined XI (Tasmania) 123	Queensland 12
Combined XI (Western Australia 10	Rockhampton 51
Compton, D.C.S. 7	Second Test 52
Cowdrey, M.C. 7	Sheppard, D.S. 7
Davidson, A.K. 12	Simpson, R.T. 7
Edrich, W.J. 7	South Australia 10, 124
Epitome of the Tests 194	Statham, J.B. 8
Evans, T.G. 8	Sydney Tests 52, 168
Fifth Test 168	Tasmania 123
First Test 13	Third Test 89
Graveney, T.W. 7	Tyson, F.H. 8
Harvey, R.N. 12	Victoria 51, 165
Hole, G.B. 12	Wardle, J.H. 8
Hutton, L. 7	Watson, W.J. 168
Johnson, I.W. 12, 193	Western Australia 10
Johnston, W.A. 12	Western Australian Country XI 9
Langley, G.R. 12	Wilson, J.V. 8
Lindwall, R.R. 12	Yallourn 165